Now and Then Again

The Way We Were and the Way We Are

Joseph Mirsky

Introduction

I own Joseph's Jewelry in Pompton Lakes, New Jersey (not the part of New Jersey they make jokes about). I send newsletters to my customers 3 times a year. The newsletters were an instant hit when I started them in 1997. There are three four page newsletters a year, Spring, Fall, and Holiday, mailed to my customers. I compiled the first 34 newsletters into a book titled *Ornamentally Incorrect* in 2008. This was followed by two other editions in 2011 and 2013.

In addition to jewelry, the newsletters had articles about consumer and middle class issues, money, economics, and the lighter side of life. The books also had politics sections that would have been inappropriate for the newsletters.

I wrote about politics in the books mainly to see if I could. It's not so easy. See *Tabula Rasa* on page 150. The politics are pretty mild, unless you're not. See *Theory of Relativity* on page 137.

Since there's nothing to watch on TV, I write. In addition to the 56 newsletters I've written so far, at this point I've accumulated so many articles about just about everything that I reorganized them into *Now and Then Again*. The jewelry articles are now in one section, *Bijoux and Beyond*. I wrote many articles about the past which, juxtaposed with contemporary articles, are eerily resonant, hence the title. There were originally 13 sections, but after I wrote *The Cat Who Came to Dinner* (page 21) I prudently added a 14th.

There's no detailed table of contents. There are at least 804 articles (you can count them different ways), not including 70 notes and the 49½ pithy profundities styled *Deep Thought* scattered through the book, so it's not feasible. It's a nonlinear book anyway. Feel free to jump around in it. A small number at the upper left or lower right of an article indicates the page number of a note.

About the cover: see *Back to the Future* on page 264. The front cover center photograph is of the Space Shuttle Discovery taking off from Cape Kennedy October 23, 2007, courtesy of NASA.

Contents

Cheers!

Prosit! Skoal! Here's How!

Those were the joyous toasts in the House restaurant on April 17, 1933 after President Roosevelt signed an amendment to the Volstead Act permitting 3.2 beer according to the New York Times in an article titled *Rush for First Beer in House Restaurant Drains 720 bottles in Four Hours' Service,* April 18, 1933.

Chairman Lindsay Warren of the House Accounts Committee that ran the restaurant said that the beer sales at 20¢ a bottle will help reduce the restaurant's $10,000 a year deficit.

On April 7, the day Roosevelt signed the bill, two sons of August Busch Sr., president of Anheuser-Busch, presented him with a surprise gift of a team of Clydesdale horses. The company arranged for a second team of horses to present a case of Budweiser to prohibition opponent former Governor Alfred E. Smith at the Empire State Building and also had a case shipped by air to the White House, later reenacted with the Clydesdales.

Wet Your Dry Whistle with This

Of course, there is the Volstead Cocktail, named after the father of prohibition, Andrew Volstead. (See *Medicinal Beer* on p. 3)
2 Parts Rye Whiskey
2 Parts Swedish Punsch
1 Part Orange Juice
1 Part Raspberry Juice
1 Dash Anisette
Fill a shaker with ice cubes. Add all ingredients. Shake and strain into a chilled cocktail glass.

"This cocktail was invented at Harry's New York Bar, Paris, in honor of Mr. Andrew J. Volstead, who brought out the Dry Act in U.S.A. and was the means of sending to Europe such large numbers of Americans to quench their thirst."
— Barflies and Cocktails, Harry McElhone, 1927

In 1911, an American jockey, Tod Sloan and a partner bought a bistro in Paris, dismantled a New York bar and shipped it to Paris where it opened as *New York Bar.* A Scot from Dundee, Harry McElhone, who once worked the bar at the Plaza in New York, was hired to run it. McElhone bought it in 1923 and renamed it *Harry's New York Bar.*

Harry's New York Bar became the watering hole for celebrities, including Ernest Hemingway, Gertrude Stein, Coco Chanel, Humphrey Bogart, Rita Hayworth, and Ian Fleming. (See below.)

Harry's claims to have invented the Bloody Mary (1921), the White Lady (1929) and the Side Car (1931), among others.

Since 1924, Harry's has conducted straw polls of American expatriates that have correctly predicted presidential elections, missing only Jimmy Carter in 1976 and George W. Bush in 2004. (The polls were not conducted during the war.)

Le James Bond

Into a champagne glass, drop a lump of sugar soaked in Angostura
Add some crushed ice
Pour in two ounces of vodka
Top up with champagne
Add a twist of lemon peel

Harry's New York Bar in Paris invented the James Bond cocktail in 1963. In the 1960 James Bond short story *From a View to a Kill* (in the book of short stories *For Your Eyes Only*), Bond, "on his first ignorant visit to Paris" went to Harry's and "That had started one of the memorable evenings of his life, culminating in the loss, almost simultaneous, of his virginity and his notecase".

By the way, a study by the University of Western Ontario found that a shaken martini has more antioxidants than a stirred one.

Vintage Car

Prince Charles has converted his vintage Aston Martin DB6* to run on vintage.

The 1969 blue sports car was a 21st birthday gift from his mum, the Queen. Prince Charles converted it to run on ethanol made from wine from a vineyard in Swindon near his country estate.

There is a European Union quota for wine production and the vineyard sells its excess to a nearby plant to be converted into bioethanol. The idea is a smaller carbon footprint. Charles has converted a couple of Jaguars, an Audi and a Range Rover to run on biodiesel from recycled cooking oil. It's not easy being green.

The Prince drives the car 300 miles a year and gets 4.5 bottles to the mile.

* James Bond drove a DB5 in Goldfinger in 1964

Silver Bullet

Before the Lone Ranger, silver bullets were mentioned in folklore as effective against various supernatural beings as early as the 18th century. In *The Two Brothers* from *Grimm's Fairy Tales* (1812) a man tore off silver buttons and used them to shoot a witch who was impervious to lead bullets, wounded her and made her restore his brother whom the witch had turned to stone.

The figurative use of "silver bullet" as a quick fix for a problem dates to its use by The Bedford Gazette, a Pennsylvania newspaper, in 1951:

"There are those who warn against viewing the atom as a magic weapon. I agree. This is not a silver bullet which can deliver itself or otherwise work military miracles."

½ gin, ¼ lemon juice, ¼ Kummel (a sweet, colorless liqueur flavored with caraway seed, cumin, and fennel). Shake well and strain into a cocktail glass.

That's the recipe for the Silver Bullet Cocktail from the Savoy Cocktail Book, published in 1930 by Harry Craddock, the head bartender at the Savoy Hotel in London.

Cheers.

Mid-Air Refueling

Aviation writer Howard Mingos (1891-1955) tells of a mid-air refueling flight gone awry over Lake Osakis, Minnesota, as quoted in the Literary Digest April 4, 1931.

Two ice fisherman reported a rain of whiskey from the sky as one airplane attempted to transfer 100 gallons of bootleg whisky to another below it through a hose that came loose.

He tells of another airman flying from Canada into New England at night with a load of bootleg booze when a blocked fuel line forced him down. He dropped a parachute flare and was able to see to land safely. Unfortunately, the flare set on fire "the finest haystack in New England", according to the farmer who owned it and who demanded payment.

The fire had attracted neighbors who would back up the farmer. The pilot said he was flying mail and offered a check in payment, which was refused.

The pilot took the farmer aside. " I owe you about six hundred dollars for that hay; but you haven't a Chinaman's chance to collect unless you accept my proposition.

I'm not flying mail but liquor. When the crowd leaves I'll unload enough to cover your loss. Squeal, and the Government will get the booze and the ship. I'll go to jail, and you—well, you can raise more hay. What say? "

The next day, the pilot fixed the plane and flew away.

Goldwater

"Clear with floating gold flakes. Sweet, star anise and medicinal herb aromas. A round, spicy entry leads to a glycerous moderately sweet medium to full-bodied palate with spicy and peppery licorice, menthol flavors. Finishes with a bitter-sweet medicinal bark fade."

That's a review of Der Lachs Original Danziger Goldwasser Liqueur. Goldwasser ("gold water" in German) is an 80 proof liqueur with small flakes of 22 karat gold floating in it and no tour of Gdansk, Poland is complete without a sip of it.

Ambrose Vermollen, a Dutchman living in the then German city of Danzig, invented this concoction of 20 herbs and roots in 1598. His distillery featured a salmon ("lachs" in German) sign.*

The gold flake gimmick was an immediate hit with royalty and commoners alike, since the minute gold flakes added little to the cost. (It's 25 - 40 bucks today.)

The secret recipe has remained in the family for over 400 years now, although it went to Germany after Danzig was separated from Germany after World War I and is today produced in Berlin.

The original distillery is still in Gdansk, now an exclusive restaurant, Pod Łososiem, "Under the Salmon"

* At that time it was common for businesses to use symbols or animals instead of numbers.

Attention Winos

Beer is proof that God loves us and wants us to be happy. You'll see this on T-shirts, mugs, etc. attributed to Benjamin Franklin.

But this is what he really said, in a letter to French Philosophe André Morellet in 1779:

Behold the rain which descends from heaven upon our vineyards, there it enters the roots of the vines, to be changed into wine, a constant proof that God loves us, and loves to see us happy.

Medicinal Beer

"...a person may, without a permit, purchase and use liquor for medicinal purposes when prescribed by a physician..."
— Volstead Act

The National Prohibition Act, known as the Volstead Act after Republican House Judiciary Committee Chairman Minnesota Congressman Andrew Volstead, was the law that put into effect the 18th amendment — prohibition. It was passed on October 28, 1919, overriding President Wilson's veto, and went into effect January 17, 1920.

Outgoing Attorney General A. Mitchell Palmer endorsed "medicinal beer" on March 3, 1921, the day before he left office, saying that since Congress could have restricted the quantity of liquor for medicinal purposes but didn't, "I think it was the intention of Congress that all reputable drug-stores authorized to compound and dispense medicine prescribed by physicians should be entitled to a permit to sell liquor at retail on such prescriptions."

The American Medical Association's House of Delegates agreed: "Legislative bodies composed of laymen should not enact restrictive laws regulating the administration of any therapeutic agent by physicians legally qualified to practice medicine."

Congress disagreed, "Pass Anti-Beer Bill in House 250 to 93" headlined the New York Times on June 28,1921, "after four hours of stormy debate."

In November, President Warren G. Harding signed the Willis-Campbell Act, also known as the anti-beer bill, restricting medicinal beer to one pint every ten days.

There were other ways to get your kick. On the fourth floor of the Treasury building in Washington was a laboratory where chemists analyzed "every conceivable concoction and many inconceivable ones: celery tonic, raspberry tonic, pear wine, elixir of life, liquid panacea, beet-root sherry, pear-leaf champagne, apple-cheese menthe, wheat juice, silo lightning; some that attempt to hide their shame under passwords like 'C. P. B.' and others that brazenly flaunt their sin to the world, like Cactus Cordial; hair tonics, rheumatism salves, quack remedies— they are all there, and many others," according to the the Kansas City Star.

Andrew Volstead (1860-1947)

He looks like he needs a drink. See *Wet Your Dry Whistle with This* on p. 1

Tache Tax

Guinness brewers estimate that 92,749 liters of beer are lost each year in Great Britain, as froth stuck to moustaches.

The giant brewery's scientists discovered this while working on Guinness bottled draught beer. .56 ml of beer per sip stays on a moustache, it takes an average of 10 sips to down a pint and there are an estimated 92,370 Guinness drinkers with face shrubbery in the UK, drinking 180 pints each a year.

It all adds up to £423,070 worth of suds wasted, dubbed a "tache tax."

But if you drink your Guinness from a glass, you would lose 81 times more. "We hope our moustached drinkers will turn to Guinness in a bottle to enjoy a less wasteful drink," said Guinness.

Eliot Ness Amber Lager

Famed "untouchable" prohibition agent Eliot Ness has a beer named after him. The Great Lakes Brewing Company in Cleveland makes it.

Ness became Cleveland's Director of Public Safety after prohibition, serving from 1935-1941. He frequented a bar on the site of what is now the Great Lakes Brewing Company's Brewpub. If you go, ask the bartender to point out the bullet holes said to have been put there by Ness.

Ness began drinking more heavily later in life after divorce and losing a job. He died in 1957 at 54.

Whiskey While You Wait

During prohibition, non-beverage alcohol for hair tonic, cologne, and patent medicine was allowed.

"The nonbeverage alcohol was manufactured under the war-time food control law and cost $240 a barrel. When the saloon keeper obtained it his next business operation was to buy a half dozen empty barrels and dilute it. Then, with his stock of prune juice and caramel at hand and his bartender ready he served his disguised stock by the small glass, making a profit of anything from $1,000 to $3,000, according to how much heart he had for his customers."

—The Indianapolis Star, Indianapolis, Indiana, November 11, 1919.

Canteen Drinking

The Army Reorganization Act of 1901, known as the Canteen Act, prohibited serving beer and wine in army canteens. This was pushed by the Anti-Saloon League and the WCTU (Women's Christian Temperance Union) as a dress rehearsal for prohibition.

Needless to say, soldiers managed to cope. From The Outlook, February 9, 1901:

"The private soldier sees no reason, nor should he see any reason, why he may not drink beer and wine if his officers drink beer and wine...."

"...about the gates of every Government post and garrison are clustered a nest of low and. vicious groggeries, whose proprietors use all sorts of wiles and temptations to get the monthly pay of enlisted men in exchange for liquors of a vile quality."

From The Literary Digest, April 27, 1901:

"Last month the soldiers at Fort Sheridan invaded Highwood in such numbers and consumed so much bad liquor that a riot call was turned in and a posse of special officers was called out to patrol the town. Last Saturday was the second payday since the canteen was abolished, and yesterday it was reported that a number of Uncle Sam's warriors were locked up in the jail at Waukegan as 'drunk and disorderly,' while others had entirely disappeared and were in danger of arrest as deserters."

In 1917, Congress extended prohibition to a 5 mile zone around army posts and made it illegal to serve alcohol to servicemen in uniform anywhere. In 1918, the Judge Advocate General's office defined intoxicating beverages as containing 1.4% alcohol or more.

Even after the repeal of prohibition in 1933, the army continued its 1.4% standard until World War II when it raised it to 3.2%. This stayed in effect until 1953 when the Canteen Act was deemed repealed by 1951 amendments to the Universal Military Training and Selective Service Act. One of the amendments authorized the Secretary of Defense to regulate liquor sales on and around military installations as he saw fit.

Close call. Only 12 years later I was able to order Singapore Slings in the club on Clark Air Base in the Philippines.

The Biggest Bootlegger

In 1922, August Busch, president of Anheuser-Busch brewers, wrote a letter to his associates in St; Louis. The letter was written while aboard the SS George Washington bound for France and mailed from Cherbourg on May 15.

His son, Adolphus Busch III, forwarded the letter to President Warren G. Harding on June 8 along with a copy of the wine list from the George Washington, "enumerating intoxicating liquors of every character." August Busch called the U.S. Government "Incomparably the biggest bootlegger in the world," and accused it of violating prohibition and the Constitution by serving alcohol since it owned the ship.

In 1916 the U.S. Shipping Board was created to ensure there would be enough merchant shipping during World War I.

In 1917, the Shipping Board set up the  Emergency Fleet Corporation to build the ships for a merchant fleet, owned and operated by the U.S. Government. 2247 ships were built or commandeered by the EFC.

The Shipping Board had to serve liquor or lose business to European competition.

Albert Lasker, chairman of the Shipping Board, said in a public reply to Busch in the New York Times June 14, 1922 that the Board's lawyers had ruled it legal to sell liquor on the ships outside the 3 mile

U.S. Territorial limit.

Lasker then questioned the motives of August Busch: "I believe you to be thoroughly selfish, and that you are acting in the hope of creating a revolt against prohibition so that you may again revive the sale of your liquors, utterly regardless of how you might hurt the American merchant marine in your effort to create a situation to benefit your brewery."

Lasker pointed out that the founder of Anheuser-Busch, Adolphus Busch, was a friend of the Kaiser, that the family still had a castle in Germany, and said that the Busch family friends hoped that a restored German merchant marine would hurt America's. "In my opinion you do not come before the bar of public opinion with clean hands," he concluded.

The George Washington was a luxurious German passenger ship launched in 1908, interned by the U.S. in 1917, used as a troop ship during the war, and carried Woodrow Wilson to the Paris Peace conference. It was turned over to the Shipping Board in 1920 and refurbished for passenger service.

MAKE EVERY MINUTE COUNT for PERSHING

UNITED STATES SHIPPING BOARD
EMERGENCY FLEET CORPORATION

Recreational Hazard

A Toronto doctor has described a new malady: beer drinker's finger. Screw top beer bottles can cause "callus formation on the palmar aspect of the thumb and index finger from persistent use."

He suggests it be called "screw-top fingers" or "molsodactyly."

Attention Winos

The British government keeps an extensive wine cellar for official functions, It came out that $28,000 had been spent to buy wine in just the month after the May, 2010 election to add to the 39,500 bottles already there, worth $1.4 million.

After the MP expense scandal of 2009 (one MP named Hogg billed the government to clean the moat on his estate) and austerity consequent to the recent financial unpleasantness, British taxpayers were not amused to learn of the bibulous hospitality of their government.

There's some pretty pricey wine, worth up to $4000 a bottle. The oldest is an 1878 cognac. Government Hospitality, the section of the Foreign Office responsible for the wine cellar, said after a review that they would sell off the expensive stuff, but keep the cellar.

The White House only has about 500 bottles of wine. President Johnson decreed in 1965 that only domestic wines would be served at official functions and that policy is still followed.

President Obama brews his own beer. White House chefs made a batch of White House Honey Ale from a pound of honey from the First Bees living in a hive on the South Lawn for 200 guests at the 2011 Super Bowl party.

Meanwhile, the Live-Ex 100, a price index of the 100 most sought after wines was up 19% since a year ago (August, 2010) and the Claret Chip Index of top-rated Bordeaux First Growths only, was up 22%. Gold was up 40%.

My Saturday night bottle of wine is still holding at 7 bucks.

Women and Wine

That's the title of an article in the Literary Digest from January 20,1900 about "an alleged increase of drunkenness among women." The article quotes the Chicago Journal:

"With greater independence, heavier cares, and a livelier intellectual life than her grandmother enjoyed—or suffered— the twentieth-century girl may be expected to seek much the same method of securing relief or stimulus as her brother does."

A New York hotel reports that women order drinks from their rooms and that women of both higher and lower classes are drinking more.

Izzy and Moe

After the 18th amendment went into effect at 12:01 A.M. January 17th, 1920, 16,000 saloons in New York City went out of business and were replaced by anywhere from 30,000 to 100,000 speakeasies. With only 1500 agents in the whole country, a woefully understaffed Bureau of Prohibition was tasked with enforcing the unenforceable. But Izzy Einstein and Moe Smith, prohibition agents extraordinaire, made a comic opera and highly successful attempt.

"Dere's sad news here. You're under arrest." Those were the words used by Izzy and Moe when they pinched violators of the Volstead Act. The sad news was heard by 4932 people between 1920 and 1925, with an extraordinary 95% conviction rate.

Isador Einstein was born in Tarnow, Poland, then part of the Austro-Hungarian Empire, circa 1880 and emigrated to New York in 1901. The 1920 census shows him as a mail sorter for the Post Office. He applied for a job as a prohibition agent in 1920. Five foot five and 225 pounds he didn't look the part but he convinced James Shevlin, head of the southern New York Bureau that he could blend in. He was fluent in Yiddish, Polish, German, and Hungarian, and could get by in French, Russian, and Italian. He could play the violin and trombone, too.

On his first raid, Izzy went to a speakeasy in Brooklyn that agents hadn't been able to get into and when the peephole opened, he demanded a drink saying he was a new prohibition agent. The joke was appreciated and the drink was poured. Izzy downed it but before he could arrest the bartender, he grabbed the bottle and escaped out the back leaving Izzy with no evidence. Thereafter, Izzy rigged a funnel in a vest pocket with a rubber tube leading to a hidden flask.

Izzy's friend Moe Smith owned a cigar store. He was a few inches taller than Izzy but weighed 250 pounds, twice his weight as a featherweight boxer in his youth. Izzy talked Moe into becoming a prohibition agent and the pair were off into the headlines.

Izzy impersonated "a German pickle packer, a Polish count, a Hungarian violinist, a Jewish gravedigger, a French maitre d', an Italian fruit vendor, a Russian fisherman and a Chinese launderer. His disguises included a streetcar conductor, an ice deliverer, an opera singer, a truck driver, a judge, a traveling cigar salesman, a street cleaner, a Texas cattleman, a movie extra, a football player, a beauty contest judge, a grocer, a lawyer, a librarian, a rabbi, a college student, a musician, a plumber and a delegate from Kentucky to the Democratic National convention," according to the SUNY Potsdam web site.

"In Coney Island, he entered a drinking joint in a wet bathing suit, shivering and gasping for aid. Wearing an attendant's white jacket, he shut another saloon near a hospital." "Izzy once tossed his agent's badge on the bar of a Bowery saloon and — this fat, unkempt individual — asked for a pint of whisky for 'a deserving prohibition agent.' The bartender sold it to him, thinking him a great wit," reported a Canadian Masonic web site in a reprint from Empire State Mason magazine. (Izzy and Moe were both Masons, which is probably how they met.)

Izzy was proud of one his early exploits. There was a a wet parade up Fifth Avenue on July 4, 1921, with bands playing *How Dry I Am*, and a sign with a quote from the Bible "Use a little wine for they stomach's sake" (1 Timothy 5:23). Izzy marched in the parade and "He followed some of them into the by-paths, with devastating effect on the unsuspecting dealers in the very article for which the demonstrators were perspiringly parading," said Truman H. Talley in the New York Times March 26, 1922.

In Detroit, a newspaper article announced that Izzy was in town. Izzy got into an argument with the bartender in a speakeasy by insisting that the agent's name was Izzy Epstein. The bartender bet Izzy drinks on the house that it was Einstein. When shown the newspaper, Izzy conceded defeat, paid for the drinks, and pinched the bartender.

The Smithsonian web site tells a story of Izzy and Moe going into a cabaret as violinists dressed in tuxedos. They "sat down and asked a waiter for some 'real stuff.' The waiter consulted with the proprietor, who thought he recognized the musicians as performers from a nightclub down the street."

"'Hello, Jake,' he called to Izzy. 'Glad to see you. Enjoyed your music many a time.' He told the waiter to serve the musicians anything they wanted. Moments later, the proprietor approached their table and asked if they might play 'something by Strauss' for the room." "'No,' Izzy replied, 'but I'll play you the 'Revenue Agent's March'. He flashed

6

his badge, and the proprietor suffered a heart attack on the spot."

Time Magazine reported Oct 31, 1932 in a review of his book (see below) that at a German beer-garden, "Izzy made so much noise he was asked to sing a solo, which he did with great gusto. Then he announced: 'This concludes the evening's entertainment, ladies & gentlemen. The place is pinched. For I am Izzy Einstein, the Prohibition Agent.'"

Izzy was fast, too. He found liquor in 21 minutes in Chicago, 17 minutes in Atlanta, and in New Orleans an impressive 35 seconds: he got into a cab, asked where he could get a drink and the cabby turned around and offered to sell a him a bottle.

Moe told a story of how famous they had become. "'One time we went from Monticello to Port Jervis on the train, and the engineer, when we got to Port Jervis, got off and ran from gin mill to gin mill yelling 'they're coming, Izzy and Moe is coming.' Talk about Paul Revere!'" — From Izzy's obituary in The Milwaukee Journal February 18,1938.

Sometimes the disguises didn't work. On Palm Sunday, they put pieces of palm in their hats and went into a saloon owned by an Irishman. Izzy said "He took one look at me, then at the palm in my hat and said: 'Get the hell out of here. What do you think this is, Yom Kippur?'" reported the Times April 10, 1922.

There are hundreds of stories, best summarized by a listing of headlines of some of the 45 articles I was able to uncover about Izzy and Moe in the New York Times, in date order.

- Izzy Einstein in Disguise. Posing as Butcher, Dry Agent Arrests Employees in Drug Store. July 5, 1921
- Izzy the Rum Hound Tells How It's Done. Champion Hootch Hunter Says Keen Scent Protects New York Agents From Poisonous Liquor. January 1, 1922
- Dry Raid Empties Jack's Secret Room. January 7, 1922
- Rum Stills Found Near a Graveyard. Izzy Einstein, Posing as a Farmer Seizes Two Plants in Barns Up-State. Raiding Party in Sleigh. January 26, 1922
- Gentiles Lose Wine Ordered By Rabbis. Izzy Einstein Seizes Truck Load After One Buyer Admits He Is a Protestant. January 28, 1922
- Izzy and Moe Raid Thespian Retreat. Beguile Occupants With Tank Town Tales and Order Auto Load of Scotch. February 26, 1922
- Izzy, Ebon In Hue, Raids Rum Bazaar. March 3, 1922
Izzy and Moe in Harlem "with blackened faces and hands and a fluent flow of negro dialect."
- Izzy 'Grave Digger' Captures 3 Stills. Einstein and Fellow Agents Wield Spades to Stalk Moonshine Plant. March 4, 1922
- Izzy and Moe Make Sunday Liquor Raids. Rum In Talking Machine. New Hiding Place Yields Seven Quarts. April 17, 1922
- 'Izzy' Seizes 'Nozo', 3% At 20 Cts. a Pint. They Call It Beer, but It's Made of Bread and It has More Kick Than Volstead Allows. April 22, 1922
- Face on Barroom Wall Was Izzy's. But No One Recognized the Dangerous Einstein as He Stood Undisguised Beneath It. June 27, 1922
- Sees Izzy and Moe, Bartender Faints. Another Collapses and Doctor Is Required When Dry Agents Reveal Identity. July 17, 1922
- Izzy Einstein Found Providence Wide Open. More Than 700 Places, He Says, Where Whiskey can be Bought, Some at 20 Cents. September 11, 1922
- Izzy and Moe Seize 'Sacramental' Wine. Purchase 10 Cases After Giving Password and Using Marked Bank Notes. October 19, 1922
- In White Wing Garb Izzy and Moe Nab 71. Carrying Street Cleaning Brushes, Dry Agents Set Record for Day's Catch. Woman Kisses Einstein. Enthusiastic Worshipper at Church Near Raided Saloon Shows Her Approval. November 20, 1922
- 53 Barrels of Wine In Stable Seized. Izzy and Moe, Posing as Fruit Vendors, Hire Wagon and Find Liquor. November 22, 1922
- Izzy and Moe Don Evening Clothes. Visit Delicatessen Shop and Later Seize $10,000 of Imported Liquor. January 13, 1923

- Izzy Pawns Coat Gets $10,000 Rum. Doubted That Throng Leaving Pawn shop With Bundles Had All Redeemed Pledges. April 12, 1923
- Einstein Has Laugh On Chicago Saloons. Izzy Keeps Their Hired Detectives Busy While Moe Smith Works Unmolested. January 13, 1924
- Izzy and Moe End Gay Careers as Dry Agents; Picturesque Pair Among 35 Finally Dropped. November 15, 1925

Retired Brigadier General Lincoln C. Andrews was appointed Assistant Secretary of the Treasury in charge of Prohibition in April, 1925 and set about reorganizing the Bureau, consolidating 48 state offices to 22 districts. All 180 prohibition agents in the Manhattan office were notified that they were terminated and instructed to report to headquarters. 145 were reinstated and 35 were let go, among them Izzy and Moe.

"General Andrews does not like prohibition agents who get too much publicity. Two months ago General Andrews gave orders that if the name of Izzy Einstein or Moe Smith appeared once in print, they would be fired. For two months their exploits have been hidden from the public eye." — Time Magazine November 23,1925.

Despite offers from vaudeville, radio, and movies both Izzy and Moe went to work for the New York Life Insurance Company, in different offices. Izzy was reputed to have said "Yes, sir! What was good enough for ex-President Coolidge is good enough for ex-Agent Izzy Einstein!" They did very well at it, both being in the company's 400 Club, writing at least $400,000 in business, according to the New Yorker June 6, 1936.

The New Yorker article tells of when Izzy Einstein met Albert Einstein. When Izzy asked him what line of work he was in, Albert said he was a discoverer. Izzy asked what he discovered and he said "'stars in the sky.'" "'So I'm a discoverer, too, I told him, only I discover in the basements. We both laughed.'"

Izzy went back to Tarnow to visit in 1928. The town held a parade in his honor and "the ovation he received was proportionately as enthusiastic as the one accorded the trans-Atlantic flyer [Lindbergh]," reported the Ogden Standard Examiner (Utah), July 8, 1928.

Izzy wrote a book, *Prohibition Agent No. 1,* in 1932. The Pittsburgh Press reported October 27, 1932 that Izzy dictated the book to his four sons. "'When one got dizzy, then I'd start dictating to another,'" Only four reporters showed up at the book's premiere. "'What good is it to be famous yet when they forget you so soon?'" Izzy said. When Izzy tried to hand out books to various dignitaries, President Hoover wouldn't see him and other politicians were "too busy." But Henry Ford responded that if Izzy would go to Detroit he would see him,

The New Yorker reported that Moe said he would sue if he were mentioned by name in the book since that would make him agent no. 2. Izzy cut out Moe's name and they remained friends. "The book sold 575 copies. 'the publishers sent me a free copy,' said Moe. 'Izzy would have sent me a copy, too, if I had sent him two dollars.'" Unfortunately Izzy's book was not reprinted and is now a rare book selling for $600.

Izzy died February 17, 1938 at 57 after an operation to amputate his right leg after an infection. Moe died in Yonkers, N.Y. December 21,1960 at 73.

Izzy, left, as a rabbi, and Moe in drag.

Izzy, left, and Moe having a drink in 1935.

Agitate - Educate - Legislate

That's the motto of the W.C.T.U. the Women's Christian Temperance Union. They did the agitate part by invading bars in Pasadena, California in 1947.

W.C.T.U Marches
on Pasadena Bars

California Women attack liquor
with prayers instead of hatchets

These were the headlines in an article in Life Magazine, May 19,1947.

One of the photos in a bar shows women pointing up at a sign that says "Wealth liquor or education never made a fool of anyone although any one of them may give a natural born fool a broader stage and a larger audience"

"Ladies register stern disapproval of barroom sentiment" reads the caption.

The W.C.T.U. was founded in 1874 and is still around, although down to 5000 members in 2012 from the peak of 372,000 in 1931.

This Spuds' for You

In a Bud Light ad for Superbowl XXI in 1987, a limousine rolls up to a disco, the chauffeur opens the door and out comes Spuds MacKenzie, "The Original Party Animal," a white bull terrier with a black splotch over one eye, wearing a white dinner jacket and black tie. Women boogie while a stein of beer slides down the bar in front of Spuds.

Mad Dog Spuds then joined Nipper (1884-1895), who listened to his master's voice on the gramophone, Morris the Cat (d. 1968), and Charlie the Tuna (reported dead of mercury poisoning by George Carlin in the 1980's) in the Mad Animal hall of fame, paving the way for the Cockney gecko and the toilet paper bears. (And here I thought a bear shits in the woods.)

Spuds donned a Santa suit and piloted a sleigh with a bag full of Bud twelve packs on Christmas, 1987. He should have consulted his lawyer first. There is a law in Ohio forbidding Santa to promote liquor and the The Ohio Department of Liquor Control made Anheuser-Busch remove the beer in the offending cartons.

84 year old Senator Strom Thurmond (R-SC), a teetotaler, spoke on the Senate floor waving a Spuds plush doll accusing Anheuser-Busch of promoting drinking among children with its Spuds toys and kid size T-shirts.

Spuds gave an interview on The Dick Clark Show dressed in a tux, speaking through his interpreters, three women Spudettes. Spuds was mellow, sitting up on the lap of a Spudette looking at the audience except when he turned to give her a wet kiss. When Clark asks Spuds if there is any truth to the "vicious rumors" that he is actually a girl, a Spudette answers that his three women wouldn't be following him if he were and Clark jumped in to say "He's a full-out macho guy."

Actually, Spuds was a girl named Honey Tree Evil Eye, Evie, from Malvern, Pa. Spuds retired in 1989 and passed away of kidney failure in 1993. She was 9 years old.

Hard Liquor

Mexican scientists have made diamond from tequila. It turns out that 80 proof tequila is perfect for making thin diamond films. The cheap stuff works just fine.

The tequila is heated to 536° to vaporize it, then the vapor is heated to 1470° to break down the alcohol molecules and the carbon in them is deposited as nano-size diamond crystals in a thin film.

Diamond films are used to coat cutting tools and semiconductors.

The First Bootleggers

Masked Robbers Hold Up Chicago Railroad Yard and Loot Box Cars headlined the New York Times January 17, 1920.

The Times reported that six armed men in masks bound the yardmaster and watchman for the Coca Cola company and six trainmen in a shanty and stole $75,000 to $100,000 worth of whiskey from two box cars.

According to Wikipedia the robbers took the "medicinal whiskey" at 12:59 A.M. on January 17, 1920, 59 minutes after the start of Prohibition.

The Fools of Bruges

De Halve Maan (half moon) brewery in the medieval Belgian city of Bruges dates back to at least 1564 and has been owned by the Maes family since 1856.

Both brewing and bottling were done on the premises in the historic downtown until 2010, when bottling was moved to an industrial park outside of town. Unfortunately, that has meant 500 trucks a year, 85% of all truck traffic, rumbling over Bruges' quaint cobblestone streets.

The solution is an underground beer pipeline two miles long that will deliver 1500 gallons an hour, a delicate operation that will have to tunnel under the canals of Bruges. Construction is to begin in 2015.

The most famous beer brewed by De Halve Mann is Brugse Zot, meaning Bruges Fool. Maximillian of Austria (see *The First Engagement Ring* on p. 203), ruler of Flanders in the 15th century, attended the Procession of the Holy Blood, a famous celebration with a costumed parade and jesters and minstrels in Bruges (in 1479?). Afterwards, he was asked to fund a "fools house", a mental institution and he replied that the town should simply close its gates for the town was already filled with fools.

The mental hospital was eventually opened in the early 16th century. In 1856 the director, Canon (reverend) Peter John Maes gave money to his nephew Leon Maes to open a brewery on the premises. This was the year the Maes family bought De Halve Maan and the Bruges fools became the first big customers.

There is precedent for piped in beer. In Gelsenkirchen, Germany, 3 miles of pipes connect over 100 bars and restaurants in a soccer arena, pumping out 14 liters a minute to each. Four cooling centers underneath the stadium store 52,000 liters of beer. There are noticeable fluctuations in the beer flow depending on if the home team is winning or losing.

The First Cocktail

Mix chuchuhuasi tree bark with aguardiente (a fiery liquor made from fermented and distilled sugar cane juice), raw sugar cane juice, lime and mint. It'll cure what ails you, as it did for the crew of Sir Francis Drake. It's the world's oldest cocktail, El Draque, The Dragon, the Spanish nickname for Sir Francis Drake.

In 1586, while pillaging Spanish settlements in the Caribbean, Sir Francis' crew took sick and he sent a shore party to Matecumbe, a Florida key, to find the ingredients for this native medicinal drink. It worked. His crew recovered enough to attack St. Augustine.

Today, the recipe has been modified into the Mojito, with rum instead of aguardiente and without the chuchuhuasi bark. This is the recipe from Bucket List Bars web site:

Whole lime peeled and sliced
2 tsp sugar
4-6 mint leaves
2 oz rum

(continued next page)

10

In a rocks glass combine the whole lime, sugar and mint leaves and proceed to give it a good muddling. Add the rum and ice and either shake (which will really help to dissolve the remaining sugar) or stir (which will help to not let the drink get too watered down.) Garnish with a sprig of mint which has been slapped a couple of times to help it release its aroma.

But if you're a purist, you can buy "Nature's Mojo Chuchuhuasi Bark Powder" on Amazon for $26 a pound. You can find aguardiente from a variety of South American countries at your local liquor store.

270 **Fowl Play**

In Oban, Scotland in 1896, John Turner sued a distillery for £12 ($1600 2015 equivalent) for allowing intoxicating material to flow into the stream from which his hens drank, causing them to get drunk and be unable to fulfill their fowl duties.

Since the distillery started up, his hens and ducks were drunk and would not eat. By Sunday, when the distillery was shut down, they were in bad shape, but Mondays were the worst "for then the hens drank excessively, fell into the burn [stream] frequently, and lately he had to keep a boy to look after them on Monday mornings." They wouldn't eat until they first went to the stream. He blamed a hen bought at Fort William for discovering the stream, then leading the others to it.

The Fort William hen was placed on a courtroom bench in a wicker cage. Asked if the hen was sober, Turner replied that it was not. This was obvious because "it sat on the bottom of the cage and put its long neck through the bars, looked sideways at the ceiling, crooning to itself in what was described as a 'maudlin style'." The hen was removed after it made "some forcible remarks to his lordship."

This was the only hen in good enough shape to make it to the court, the rest were too drunk.

The defense contended that the hen might have had influenza and his lordship postponed judgement due to it being a peculiar case.

The hen was of much interest and "A thoughtful individual presented to it fully half a glass of whiskey, which it took greedily. This revived it considerably and it cackled at a great rate, to the intense enjoyment of the bystanders."

This is from an article in The Hawke's Bay Herald (New Zealand), January 16, 1897, quoting the Westminster Gazette.

Attention Winos

You have been declared non-essential. Only essential government services were up and running during the 2013 government shutdown, and approving wine labels wasn't essential.

Wine labels have to be approved by the Alcohol and Tobacco Tax and Trade Bureau, TTB, an arm of the Treasury that approves 152,000 labels each year and collects $26 billion in fees from its various operations.

Like food labels, you have to say what's in it, where it's from, additives, etc. Château Napa Organic Plonk 2013 has to be made from grapes organically grown in Napa county and trampled out in 2013 by people with government inspected feet.

The Ghost Ingredient is Back!

Barney Barnato Cocktail
1 Dash Angostura Bitters.
1 Dash Curacao.
1/2 Caperitif.
1/2 Brandy.
Stir well and strain into cocktail glass.

This recipe from the Savoy Cocktail Book by Harry Craddock is named after South Africa's favorite rascal (see *The Largest Check Ever Written* on p. 206) calls for a native ingredient, Caperitif, a white wine based aperitif from South Africa, 20% alcohol, that was flavored with herbs and quinine. Caperitif was popular in the early 20th century but vanished and was listed as "defunct" until its rebirth in 2014. "The Ghost Ingredient is Back!" announced its maker, AA Badenhorst Family Wines in South Africa.

After your cocktail, dinner is served. (*See the Cat Who Came to Dinner* on p. 21.)

Slipping Across the Border for a Drink

Although publicly supporting Prohibition, Commerce Secretary Herbert Hoover would slip into the Belgian embassy, technically foreign soil, for a martini on the way home.

Hoover had organized massive food relief for Belgium during World War I.

Sabrage

Champagne! In victory one deserves it; in defeat one needs it.

— Napoleon Bonaparte

Napoleon's troops would open their champagne bottles with their sabers. The technique, called sabrage, is still used today.

There are special champagne sabers, $75 - 300 depending on the hoity-toitiness of the seller.

They are short swords with a blunt business edge. Where the mold seam line meets the opening lip of the bottle, the glass has the most stress and a sharp blow cracks off the whole top of the bottle, cork and all. You don't need sharp, just a whack.

Be sure to take off the foil and the wire cage first and slide your weapon up the bottle at a low angle with force. You may get bits of broken glass and you'll lose an ounce of bubbly in the process and the bottle lip with the cork will fly across the room. One web site reports that a novice did it perfectly, except that the projectile glass with cork flew across the room and killed a $3000 bottle of cognac.

Actually, you could use any steel blade instrument to guillotine a champagne bottle.

I know it's not as macho, but I've found that grip, twist, wiggle works just fine with no collateral damage.

Happy New Year!

Champagne Charlies

Champagne Charlie is my name
Champagne drinking is my game
— Champagne Charlie, English music hall song by George Leybourne & Alfred Lee, 1867

A former clerk of the House of Commons testified in 2014 before a committee looking into how the Palace of Westminster, home of the British parliament, was run that the House of Lords rejected combining the catering services of Lords and Commons to save money "because the Lords feared that the quality of champagne would not be as good if they chose a joint service."

This so astonished the chairman of the committee that he asked "Is that true? Did you make that up?" He was assured that it was true.

In the teeth of Prime Minister David Cameron's austerity budget, the House of Lords has spent over $400,000 for 17,000 bottles of champagne, more than 5 bottles a year for each of the 780 peers, since he took office in 2010. However, a peer pointed out that the champagne was sold to milords and ladies at a profit for their occasions. (The House of Lords gift shop will sell you a bottle of vintage champagne for $53.)

A columnist for the Independent suggested one economy would be to just add fizzy lemonade to a bottle of German plonk. "After the first three glasses you can't tell the difference anyway."

The Toothpick Won't Work

The Ritz-Carlton Hotel in Tokyo is offering the Diamond-tini, a vodka martini with a 1 carat diamond in the glass instead of an olive.

The cocktail is served with the strains of "Diamonds are Forever" from the 1971 James Bond film in the background. The price includes setting the diamond in a ring by a local jeweler.

$15,000. Sip, don't chug.

Beer Drinking Song

[The Working Man:]
I want my beer, I want my beer
And there are no two ways about it
I want my beer, I want my beer
I won't do any work without it
The working man must have his can
To do his work from year to year
Oh, how I wish again
That I was a fish again
Swimming in an ocean of beer
— Irving Berlin, *Prohibition*

"The return to beer will have a tremendous influence sociologically and this influence will be manifested in popular music by a return to the singable song."
— Irving Berlin as quoted in the Literary Digest April 7, 1934

Berlin also wrote a song titled *You Cannot Make Your Shimmy Shake On Tea.*

Bon Appétit!

A Twinkie is Forever

Roger Bennatti, a science teacher in Blue Hill, Maine bought a two-pack of Twinkies around 1974, ate one, and put the other one above his blackboard.

In 2005 Bennatti said "It's starting to flake off just a tad. But it's sort of an off-yellow, dusty--the bottom, you know, appears to be a little, you know, perhaps moldy, but just a little bit of the bottom of it." Mr. Bennatti retired but the twinkie lives on in a bespoke glass case provided by his successor

A Twinkie spokesman said that the official shelf life of a Twinkie is 25 days.

You can find out what's in a Twinkie, if you dare, by reading *Twinkie, Deconstructed* by Steve Ettinger. There are 37 ingredients, high fructose corn syrup, of course, a whole bunch of the usual suspects food chemicals, and a number of ingredients that are mined, like calcium sulfate, food grade plaster of Paris.

The Japanese hot dog eating champion (69 in 10 minutes) set the Guinness world record by downing 14 Twinkies in a minute in 2012.

As for the oldest Twinkie actually eaten: "We nibbled our 16 year old Twinkies a teeny-tiny bit just to see what they tasted like. Guess what? They tasted exactly like a normal Twinkie. Very scary indeed."

Mountain Dew was sued by someone claiming a dead mouse was found in a can of it. Pepsico's lawyers said it couldn't be because Mountain Dew would have dissolved the mouse into "a jelly-like substance" in the 15 months it sat on the shelf. This inspired the National Public Radio Science Desk to run an experiment in January, 2012 to see how long a Twinkie would last in Mountain Dew. After two hours the Twinkie was still intact.

Mountain Dew's tag line is "it'll tickle yore innards". What Twinkies do to yore innards is the heart of the "Twinkie defense", that a junk food sugar rush turned you into a monster, a misinterpretation of the defense in a famous murder trial

In 1978, Dan White, a former San Francisco city supervisor shot and killed the mayor, George Moscone, and supervisor Harvey Milk.* White was a health food fanatic and his lawyers argued that his switch to junk food, along with other behavioral changes were one of the symptoms, not a cause, of his depression, and hence diminished capacity. White was convicted of the lesser charge of voluntary manslaughter and sentenced to 7 years, 8 months.

Twinkies were mentioned only in passing during the trial, but reporters coined the term "Twinkie defense", which then passed into urban legend.

Hostess, maker of Twinkies as well as Wonder Bread, filed for bankruptcy a second time since 2004 in January, 2012 and went out of business in November after a bakers strike. Hostess said it had been making 500 million Twinkies a year. The last 20,000 Twinkies went to a Chicago supermarket in December, 2012.

But a Twinkie really is forever. Twinkies was sold in March, 2013 along with Dolly Madison Snack Cakes for $410 million and was resurrected July 15, 2013.

Twinkies have been around since 1930 (Wonder Bread since 1921). 2011 sales of Twinkies were 36 million packages, down 2% from the year before.

*Harvey Milk was gay. After the lenient sentence was announced on May 21, 1979, the gay community rioted. Over 5000 people stormed city hall in the White Knight riots, causing considerable damage as well as injuries to police officers. White was paroled after 5 years and committed suicide in 1985.

Let Them Eat Porridge

At a time of increased hunger and use of foodbanks in Britain. One peer, Baroness Anne Jenkin, explained that the problem is what the simple folk do: "Poor people don't know how to cook." "I had a large bowl of porridge today, which cost 4p. A large bowl of sugary cereals will cost you 25p."

"Let Them Eat Porridge" headlined the Morning Star, December 9, 2014.

Jenkin sits on the Lords' Refreshment Committee that spent over $400,000 on champagne for the use of the upper house. See *Champagne Charlies* on p. 12.

Big Gulp

A New Mexico man decided on a surprise proposal to his girlfriend. The couple and a group of friends went to a Wendy's for Frosties. The man put the engagement ring into the milkshake, counting on a pleasant surprise.

The friends were in on the surprise and the women in the group challenged the bride-to-be to a chug-a-lug race to speed things up. She won the race, but there was no ring in the bottom of the cup.

After a trip to the hospital, the man proposed on bended knee holding the X-ray of the ring.

After a day of eating prunes and high-fiber cereal, the ring arrived the following morning.

Fishy Chips

Walkers Potato Crisps recently redid some of their flavoured crisps products. The British company, owned by Pepsico, is now using real meat in its smoky bacon and roast chicken crisps.

Walkers is using extracts of British pork certified ethical by the Royal Society for the Prevention of Cruelty to Animals and free-range chickens.

Previously, the flavors were fake and were labeled "suitable for vegetarians." According to the Daily Mail Online, "vegetarians have reacted with horror" to the new critter crisps and have urged Walkers to reconsider.

Fortunately, Walkers Cajun Squirrel Flavour Potato Crisps contain no squirrel.

The Brits say crisps and we say chips. They say chips and we say fries. We say crisps for fake chips: Munchos Potato Crisps "A light tasting crispy snack!"

Ingredients: dried potatoes, vegetable oil (corn, canola, soybean, and/or sun-flower oil), enriched corn meal (corn meal, ferrous sulfate, niacin, thiamin mononitrate, riboflavin, and folic acid), potato starch, salt, and yeast. Enjoy!

Deep Thought

Buy for yourself, not for the approval of others.

Silver Plate

Indian cooking uses pure silver leaf as edible decoration. Typical are dragees, little silver-coated sugar beads used to decorate pastries, and varc or warq, silver leaf used to cover a variety of sweets.

Silver generally has low toxicity, but if you eat too much of it you'll get argyria — your skin will turn amazingly blue-gray and you'll look like a Smurf. The silver accumulates and lodges in the skin and reacts with exposure to sunlight and darkens, just like in photography. (Google "argyria" in images. It's just amazing.)

The amounts in Indian sweets are minuscule, as the metal leaf is only a few hundred-thousandths of a millimeter thick and Indians have been eating it for centuries without ill effect.

But a Napa, California attorney sued some big names in the food business, including Martha Stewart, in 2003 over selling silver dragees. He cited EPA information that silver is toxic in amounts greater than a few tenths of a milligram per day.

The lawsuit was settled with the agreement not to sell silver dragees in California. Silver dragees are now sold everywhere else "for decoration only". You can buy a 3.3 ounce jar on Amazon for $14.99.

But if you get your vark or dragees direct from India, "only Lord Shiva knows exactly what they mix in their silver" according to an Indian web site.

Fairy Floss

You'd think that the National Confectioners Association would have picked a day other than December 7 for National Cotton Candy Day. You know about "a date which will live in infamy", right?

Spun sugar as an expensive luxury goes back to the 18th century. A dentist (!) and a confectioner invented the cotton candy machine in 1897. The machine debuted at the 1904 World's Fair in St. Louis. Their "Fairy Floss" sold 68,655 boxes at 25¢, $6.50 2015 equivalent.

A large cone of cotton candy has less sugar than a can of soda, because it's mainly air. Tootsie Roll is the largest manufacturer of cotton candy.

Why December? County fair season is in the summer. July 4th would be better. Then you could call it Freedom Floss.

M&M's

In 2006, a single brown M&M was auctioned for $1500. "This brown M&M® (.5" diameter) has been sealed in an archival sleeve and professionally matted and framed (to 7.25 x 8" in an appropriately chocolate brown frame!)" reads the auction catalog.

The M&M was flown aboard SpaceShipOne on June 21,2004, reaching an altitude of 328,391 feet on the first private space flight. Pilot Mike Melvill (MM) took some M&Ms out of his pocket and let them float weightlessly. "And they just spun around like like little sparkling things. And I was so blown away I couldn't even fly the airplane."

"The exterior coating and the white 'M' logo on the M&M are a bit scuffed from tumbling around SpaceShipOne during its 'flight'." But there was no structural damage "unlike many of its fellow M&M's" it is "intact (i.e. not squished or broken!)....A certificate of authenticity signed by Melvill is included."

M&M's were invented by Forrest Mars Sr., founder of the Mars candy company. He saw soldiers during the Spanish Civil War (1936-39) eating chocolate pellets with a hard shell around them to keep them from melting. He patented his own process and began making the candy in Newark in 1941.

The other "M" was for Bruce Murrie, son of the Hershey president. Chocolate was rationed during the war and this arrangement allowed the candy to be made with Hershey's which had a deal with the government for the bulk of the chocolate.

The first M&M's came in 5 colors in a cardboard tube. During the war, only the military could get M&M's.

M's were printed on the candies starting in in 1950, in black, and changed to white in 1954.

"There will be no brown M&M's in the backstage area, upon pain of forfeiture of the show, with full compensation." This was article 126 of the rock band Van Halen's standard contract. This was reinforced with a list titled "Munchies" that specified:

Potato chips with assorted dips

Nuts

Pretzels

M&M's (Warning: Absolutely No Brown Ones)

Twelve (12) Reese's peanut butter Cups

Twelve (12) assorted Dannon yogurt (on ice)

In 1980, at the University of Southern Colorado at Pueblo, David Lee Roth, Van Halen's lead singer, found brown M&M's backstage and trashed the dressing room causing $12,000 in damage. But the weight of the band's equipment caused the stage to collapse causing $80,000 in damage to the gym floor.

That was the reason the M&M clause was in the contract: to determine if the complex contract had actually been read. The band was a huge production, with nine 18 wheelers to carry all the gear. There were detailed technical specifications about all aspects of the concert, including electrical requirements and load bearing structures. Obviously, the school didn't read them.

---

270   Smelling the Roses

Deo Pefume Candy from Bulgaria contains rose oil component geraniol. Geraniol, like garlic, comes out of your pores if you eat it, so you'll smell like a rose. Bulgaria produces 70% of the world's rose oil.

In Victorian times, women used rose-flavored cachous, lozenges like breath mints. Victorian cachou boxes are collectibles.

Bond villain Ernst Stavro Blofeld, head of SPECTRE, put a violet scented cachou in his mouth to sweeten his breath when he had to deliver bad, probably fatal, news.

Slip Sliding Away

MIT wizards have invented a bottle coating that lets ketchup pour out like milk. No more bottle-thumping followed by a bloody mess. Ketchup is a non-Newtonian fluid (don't ask), but LiquiGlide brings out its inner Newtonness.

LiquiGlide is an edible plant-based material made of FDA approved ingredients (the inventors aren't telling which ones).

The inventors estimate that 1 million tons of ketchup and other viscous condiments would be saved by this good-to-the-last-drop technology.

Fighting the Kaiser in the Kitchen

Lemon tree very pretty and the lemon flower is sweet
But the fruit of the poor lemon is impossible to eat
— Lemon Tree

Lemon-drops candy was so popular with the doughboys in World War I that the Subsistence Division of of the Quartermaster Corps of the U.S. Army had trouble supplying enough of them, according to the American Journal of Clinical Medicine in March, 1919.

200,000 pounds of lemon-drops were eaten each month, 15% of the candy supplied to the troops.

The lemon-drops were made of pure granulated sugar with an emulsion of lemon rind. "It is found that an extra sour lemon-drop is the favorite with the soldiers. The product made from the formula used has the thirst-quenching quality of lemon-ade."

M&M's were the favorite of the GIs in World War II. The first M&M's came in 5 colors in a cardboard tube. During the war, only the military could get M&M's.

A Moo Down Milk Lane

That was the winning tune in an online contest in British Columbia, Canada in October, 2012 to see which music would inspire cows to give the most milk. The contest was called "Music Makes More Milk".

The contest kicked off with tuxedoed classical musicians warming up the cows of a farmer in Agassiz, B.C. who had been playing music for his cows for years.

A Moo Down Milk Lane by Tzu Deng Jerry D of Vancouver topped the bovine charts with 7230 liters the day it was played, the highest of the week. It's a simple upbeat melody on the piano. You can listen to it online.

A 2001 study by psychologists at the University of Leicester in England played different types of music to a thousand cows and measured the milk output. *Bridge Over Troubled Waters*, *Moon river*, and Beethoven's *Pastoral Symphony* were among the winners.

Fast music, including *Size of a Cow* by The Wonder Stuff, a British alternative rock band, was a turnoff for the cows.

This is not new. A March 26, 1927 Literary Digest article cites a German report that music played to cows increases milk yield and adds "it is probable that some enterprising farmer will try soon the effects of milking-time radio programs or of phonograph concerts on his milk-yielding stock."

And in 1930, The Ingenues, an all-girl band, serenaded cows in a dairy barn at the University of Wisconsin in Madison in a test to see if music would produce more milk. No word on results.

Don't Wolf Your Food!

This has got to be the dumbest thing I ever saw in a catalog: "The faster you eat, the more you eat. So slow down with HAPIfork! It alerts you with vibration and LED lights when you're eating too fast." And it's a bluetooth fork: it will wirelessly upload how much you ate to your computer and your mom will see how you pigged out.

According to WebMD, people who eat too fast are fatter because It takes 20 minutes for your stomach to tell your brain it's full so fast eaters shovel in more than slow eaters.

But other than an artfully concealed small pot belly, I'm pretty thin and I wolf down dinner faster than my dog.

For more dumb forkiness see *Great Gift for Italian Food Lovers* on p. 20.

Available in hot pink, green, blue, black and white.

They Don't Serve Horse at McDonald's

A woman showed up in July, 2013 at the drive-thru window at a McDonald's in Whitefield, England, near Manchester, riding a horse. Her daughter was along, too, riding a pony. She was refused service.

The woman then led her horse into the restaurant where it pooped on the floor. The police were called and the woman was cited and fined.

"The staff refused to serve the woman due to company policy. The woman then took the horse into the restaurant, who ended up doing his business on the floor," the Manchester police said on Facebook."

McDonald's has a horseback service policy?

Until McDonald's gets a hitching post, you equestrians can make your own Big Macs: two all-beef patties, special sauce, lettuce, cheese, pickles, onions – on a sesame seed bun. (All-beef means contains no horsemeat.)

As for the "special sauce", in 1969 McDonalds printed the recipe for its secret Big Mac sauce in a manager's handbook. The idea was that if a McDonalds ran out of the pre-packaged sauce, it could be whipped up on the spot. The page was pulled, but the formula got out.

•1/4 cup salad dressing, i.e. Miracle Whip

•1/4 cup mayonnaise

•3 tbsp French salad dressing

•1/2 tbsp sweet pickle relish

•1 1/2 tbsp dill pickle relish

•1 tsp sugar

•1 tsp dried, minced onion

•1 tsp white vinegar

•1 tsp ketchup

•1/8 tsp salt

Mix all ingredients, and stir well in a small container. Microwave on high for 25 seconds, and stir well. Enough for 8 burgers.

April Fools'

The BBC broadcast a three minute report on April 1, 1957 showing a family in the southern Swiss canton of Ticino harvesting spaghetti from spaghetti trees. A mild winter and no spaghetti weevils produced a bumper crop.

"After picking, the spaghetti is laid out to dry in the warm Alpine air. Many people are very puzzled by the fact that spaghetti is produced in such uniform lengths. This is the result of many years of patient endeavour by plant breeders who succeeded in producing the perfect spaghetti."

There were scenes of a harvest festival meal with spaghetti "....picked early in the day, dried in the sun, and so brought fresh from garden to table at the very peak of condition. For those who love this dish, there is nothing like real home-grown spaghetti."

The British were not that familiar with spaghetti at that time and people phoned in the next day for tips on growing their own spaghetti trees. "Place a sprig of spaghetti in a tin of tomato sauce and hope for the best," they were told.

Where's the Beef?

Google co-founder Sergei Brin spent $337,000 to develop the world's first fake hamburger in 2013.

Stem cells from cows were were gown into muscle fibers at Maastricht University in the Netherlands. 20,000 little hoops of muscle were each cultured in individual compartments. After a few weeks, the hoops were cut open by hand, straightened out and pressed together, colored with beet juice and mixed with saffron and breadcrumbs to form the first synthetic hamburger, the Googleburger.

The Googleburger was cooked and eaten at an event in London August 5. The burger was given high marks for mouth feel but lacked juiciness due to lack of fat, but they're working on the fat problem. Googleburgers are highly efficient, with one cow providing enough material to produce 175 million burgers as opposed to 440,000 cows to make them the old-fashioned way.

So what took so long? An article in the January 13, 1906 Literary Digest titled *Food by Chemical Synthesis?* recounts an article in the Parisian journal Cosmos that tells of a German chemist who "has discovered in it [coal] a food-stuff of the first rank, whose formula, which is not yet divulged, is sensibly the same as that of animal flesh. If this announcement is not a 'bluff' we must ask whether we shall not, some day, see food derivatives of coal make their appearance on the market."

Chemists have synthesized lecithin, an ingredient in eggs, so "When shall we have the synthesis of beefsteak?"

Free Lunch

CARRY LUNCH IN YOUR POCKET

Lunch is a troublesome matter with the busy business man. Eating at a crowded restaurant wastes time, creates ill humor, and sends you back to work unsettled for the tasks of the afternoon. The brain, dull because its blood supply has been called to the stomach by heavy food, refuses to work."

Should you try to avoid the restaurant nuisance by bringing your lunch, you are no better off. Cold food is seldom good food. Lacking appetisers to stimulate the digestive juices, it makes double work for the stomach.

Avoid the bother of lunch. Eat half a dozen or a dozen (more if desired)

Horlick's Malted Milk Lunch Tablets

You save time, money, bother, and give the stomach a new lease on life. This partially pre-digested lunch does not tax digestion. The brain bright and alert, not robbed of its blood supply, turns off the afternoon work as fast as the morning. The satisfaction of tasks well done, and the keen appetite for the evening meal, sets you at ease with yourself...The famous HORLICK'S MALTED MILK, pressed into lozenges and flavored with chocolate or vanilla.

This is an ad from the January 26, 1907 issue of The Literary Digest. And yes, there is free lunch. You could send in a coupon for a free "Horlick's Special Vest Pocket Lunch Case filled with Malted Milk Lunch Tablets." After you eat them "The result will lead the reasoning man, who wishes to save time, his digestion, and increase his thinking capacity, straight to the druggist for more tablets."

Founded in 1873 by two brothers named Horlick, the company produced a powdered malted milk hot drink, which is still available, mainly overseas. The drink was popular during World War I. Horlick's tablets were sold as candy in the U.S. and were popular during World War II and were part of aircrew survival kits. The brand is now owned by GlaxoSmithKline.

You Are What You Ate

It seems like diet is the cure for what ails you. It doesn't affect me, though. I can eat anything I want any time I want with no ill effects. This is because I grew up before they found out that food was bad for you.

The Artichoke King

Mayor Puts a Ban on Artichoke Sale to Curb Rackets

With Trumpet Fanfare at Dawn in Bronx He Proclaims an Emergency in City Markets.

Toll at $1,000,000 a Year

Dealers Cynical, Seeing Corner in Broccoli Next, But Growers in the West are Jubilant.

These headlines are from an article in The New York Times from December 22, 1935. The Mayor is Fiorello La Guardia.

At 6:50 a.m., at the Bronx Terminal Market, two police buglers heralded the Mayor from the back of a truck, after one bugler faltered in the bitter cold. The mayor clambered up onto the truck and read a proclamation banning small artichokes, which were primarily sold to Italian-Americans.

"Artichoke King" Ciro Terranova, a mobster from — where else? — Corleone in Sicily had muscled in on the artichoke trade, jacking up prices and intimidating merchants. He bought artichokes for $6 a crate and resold them at a 30-40% profit, or else.

The artichoke farmers of California were not happy; the artichoke racket had hurt them, too. But one of the merchants in the market was skeptical: "If they squeeze the racketeers in artichokes, the racketeers will just corner something else — probably broccoli."

The ban was lifted on its third day when the 5 dealers who bought the artichokes in California signed an agreement not to deal with the Union Pacific Produce Company, Terranova's company, that had forced them sell only to it, which closed the same day.

LaGuardia then got the Department of Agriculture in Washington to revoke Union Pacific's license to sell food to head off Terranova's lawyers.

Terranova lived in Westchester County, north of New York City, and whenever he crossed the border into New York he was arrested for vagrancy on the Mayor's orders. He died in poverty in February, 1938 at 49.

Terranova was played in the TV series The Untouchables by Jack Weston.

Eeeeew!

Larvets, "Original Worm Snax in BBQ, Cheddar Cheese, and Mexican Spice flavored worms for your snacking pleasure. Savor the CRUNCH!" They're fried mealworms.

These and other insect candies are available from Hotlix. "For over 20 years HOTLIX has been making people cringe with delight with their outrageous confections featuring real insects embedded inside the candy!" Try the Lollipops with a real scorpion inside. $2.95.

The Arizona Exposition & State Fair's Chef du' Jour booth sold caramel apples dipped in mealworms in 2011.

Mealworms grow up to become beetles. Bon appétit!

To Boil Pig's Pettitoes*

"Boil the heart, liver, and lights* of one or more pigs ten minutes, and then shred them pretty small. Let the feet boil until they are pretty tender, and take them out and split them. Thicken your gravy with flour and butter, put in your mincemeat, a slice of lemon, a spoonful of white wine, a little salt, and let them boil a little. Beat the yolk of an egg, add to it two spoonfuls of good cream, and a little grated nutmeg. Put in your pettitoes, shake them over the fire, but do not let them boil. Lay sippets* round your dish, pour in your mincemeat, lay the feet over them, the skin side upwards, and serve them up."

— The Accomplished Housekeeper and Universal Cook by T. Williams and the principal cooks at the London and Crown and Anchor Taverns, 1797.

The preface stresses cleanliness, both of cooks and kitchenware, referencing the "melancholy affair at Salt-hill", food poisoning from a dinner at the Castle Inn in 1773 resulting in the deaths of 19 people.

* Pettitoes — pig's feet, lights — lungs, sippets — small pieces of bread fried with herbs and butter. The London Tavern and the Crown and Anchor Tavern are still there.

Pacific Pacifier

On Canada Day, July 1, the celebrants can get rowdy after the bars let out. A city councilor in Victoria, the capital of British Columbia on Vancouver Island, had the idea of handing out lollipops to soothe the savages. 11,000 red and blue lollipops were given out by police.

It worked. It's hard to yell at someone with a lollipop in your mouth, it boosts low blood sugar, and sucking on something has a pacifying effect, as any mother knows.

What's for Dinner?

Here's the cost of living large in the Depression, from the Nov. 7, 1936 Literary Digest. Multiply by 17.02 for 2015 dollars.

GOURMET'S PRICE LIST
(New York Quotations)

Caviar $12 per 14 oz.

Terrapin $3.75 per No. 2 tin

Snails $1.15 per 7 oz.

Pate de foie gras 90c. per 2 oz.

Goose-breast $3 per lb.

Goose-livers $3 per 12 oz.

Frogs' legs 50c. per 5½ oz.

Cocks' combs $2.70 per 8 oz.

Pigs' feet 33c. per 14 oz.

Rattlesnake meat $1.20 per 5 oz.

Scotch grouse $4.50 per pair

Red-leg partridges, French $3.50 a pair

English partridges, 90c. each

English pheasants $4.50 per pair

South American quail 75c. each

Venison 75c. per lb.

Hazel hens $1.10 each

For an update see *Got A Clew* on p. 27.

Waste Management

In January, 2011 the FDA announced a recall of candy made in Pakistan, the *Toxic Waste Nuclear Sludge Cherry Chew Bar.* It seems there was some toxic waste in the toxic waste: lead.

Toxic Waste Nuclear Sludge Green Apple and *Toxic Waste Nuclear Sludge Blue Raspberry* chew bars were also recalled.

But not to worry. *Lick Your Wounds Candy Scabs* should fill in nicely. You stick the band-aid replica on your arm and open a little compartment to lick a blob of candy that looks like a scab.

Great Gift For Lazy Italian Food Lovers

That's how one web site characterizes this motorized spaghetti fork.

"A thumb-activated button on the handle sets the prongs turning at 22 rpm, smoothly winding pasta into a mess-free mouthful, rather than fumbling awkwardly with a helper spoon or slurping up long noodles", says another.

$29.95 for a pair at Hammacher Schlemmer, but only $9.99 each at Stupid.com. Batteries (2 AAA's) not included.

Truth in Labeling

Lea & Perrins, makers of Worcester-shire Sauce, "pronounced by connois-seurs to be the only good sauce, and applicable to every variety of dish," ran a notice in the January 26, 1858 Argus (Montreal) of "extensive frauds." Fake Worcestershire sauce was found in for-eign markets with labels closely resem-bling the real thing, some with the Lea & Perrins name forged. The genuine article has "Lea & Perrins" on the "wrapper, label, stopper, and bottle."

Of course, you could also take a genuine bottle and fill it with your own inferior stuff. A 1917 article in *Modern Business Talks* says the cure may be a non-refillable bottle:

"The manufacturers of Lea & Perrins Sauce are constantly called upon to pre-vent the use of substitutes which are of-fered for consumption in a Lea & Perrins bottle bearing the genuine label.... The non-refillable bottle and the pasting of a genuine label over the cork are precau-tions against this kind of substitution."

There were a rash of patents for non-refillable bottles in the early 1900's. An article in the August 23, 1902 Literary Di-gest mocked the concept:

The bottles "are fearful and wonderful mechanisms with complicated valves and pumps, which are perhaps interesting as

curiosities, but useless for any other pur-pose."

The article then quotes *The American Inventor*: "Take the case of the most-often used bottle for illegitimate purposes, which is that holding a certain sauce found on all restaurant tables. . . . The better class of restaurants of course use this sauce new and fresh for their customers, but the num-berless smaller eating-houses throughout the country will buy perhaps a dozen bot-tles of the condiment in question and then continue to refill them after they have been emptied of their original contents." The arti-cle goes on to say that the loss to the maker of the sauce is minuscule compared to its profits and that non-refillable bottles are far too expensive

"Assurance for Nothing. That is what the new Johnnie Walker non-refillable bottle gives the purveyor...Read how to pour and don't worry about the whiskey."

This is from a large ad on the front page of The Cairns Post (Queensland, Australia) on October 3, 1913. There is an illustration of whiskey pouring into a glass from a bottle held almost vertically. "Tilt the bottle (at the angle shewn in the illustration) and the whiskey will flow freely."

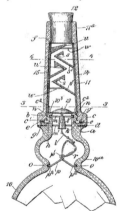

Illustration from the 1902 patent of George McCracken.

Waste Management

Coffee beans are seeds of the coffee plant that are inside the bright red fruit, called a coffee cherry. Coffee cherries are sweet and Elephants love them.

In northern Thailand some 20 elephants are fed coffee cherries grown on nearby coffee plantations. Coffee cherries go in and coffee beans come out the other end of the elephant. The beans are plucked from the dung and sun dried and roasted.

It takes 10,000 coffee cherries to make a kilogram of Black Ivory coffee, the most expensive in the world at $50 a cup and $500 a pound. The coffee is said to be exceptionally smooth thanks to the digestive enzymes of the elephant.

In Indonesia, coffee cherries are fed to civets and the beans collected from their droppings. Civet coffee is $320 a pound.

Dining Out

World War II canned K-rations were superseded by the C-rations I ate in Viet Nam and they in turn were updated to MRE's, Meals Ready to Eat, in lightweight pouches. There are 24 menu choices, including lemon pepper tuna and Mediterranean chicken, which may be contrasted with the execrable ham and lima beans C-rations.

The shelf life of MRE's is 3 years. (As opposed to infinite for C-rations.) The holy grail is pizza, and the U.S. Army Natick Soldier Research, Development and Engineering Center in Natick, Mass. is almost there. The prototype tastes pretty good according to the pizza scientists who are developing it.

The trick was to add ingredients to prevent moisture in the tomato sauce, cheese. and toppings from migrating into the dough, making it soggy and bacteria-friendly. The correct acidity of the ingredients inhibits bacteria also and iron filings in the pouch absorb remaining oxygen.

 You would open your C-rations with your handy P-38 can opener. Only 1½ inches long, it was worn on the chain with your dog tags. C-ration peanut butter came in a little can. It wasn't homogenized, so it was best to turn the can upside down for a day or so before you opened it with your P-38. Otherwise you would get a layer of oil on top of peanut plaster.

But not all field rations were canned. Major General Terry de la Mesa Allen, commander of the First Infantry Division (Big Red One) in North Africa in 1943 often served his men "casualty beef", which he claimed was the result of cattle killed by enemy fire.

The courtesy was not reciprocated. When Major General Ernest Harmon, commander of the First Armored Division, took the surrender of German officers in in full dress uniforms in Tunisia May 9, 1943 they were handed K-rations for lunch. "You would have thought the bastards were going to a wedding", Harmon told General Bradley.

Stop the Music

Beans, beans, the musical fruit
The more you eat the more you toot.

The Japanese have figured out how to pass on the gas when eating beans. Just cook them with a strip of kombu, edible kelp seaweed. "Tender fronds Arctic current nurtured off Hokkaido." 60 g. $9.05.

In a 1993 episode of The Simpsons, Bart is expelled from Springfield Elementary School. He was then enrolled in Springfield Christian School and when asked to recite a psalm, Bart is chased from the school after singing "Beans, beans, the musical fruit, the more you eat, the more you toot." In a 1994 episode, Bart writes on the blackboard "Beans are neither fruit nor musical."

The Cat Who Came to Dinner

In 1898, Woolf Joel, nephew of South African diamond magnate Barney Barnato (see *The Largest Check Ever Written* on p, 206), gave a dinner for 14 at the Savoy Hotel in London. One guest canceled, leaving an unlucky 13. A guest predicted that the first one to leave would die. Woolf scoffed at this superstition and left first. A few weeks later, on March 14, 1898, he was shot dead in his office in Kimberley by a blackmailer.

Thereafter, the Savoy volunteered a staff member to sit in on parties of 13, but it was awkward having a stranger and in 1927 noted British architect Basil Ionides sculpted Kaspar, a 3 foot high wooden black cat to be the 14th guest.

 Kaspar is given his own place setting, a napkin is wrapped around his neck, and is served each course.

Winston Churchill liked Kaspar so much he insisted that he join him no matter the number of guests. Kaspar was catnapped during the war in an RAF prank. He was returned, slight damage repaired, after intercession by an Air Commodore whose dinner guests, officers of an air squadron, unknown to him, had done the catnapping.

Speaking of the Savoy Hotel there is a Barney Barnato cocktail listed in the *Savoy Cocktail Book* (1930) by Harry Craddock, head bartender at the Savoy. (See *The Ghost Ingredient is Back!* on p. 11.)

Ad Nauseum*

If the flying didn't didn't make you sick, the barf bag will. Spirit Airlines has ads on its dishonorable discharge containers. If you want people to remember your product every time they get sick it'll cost you $30,000 per quarter to put your ad on 150,000 barf bags.

For $60,000 per quarter for 350,000 the wretched retchers can tidy up with your bespoke napkins. Stewardess aprons, cups, boarding passes, and ticket jackets will also tout your product.

But why not go all the way with a flying billboard? Get a plane wrap for $400,000 per quarter for 1 one plane.

People collect barf bags, too. A Dutchman holds the Guinness record with 5468 of them.

And, of course, there are designer barf bags. In 2004 Virgin Atlantic "introduced 20 limited edition sickbags designed by artists from around the globe." I like this Japanese design.

* This irresistible title was gleefully stolen from the New York Times Magazine May 4, 2014. Runner up was "Queasy Rider" which I saw somewhere on the Internet and which was also stolen, from a 2003 King of the Hill episode.

Potlikker Politics

After you boil up your mess of greens, the liquid in the bottom of the pot is potlikker. It's a Southern delicacy, especially when served with corn-pone.

In February, 1931, the Atlanta Constitution ran an Associated Press article about how Louisiana Governor Huey Long had saved the state $600,000 on highway bonds by serving corn-pone and potlikker to the representative of a bond syndicate, who gave a lower interest rate in appreciation. The article explained to the Yankees that Long dunked the cornbread in the potlikker.

An editor at the Constitution, Julian Harris, appended an editor's note: "Corn-pone, so-called, that can be 'dunked' is not genuine corn-pone." That touched off a three week battle in the press over whether corn-pone should be dunked or crumbled into the potlikker.

Huey Long sent a telegram to the Constitution demanding a retraction. The Constitution replied with its telegram, citing its 60 year status as "a patriotic arbiter of all matters appertaining to potlicker, cornpone, dumplings, fried collards, sweet 'tater biscuits and 'simmon beer and 'possum, reiterates its assertion that cornpone is crumbled into the potlicker and not dunked." It gave Long two hours to reply.

Not hearing from Long, the paper put the dunking vs. crumbling question to Southern governors. None agreed with Long. New York Governor Franklin D. Roosevelt, an honorary Southerner due to his second home at Warm Springs, Georgia, sent a telegram to the "Potlikker and Cornpone Department" of the Constitution diplomatically suggesting that the matter be referred to the platform committee of the Democratic National Convention due to meet shortly in Washington, but added "I must admit I crumble mine."

Emily Post waffled on potlikker etiquette, suggesting "dunk with dunkers, crumble with others" in the New York Times February 19, 1931.

An article in the Oxford American Magazine (Miss.) March 13, 2014, said the Constitution had received over 600 letters to the editor about dunking and crumbling, including one from an 85 year old Confederate Civil War veteran asking "does it not depend in a great measure if the users have two sets, upper and lower teeth?"

Spam

Now I lay me down to sleep
And pray the Lord the Spam don't keep
— WWII GI prayer, Life, March 11, 1946

Life Magazine had a long article about Spam. Jay Hormel, son of Hormel Foods founder George Hormel, had a contest at a 1936 New Year's Eve party at his house. 65 guests were told that the price of each drink would be an entry for the name of a new Hormel product. But it was the butler* who came up with the winner: "Spam."

Spam was launched in 1937 with a corny jingle to the tune of Bring Back My Bonnie to Me:

SPAM, SPAM, SPAM, SPAM
Hormel's new miracle meat in the can,
Tastes fine, saves time,
If you want something grand ask for SPAM.

But it turns out that the GI prayer was for the wrong stuff. According to Life, "A lively correspondence" between *Yank* [Army weekly magazine] and Hormel revealed that real Spam was only shipped in 12 ounce packages, not the bulk cans of ersatz Spam supplied to the Army by various manufacturers from a recipe supplied by the Quartermaster Corps.

Hormel shipped Spam, "a special high-grade compound of ham and pork shoulder", to England and Russia under Lend-Lease, "but little to the Army."

Hormel pointed out that "dainty, tasty Spam retained liquids in the meat, whereas the bulky Army preparation was guilty of the worst sin in the tinned-meat world—the presence of 'loose juice.'" Yank ended the article with "What's in a name? That which we call Spam by any other name would taste as lousy."

Spam is considered a delicacy in Korea, where it was the only meat available, and only to the rich with GI connections to get it from the PX, during the privations of the Korean War and subsequent occupation. It is also served with kim-chi in "military stew", and is considered a special gift.

Then there's the lousy tasting spam you get in your inbox. The use of "spam" for email comes from a 1970 Monty Python skit in which everything on a restaurant menu involves Spam. A group of Vikings start singing "SPAM,SPAM,SPAM..." drowning out everyone else. The first instances of the term "spam" reference the skit.

The BBC reports that a fridge was one of more than 100,000 smart appliances that were hacked to send out spam at the end of 2013.

According to the Radicati Group, a tech research firm, there are 4 billion 116 million email accounts,191.4 billion emails are sent per day and 84% of emails are spam. That works out to 58.7 trillion spam emails a year, or about 8400 for every person on earth!

A 2004 article on the BBC web site says Bill Gates is the most spammed person in the world, with 4 million emails a day, most of them spam. Gates gives out his email address in speeches. There is an entire department at Microsoft devoted to sorting his email.

Gates said in a 2003 Wall Street Journal article that "much of it offers to help me get out of debt or get rich quick."

*The official Spam web site says Kenneth Daigneau, an actor and brother of a Hormel vice-president won the contest and was awarded $100. The site also says that from 1941-1945 "More than 100 million pounds of Spam luncheon meat are shipped abroad to feed allied troops during WWII."

I emailed Hormel asking about the contradictions between the Life article and their web site. I got an initial response insisting that Daigneau, not the butler, did it. I sent the link to the Life article and was promised definitive answers after more research, but they never got back to me.

The email said "I do know that we sent 12 oz cans of SPAM® to our allies as part of the Lend-Lease program. But for our own military it was sent in a large 6 lb can and was also a different formula, so it was indeed not true SPAM®."

No word on the loose juice problem.

Shoe Leather

271

In the 1925 silent *The Gold Rush,* a starving Charlie Chaplin boils a shoe for Thanksgiving dinner. The shoe was made of licorice and the meticulous Chaplin needed 63 takes to nail the scene. Some accounts have Chaplin rushed to a hospital for an insulin shot, although Chaplin in an interview says only "The shoe was made of licorice— it's very laxative you know—and we had two days of retakes on it. The poor fellow who played the big man, he finally said, 'I cannot eat any more of that shoe.'"

You're Toast!

Listen up narcissists. Now you can really be full of yourself. Just send a high resolution photo to the Vermont Novelty Toaster Corporation and they'll send you a selfie toaster for only $75.00.

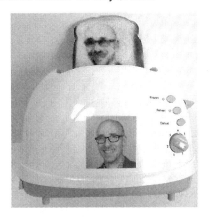

The company had a big hit making Jesus toasters for Amazon and they became the 32nd best selling toaster. "Pretty good for a product created by a slacker pothead," the company tweeted.

But Amazon was too big for the company's britches, withholding half their money at Christmas when sales went above their "limited velocity amount" and triggered an account review. On top of that, Amazon had other onerous fees.

So the company pulled their Jesus toasters from Amazon along with Virgin Mary, Sarah Palin, Obama, butterfly, peace sign, marijuana leaf, and paw print toasters.

Too bad. In a review on Amazon, one fellow said that one day so many people showed up at his house he didn't know what to do until a small boy offered him two small loaves and he put them in the Jesus toaster and so much toast came out he fed 5000 people.

The company staff evidently wishes to remain Anonymous. Their web site shows three of them hiding their faces behind Guy Fawkes toast.

Hot Chocolate

In 1945, Percy Spencer, who was in charge of manufacturing the magnetron tubes that generated microwaves for radars for Raytheon, was standing in front of one of the tubes when he noticed the chocolate candy bar in his pocket had melted.

Intrigued, Spencer experimented with various foods, making the first microwave popcorn and cooking an egg which exploded in the face of a co-worker. He patented the microwave oven in October, 1945, which became the Radarrange. The first microwave ovens were 6 feet tall and weighed 750 pounds. The first countertop microwave was introduced in 1967.

Now it's your turn to melt a chocolate bar with microwaves. Get a large chocolate bar, take out the rotating glass plate in the microwave so the chocolate bar won't move, and put it inside. Zap it for 20 seconds or so until you see two melted spots. Measure the distance between the centers of the melted spots. Multiply the measurement by 2 and then by .0254 and finally by 2,450,000,000.

Congratulations! You just measured the speed of light.

You should get about 2.4 inches for your measurement. The hot spots in the chocolate are at the peaks of the micro-wave so you measured half its wavelength and have to multiply by 2. Multiplying by .0254 converts the inches you measured to meters. The standard frequency of the of microwave ovens is 2.45 gigahertz or 2,450,000,000 cycles per second. Micro-waves are electromagnetic radiation like visible light but at a lower frequency. Speed is how many wavelengths go by in a second.

2.4 x 2 x .0254 x 2,450,000,000 = 298,704,000 meters per second. That's pretty close to the actual value of 299,792,458.

For more fooling around with waves see *Mercury Made From Gold* on p. 229.

Cartoon Cow Comes to Life

A man named Gail Borden invented condensed milk in 1856 and founded the Borden company. In 1936, one of four cows in popular cartoon ads in medical journals, Elsie, wrote a letter to a radio commentator: "Dear Mama, I'm so excited I can hardly chew! We girls are sending our milk to Borden's now. Love, Elsie." Other letters followed and by 1939 Elsie was featured in magazine ads which were voted best of the year by the Jury of the 1939 Annual Advertising Awards.

At the 1939 New York World's Fair, Borden installed a "Rotolacter", a glass enclosed turntable on which cows were milked twice a day by automated milking machines. Surveys revealed that 60% of questions about the exhibit asked "Which cow is Elsie?" Borden selected a cow named You'll Do Lobelia from the herd of 150 and renamed her Elsie.

Elsie appeared on the Rotolacter between milkings in a green blanket with her name embroidered on it, a bow on her tail and a wreath of black-eyed susans around her neck. She was a hit, becoming the Fair's #1 attraction.

Elsie became one of the most recognizable advertising characters of the 20th century, going on tour in her 18 wheeler "Cowdillac" and appearing in the film *Little Men* as Buttercup.

In 1941, Elsie was on her way to New York City when the Cowdillac was hit by a truck from behind at a traffic light in Rahway, New Jersey. She suffered spine injuries from which veterinarians said she could not recover and was put down on her home farm in Plainsboro, New Jersey.

Successor Elsies, at least 32 of them since 1939, continue to tour the country.

It Tastes Offal

Ye Pow'rs, wha mak mankind your care,
And dish them out their bill o fare,
Auld Scotland wants nae skinking ware
That jaups in luggies:
But, if ye wish her gratefu prayer,
Gie her a Haggis*
— Robert Burns, Address to a Haggis, eighth stanza

Haggis is a Scottish delicacy, a pudding made from sheep's pluck: heart, liver, windpipe and lungs, with minced onions, oatmeal, suet, spices and salt cooked and served in the sheep's stomach.

Although available year-round, it is traditionally served in the Burns Supper, a celebration of Scottish poet Robert Burns, held on January 25th.

Guests are piped in, the host gives a short speech, the Selkirk Grace, written by Robert Burns in 1787 and delivered by him at a meal hosted by the Earl of Selkirk in 1794, is recited:

Some hae meat an
canna eat,
And some wad eat that want it;
But we hae meat, and we can eat,
And sae let the Lord be thankit.

Soup is served, then everyone stands as the haggis is brought in, accompanied by bagpipes, traditionally playing *A Man's a Man for A' That*, a 1795 song by Burns.

Then the Address to a Haggis is read (above is the last of 8 stanzas). The haggis is toasted with Scotch whiskey, then everyone sits to eat it.

But you'll have to go to Scotland to eat haggis: it's been banned in the United States since 1971. The problem is the lungs, deemed inedible by the Department of Agriculture. (See *To Boil Pig's Pettitoes* on p. 19.)

If you really need your haggis fix, you could make your own if you're up to slaughtering a sheep. But the only platter of haggis you'll find on the black market is a CD. Black Market Haggis is the name of an Alabama band ("Better Than it Sounds") that plays Irish and Celtic music.

* You powers, who make mankind your care,
And dish them out their bill of fare,
Old Scotland wants no watery stuff,
That splashes in small wooden dishes;
But if you wish her grateful prayer,
Give her a Haggis!

Conspicuous Consumption

Cosmetic Sturgeon

If smearing the gold on your face (see *Cosmetology* on p. 35) didn't make you any younger, try caviar.

"The extract of caviar is a complete cocktail of pure and concentrated marine substances favouring considerably the process of rejuvenization of the skin."

"The specific talent of caviar is that of teaching our skin how to return to its youthful stage."

"Penetrates Over 7 Layers Deep Into Your Skin!"

$25-52 for various brands.

The top of the line is La Prairie Skin Caviar Luxe Cream 3.4 oz. $780.00. "Protein-rich Caviar Extract combines energizing vitamins, humectants and emollients in caviar-like beads."

You can eat caviar, too. Petrossian Special Reserve Ossetra Caviar, 1000 grams (2.2 lbs), $12,500.

As Inspector Doppler (Michael Caine) said to Andrew Wyke (Laurence Olivier) in the 1972 movie *Sleuth* after sampling this upper class fare, "Caviar, eh? Can't say I like it. Tastes of fish eggs."

Consume Delicious Awake Up Chow at Tiffany

The ustiffany4sale web site offers amazingly discounted jewelry advertised as overstock from genuine Tiffany manufacturers. Why pay $1200 for a key pendant from Tiffany when you can get it for $64.99?

Tiffany, of course, is not amused. They are suing them and other similar knockoff sites.

The site says "Tiffany & Co jewelry is interantional famous brands. It had become legendary for a long time because of the movie- BREAKFAST AT TIFFANY'S (1961) and Audrey Hepburn."

And you will be more than satisfied: "all will surely give a loud hooting cry of exultation or excitement."

Wretched Excess Dept.

Here's the latest for overrich twits.

A company called *It's My Binky* gave a solid white gold pacifier set with 3 carats of diamonds to Brangelina baby Shiloh.

You can get your kid off to the right start with baby bling, too, for $17,000.

Arachnophilia

For the July, 2004 London premiere of Spiderman II, British singer Samantha Mumba wore a $9 million dress with diamonds woven into a spiderweb pattern over a black background.

It's the most expensive dress ever made.

Underwear Dept.

Victoria's Secret is offering a bra with over 2000 rubies and emeralds, in a rose and leaf pattern, with a 60 carat flawless pear-shaped diamond in the center. Matching panties with rubies, emeralds and diamonds complete the ensemble. Sizes not given. $10 million. [2003]

Attention Winos

If you want to drown your sorrows about the high price of gold in a glass of wine, you'd better hop on the wagon.

The London International Vintners Index, Live-ex, rose 40% in 2007. Gold rose 31%. Live-ex tracks prices of the top 100 wines. It's even listed on Bloomberg. Needless to say it's not for plonk.

I guess I'm not a wino — excuse me, oenophile. I never did taste those notes of raspberry, black cherry, sweet oak(?), or currants. Basically, I drink for effect: a convivial euphoria followed by a snooze in the barcalounger. It just shouldn't taste bad. If I wanted something delicious to drink, I'd have a glass of chocolate milk.

I spend 7 bucks for a bottle of wine every Saturday night, chosen from the Phil-ex.*

*I don't know why the Philistines get such a bad rap. They make good wine.

Precious Skin

That's the name of a shop in Dubai that will give you a temporary tattoo made of gold or platinum.

A thin film of precious metal is applied to the skin. The tattoos last about a week and start at $55, twice as much for platinum, and go to over $5000 for large, elaborate designs. The application takes about ten minutes.

The company opened in Dubai and plans to expand to other Middle Eastern countries. The Middle East has a tradition of temporary henna tattoos dating back to the bronze age.

Got a Clew?

CLEW, The Cost of Living Extremely Well, a basket of 40 luxury products tracked by Forbes Magazine only rose 1% in 2009. In 2008 it went up 12%.

Here are some products on the list:

Gucci loafers, $460
A dozen bespoke cotton shirts from Turnbull & Asser in London $3900
Men's black calf wingtip shoes, custom-made by John Lobb in London $5,075
Estate planning hourly fee for a Schlesinger, Gannon & Lazetera partner, $850
1 kilo of Petrossian Imperial Special Reserve Persicus caviar, $24,400
A year at Harvard, $47,215
45 minutes with a shrink on the Upper East Side, $325
Rolls-Royce Phantom, $345,750
Hatteras 80 MY yacht, $5,273,000
Learjet 40XR, $9,259,000
Facelift, $17,000
Hermes "Kelly" calfskin bag, $7,150
Forbes, 1-year subscription $60

But — attention winos — the Live-Ex Fine Wine 100 Index that tracks the prices of 100 of the most sought-after wines was up 15% in 2009 and 32% so far for 2010.

Maybe the Great Recession has driven the wealthy to drink.

Bathing Beauty

An 18 karat gold bathtub weighing 176 pounds worth $1.3 million was stolen in 2007 from a resort hotel south of Tokyo. Someone cut the chain on a door leading to the tub room and made off with the tub, which wasn't nailed down. The police have no clue. Maybe it's in the Hong Kong jewelry store with the gold toilet that was taken off the tourist list because of rude remarks by the staff. (See *Chinese Capitalist Fulfills Russian Communist's Dream* on p. 29.)

Deep Thought
A good deal on a bad diamond is no bargain.

Spring Bling

Bling H2O – The Dubai Series is "a limited edition bottle of mountain spring water encrusted with 10,000 hand-applied Swarovski crystals". The water "is bottled at Dandridge, Tennessee using a nine step purification process that includes ozone, ultra violet, and micro-filtration" and "won the gold medal for best tasting at the Berkeley Springs [West Virginia] International Water Tasting Festival."

The bottle comes "packed in a museum-quality case along with a letter of authenticity and a pair of white gloves to avoid smudging." 750 ml $2600.

On a hydration budget? Get the "Standard Edition" with "Bling" spelled out on the frosted glass bottle in Swarovski crystals. 750 ml, $40.

As for me, strange — love distilled water. It has a two-step purification process. It tastes like water. 1 gal., 99¢. It's the essence of purity.

Toot Your Horn

Now you can be obnoxious in style. An Austrian goldsmith made a deluxe vuvuzela, the plastic horn blasted continuously at the 2010 World Cup soccer matches.

With white gold trim and diamonds, the $21,343 horn was bought by a Russian businessman just in time to join the din at the World Cup final in Johannesburg, South Africa in July, 2010.

And, of course, there is Vuvuzela Radio, "a station dedicated to playing the sound of the vuvuzela......We are broadcasting non-stop, without commercial breaks." It's a constant B flat buzz.

Soccer sponsor Hyundai built a 115 foot vuvuzela on an unfinished bridge to nowhere in Cape Town before the World Cup final. It was painted blue with the Hyundai logo and slogan "Hyundai Brings the Gees" ("spirit" in Afrikaans) in white. A truck horn was blown through it. But after tests the authorities put a sock in it — too loud.

The Cape Town Sports Council banned vuvuzelas in July, 2010 three days after the World Cup final. Cape Town can now look forward to being a "vuvu free city".

Austria had banned vuvuzelas in 2009, not as too noisy, but for their potential use as missiles by soccer hooligans.

Vuvuzelas are also used to scare off marauding elephants in Uganda.

Pavement

A Bern, Switzerland company is offering jewelry made from paving stones from the street in front of Albert Einstein's ex-house.

Beads, rings, and pendants accented with 18 karat gold, diamonds and citrines have been made from more than half a ton of of rocks that Einstein's shoes once trod. And the jewelry is pricey – $250-300 just for a bead necklace.

Any of Einstein's shoe leather left on the pavement would have been polished off in cutting up the stones. And in any case, you'd be getting the wrong end of the Einstein.

But at least you won't have to worry about provenance: the stones were notarized for authenticity. How do you notarize a stone?

Deep Thought

A fool knows the price of everything and the value of nothing.

— Adapted from Oscar Wilde

ET* Phone Home

You can make the world's most expensive phone call for £5 million, or a little over $8 million, with a gold and diamond IPhone 4 from British firm Stuart Hughes Exclusive Elite Gadgets

The back is made from 18 karat rose gold. Set in the edge of the phone are 500 flawless diamonds, over 100 carats.

The Apple logo on the back is formed from 53 diamonds and the platinum main navigation button below the screen holds a 7.4 carat pink single-cut diamond which can be changed to a 8 carat flawless white single-cut diamond. (This is very odd. Single-cut diamonds have only 17 facets instead of 58 and usually are quite small, less than .05 carat, and they don't sparkle as much as full cuts.)

The phone comes in a granite chest lined with nubuck leather.

Better hurry, only two wil be made.

For the heck of it, I clicked on the "Purchase" button. You can't buy it until you create an account. They want a lot of information.

* Extravagant Twit

Your Weight in Gold

Dubai is a very rich, and very fat, country. It has the second-highest incidence of diabetes, half the people are considered overweight, and one in three children are obese, almost twice the rate in the U.S.

In July, 2013, the Dubai government offered a 30 day gold for weight loss contest. After registering and weighing in, participants were offered 1 gram of gold (about $45) for each kilogram (2.2 pounds) lost, with a 2 kilogram minimum but with no limit. The contest attracted 10,000 participants.

The biggest loser was a 29 year old engineer who shed 24 kilograms, about 53 pounds. He got almost $1100 and said he would use the gold to buy a gift for his mum.

A Human Is Forever

You are a carbon-based life-form (according to Mr. Spock). And, as you know, diamonds are pure carbon. Now you can be a diamond, too.

A company called LifeGem will turn you into a diamond after you're gone. The company will heat your specially prepared "cremains" in a vacuum at 5400° to reduce you to pure carbon, then will squeeze you into a diamond. A blue diamond. That's all they're doing now. The 18 milligrams (.09 carat) of boron in your body turns it blue. But yellow, red, and white are in the offing. You've got about 50 diamonds of various sizes in what remains of you. Cost is $22,000 per carat, with a ¼ carat minimum at $4000. A human is forever.

And you don't have to spend forever without your best friend. Rover can join you when his time comes. The company reports that half its business is for pets.

Snake Shoes

Harrods, the luxe London department store rented an Egyptian cobra to guard a pair of ruby, sapphire, and diamond encrusted sandals worth $120,000 on display in the shoe department.

They should have just hired Emily. She's our high-mileage used dog, a strawberry blonde Cocker Spaniel who came with a shoe fetish. If we leave shoes on the floor she guards them ferociously.

There's anti-venom for snakebites, but a one-handed thief is out of business.

Golden Garnish

Nieman Marcus will sell you 150 mg of 23 karat edible gold flakes to sprinkle on your food for $40. 150 mg, or .15 gram of gold is worth $5.31 at $1100 gold.

"Crafted in Italy", the gold meets FDA guidelines for edibility and is certified kosher. What would non-kosher gold be?

Pot of Gold

Harrods department store in London offered a saucepan in 2008 with gold handles and logo and 200 diamonds for £100,000.

After you've cooked your food in it, you can eat it with the chopsticks with gold flakes between them that drop into the food when you break them apart. ($40 for two sets of five).

A culinary school chef commented on edible gold:

"There is something psychological about consuming gold. It says that you have arrived, that you are on top of the world! You can truly say that you are among the very elite who can enjoy such a luxury. That, and rich people like to see their crap sparkle."

Chinese Capitalist Fulfills Russian Communist's Dream

"When we are victorious on a world scale, I think we shall use gold for the purpose of building public lavatories in the streets of some of the largest cities in the world."
—Vladimir Lenin, Pravda, November 5, 1921

One of Hong Kong's most popular tourist attractions is a solid gold toilet in a jewelry store in Kowloon. Inspired by Lenin's statement as a boy in China, Lam Sai Wing, chairman of a Hong Kong Jewelry firm, installed the 24 karat commode in 2001. (I think he got the meaning of Lenin's statement backwards, though).

The toilet is in a bathroom with solid gold sinks, toilet brushes, toilet paper holders, mirror frames, and wall tiles. There are also gold bars embedded in the floor. The store gets 5-6,000 visitors a day. Looking is free, but you can use the facilities if you

remove your shoes to avoid scuffing the floor and spend $138 on jewelry.

But if you go, you won't find the address from the Hong Kong Tourism Board. The Board removed it from the list of attractions in February, 2005 after store staff were rude to customers.

Time of Reflection

Russian Orthodox Patriarch Kiril I was photographed in April, 2012 wearing his simple long-sleeve black robe.

But he was sitting at a highly polished wood table which showed a reflection of a not-so-simple watch, a $30,000 Breguet (see *Chronology* on p. 340).

The photo was posted on the church's web site but with the watch Photoshopped into oblivion by extending his sleeve a bit. But the editors didn't notice the reflection and left it in the photo.

The church apologized and restored the original photo to its web site. But Kiril then denied having worn the watch and accused someone of Photoshopping the watch onto his wrist.

Rummaging through all the stuff he had been given as gifts, Kiril then said he found the watch.

Kiril was first spotted wearing the Breguet in 2009 during a televised lecture on the importance of asceticism.

House Of Pearls

Before cultured pearls came on the market in 1921, there were only natural pearls and they were next to diamonds in value.

In 1917, railroad investor Morton Plant gave in to the inevitable commercial desecration of his tony Fifth Avenue and 52nd Street residential neighborhood by selling out to Cartier.

Plant's wife Mae admired a two-strand pearl necklace that Cartier had. Plant agreed to swap his mansion for the pearls, valued then at $1 million.

In 1956 the pearl necklace was auctioned for $151,000, so had natural pearls fallen in value after the introduction of cultured pearls.

No one knows where the pearls are now.

Ruffles and Flourishes

"It was profusely laced, plaited, and apparently divergent from a centre on the back of her neck; it was very broad, extending on each side of her face, with the extremities reposing on her bosom, from which rose two wings of lawn, edged with jewels, stiffened with wire, and reaching to the top of her hair, which was moulded into the shape of a cushion, and richly covered with gems."

This is a description of Queen Elizabeth I's ruffled collar by Phillip Stubbs in his *Anatomie of Abuses,* a Puritan screed published in 1583. Stubbs was a pamphleteer who attacked the evil customs of the Elizabethan era. His accounts of the dress and manners of the time are so detailed they are a valuable historical resource.

He especially didn't like those large ruffled collars, the ones you see in old paintings that look like car air cleaner elements: "They have great and monsterous ruffes...whereof some be a quarter of a yard deep..."

The ornamentation of the ruff was as offensive as the collar itself: "Some are wrought with open woork down to the midst of the ruffe and further, some with purled lace so cloyd, and other gewgawes so pestered, as the ruffe is the least parte of it self."

It's all the work of the devil, of course. "The devil, as he in the fulnes of his malice, first invented these great ruffes..."

"...a certaine kinde of liquide matter which they call Starch, wherin the devill hath willed them to wash and dive his ruffes wel, which when they be dry, wil then stand stiffe and inflexible about their neck."

Hail to the Chief

Harry and James Kazanjian immigrated to the United States in 1912. In 1918, they founded Kazanjian Brothers in Beverly Hills, which became one of the premier international estate jewelers and dealers in rare gems, including the largest red diamond in the world (see *Seeing Red* on p. 166).

In gratitude to their adopted country, their foundation commissioned the carving of four large Australian sapphires into busts of George Washington, Thomas Jefferson, Abraham Lincoln and Dwight D. Eisenhower, President when the carvings were finished.

The busts range from 1056 to 1444 carats. The busts were donated to the nation in 1988 by the Kazanjian Foundation in a White House ceremony with President Reagan. They still reside at the White House.

Technical advisor for the carvings was Lincoln Borglum, who succeeded his father, Gutzon Borglum, as sculptor of Mount Rushmore in 1941.

The Foundation also commissioned a 3294 carat sapphire sculpture of Martin Luther King and a 5½ inch tall 8500 carat carving of the Liberty Bell under the wings of a bald eagle carved from a huge ruby weighing over 7 pounds that was presented for the 1976 bicentennial.

Silver Spoon

The expression "born with a silver spoon in your mouth" dates from the 18th century, when a doctor would put a silver spoon in the mouth of a child born sick. Silver kills germs and silver's ability to prevent disease has been know since antiquity, long before the discovery of microbes.

This is the basis of the tradition of giving babies silver rattles and cups – it helped them survive.

I reported to you that socks made with silver-coated fiber will kill stinky feet germs (see *Silverwear* on p. 46). But you should hold off buying the washing machine I told you about (see *Silver Lining* on page 210) that sprays nano size silver particles on your clothes and keeps them germ-free for a month. It turns out that the waste water also kills good germs in the environment.

Skullduggery

British artist Damien Hirst claims to have "sold" his latest artwork to a consortium that included Hirst himself for $100 million in 2007. Called *For the Love Of God*, It's a platinum skull encrusted with 8601 diamonds weighing 1106 carats, including a large pink diamond worth $8 million in the center of the forehead.

The skull was cast from a mold made from an actual 18th century dead guy. The teeth are original. Hirst said the skull cost $20 million to produce. Five time markup. Not bad.

Other works by Hirst include pigs, sheep, and a shark suspended in formaldehyde, a cabinet full of old drug bottles, and a painting with a bunch of dots, all sold for big bucks.

You can get your or your pet's ashes squeezed into a diamond, Beethoven's hair was made into diamonds (see p.167). What's with death and diamonds? I guess both are forever. I like the diamond bra and panties better.

In 1999, the Brooklyn Museum of Art displayed a few of Hirst's works including a composition of a cow's head, flies, maggots, sugar and water and a split pig carcass floating in formaldehyde. Then mayor Rudolf Giuliani threatened to cut off funding to the museum saying "If I can do it, it's not art." (Update on next page.)

Gold to Go

If you happen to be passing through the Frankfurt, Germany airport, you can pick up a little gold from a vending machine.

The prototype *Gold to Go* machine offers a 1 gram or 10 gram bar and gold coins at 30% over the gold price. The gold comes in a presentation box with a certificate of authenticity.

The machine is connected to the gold market and updates the price every few minutes.

The machines will be installed at 500 locations across Germany. The Germans in particular have an interest in holding gold in hard times since they have lost everything twice in the two world wars and went through the hyperinflation of the Weimar Republic. In 1923 prices were doubling every two days and the mark fell to 4.2 trillion to the dollar.

I'll beat the machine. I'll sell you all the gold you want at only 25% over the market.

Cosmetology

The venerable House of Guerlain, French perfumers since 1828, is selling a lipstick called KissKiss for $62,000.

The lipstick features a 110 gram 18 karat gold case studded with 199 diamonds weighing 2.2 carats. If you want to pick up a tube, you can just hop on the bus to New York; it will be sold exclusively at Bergdorf Goodman by appointment.

I estimate the cost to produce it at $5200, assuming the lipstick itself costs pennies. (In 2008.)

China Time

"A well-equipped Chinaman, I have been told, carries a watch on each side of his breast, that he may be able to regulate the one by the other. Wealthy Chinese cover the walls of their rooms with watches." This is from an article in the April, 1861 issue of Scientific American. The article was about a visit to a pocket watch factory in Switzerland.

Edouard Bovet (1797-1849) was the son of a watchmaker from Fleurier, Switzerland. He went to London, then the center of the watch trade, in 1814 to study watchmaking. in 1818, he was sent to Canton, China, then the only port open to westerners, by his employer and Immediately sold 4 watches for 10,000 Swiss Francs, the equivalent of $1 million today.

In 1822, Bovet founded the Bovet-Fleurier watch company for the sole purpose of manufacturing pocket watches for the Chinese market. Demand was so high the company had to contract with other Swiss manufacturers to meet it.

The Chinese watch market declined for the Swiss after 1855 due to French and U.S. competition and, of course, cheap Chinese knockoffs.

The company was sold many times since the 19th century but still exists. Bovet-Fleurier makes about 2000 high-end watches a year today.

Remount

In honor of the 50th anniversary of Harry Winston donating the Hope diamond* to the Smithsonian, the 45.52 carat deep blue stone has been removed from its setting. It will be displayed as a loose stone until May of next year, when it will put in a new setting. The necklace was chosen from three designs by the Harry Winston company in an online poll. The Hope will then be returned to its original platinum setting in late 2010, 100 years after Pierre Cartier designed it for Washington socialite Evalyn Walsh Mclean.

* He sent it registered mail in a plain brown box. See *You've Got Mail* on p. 166

Original Cartier setting. It was hung from a chain of 45 diamonds

New Harry Winston setting

Con Art

Conceptual art is what artists who can't draw or sculpt do. The king of con art is surely Damien Hirst. I told you about Hirst and his $100 million diamond skull* on p. 31.

His latest work is *For Heaven's Sake*, a platinum baby skull set with more than 8128 pink and white diamonds (right). And now for the ick factor: the skull was cast from a mold made from a dead newborn less than 2 weeks old. Hirst bought a 19th century pathology collection that included the skull. Price upon request.

But hey, we're in the Great Recession, so Hirst has conjured up some downmarket skulls: plastic, brightly colored with "household gloss" paint for $58,000. *Hallucinatory Head* comes in a limited edition of 50, each one different (left 2).

An art critic who called Hirst a con artist was barred from a Hirst exhibition at the Tate Modern Art Gallery in London in 2012.

Hirst is reckoned to be the Britain's richest artist worth $284 million in 2010.

* Hirst claims to have sold the diamond skull to a consortium of buyers including himself for $100 million in 2007. "Everyone in the art world knows Hirst hasn't sold the skull. It's clearly just an elaborate ruse to drum up publicity and rewrite the book value of all his other work," according to one art critic.

 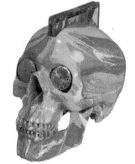 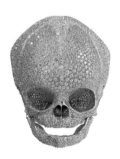

The Write Stuff

Montblanc has created a pen, the Classique Bohème Royal, set with 1430 diamonds weighing 15 carats.

You'll have to pull out your Bic and pen a check for $150,000 to use it.

For the Serious Vampire

That's how vampireteeth.com describes its "14K real gold fangs." $649.99.

And "if your a real baller", you can get them with a diamond set in each.. $1149.99.

The Man With the Golden Shirt

Datta Phuge, a finance entrepreneur from Pimpri, India shows off his wealth by wearing a gold shirt weighing 3.2 kilograms (7 pounds). He paid $230,888 for the shirt.

15 goldsmiths worked 16 hours a day for two weeks on the shirt which is made of 14,000 pieces of 22 karat gold sewn to white velvet lining. Matching cuffs and rings were made from the leftover gold.

Phuge said that the shirt "will be an embellishment to my reputation as the gold man of Pimpri." It will impress the chicks, too: "I know I am not the best looking man in the world but surely no woman could fail to be dazzled by this shirt."

Cosmetology

For some reason, women like to start the day with a schmear.

Chantecaille Nan Gold Energizing Face Cream has teeny silk fibers coated with gold that are supposed to penetrate the skin and cure wrinkles. $420 for a teeny jar.

Beaubelle's Amazing Luminance luxury anti-aging cream has diamond dust in it. It irons out your wrinkles and leaves a shimmering afterglow. $162 for 1.8 ounces.

La Prairie's Cellular Cream Platinum Rare has platinum in it. It's supposed to make it easier for your skin to absorb nutrients (isn't that the stomach's job?) and keep your skin in electrical balance. I didn't know skin had electricity to balance. Dr. Google didn't know either. $1000 for 1.7 ounces. It doesn't say how much platinum is in it.

Santa Loses Title!

Santa Claus was dethroned from the head of the list of the Forbes Fictional 15 in 2006. Although his wealth is still listed as infinite, letters from outraged children plus the evidence of toys delivered and milk and cookies eaten tipped the scales of prudence and Claus was removed from the list as possibly non-fictional.

Replacing him at the number 1 spot was Oliver "Daddy" Warbucks. His net worth is $36.2 billion, from military contracts. Here is the rest of the list. Amounts are in billions.

2. C. Montgomery Burns, $16.8, energy. Springfield nuclear plant very profitable.

3. Scrooge McDuck, $10.9, mining and treasure hunting.

4. Richie Rich, $10.7, inheritance.

5. Jed Clampett, $7.7, oil, gas, banking

6. Mr. Monopoly, $7.1, Atlantic City real estate.

7. Bruce Wayne, $6.8, inheritance, defense.

8. Tony Stark, $3.0, defense.

9. Prince Abakaliki of Nigeria, $2.8, telecommunications. (If you answer one of his emails, you can be rich, too.)

10. Thurston Howell III, TV character, $2.7, Howell industries. Unfortunately, can't enjoy his fortune stuck on Gilligan's Island.

11. Willy Wonka, $2.0, chocolate.

12. Lucius Malfoy, $1.3, inheritance, but wizardry can't get him out of Azkaban.

13. Tony Montana, $1.0, cocaine.

14. Lara Croft, $1.0, inheritance, antiques.

15. Mario, $1.0, commodities. Plumbers find lots of gold coins in the sewers.

Paper Profit

Elizabeth Taylor's jewels were sold at auction by Christie's in New York in two sessions, December 13-14, 2011. The total was $137,235,575, a world record, eclipsing the 1987 sale of the Duchess of Windsor's jewels for $50.3 million.

La Peregrina, a 51 carat 16th century pearl sold for $11.8 million, a record for a pearl and the Krupp diamond, a 33.19

carat asscher cut (square emerald cut) for $8.8 million.*

But the priciest lot was a suite with a necklace, earrings and ear clips that sold for $6875. Huh? It was paper cutouts of jewelry, a gag gift from Malcolm Forbes. It was bought by a Virginia jeweler for its publicity value. The pre-sale estimate was $200-300.

*See Close Encounters of the Canine Kind bottom right and Robbery at Spring Mountain Ranch on p. 167

Chronology

The first wristwatch was made by Abraham-Louis Breguet. It was commiss-ioned by the Queen of Naples in 1810. The watch took 2½ years to complete and was a marvel of slender elegance and complication. The French watchmaker (1747-1823) is generally considered the greatest watchmaker of all time. The Breguet brand is still sold today (expen-sive).

Brazilian aviation pioneer Alberto Santos-Dumont asked his friend Louis Cartier to make a wristwatch after a dirigible flight around the Eiffel Tower in 1900 so he could keep his hands on the controls. Men used pocket watches at that time. The result is the first man's wristwatch, in 1904.

Underwear Dept.

I told you about the $10 million Victoria's Secret bra and panties with diamonds, rubies, and emeralds (p. 26).

This year [2006] it's a bra with 2000 diamonds weighing 800 carats set in white gold. $6.5 million. Size not given.

At a Korean fashion show, a solid gold bra worth $1.89 million was shown. The model looked really uncomfortable.

Close Shave

For $100,000 your shave with the Zaffiro razor better be close. The razor features a handle made from iridium, a rare metal in the platinum group, and solid white synthetic sapphire blades honed to atomic sharpness. The blades come with a 20 year guarantee — if your beard is so tough it dulls the blades, the company will sharpen them for free.

Iridium is quite rare, with only about 3 tons produced a year. Your platinum ring may be stamped 90PLAT10 IRID, mean-ing it's made from 90% platinum, 10%

iridium, the standard platinum alloy until recently. (95% platinum, 5% cobalt is of-ten used today.) The iridium hardens the soft platinum.

Iridium cost $1050 a troy ounce in 2011 when the razor was introduced, (about half of that by 2015), and the synthetic white sapphire used in the blades is not expensive. Amazon sells a knife with a sapphire blade for $82 and you can buy a sapphire microtome (instrument for slicing tissue specimens) blade for $175.

They skimped on the iridium, too. The handle is hollowed out with grooves and rectangular holes. If my Gillette razor were made of iridium it would weigh about 9.4 troy ounces (with a rough calculation of its volume of 13 cc).* Figure maybe half that for the hollowed out Zaffiro, $5000 in ma-terials, tops (with the platinum screws that hold it together).

So where's the $100K price come from? They're making it up. "At that price, it better be able to kill vampires and werewolves, automatically." according to one review.

Better hurry. Only 99 were made.

* Iridium is only a smidge less dense than osmium, the densest element. Iridium is 500 times more abundant in meteorites than in the earth's crust, so a thin layer of iridium-rich clay dating to the time the dinosaurs disappeared 65 million years ago is thought to be evidence that they were wiped out by a meteorite.

Rodent Dept.

For the luxe computer experience there is an 18 karat white gold mouse with 59 diamonds, about 2 carats, arranged either as a flower or in a scattered design. You can also have it in yellow or rose gold. Made in Switzerland. $26,730.

Close Encounters
of the Canine Kind

La Peregrina (pilgrim or wanderer) is a large pear-shaped pearl weighing about 51 carats. It was discovered in the mid 16th century by an African slave off an island in the Gulf of Panama.

The slave was given his freedom and the administrator of the Spanish colony gave it to King Phillip II who presented it to his wife, Queen Mary I of England. There were several portraits painted of Mary wearing the pearl.

On Mary's death in 1558, the pearl was returned to the crown jewels of Spain, where it remained until Joseph Bonaparte*, who had been made king of Spain by his older brother Napoleon, lost a battle and had to abdicate in 1813. He took the pearl with him back to France. This is when the pearl got it's name as the wanderer.

Joseph Bonaparte left the pearl to his nephew (the future Emporer Napoleon III), who, while exiled in England, sold the pearl to the Duke of Abercorn. It remained in his family until it was auctioned by Sotheby's in 1969.

Richard Burton bought it for $37,000 (about $239,000 today) for his wife Elizabeth Taylor's 37th birthday.

Shortly after receiving the pearl, Elizabeth Taylor was in her hotel room at Caesar's Palace in Las Vegas when she noticed the pearl had vanished from the chain from which it hung.

After a frantic search, and without telling Richard, she noticed one of her Pekingese dogs chewing on something. She opened the dog's mouth and extracted the pearl, unharmed.

The pearl was sold in 2011 for $11.8 million. See *Paper Profit* on p.33

* Joseph Bonaparte spent part of his exile in New Jersey, arriving in 1817. He established a thousand acre estate near Bordentown, on the Delaware River, called Point Breeze.

Cosmetology

UMO 24 Karat Gold Facial lifts and firms, and reduces the appearance of fine lines, wrinkles, sun damage and sun spots.

For $110 you get "one full face 24k gold mask sheet with one free age defying serum (3ml)." You put the serum on your steamed face, rub it in, then put the gold mask on and rub it in until it is absorbed. (I didn't know that the skin could absorb metals.)

But for best result "We recommend you use the Pur Vous 24k gold collagen serum after the gold treatment." 1 fl. oz is $227.

The gold mask is 8" x 7.5" and has .004 oz. of gold in it. That works out to 6.5 millionths of an inch thick, the thickness of gold leaf, worth $4.40 at $1100 gold.

They don't say how much gold is in the Pur Vous serum.

In a May 27, 2010 article in the New York Times, two dermatologists were interviewed about gold face creams. "At best, they do nothing, and at worst, they can give you irritation of the skin," one said.

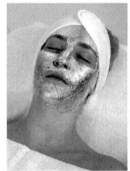

"There are absolutely no scientific studies that show that gold has any effect in firming or revitalizing the skin, nor that it reduces wrinkles or gives skin a plumped, golden glow" said the other.

Hallucination

Super luxury jeweler Laurence Graff has unveiled a $55 million watch at the 2014 Basel watch and jewelry show.

The watch, dubbed "Hallucination" sports 110 carats of rare natural colored diamonds of every color and took thousands of hours to produce. That works out to a half million bucks a carat.

The teeny circle in the center is the dial. No word on whether it's a battery watch or a wind-up.

Cosmetology

Now you can dust your face with gold.

"The first special occasion powder to contain real gold. Precious metals in makeup, at last! Yes, Jane Iredale use [sic] real gold and food-grade at that!"*

You get 1.8 grams of face powder with 24 karat gold dust in it for $12. How much gold is in that 1.8 grams isn't specified. 1.8 grams of 24 karat gold would cost about $64 at $1100 gold so it must be seriously diluted. I doubt that it contains more than $3.00 worth of gold. That would be .08 gram and would make the powder .04% gold, or about1 karat.

I guess the food-grade gold is in case the dog, baby, or man licks your face.*

* You can eat pure gold. See the mildy vulgar article about chopsticks with gold flakes between them that drop into the food when you break them apart on page 29

Glamburger

Head chef Chris Large at the Honky Tonk restaurant in London ("American flavour, British behaviour") has cooked up the Glamburger, the ultimate burger, costing £1100 ($1771 — plus 12.5% service).

"The burger patty is made from 220 grams of Kobe Wagyu beef minced with 60 grams of New Zealand venison to perfectly balance the fat content, and a rich center of black truffle brie to create a liquid pocket once the meat has cooked."

"The burger patty is then seasoned with smoked Himalayan salt and served with a Canadian lobster poached in Iranian saffron. Atop the lobster... is maple syrup-coated streaky bacon, Beluga caviar and a hickory-smoked duck egg intricately covered in edible gold leaf. The bun is seasoned with a Japanese matcha and cream mayonnaise and coated in gold leaf. Finishing touches come in the form of a mango and champagne jus and grated white truffle." 2600 calories.

That's the recipe from Groupon UK which sponsored the Glamburger to celebrate its 5 millionth food and drink voucher. A Groupon voucher purchase enters you in a drawing for the burger. Winners get round-trip travel costs thrown in.

"An American-inspired dining concept, Honky Tonk brings homespun grub, craft beer and music to venues in Chelsea and Clapham. Menus feature wings, chili dogs and waffles in their array of classics. The bar stocks a wide selection of bourbons, to be taken neat or as a cocktail."

Luxebrush

After you've eaten your Glamburger you can clean your choppers with the $4000 solid titanium toothbrush by Reinast

Four years in the making, Reinast enlisted control groups for "haptic feedback tests" (how it feels). The shape of the toothbrush was inspired by an ancient natural toothbrush, a miswak stick, a twig of *Salvadora persica*, the tooth-brush tree, native to the Middle East and Africa.

Underneath the replaceable bristle head is an anti-bacterial coating. If you don't like that metallic taste, you can accessorize with matching plastic bumpers that cover the part of the brush that goes in your mouth.

The bristle heads and bumpers have to be changed every two months and you have to sign up with a plan to do it: 5 years for $400, 7 years for $800, or 11 years for $1,600.

The toothbrush comes in four colors: titanium, champagne, rose, and matte-black (with matching bumpers) and has a lifetime guarantee.

So who's buying it? People "with an incredibly high net worth. People who have their own yachts, people who have their own private jets." One Middle Eastern sultan buys 'em by the dozen to hand out as gifts.

But why not just go natural? Miswak sticks have anti-microbial properties and are used all over the Middle East and Africa. For replacement bristles, just cut off the worn ones and peel the bark for new ones. Al-Khair freshly harvested miswaks (1 box 36 miswaks) $23.95 from Amazon.

Conspicuous Elimination

22 Carat Gold Toilet Paper - 1 Roll
Price: $1,376,900.00
Availability: Delivered Personally with a bottle of Champagne
Current Stock: 1
Quantity: 1   [Add To Cart]

Inevitably the Glamburger will make its final curtain, so why not go in style? Might as well use the golden toilet, too (see *Chinese Capitalist Fulfills Russian Communist's Dream* on p. 29).

An Australian company, Toilet Paper Man, offers this deluxe bathroom tissue on its web site as above.

"This is the most expensive toilet paper roll in the world. A quality 3-ply toilet paper with 22-carat gold through the roll,"

"As you use the toilet paper 22-carat gold flakes will fall onto the floor and your behind taking you to another level of sophistication."

Talk about flushing money down the toilet!

Jurassic Perk

Here's the perfect status symbol for the corner office of the hard-charging CEO: Stan, the fake T. Rex.

Just add to cart from Hammacher Schlemmer and soon a life-size 1500 pound replica of the baddest bad boy ever will give your visitors something to think about.

"Spanning 40' from tail to snout, this is the life-size replica fossil skeleton of Stan, a Tyrannosaur first unearthed in South Dakota's Black Hills in 1992."

"Whether you want your STAN walking, stalking, attacking, running, jumping or looking your visitors right in the eye, we welcome your input, so long as the pose requested is natural and anatomically possible…assembled by an experienced crew of six in just under an hour!" according to the Black Hills Institute of Geological Research which also sells it.

Stan comes warts and all. "This museum-quality replica is expertly crafted using GI-1000-grade silicone molds that impart stunning, authentic detail to the polyurethane resin casts that faithfully preserve the healed injuries Stan suffered during life, including a broken neck and ribs as well as puncture wounds in his skull and lower jaw", says Hammacher Schlemmer.

$100,000 from Hammacher Schlemmer or the Black Hills Institute. Or you can lease for $10,000 a month from the Black Hills Institute. "Crate and packing fees apply."

If you want the real deal, Sue, a girl T. Rex sold at Sotheby's in 1997 for $7.6 million (plus $862,500 commission).

So how can they tell the boys from the girls? The girls have wider hips.

Fifth Avenue

Somehow I got on the mailing list of one of those internationally famous Fifth Avenue jewelry stores, as a civilian, not as a jeweler.

It's pretty hard to evaluate complex jewelry from a catalog picture, but one item was easy: a ½ carat round diamond in a plain 18 karat gold ring. Gotcha! Three time markup. We purveyors of jewels to the unrich and unfamous would be lucky to get half of that.

Walking on Ice

Luxe jewelry store Leon's of Beverly Hills is offering a pair of $1 million diamond shoes. The size 6 Giuseppe Zanotti peep-toe pumps with 5 inch stiletto heels are covered with 11,000 diamonds ranging from .03 to .4 carats. How many carats you get for your million bucks wasn't given.

The shoes were customized with diamonds by Crystal Heels, also in Beverly Hills. The job took three weeks.

Crystal Heels also offers some down-market heels with rhinestones starting at $500. The shoes are "hand strassed", done one crystal at a time by hand.

You can send in your shoes to be crystallized, too, $295 for the heels only, $1450 for pumps, and $1700 for boots. Allow 5 weeks, 10 day rush job $300 extra.

Denture Dept.

Rap star Kanye West made a surprise appearance on the Ellen Degeneris show on October 19, 2010 to show off his new diamond choppers.

His bottom teeth were damaged in a car accident in 2002 and he now sports diamond dentures.

Diamonds are a lot harder than teeth and he will probably wear down his top teeth over time.

Deep Thought
Image is bought,
reputation earned.

Conspicuous Elimination

Haven't Got a Pot to Piss in?
A rare George II Chamberpot made for
the Earl of Warrington
$125,000

This is from an ad in the New Yorker December 8, 2014 by S.J. Shrubsole.
"Solving upper-class problems since 1912"

Message to the 1% of the 1%

Forget gold or platinum. That's for paupers. The JPMorgan Chase Palladium Card is for you ultra-high net worthies — $25 million+. Oh, and you have to be a Chase private client:

"A Private Client Banker will oversee your entire banking relationship and seamlessly connect you to other professionals dedicated to meeting your financial needs."

It's a Visa card with your signature laser-burned into it. It comes with a $595 annual fee, but no foreign transaction fees, no late fees, and no over limit fees. And you can pull out $5,000 a day cash from an ATM (that's 250 twenties!).

Many web sites, including Bloomberg, erroneously report that the card is actually made from palladium (with some 23 karat gold thrown in), a precious metal in the platinum family.

This is physically impossible. All reports give the weight of the card at about 27 grams (your plastic card weighs 5 grams). Since credit cards have standard dimensions, it is possible to calculate the weight of a palladium card: 42.19 grams.

One forum reports an actual assay of the card as 68% copper, 28% zinc, 3.5% nickel, .3% palladium, probably non-destructively by x-ray fluorescence analyzer (see *Selling Your Gold* on p. 216).

Reports are that there are 5,000 Palladium cards out there. There are 199,235 people with a net worth of 30 million or more and 2170 billionaires in the world. I am not one of them.

Chopstick Smackdown

CNN ran a Chopstick Challenge in 2010, Carbon Fiber vs. Louis Vuitton.

"Wearing the black silk trunks, weighing in at US$149.95 and looking mighty shiny over in the 'completely unnecessary accessory' corner", the carbon fiber chopsticks were awarded 3 points. The plusses were that they could be heated to over 400 degrees and were completely non-toxic, and had a tensile strength of 1.8 million PSI. But points were subtracted for only one pair for the money and being hand-made in the USA — "sorry, we're in Asia, this doesn't count for much here."

"Sporting the fashionable LV trunks and weighing in at over US$500 on eBay", the Louis Vuitton chopsticks were rated 4 points for two pairs in the set, being hand carved from rosewood, packaged in a lucite box, and "LV branding for the fashionably inclined." A minus for being out of production was offset by a plus for being a collectors item.

By the way, the ultimate chopstick test for you native forkers is Bún, Vietnamese soup with a pig's foot in it.

Diamond Suit

We're not playing cards, we're dressing up. English luxury designer Stuart Hughes (see *ET Phone Home* on p. 28) in collaboration with tailor Richard Jewels (really!) have come up with the world's most expensive suit. The cashmere and wool suit has piping of 480 half carat diamonds. It took 600 man-hours to make in 2009. £599,000 (over $900,000 in 2015). Better hurry, only three were made. Maybe not. The suit was still being offered in 2012. If you buy it you'll get an all-expenses paid trip to St. Lucia, where you can wear it on the beach.

Runner up was Indian Prime Minister Modi's suit he wore when he met with President Obama in January, 2015. The navy blue suit had pinstripes of tiny yellow letters that spelled out his name, Narendra Damodardas Modi. The suit was given to him by a friend.

Close-ups of the selfie suit went viral generating ridicule. Modi auctioned the suit in February for $691,890. It was bought by a wealthy diamond merchant.

The money will go to help clean up the Ganges, India's holy river, which is pretty dirty.

Shop Till You Drop
Verbal Abuse

Confucius called for the rectification of names. This is an excellent concept, roughly translated as "cut the crap". Here are some candidates for rectification in the retail sphere.

Discount — From what?

Designer — Who?

Sale — When is it not on sale? see also **Discount.**

List Price — You *can* fool some of the people all of the time.

Selected Items — Turkeys. After they're sold, Thanksgiving.

Retail Price (TV shopping) — see **List Price.**

Wholesale to the Public — We're honored.

Open to the Public — We're honored.

Overstocks — see **Selected Items.**

Sales Associate — Clerk. Better yet, clark, a good old-fashioned word.

50-60% Off, etc — They're not supposed to mark it up that much in the first place.

Starting at/as low as — You won't want that one.

America's Leading Jeweler™ — The self-awarded title of Service Merchandise*. Eat your heart out Tiffany.

*Since defunct. That can happen when you sell crap.

Exclusive Gourmet Discount Hand-Crafted Designer Products For All

I opened the refrigerator to get milk to put in my coffee and there it was: *Land O Lakes Gourmet Half-and-Half**. "Gourmet" was done up in fancy script, too. The carton contained no information that would save the name from being an oxymoron, i.e., "from hand-milked cows" or "extra-virgin cream".

A lot of words like "gourmet" and "designer" are bandied about today. I suppose everything is designed by someone, but prefixing a product with "designer" should mean it was designed by someone you've heard of.

Hand-crafted is also abused. I was once in a fast-food chicken joint and, knowing the mashed potatoes were of the instant ilk, I declined them. Well, the girl behind the counter was offended and she proudly told me that she had personally hand-mixed the potato powder. A lot of that "hand-crafted" Indian jewelry you see was just soldered together from cast-from-a-mold components. The FTC regulates such claims: hand-made jewelry is supposed to be made from scratch with hand tools.

Then there's "discount." Discount from what? Other than for watches, there's no list price on jewelry to discount from. Actually, "discount" is a code word for cheap stuff cheap. Good stuff cheap is hard to find, since the minute a store starts pushing "discount", it attracts people who only want to hear price, not quality, which forces the store to adjust its products accordingly.

"Exclusive" and "imported" are a few other words to make you think you're not just getting a mass-produced product. I like the beer ad jingle that claims the stuff "never tasted so imported." What does imported taste like?

I used the milk.

* since renamed "Traditional Half-and-Half", no doubt from the original pilgrims' recipe.

Deep Thought

Don't count new money for old things or old money for new things

Joe Shmoe

"Joe, we saved your car insurance quote." That was on the junk mail postcard that came to the store from esurance. The address was right but I think they got the wrong Joe. It was addressed to Joe Shmoe.

Maybe they'll have better luck with John or Jane.

Ring Around the Collar

In the 19th century people changed their shirts once a week. Shirt collars got dirty before the shirts since men wore undershirts. Laundry then was quite a chore. In 1827, Hannah Montague of Troy, New York cut off the collar of her husband's shirt, washed it, then sewed two pieces of white tape to it so it could be tied back on to the shirt, a detachable collar.

The idea was popular with other housewives of Troy, and Hannah began making "string collars" for sale.

In 1829, a retired Methodist minister, Ebenezer Brown, owner of a small dry goods store, put his wife and daughters to work making collars in the back of the store. Soon he was contracting the work out to local women to make them at home in exchange for credit at his store. He sold them for 25¢ (About $6 in 2015)

In 1834, Hannah's husband, Orlando Montague started his own collar factory with a partner. A few years later another collar maker started a laundry to wash collars. This idea spread and "Troy laundries" appeared throughout the country.

Troy became "Collar City" as other collar manufacturers started up. By the early 20th century 90% of collars were made in Troy.

Gaps between collar and shirt led to the invention of the collar that buttoned on. There was one button used to attach the collar to the shirt in the back and one in the front.

Krementz, a Newark, New Jersey manufacturer, invented the one-piece collar button in 1884 and by the turn of the century dominated the world collar button business.

Linen collars had to be laundered, pressed, and starched. In the 1880's the celluloid collar was invented. Linen was heat laminated between two pieces of celluloid plastic. This gave a stiff collar that could be easily wiped clean.

Krementz
collar button

The term "white-collar worker" came from these stiff white collars as those who wore them were office workers. "White collar" was used as early as 1911, and was used in the Wall Street Journal in 1923. Detachable collars went out in the 1930's with changes in fashion.

There were also detachable cuffs. A New York Times article from September 15, 1911 speaks of a revival of them whereas detachable collars were going strong then. A plastics industry publication estimates that nearly half the plastics manufactured annually by the turn of the 20th century was celluloid for collars and cuffs.

Some collars and cuffs were disposable. An 1899 ad for linene (cotton bonded to cardboard) collars touted "No Laundry Work. When soiled discard. A box of 10 collars, or 5 pairs of cuffs, 25 cts. By mail 30 cts."

You can still buy detachable collars and cuffs and the tunic shirts they fasten to, mainly at the high end: "Be the nobbiest gent in town with one of our splendid men's collars!" ($7.95, collar buttons not included.) The Brits have the biggest selection. One web site shows "Prince Charles in Blue White Striped Winchester Morning Dress Shirt with Detachable Turndown Collar."

99 Cent Sale

People often remember the price of something in the store as, say, $299.99. But the price is actually $299.00. So habituated are they by the chain store practice of giving a penny off to make you think the price is closer to 200 bucks than 300 bucks, that they mentally add the extra 99 cents. (I'm waiting for stores to add an extra 9/10ths of a cent, like gas stations.)

Well, at Joseph's you get a whole dollar off, not just a penny.

What's in Your Wallet?

Credit card propaganda would have you think we're moving toward a cashless society. You'll know we've arrived when people who sell their gold start demanding checks. Ha!

And don't charge that $7 watch battery. Watch batteries are why God invented cash.

Buy Him Anything He Wants

85% of diamonds are bought as a gift from a man to a woman, according to DeBeers.

Shoddy Goods

"With respect to the tagging of goods containing shoddy, we may say that the purchaser of the goods is clearly entitled to protection from fraud; but no purchaser of an eight-dollar ($216 in 2014 dollars) heavy overcoat needs to be told, if he has fairly good sense, that the fabric is not made of long-staple wool. Shoddy properly used is a valuable commodity to manufacturer and wearer."

— The Textile [World] Record, March 1902 quoted in the Literary Digest April 12, 1902.

Shoddy is recycled wool. Existing wool fabric is torn apart and the fibers respun. This process makes the fibers shorter and inferior to the original. Shoddy is often mixed with other fibers which increases the average fiber length. These composite yarns are used as the weft (crosswise) strands in fabrics as the warp yarn needs to be stronger because it is stretched on a frame for weaving.

The main disadvantage to fabrics containing shoddy is that the short shoddy fibers come out of the yarn with abrasion and cause pilling, little tangles of fiber on the surface.

Manufacture of shoddy was big business, 210 million pounds, almost 25% of the total of animal fibers produced in the United States, was shoddy in 1907 according to an article in the Textile World Record in 1909.

The 1902 article goes on to oppose a proposed truth-in-fabric law, saying that if a manufacturer misrepresented his goods "this would be perfectly useless, for the dealer who buys from him is quite able to determine the nature of the stock in the fabric." It explains "That he [the poor man] will be any happier, any more comfortable, any richer, if he shall get an analytical statement with his suit, explaining what it is made of, seems to us unlikely."

The article compares shoddy to oleomargarine: "when the product is sold for exactly what it is, no one is harmed." This is an odd analogy since the article argues the opposite: that shoddy should not be sold for exactly what it is. And oleomargarine was not sold mixed with various quantities of butter as is fabric that contains shoddy as a component fiber. In fact, it was illegal in many states to sell yellow oleomargarine.*

No doubt the problem is the word "shoddy" itself. "Shoddy has a far worse name than it deserves, but only among people who know little about the matter..." In other words, fear that the label will freak out consumers is really behind opposition to labeling by the garment industry. During the Civil War, "shoddy millionaires" sold inferior uniforms to the Union army made from shoddy, or worse. (Brooks Brothers was a prime offender — google "Brooks Brothers scandal".) Indeed, there would be no need for the term "virgin wool" were it not for shoddy. The first known usage of "virgin wool" was in 1915.

This was the first skirmish in truth-in-fabric laws. In 1920 the matter was debated in the House and Senate with no result. The New York Times had an article on February 29, 1920 headlined "Misleading Ideas As To Virgin Wool and Why Proposed 'Truth in Fabric' Law Will Be of no Service to the Public."

The article presented the argument of the American Association of Woolen and Worsted Manufacturers that it would "place virgin wool on a pedestal of public esteem regardless of how poor a quality this wool might be." Fine quality fabric that contained some shoddy would be deprecated whereas "card waste and burr waste, two of the poorest fibres known in the woolen trade, would be labeled virgin wool."

The bill was backed by the National Sheep and Wool Bureau of Chicago representing the sheep raising industry in hopes that it would raise wool prices.

In 1924, "Truth-in-Fabric and Misbranding Bills" were again debated in Congress with hearings held but with no law passed. It was not until 1939 that the Wool Products Labeling Act was passed.

To see if you're wearing shoddy clothes, look for "recycled wool" on the label.

If you want to make your own, you can buy shoddy wool yarn from India, "used for knitting and weaving purpose. This would reduce your cost by many folds." Wool/polyester. 1000 kilogram minimum, $5-10/kg.

* I remember as a kid circa 1952 margarine was white and came in a plastic package with a dot of yellow coloring that you had to knead in to make it yellow. The butter lobby in Pennsylvania was powerful.

Sales Tax Tokens

The first general retail sales taxes in America were enacted in 1930 in Kentucky and Mississippi. 22 other states followed in the 1930's.

12 states* adopted tokens to pay for the fractions of a cent generated by the sales tax math rather than just rounding up or down to the nearest cent. The tokens came in denominations of 1 to 5 mils, tenths of a cent. There was even a 1.5 mil token in Illinois. Washington State had a I mil token marked "tax on purchases 10 cents or less"

The tokens were made of aluminum, brass, copper, pewter, zinc, red, green, blue, white or gray plastic, and even cardboard.

So if you bought an item for $1.50 with a 3% sales tax, you owed $1.545. You would pay $1.55 and get change of a 5 mil (half cent) token. The next time you bought something for $1.50, you would pay $1.54 plus the half cent token.

The Louisiana token shown was called a Luxury Tax Token because necessities were supposedly exempt, but in fact many were taxed, like clothes and medicine, and many luxury items, such as tobacco alcohol, and New Orleans nightclubs were exempt.

Sales tax tokens were mostly discontinued after World War II, the last of them in 1961.

* Alabama, Arizona, Colorado, Illinois, Kansas, Louisiana, Mississippi, Missouri, New Mexico, Oklahoma, Utah, and Washington state.

Deep Thought

If you want jewelry, don't shop where they just sell merchandise.

Waste Management

I spotted this useful item in a catalog:

"When gas sneaks up on you, there's no worry you'll be found out with this ultra-thin polyester mat. Perfect for those on medication or who love spicy food."

You put it on your chair and sit on it. It's an anti-whoopee cushion. The secret ingredient is activated charcoal.

And if it doesn't work, you can always blame the dog.

You're Fired!

An article in the May, 1912 issue of Scientific American tells of a strange occupation, the department store "goat". The goat was an employee whose job was to be fired, as often as necessary.

If a customer complained of poor treatment by a store clerk, the goat would be summoned to the office along with the customer, who was told that the goat was the manager of the department involved. The goat would be chewed out and fired on the spot, to the satisfaction of the customer.

How widespread was this practice I don't know, but a movie was made about it, *The Professional Scape Goat*, a 1914 silent comedy,

First Supper

In 1949, Frank McNamara went to a New York restaurant, Major's Cabin Grill, to entertain a group of dinner guests

He had changed suits before he went and when the bill was presented, he realized his wallet was in his other suit. Fortunately, he knew the owner and his IOU was accepted.

That night he had an idea: why not charge it? He and a partner, his attorney, started the first credit card, the Diners Club.

In February, 1950, McNamara and his partner returned to Major's Cabin Grill and paid for dinner with his Diners Club card. This seminal event is known in the credit card business as "The First Supper."

Initially, the Diners Club card had 200 subscribers, mostly friends and acquaintances, and was accepted in 14 New York restaurants. By the end of the year, 20,000 people carried the card.

Today, it is accepted by 13 million establishments in 200 countries.

Sorry, I don't take Diners Club cards. But you can buy me lunch.

The Great Civilizer

The Singer Manufacturing Company, the sewing machine maker, put out a series of 36 trade cards in time for the World's Columbian Exposition* in 1893, *Costumes of the World*, with photographs of people of various countries in traditional dress using Singer sewing machines. Millions of the cards were given away at the fair and proved so popular that the series was extended, running up to World War I.

Singer called its sewing machine "The Great Civilizer." "The Singer Machines has been a factor in helping the people of India towards a better civilization for nearly twenty years, and thousands of them are in use", read the back of a card for India.

An ad with the picture above reads "MISSIONARY WORK OF THE SINGER MANUFACTURING COMPANY."

"At the close of the recent war [Spanish-American War,1898] the King of Ou (Caroline Islands) came to pay homage to the Government of Manila. As the best means of advancing and establishing a condition of things that would prevent all future outbreaks, the King was introduced to the "Great Civilizer," the Singer sewing machine, and we have here his photograph, seated at the Singer sewing machine, with his Secretary of State standing beside him."

Spain sold the Carolines to Germany in 1899. Japan occupied the Carolines in 1914 under a League of Nations mandate. Truk was a large Japanese naval base that was bombed in February, 1944. Palau (Peleliu) was assaulted by Marines in a bloody battle Sept.-Nov. 1944. Yap is famous for its stone money the size of millstones. See *Big Money* on p. 124.

*Chicago World's Fair

Givers Keepers

In a 1999 ruling by the Pennsylvania Supreme Court, a jilted bride had to give her $17,000 diamond engagement ring back to the guy who dumped her. The court ruled that the ring was "a conditional gift."

Deep Thought

Discount means cheap stuff cheap, not good stuff cheap.

271

Zip Your Lip

The California Supreme Court ruled unanimously that you don't have to give out your zip code when you charge something in a store. The court held that zip codes are "personal identification information" and none of a business's business.

The simplest solution to this invasion of privacy is to move to Beverly Hills. Whenever I'm asked my zip code I tell them 90210.

Prix Fixe

Price tags were invented by John Wanamaker (1838-1922), the founder of Wanamaker's department store. Before that you had to haggle for everything. A devout Christian, Wanamaker believed that if everyone was equal before God, they should be equal before price.

Wanamaker opened a men's clothing store in Philadelphia with his brother-in-law, called Oak Hall in 1861. In 1876, Wanamaker bought the abandoned Pennsylvania Railroad station and turned it into one of the the first department stores, Wanamaker's.

He instituted a radical retail policy: "One price and goods returnable." He guaranteed the quality of his merchandise in print.

Wanamaker's added an in-store restaurant in 1876, electric lights in 1878, a telephone in 1879 and elevators in 1889. Wanamaker's also invented the white sale.

In its heyday in the early 20th century, Wanamaker's was a magnificent retail emporium, with the world's largest organ in the Grand Court along with a large bronze eagle from the St. Louis World's Fair of 1904. The organ, with 28,000 pipes, is still played today at Macy's which now occupies the building.

Wanamaker treated his employees with respect, giving them free medical care, recreational facilities, profit sharing plans, and pensions.

John Wanamaker was appointed Postmaster General by president Benjamin Harrison in 1889 and served until 1893. (See You've got Mail on p. 259.) Wanamaker died in 1922 at 84.

Wanamaker's died in 1995, joining a distinguished list of defunct palaces of consumption: B. Altman, Alexanders, Bambergers, Gimbels, Stern's, and Watt & Shand, (1878 - 1995) on the square in Lancaster, Pa., where I grew up.

But Wait, There's No More!

We note the passing in June, 2012 of Barry Becher, the originator of the Ginsu knife and the cult classic Ginsu knife commercial. The Ginsu knife would be shown cutting through a can, nail or a rubber hose, then effortlessly parting a tomato.

The knives were made in the USA, in Ohio. Becher and his partner Ed Valenti

sold $30 million worth of Ginsu knives before Warren Buffet bought the parent company of Ginsu, Scott Fetzer, in 1985 for $315 million.

Ginsu sounds very Samuri in English, but it has no meaning in Japanese. When asked what Ginsu means, Becher would translate "I never have to work again."

Pet Dept.

Remember pet rocks? They were a 1975 fad, an ordinary gray rock in a straw bed in a box with air holes.

California advertising executive Gary Dahl came up with the idea of the no-maintenance pet while listening to friends complain about their pets in a bar.

Pet Rocks came with a 32 page manual that was mainly a joke book. Pet rocks would obey simple commands such as sit or stay. They would follow advanced commands like roll over or attack with an assist from their master.

After an article in Newsweek and Pet Rocks being picked up by Nieman Marcus, Dahl sold 1.5 million of them at $4 in the six months the fad lasted.

Dahl kept a low profile after that saying that "a bunch of wackos" came out of the woodwork with death threats and lawsuits seeking money. He even turned down an appearance on the Oprah Winfrey show.

Pet Rocks now sell for 10 bucks on Ebay.

ThinkGeek (see April Fools' on p. 46), a nerdy gadget site, has brought the Pet Rock into the 21st century with one that hooks up to your computer. "Plug-n-play. Just plug it into your USB port. No feed or care needed, draws no power." $9.99.

I like the cartoon at the time that showed an exasperated man standing over his Pet Rock looking at the puddle it had made on the floor.

And Now a Word From Our Sponsor

The first TV license was granted by the FCC in 1941 to NBC's New York City station, WNBT-TV, now WNBC-TV.

Of course, the first commercial ran on its first day on the air, July 1, 1941 during a baseball game between the Brooklyn Dodgers and the Philadelphia Phillies.

The 10 second spot was for Bulova watches and featured a Bulova clock over a map of the United States. "America runs on Bulova time" was the voiceover.

The ad cost $9 ($145 in 2015) and was viewed on 4000 television sets. That's 3.6¢ per set in today's dollars. A Super Bowl spot cost $4 million in 2015 and reached 53 million households, 7.5¢ per set. But the Bulova ad only ran for 10 seconds versus the Super Bowl's 30 seconds, or .36¢ per set-second, 1.4 times the .25¢ for the Super Bowl.

The Phillies won 6-4.

And Now a Word From Our Sponsor

Annoying, isn't it, when your TV show goes to commercial: **CAN YOU HEAR ME NOW?**

Help is on the way for commercials that spike so much louder than the program. CALM, The Commercial Advertisement Loudness Mitigation Act, passed the House at the end of 2009.

The FCC has received complaints about loud commercials since the 1960's. Remember your ultimate weapon, the mute button.

A California representative introduced the bill after a loud commercial interrupted a family dinner and her brother-in-law said "Well, you're the congresswoman. Why don't you do something about it?" (Update next page.)

Floods O' Suds

In 1947, Life Magazine challenged Colgate-Palmolive to prove the claim in a Super Suds ad that "Just one package could all but fill 2 trailer trucks with suds!" The ad showed two trucks filled with suds perched on top of the soap box.

Colgate manned up and tried it. They got one large truck equivalent to the two 800 cubic foot trucks in the ad, put in three troughs filled with soft water and sprinkled in a box of Super Suds. Perforated pipes pumped air into the soapy water and suds bubbled up to fill the 1250 cubic foot truck

and then some, with an estimated 300 cubic foot overflow, proving the claim.

Life documented the test in its October 20, 1947 issue, with a photo of the Procter and Gamble vice president for advertising standing on a ladder by the overflowing truck blowing puffs of Super Suds in the air.

Super Suds — Floods O' Suds For Dishes and Duds

Honey, Did You Order Dog Food?

A San Francisco area man ordered parts for his Harley motorcycle online in and shortly afterward started getting tons of spam email, so he signed up his dog, a pug named Clifford for an email account as cliffordjdawg at hotmail that he would use for online ordering.

Soon Clifford started getting spam. Then Chase Manhattan Bank sent an email saying that Clifford J. Dawg was pre-approved for a credit card.

The man signed up saying that Mr. Dawg worked at the Pupperoni Factory (Pupperoni is Cliff's favorite treat) and that his mother's maiden name was Pugsy Malone. He even put a note on the application: "You are sending an application to a dog! Ha ha ha."

In January, 2004 a credit card with a $1500 limit arrived in the mail. The man called and canceled the card the next day. Chase explained that Mr. Dawg was on a list they bought and suggested that they might want to use the incident in a commercial.

Clifford should have kept the card. They wouldn't dare raise the interest rate. Think jaws.

Artificial Stupidity

If you flunked the Turing test, Amazon has a job for you: picking the appropriate ads to show on a book's page.

On the Amazon page of *Ornamentally Incorrect, Luxe et Veritas*, are ads for related products:

"Discount on Lux. Save up to 73% while stocks last!" Cheap.org will sell you various Yale tchotchkes. Lux et Veritas, Light and Truth, is the Yale motto.

"Fast shipping and best prices on Lux et Veritas, buy now!" Sale-Hot.com has a luxe lux et veritas: an antique Yale watch fob with the motto for $95.

BE CALM!

I reported to you on the previous page that a new law, CALM, The Commercial Advertisement Loudness Mitigation Act, prohibiting commercials on TV from blasting your ears was in the works. (I never understood why they made commercials so loud. Like I'm going to buy your stuff if you aggravate me.)

The President signed it into law in December, 2010. The law directs the FCC to make broadcasters and cable operators pipe down.

The FCC has a year to make new regulations per recommendations of ATSC, the Advanced Television Systems Committee, an industry organization, and TV has another year to comply.The ATSC has a 72 page manual with lots of diagrams on how to do it.

Here's a one page manual with one diagram:

1. Locate the knob marked "Vol".
2. Turn it to the left.

The New White Meat

ThinkGeek, a nerdy gadget site, sells a faux product on its web site every April Fools' day. The USB Desktop Tanning Center — get a golden glow without ever leaving the office! — or a Fondue set that plugs into your computer were a few.

In 2010 it was Canned Unicorn Meat. *Pâté is passé. Unicorn, the new white meat* was the tag line. That was too much for the other white meat. ThinkGeek got a

cease and desist letter from the National Pork Board.

ThinkGeek apologized to the Pork Board

on its web site for possible confusion between unicorn and pork: "It was never our intention to cause a national crisis and misguide American citizens regarding the differences between the pig and the unicorn. In fact, ThinkGeek's canned unicorn meat is sparkly, a bit red, and not approved by any government entity."

Deep Thought

If everything is a bargain, nothing is a bargain.

Silverwear

You don't have to just accessorize your clothing with silver. Now your clothing can be silver. A company has patented X-static, a fiber coated with a layer of pure silver and clothes are made from it.

Silver kills germs. This has been known since ancient times. Cyrus the Great, the fifth century B.C. Persian emperor, equipped his troops with silver vessels to carry drinking water — no Babylon belly for them. Today, medical products containing silver are used to prevent infection.

Socks made from X-static will keep your feet fresh and will cure your plantar hyperhidrosis (stinky feet) by killing the germs that cause it. And they will also prevent that little lightening bolt from coming out of your finger when you walk around on the carpet. This is because silver has the highest electrical conductivity of any element and prevents the build-up of static electricity.

Silver also reflects, holds, and transfers heat very well. That's why they make sheets from X-static. You'll stay toasty in the winter and cool in the summer. And if you're a soldier, wearing a uniform made from silver-coated fiber will keep you from showing up in the night-vision scope.

The Hard-Boiled Collars of Palm Beach

That's the title of an article in the May 5, 1923 Literary Digest. Evidently the stiff detachable collars of that era were uncomfortable (see *Ring Around the Collar* on p. 40).

"The man whose neck is worn ragged by a starched collar and who wriggles as much as politeness permits because the button in back is pressing upon a knob in his spine can hardly feel anything but loathing for his fellow guest whose throat is open to the breezes," writes Heywood Broun.

Broun was commenting on a textile trade magazine article *Complete Analysis Chart of Apparel Worn by Over 300 of the Best Drest* Men of Palm Beach*. Only 1 percent, or three men, wore soft collars. "Apparently the revolt against the tyranny of starch has hardly begun, or at any rate it has not yet touched the upper orders."

* See *Language Isn't Fixt* on p. 254

Fashion Police Arrest Counterfeiters

The Chinese burn paper or cardboard replicas of things the recently deceased will need in the next world at funerals.

Houses, sometimes complete with paper servants and furniture, televisons, $10,000 bills, and, of course, brand name luxuries — Mercedes, Rolexes, and expensive handbags are among the offerings.

Police in New York busted a Chinatown store clerk for selling fake Louis Vuitton and Burberry handbags — cardboard fake fakes, not real fakes.

The charge was copyright infringment. The clerk was taken away in handcuffs, jailed overnight and arraigned the next morning.

The other store employees then prudently covered up the insignia on a four foot fake fake BMW.

Pecunia ex Machina

Inserito scidulam quaeso ut faciundam cognoscas rationem

Those are the instructions in Latin for the ATM machine in the Vatican. Translation: Insert your card so that the account may be recognized.

Spend it wisely. Pecunia in arbotis non crescit! (Money doesn't grow on trees.)

This Spud's for You

Menthol cigarettes were invented by Lloyd "Spud" Hughes of Mingo Junction, Ohio in 1924.

Hughes suffered from asthma and inhaled the vapors from menthol crystals his mother had given him. He hid his cigarettes in a tin with the menthol and he noticed that the cigarettes became flavored with the menthol.

Hughes patented menthol cigarettes in 1925. He formed the Spud Cigarette Corporation with a Wheeling, West virginia businessman, contracted with a tobacco company to manufacture them, and hit the road, selling them from his car for 20¢ a pack, a premium price; other cigarettes sold for 15¢.

Hughes then contacted the Axton-Fisher Tobacco Company of Louisville, Kentucky, maker of Clown cigarettes, to make more Spuds. Axton saw the potential of menthol cigarettes and offered Hughes $90,000 ($1.2 million inflation adjusted to 2015) for the brand and patent in 1926.

Axton-Fisher hired a New York advertising agency ("Be Mouth-Happy") and Spud became the fifth best selling cigarette by 1932. Kool was introduced in 1933, and Spud reduced its price to 15¢ to compete.

In 1944, Phillip Morris bought Axton-Fisher. Spuds were discontinued in the U.S. In 1963 and everywhere in 1999.

Spud Hughes took the money and ran through it in two years, buying cars and airplanes. He died in 1967. He was 67.

Deep Thought
The cheaper the merchandise, the louder the advertising.

47

Trademark of the Beast

In the early 80's, rumors began circulating that Procter and Gamble's logo with the man in the moon and 13 stars is secretly a satanic symbol with "666" concealed in the curls of the beard and that the hair and beard taper into devil's horns.

The rumors also held that the president of P&G had come out as a Satanist on a talk show and that the company had given large sums to the Church of Satan. (There really is a Church of Satan.)

Boycotts of Procter and Gamble products were organized and hundreds of thousands of inquiries poured into the company from all over the world.

P&G sued a few individuals for spreading these rumors in the 1980's. In 1990, P&G sued a Kansas couple who were Amway distributors (and P&G competitors), charging that they had distributed literature to their customers with the satanic rumors. P&G was awarded $75,000 in damages.

P&G found out that other Amway distributors had used the company's voicemail system to revive the satanic rumors and in 1995 sued Amway and some of its distributors.

After 12 years of dismissals and appeals, Procter and Gamble won a judgement against four Amway distributors for $19.5 million in 2007.

Procter and Gamble had retired the man-in-the-moon logo in 1985 due to the controversy.

The devil-under-the-bed types are still out there, though more liability conscious. One web site carefully insinuates satanic associations by posing questions for you to answer. Does the Lucent logo, a roughly drawn red circle, represent the flames of hell and does Apple's logo depict a bite out of the forbidden fruit? And it noted that the price of the first Apple in 1977 was $666 (it really was).

Even Disney is not immune. They prod you to find "666" in the curlicues of the Walt Disney signature. The Lucifer Lighting Company was automatically diabolical.

Speaking of Lucifer lighting, one of the first matches was patented in 1828 and sold under the name "Lucifer." The name stuck. Even into the 20th century you could light your fag with a Lucifer, as immortalized in a World War I song.

Pack Up Your Troubles
in Your Old Kit Bag

Pack up your troubles in your old kit-bag,
And smile, smile, smile,
While you've a Lucifer to light your fag,
Smile, boys, that's the style.
What's the use of worrying?
It never was worth while, so
Pack up your troubles in your old kit-bag,
And smile, smile, smile.

Mercare Donec Succumbas*

The first shopping mall was Trajan's Market, built 100-110 A.D., in old Rome. Built from brick and concrete, It was 6 stories high with 150 shops, tabernae in Latin, and offices. A taberna was a barrel-vaulted room with a wide entrance.

There was often a taberna in a room in the front of a Roman house with a street entrance only, and there were tabernae in insulae, apartment buildings. Our word "tavern" is derived from the Latin taberna.

Trajan's Market was only recently discovered, the excavation beginning under Mussolini in 1928. You can tour the well-preserved ruins of Trajan's Market today.

* Shop till You Drop

271   **Pardon My French**

Want to get into the perfume business? Just French it up. Call it Eau de Merde Parfum and you'll sell it. Parfum smells better than perfume. You can't go wrong with French for cosmetics. (Or for food, except for freedom fries.) Take some ordinary jeans and sew something on the back pockets, double the price, and voilà: designer jeans by Philippe Tushée.

For jewelry, a British accent works well. Spell it "jewellery". Sell it in the "Harbour Shoppes Jewellery Centre". Buffy and Biff won't be able to resist.

American English spoken at Joseph's.

See an appellation prétentieux of another sort on page 39.

Cosmetology

Get on over to Lee & Co's. Patent Medicine Store at 31 Market Street, Baltimore and pick up a bottle of The Genuine Persian Lotion.

"an invaluable cosmetic, perfectly innocent and safe, free from corrosive and repellent minerals (the basis of other lotions)..." prevents and removes "cutaneous blemishes ...of every kind, particularly, freckles, dimples, pits after small pox, inflammatory redness, scurfs, tetters, ring worms, sun burns, prickley heats, premature wrinkles, &c."

"yet its effects are speedy and permanent, rendering the skin delicately soft and smooth, improving the complexion and restoring the bloom of youth."

— Advertisement in the Herald and Eastern Shore Intelligencer, Easton, Maryland Jan. 21, 1800.

Tetters means any of various skin diseases with eruptions and itching. Scurf means skin scaling like dandruff.

Nothing much changed about a hundred years later. Ayer's Recamier Cream is guaranteed "to remove Tan, Sunburns, Pimples and Redness or Roughness of the skin, to eradicate, so-called black heads, and to cure Eczema."

According to an 1888 book, The Medical Standard, citing Western Druggist, Ayers Recamier Cream consists of zinc oxide, glycerin, water, and sprit of rose

And for the next hundred years, see *Cosmetic Sturgeon* on p. 26

Nothing has Changed but the Price

"Except for news and sports the fare is mediocre to bad." This is from an article about television in Life Magazine, December 1, 1947.

The article cites the wedding of Elizabeth and Philip in Westminster Abbey, seen only 29 hours after the event "from newsreels flown across the ocean" as one example of the good. The bad is that "Television...has cruelly disinterred some the hoariest acts of vaudeville," with "implausible dramatics, sword-swallowers, and witless chitchat." And the commercials are "a maddening chip off the old block."

There were only 122,000 sets in the country then according to the article, although it projected 2 million by 1950.

Television is "as yet no medium for products like soap flakes and breakfast cereal, it does well at selling luxuries." A Philadelphia furrier who sponsored six 15 minute shows got 94 people into the store and 38 sales totaling $11,200. The shows cost him $1500.

TV sets cost $180 to $2945 then, with the most popular model a tabletop set like this RCA with a 6½ x 8½ inch screen for $325, 11% of the average 1947 yearly wage of $2850.

Commercial

So far I've only plugged my own products in this newsletter, not counting unplugging a few banks, credit cards, and other corporate malefactors.

I am a prodigious user of paper towels, for cleaning the glass counter tops and my hands, which get black from polishing your repairs. I've tried them all. The best is Viva. Second is Bounty. The rest seem to dissolve in water.

This is an unpaid testimonial given as a public service.Viva paper towels. Jeweler-tested

Disclosure

In the last newsletter (see above) I recommended Viva paper towels as a community service. I emailed the article to Kimberly-Clark, to avoid a repeat of the Dilbert contretemps. (See *Comic Figure Gets Huge Award!* on p. 69)

They were appreciative and sent me some 50 cents off coupons. Viva Viva. No D****** points for them.

Deep Thought
Don't deny the problem because you don't like the solution.

Blueteeth

I reported to you on the $4,000 titanium manual toothbrush (see *Luxebrush* on page 36.) But that was a dumb brush.

Oral B now offers a smartbrush, a bluetooth toothbrush. It will upload your brushing data to your smartphone.

"You can use your smartphone as a 'remote control' to customize your brush to your needs, including setting your target session length and selecting your preferred modes."

"It tells you if you're brushing too hard, if you've brushed long enough and even if your brushing habits have improved. It's so intelligent it communicates while it cleans."

"Dental professionals can program patients' brushing routines in the app to help improve their brushing behaviors and focus on problems."

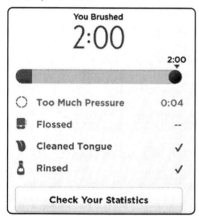

"holding the phone without splattering it with toothpaste droplets and drool is an art waiting to be mastered," said one reviewer.

I'm waiting for the smartfloss.

Tchotchkes

The Gettysburg Museum and Visitor Center bookstore removed bobblehead figures of John Wilkes Booth holding a pistol in March, 2012. A reporter had questioned selling a toy Lincoln assassin. The Abraham Lincoln Presidential Library and Museum in Springfield, Illinois followed suit a week later. However, the more tasteful Lincoln bobbleheads will continue to be sold.

Bobbleheads, also called nodders, originated in ancient China. Brass bells with deities that would nod when they were rung were used in temples. The 10th century monk Pu-Tai (d. 916), the model for the fat laughing Buddha, nodded at visitors to temples, his terra-cotta head bobbing on bamboo strips.

The Meissen porcelain factory made nodders in the early 18th century and the toy enjoyed a vogue in Victorian era Europe and England.

An 1842 short story, The Overcoat, by Nikolai Gogol described a man's neck as "like the neck of plaster cats which wag their heads".

After you've eaten the selfie toast (see *You're Toast* on p. 24), you can get the selfie bobblehead. Hammacher Schlemmer will make one for you:

"Artisans sculpt a poly-clay model head from a photograph you submit of your subject, taking up to three full weeks to capture the subtle facial contour, eye, smile, and hair nuances that reflect his or her unique character." $119.95.

Or you can get hitched in style with a bobblehead wedding cake topper. CuteBobble.com has them on sale. Starting at: ~~$149.00~~ $134.10

Bobblehead LLC in Kansas City, Missouri announced the release of an Osama bin Laden bobblehead in December, 2008, in a limited edition of 100. You could buy it in 2012 on Ebay for $799.

Seal Team Six bobbleheads are $19.95.

Deep Thought
Tomorrow's antiques are here today.

When I was a kid in the early 50's — Thanks! You're looking pretty good yourself — my dad would drive us from Lancaster to Philadelphia to visit relatives via Route 30, the Lincoln Highway. The Pennsylvania Turnpike at the time ended at Valley Forge, 20 miles northwest of Philadelphia, so it was more direct, if slow, to go through all the little towns in between.

 One of the amusements on the way was to read the Burma Shave signs, a series of 5 red signs with doggerel with the sixth being the Burma Shave logo, spaced so that they could be read from a moving car.

Burma shave's feature was that it was brushless — you would dip fingers in a jar of it or squeeze it from a tube and apply it to your face rather than whip up a lather from shaving soap in a shaving mug with a badger hair brush and slather it on your bristles as was the method at the time.

Burma Shave debuted in 1925. Clinton Odell of Edina, Minnesota formed a company that made a liniment called "Burma-Vita", so named because the ingredients, camphor, cassia, and cajeput oils, came "from the Malay Peninsula and Burma." The liniment was wonderfully effective for burns, but smelled so bad it didn't sell well and the company foundered.

A family friend owned a wholesale drug company and tried to help out with a supply of Lloyd's Euxesis, an English brushless shaving cream that had been around since 1854, for Odell to distribute, but instead he hired a chemist to develop his own shaving cream. The 143rd formulation was the winner, but this wasn't revealed until later when an old jar of #143 was tried again and it was discovered that aging for a few months was the answer.

On a drive to Illinois in 1925, a son, Alan Odell, saw a series of signs that read Gas/Restrooms/Food just before a service station and hit on the idea of the Burma Shave signs. He convinced his father to budget $200 for the signs and using old lumber he painted them himself and in 1926 put up the first signs on Route 35 south of Minneapolis.

The first signs were straightforward, see below left, but even so new orders soon started coming from drugstores which had sold out. The next year $25,000 was spent on signs across Minnesota and into Wisconsin. Eventually, 7000 sets of signs were put up in 45 states. In 1929, the company began its annual Jingle Contest. Life Magazine reported June 2, 1947 that 50,000 jingles had been sent in that year; the best 25 were chosen and the poets rewarded with $100 each.

The signs had to be properly situated so they could be read and were often put up on farmers' land and the farmers were compensated with free products and a yearly fee. The signs had to be raised from 8 feet to 10 feet because horses would break them trying

Shave the modern way Fine for the Skin Druggists have it Burma Shave 1926	Henry the Eighth Prince of friskers Lost five wives But kept His whiskers 1938	Santa's Whiskers Need no trimmin' He kisses kids Not the wimmin 1947	20 miles per gal. Says well-known car To go 10,000 Miles per gal By half-pound jar 1935
Within this vale Of toil And sin Your head grows bald But not your chin--use Burma Shave 1948	I proposed To Ida Ida refused Ida won my Ida If Ida used Burma Shave 1939	Many a wolf Is never let in Because of the hair On his Chinny-chin-chin 1943	The wolf Is shaved So neat and trim Red Riding Hood Is chasing him 1952
If Crusoe'd Kept his chin More tidy He might have found A lady Friday 1953	Twould be More fun To go by air If we could put These signs up there 1945	Let's make Hitler And Hirohito Look as sick as Old Benito Buy defense bonds 1942	Don't pass cars On curve or hill If the cops Don't get you Morticians will 1940

to scratch their backs. Burma-Vita sent farmers a magazine called Burma Shavings with an honor roll of farmers who had reported problems with the signs. A farmer from Medicine Park, Oklahoma said that teachers in his elementary school copied the jingles onto flash cards for reading lessons, according to a July, 2000 article on *Farm Collector* website.

Sometimes the signs triggered the law of unintended consequences. A 1933 jingle, left, echoing the new trend of sending in coupons backfired when scores of old fenders scavenged from junkyards or some even from toy cars, were dropped off or mailed in to the company, which honored its promise of a free jar, which sold for 50¢. (Average wages in 1933 were about $30 a week.)

> Free Offer! Free Offer!
> Rip a Fender
> Off Your Car
> Mail It in For
> A Half-Pound Jar

In 1958, the company thought surely everybody would think they were kidding about a trip to Mars. Arliss French, the manager of a Red Owl supermarket in Appleton, Wisconsin wired Burma Shave that he was ready to blast off and where should he ship the 900 jars? Burma Shave answered and there was this exchange of messages, below left.

> Free--Free
> A trip
> To Mars
> For 900
> Empty Jars

A company representative went to Appleton to visit French and found the store decorated with the trip to Mars signs, a pile of empty jars and a fake rocket ship. French had run full page ads with his picture saying "I Accept" with a facsimile of the telegram to Burma Shave and "Send Frenchie to Mars" offering to pay 15¢ each for 900 jars. Rockets, Sputnik, and men in space suits were graphics in the ad.

> If A Trip
> To Mars You Earn
> Remember, Friend
> There's No Return
>
> Let's Not Quibble
> Let's Not Fret
> Gather Your Forces
> I'm All Set
>
> Our Rockets Are Ready
> We Ain't Splitting Hairs
> Just Send Us The Jars
> And Arrange Your Affairs

French showed up at Burma Shave's offices wearing a football helmet and a silver space suit with a Red Owl logo. The 900 jars were shipped in a Brink's truck with a "Send Frenchie to Mars" sign.

He and his wife were given tickets to Moers (pronounced "Mars"), Germany and jars of Burma Shave to barter with the Moertians. He agreed to the condition of the trip that he wear his space suit and a photo of Frenchie going through customs in his space suit ran in the Racine Journal Times.

When the Frenches arrived in Moers in December, the entire population of 78 came out to greet them. They were wined and dined and when they returned the local paper headlined "Fox Cities Spaceman Returns from Mars." (Cities along the Fox River, including Appleton.)

Sales peaked in 1947 and declined after that due to superhighways, faster speeds, and changing culture. The company was sold to Gillette in 1963 and the signs had all disappeared by 1966. Alan Odell died in 1994 at 90, Arliss French in 1998 at 85.

But not everyone used Burma Shave. This jingle appeared in 1947:

Altho
We've sold
Six million others
We still can't sell
Those cough drop brothers

A Glimpse of Stocking

May 15, 1940 was N day: nylon stockings went on sale for the first time and women lined up to buy them, snapping up 4 million pairs at $1.15 - 1.35 ($23 today) in two days and 64 million by the end of the year.

DuPont invented nylon in the 1930's and first showed nylon stockings at the Golden Gate International Exposition in San Francisco and at the New York World's Fair in 1939. At a test sale at DuPont's Wilmington, Delaware headquarters October 24, 1939, 4,000 pairs were sold in 3 hours.

Before nylon, women wore rayon or silk stockings. Rayon tended to bag at the knees and ankles and silk stockings ran easily and were expensive.

In August, 1941, the government requisitioned all silk and in February, 1942, nylon. Silk was needed for the powder bags of naval guns (it burns completely with no residue) and nylon for parachutes, mosquito netting, tire cords, and other military uses.

Enter trompe l'oeil stockings. The legs were covered with makeup and a seam drawn with an eyebrow pencil. There were kits sold for this, *Leg Silque Liquid Stockings* was one, and there were improvised eyebrow pencil holder gizmos for drawing a straight seam.

On August 23, 1945 just 8 days after Emperor Hirohito broadcast the surrender of Japan, the War Production Board sent 30,000 telegrams canceling war contracts and Dupont announced it would resume nylon stocking production.

In September, the first small shipments of nylons went on sale around the country. Women heard of it by word of mouth and mobbed the stores beginning what the press dubbed "Nylon Riots."

The Augusta (Georgia) Chronicle reported "Women Risk Life and Limb in Bitter Battle for Nylons", December 16, 1945.

The New York Times headlined January 30, 1946 "30,000 Women Join in Rush for Nylons" and "Thousands More Turned Away as Gimbels Sells Entire Stock of 26,000 Pair."

On April 11, 1946, a scheduled 6:30 after hours sale of 10,800 pairs of nylons at the Weinstein department store in San Francisco was called off by the police after an officer reported that the "situation is out of hand." Many of the 15,000 women had waited in line for 3 hours. "As word of the decision passed through the packed thoroughfare, eggs, vegetables and angry words started to fly. Three women fainted. The crowd refused to disperse and set up a chant of 'we want nylons,'" reported the Salt Lake Tribune April 12, 1946.

In June, 1946 the mayor of Pittsburgh arranged for a night sale of nylons in response to a petition from 400 working women who couldn't shop during regular store hours. "Nylon Mob, 40,000 Strong, Shrieks and Sways for Mile", the Pittsburgh Press headlined June 13, 1946. In a fight for 13,000 pairs of stockings "a good old-fashioned hair-pulling, face-scratching fight broke out shortly before midnight" according to *American Plastic: A Cultural History,* quoting the article.

The demand for nylon was so great that Dupont demanded upfront payment from its customers, even Burlington Mills, which had to send a check for $100,000.

Nylon stocking production increased 30% in 1947, but there were still shortages. The New York Times reported on October 25, 1947 that idle production capacity due to the nylon yarn shortage would not be taken up by making silk stockings as consumers spurned them, spoiled by nylon. Kiplinger Magazine reported a continuing shortage of nylon yarn in September, 1948. The shortage eased by 1949 when 543 million pairs of nylons were sold.

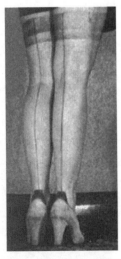

Liquid stockings, photo
courtesy of the Smithsonian

Made in the U.S.A.

"Mr. Madison was dressed in a full suit of cloth of American manufacture, made of the wool of Merinos raised in this country; his coat from the manufactory of Col. Humphreys, and his waistcoat and small clothes from that of Chancellor Livingston, the clothes being, we understand, severally presented by those gentlemen."

— Bristol County Register (Rhode Island) March 18, 1809.

President James Madison was inaugurated March 4, 1809 in the House chamber of the Capitol. Madison is credited with being the first President to wear an all-American outfit for the occasion. George Washington wore a brown woolen suit also made in the U.S.A., by the Hartford Woolen Manufactory. His white silk stockings were also native. Perhaps the less than 100% Americanness comes from his shirt, shoes, or small clothes (underwear).

Making fine wool broadcloth suitable for gentlemen's clothing was high tech in those times, requiring "expert dyeing and finishing. Finishing processes included fulling, using heat and moisture to shrink up the fabric; napping, to raise the fibers; and shearing, to trim the nap evenly", according to a Textile Society of America paper presented at a 2012 symposium.

Fine cloth at that time was made in England. "We anxiously look forward to the day, when a man may furnish himself with a good Coat, for either winter or summer, without being obliged to send 3000 miles for the Cloth", the Textile Society paper quotes the Raleigh Register (N.C.) December 28, 1809.

Washington deliberately wore an American-made suit to the ceremony. "It will not be a great while before it will be unfashionable for a gentleman to appear in any other dress," Washington wrote in a letter to the Marquis de Lafayette shortly before his inauguration.

Auction by the Candle

In the 17th and 18th centuries a candle was lit for an auction and when it went out the auction was over. This prevented auction sniping, a last-second bid just before time ran out.

Samuel Pepys (1633-1703), famous for his diary showing life in London of his time, mentions the Admiralty selling surplus ships "by an inch of candle." He also gives a tip from a successful bidder that the candle always flares up just before it goes out. Seeing this he would shout out the winning bid.

Dress Code

In 1951, Bing Crosby went to check into the Hotel Vancouver in Vancouver, Canada. He had been on a hunting trip with a friend and was wearing a denim jacket and pants (We called them "dungarees" in 1951. They came long and we rolled them up to make cuffs) and had a few day's growth of beard.

They were told they they would not be admitted to the hotel — too scruffy. Fortunately, a bellhop recognized Crosby and they were given a room.

Crosby had a ranch in Elko, Nevada, and when he went back and told this story, neighbors contacted Levi-Strauss and they made a blue denim tuxedo jacket for him. The double breasted jacket had contrasting lapels and collar of reverse denim formed by turning the fabric out. Red Levi's labels riveted in a circle formed a boutonniere on the lapel.

Inside the jacket was a large leather label putting any too-snooty hoteliers on notice that the wearer was respectable. Levi's presented the jacket to Crosby at the 1951 Silver State Stampede rodeo in Elko, where Crosby was the honorary mayor.

Virgin Airlines founder Sir Richard Branson heard the Bing Crosby anecdote from Levi's chief J.C. Curleigh at Virgin's Leadership Gathering on Necker Island in the British Virgin Islands in 2014. Branson had been rejected as too scruffy at a London club as a young man. "Later, I went back and bought the place!" The informal Branson went to Curleigh and got a Crosby denim tux to wear at the Scottish Business Awards.

Levi's brought back the Crosby tux in 2014 in a limited reproduction of 200.

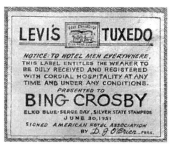

Shirt-Waists are for Pantywaists

Do you remember reading about the horrific Triangle Shirtwaist fire in 1911? The fire in Manhattan killed 146 people, mainly young women garment workers. The fire led to better safety regulations and working conditions.

Shirtwaists were very popular then; Triangle was one of many factories making them. So what is a shirtwaist? A shirtwaist is a woman's blouse constructed like a shirt, with collar and buttons. It became a symbol of the modern independent woman in the late 19th and early 20th centuries. It freed women from the voluminous floor-length dresses of their mothers. It was worn tucked into a skirt that sometimes showed a scandalous glimpse of ankle.

The popularity of shirtwaists can be traced to a dry goods merchant in Fort Wayne, Indiana, Samuel M. Foster, in 1884. During a desperately slow winter Foster recalled that boys' shirtwaists had been a good seller. He was out of them but one of his clerks had bought one for his son. The garment was retrieved and torn apart and used as a pattern to make more in the back of the store. The shirtwaists caught on with women.

Foster became a millionaire for "providing the world with the most useful and the most universally-worn garment ever devised", according to the 1917 Pictorial History of Fort Wayne, Indiana

Men at that time had to wear a coat, which was a problem in hot weather. If they took off the coat and wore just a shirt it was considered effeminate — a man in a shirtwaist, a woman's garment.

An article titled *The Shirt-Waist For Men, Again* in The Literary Digest July 13, 1901, quoting the New York Tribune, says "More and more coatless men are to be seen day by day, and certainly it can not be maintained that they are all callow youth or men readily convicted of a desire to to look like women."

The problem especially vexed postmen who had to be out and about in hot weather. A letter-carrier from New Haven summed it up: "What do they want to rig us out with shirt-waists for? Do they think we are a lot of women? Some of the men who favor shirt-waists will one of these days be calling for hoopskirts for the carriers. Give us the blouse, a man's garment."

The Tribune thought this a splendid idea: "A blouse, according to the dictionary is a loose upper garment worn by men in the place of a coat. Certainly give us the blouse, or, in other words call it a blouse and don't, for pity's sake, call it a shirt-waist. The garment will be just the same, and the resultant coolness will be just as delightful, but the stigma of aping the women will be forever removed."

Postal regulations were changed to permit shirtwaists in 1902. Postmen could wear "a neat shirt waist or loose-fitting blouse, instead of coat and vest" "during the heated term". The Times reported April 9, 1901 that Washington police, after they saw pictures of Camden, New Jersey police in shirtwaists agitated for cooler uniforms, too. "The apostles of the shirt waist for the Washington force have been ardent in their propaganda ever since they saw these enticing pictures." But police chief Sylvester "thinks a coatless officer would fail to inspire the turbulent with awe."

By the way, a pantywaist was a child's undergarment, short pants buttoned to a shirt. The first known use of pantywaist to mean a sissy was in 1936.

Evidently the nomenclature problem of summer wear for men wasn't solved in 1901. 33 years later, an August 4, 1934 article in the Literary Digest titled *Word for "Shirt-Sleeves" Is America's Crying Need* explains that "shirt-sleeves" means removing the coat but not the waistcoat so only the shirt's sleeves were exposed.

"At the time when any shirt made up without a stiff bosom was called a 'negligee,' one wearing such a shirt without coat or vest was called a 'shirt-waist man.'" (Negligee originally meant informal wear.)

If a man is "in his shirt" it implies that he is wearing neither coat nor trousers, so there is a need for a word "which would indicate that a man is wearing his trousers and his shirt without encumbrance of either coat or vest." (How about "hippie"?)

Hello Dali

In March, 1939, surrealist painter Salvador Dali was commissioned by by luxe New York City department store Bonwit Teller to create two display windows, "Night" and "Day", supposed to illustrate the Narcissus Complex, arranged by his art dealer Julien Levy.

The Day window featured a mannequin wearing a see-through negligee, a red wig, and green feathers stepping into a water-filled bathtub lined with Persian lamb fleece. Flowers floated on the surface and three wax hands holding mirrors reached up from the water.

The Night window had a mannequin lying in bed with buffalo legs and a mattress of glowing coals with a buffalo head headboard with a bloody pigeon in its mouth. Dali said it was "the decapitated head and the savage hoofs of a great somnambulist buffalo extenuated by a thousand years of sleep," according to the On This Day in Fashion web site.

Bonwit undercover agents mixed with the gawking crowds outside the windows. The indecent mannequin stepping onto the tub was the most upsetting and the store replaced both mannequins with ones in suits.

Dali arrived to survey his work and was enraged by the changes. He stormed into the Day window and upended the bathtub, which then crashed through the plate glass window onto the sidewalk along with Dali.

He was arrested by a passing policeman and charged with malicious mischief. His wife Gala rushed to find Julien Levy who told Louis Brodsky, a magistrate in the Tombs, that Dali promised never to do it again and the charges were reduced to disorderly conduct and Dali was released, Brodsky saying "these are some of the privileges that an artist with temperament seems to enjoy."

The affair made all the morning newspapers and when Dali's exhibit opened that night, the Julien Levy Gallery was thronged and more than twenty paintings were sold.

Bonwit Teller was founded in 1895. the flagship store on Fifth Avenue was bought by Donald Trump in 1980 and demolished to build Trump Tower. Bonwit moved to a smaller store around the corner with an entrance from The Trump Tower indoor mall, but went bankrupt in 1990. Dali died in 1989.

Shoveling Silver

A July 29, 1957 ad in Life Magazine featured a Canada Dry sweepstakes in which the grand prize was "all the silver dollars you can shovel in 5 minutes," with a guaranteed minimum of $15,000. Second prize was 2 minutes of shoveling with a $6,000 minimum and third prize was one minute and $3,000. And entering was easy: "No Jingles! No Puzzles! Nothing to Buy!" Just fill in the entry blank. If you win you will be flown to New York City for the shoveling. (I like the no-nonsense guard with the tommy gun.)

The winner (a man) shoveled more than $30,000, over a quarter million in 2015 dollars. Silver dollars in 1957 were just heavy money worth a dollar. At $14.50 silver, 30,000 silver dollars would be worth $335,000 just for the silver value.

The "shovel-off" was televised on the Today Show hosted by Dave Garroway, the debut host of the show in 1951.

Ad in the April 2, 1900 Baltimore Morning Herald

The Customer is Always Right

Joseph's 3 Laws Of Retail Dynamics

The Law Of Inverse Anxiety
The smaller the diamond, the bigger the worry about leaving it.

The Law Of Least Favorable Assumption
Wherever it was fixed, that's where it broke again. Or, it's not my watch, it's your battery.

The Law Of Inappropriate Negotiation
The smaller the price, the harder the bargaining.

Psychopathia Ornamentalis

Subclinical Hypoornamentation
Symptoms include subadornment of the fingers, neck, and ears, pallor of the raiment, underappreciation of the ornamental craft, ebbing of decorative desire. Can progress to systemic inelegance, atrophy of the aesthetic faculty, and, in extreme cases, arrest by the fashion police. See your jeweler for semiannual check-ups.

Ideopathic Monochromaticism
Characterized by an abnormally narrow chromatic decorative range, sometimes obessional. Subtypes include gemological monochromaticism and monometallism (see WJ Bryan, 1896).

Benign Male Hyperchronicity
This common male syndrome presents as a mild to moderate obsession with acquiring timepieces, far in excess of functional needs. This is endemic in American society due to the narrow range of socially permissible male ornamental outlets. Serendipitous benefits of this syndrome include low rates of tardiness and an obvious solution to the male birthday gift problem.

Systemic Hyperirresolution
Symptoms include excessive vacillation and indecision, often expressed as inappropriate hyperanalysis in inherently non-rational contexts. Hey – if it looks good, it is good. Make up your mind already!

Take two diamonds and call me in the morning.

Intelligence Agent
A woman came in to the store and asked if any intellectuals patronized the store. I never was asked that before. I told her that all walks of life come in. She looked dubious. I was sore tempted to ask her how one could spot an intellectual, but she was looking at something and I wanted to segue to close the sale.

She bought a chain and wanted me to shorten it. I told her she could pick it up the next day and gave her a newsletter.

She came in to pick up the chain, wearing her phi beta kappa key, and gave me back the newsletter with a few corrections highlighted in yellow.

So how could one spot an intellectual? A subtle air of superiority? Gratuitous displays of erudition? An arrest for sherry binge-drinking? Wait! Of course! The head comes to a point. And in advanced cases there is a propeller on top.

Mileage
Attention! Joseph's does not stock those 5 year watch batteries you're always asking for. They're only sold at gas stations where they also sell the 35 miles per gallon gas.

Finger Lickin' Bad
Please don't lick your finger to remove a too-tight ring and then hand it to me. Joseph's has a variety of sanitary lubricants on hand for this purpose. Thank you for your attention.

Tip Of The Hat
To all the cheerful, unneurotic customers who really are always right and don't give me something to write about.

Deep Thought
It is what it is, whether you believe it or not.

We've Got Steam Heat

People believe all sorts of cockamamie things about jewelry. This is usually due to an understandable ignorance of the technical aspects of jewelry or to general lack of mechanical intuition. But, then again, some people don't light up when you flip the switch.

The best story I've heard is about a consumer who believes that you should never let a jeweler steam your jewelry because some of the gold comes off and the jeweler collects it and sells it.

In my own experience, the best is a question I've been asked several times: "Is it true that opals bring bad luck?"

I think it's only a nasty rumor.

Actually, the origin of this superstition is known. It comes from an 1817 Sir Walter Scott novel, *Anne of Geierstein*, in which the colors of the opal the heroine wears in her hair change with her moods and fade when she dies.

Something For Nothing

Clueless? Unsure of yourself? Ornamentally challenged? Problem solved! Just buy a gift certificate and let the giftee do all the work while you get the credit!

Licensed to Drive

I accept money in any form: paper, plastic, or real. When people give me checks they often ask if I want to see their driver's license.

Showing a driver's license is a deterrent to fraud: stolen or forged checks. In that case the police can track you down.

But I know who you are. I'm concerned that the check shouldn't bounce. A driver's license won't tell me how much is in your account. So drive carefully on the way to the bank and don't lay rubber.

Dumb Question

People often announce they have a dumb question to ask. Usually they're not so dumb. I don't expect you to be aware of the technical aspects of jewelry.

But I do expect you to have a little common sense.

A woman asked me if I could do an insurance appraisal for her diamond ring without taking it off her finger. I was struck dumb by that question.

A Diamond As Big As The Ritz

I had a sign in my window saying "The Ideal Cut Diamond Sold Here." Next to the sign was a 3 inch prop diamond in a box and a copy of the previous edition of my diamond book with another sign that said "Diamond Mistake Insurance, $6.95"

One day, an elderly gentleman came in and inquired as to the price of the ideal cut diamond in the window. He was crestfallen after I gently explained that it wasn't a real diamond.

Another time, I saw two people outside the window animatedly talking and pointing at the "diamond". They came in, a grandmother with her teen-age grandson. The grandson just couldn't wait to find out if that big diamond was really $6.95. I patiently explained to him that it wasn't a real diamond. "See", the grandmother chided him, "the $6.95 is for the insurance".

A Diamond As Big As The Ritz

A 3 inch diamond would weigh over 1600 carats, or about ¾ pound, easily trumping the Cullinan I, the pear-shaped diamond in the king's scepter of the British crown jewels, the largest cut diamond at 530.2 carats.

The Cullinan diamond was found in 1905 in South Africa's Premier mine. The 3106.75 carat (1.37 lbs.) rough is thought to be itself a cleavage from a still larger stone, as yet hidden in the bosom of the earth. It was cut into 105 finished stones.

Yes, We Have No Gold Bananas

People come in all the time with all sorts of things they think are gold. Cheap watches, gold colored rolls of paper, pens, and assorted dime-store objets d'art.

But the best so far is a banana plug, one of those stereo connectors. I doubt that even Space Shuttle banana plugs are gold.

Deep Thought

Things are worth what you can sell them for.

Budget Deficit
Continuing scientific research has discovered a a new law, Joseph's Fourth Law of Retail Dynamics.

The Law of Ornamental Inflation
Jewelry always costs more than the budget. No one ever said that what was bought cost less than anticipated. So take that unrealistic number that popped out of your wallet and into your head and add at least 50%.

Mix & Match
People often ask me if it's all right to wear white gold next to yellow, or to hang a white gold pendant on a yellow gold chain. The answer is yes. The underlying principle is called free will.

There are plenty of 2-tone watches and bracelets, rings, pendants, and earrings and nobody thinks they're odd. Your diamond is set in white prongs, even if the bottom of the ring is yellow.

I hope you don't suffer from ideopathic monochromaticism! (See *Psychopathia Ornamentalis* on p. 57).

Don't Stick It To Me!
Please don't tape your broken chains to a piece of paper or cardboard before bringing them in for repair. It takes as long to remove the chain as to repair it. Plus the tape leaves stickum on it.

I once had a nurse come in with a chain nailed down completely with old-fashioned white adhesive tape. Took forever to peel it off and I had to use acetone to get the residue off.

99 Cent Sale
People often remember the price of something in the store as, say, $299.99. But the price is actually $299.00. So habituated are they by the chain store practice of giving a penny off to make you think the price is closer to 200 bucks than 300 bucks, that they mentally add the extra 99 cents. (I'm waiting for stores to add an extra 9/10ths of a cent, like gas stations.)

Well, at Joseph's you get a whole dollar off, not just a penny.

How Should I Know?
When people come in for something I don't have or don't do, they always ask where they can get it or have it done.

But when I tell them I don't know, they think I'm being difficult.

I talk to one other jeweler on a regular basis. I have a general idea of what kind of stuff he sells (pretty much the same stuff I sell). But I don't know if he or who else has the particular thing you're looking for. I have a general idea of which jewelers in the area sell the fancy stuff and which sell the cheap stuff, but that's it.

People also come in with jewelry they bought somewhere else and want to know what it's worth at a glance. Without doing a full analysis, measuring stones and diamonds, estimating carat weights, calling suppliers to see what that emerald or ruby sells for, I couldn't tell you.

As for the really cheap stuff, I don't have a clue. It's worth what stores that sell cheap stuff sell it for.

Grown-ups Play Peek-A-Boo
First, a review of my observations of quirky consumer psychology in previous newsletters.

• The Watchband Syndrome. There are two places you can adjust your foldover watch band from the clasp. One place (the end where the band attaches to the clasp) is right and the other place (the end where the folding joint attaches to the clasp) is wrong. People always choose the wrong way.

• The Tag Sale syndrome. Bracelets laid side-by-side over the half-cylinder display I have are crowded together and the price tags are jumbled so that you can't tell which tag goes to which bracelet. People always think the lowest price tag in the heap belongs to the bracelet they're interested in.

• And now, the Peek-A-Boo syndrome. I put the jewelry in a nice box, flourishing the open box for the customer to see before closing the lid. Then the paperwork and moneywork are completed. but before I can wrap the box or put it in a bag, the customer always opens the box for a second look, just to be sure it's there, I suppose. It's so common that I head them off and flip the box open for their second peek just as the impulse seizes them.

Do Not Fold, Spindle or Mutilate
When I hand out newsletters, the pamphlets on diamonds, selling gold, and the book plug, I cringe when people start fold-

ing them. Not just once but into fourths, eighths, sixteenths or a cootie catcher.

All my literature is carefully formatted to be read with the natural creases, so ask for a bag so you can carry it in your hand and not stuff it into your pocket or pocketbook.

Thank you for your attention.

271   Bad Relations

Continued probing of the consumer psyche has uncovered Joseph's Fifth Law of Retail Dynamics.

The Law of Familial Infelicity

Diamonds bought from a relative or friend in the business are not so hot.

But you probably got what you paid for.

There's a Sixth Law, but I can't tell you what it is. (Hint: it's called the Law of Inverse Proportion.)

Can We Talk?

I hate to bring up the delicate topic of sanitation (I'm sure you're all very clean), but often when I'm changing watch batteries, I find unidentifiable substances caking the back of the watch. It's packed between the lugs of the watch case, where the band connects to the watch, and around screws and grooves. It's pretty gross and sometimes it smells.

When adjusting watch bands, the space behind foldover clasps is usually pretty bad. As for what's packed in the links of a well-worn expansion band.....it's too upsetting to mention in polite company.

You might take a toothpick or a toothbrush and a little dish soap to the nooks and crannies of the back of your watch from time to time.

Go ahead. Take off your watch and look at it now.

Friends

I often get this puzzling response when showing an unusual gemstone, say, a green garnet that most would think is emerald because they don't know about green

garnets: "My friends won't know what it is." Let's call it the Friends Syndrome.

I'm tempted to reply "tell them" or "get new friends". But that would be flip. There's obviously something deep going on here.

I don't think it's a leaders and followers thing. I think it's a traditionalist thing. Garnets are supposed to be red. If garnets are also green (yellow and orange, too), then who knows what other universal truths will crumble away.

Gender Studies

I have a little joke in the newsletter section of the web site. An article titled "What's in it for Me" gives one of the reasons I do the newsletter: "Ego. Not too much, because (surprise!) I'm an old guy. Your ego gets smaller and your father gets wiser when you get older." There's a link that says "click here for old guy lessons" and a window pops up:

Old Guy Lessons
1. Wear baggy pants
2. Say what you think

Someone came to the site by searching for "guy lessons". I have no idea what that means. I don't think I want to know.

Great Expectations

Diligent investigation has revealed Joseph's Seventh Law of Retail Dynamics.

The General Law of Specific Expectation

If it has to match, you won't find it.

People are shocked!, shocked! that I don't have a matching bracelet or earrings for their necklace or a specific item they have in mind. I have one catalog with 1226 pages of jewelry and it isn't in there, either. And that's just from one company. There are thousands of manufacturers and millions of styles.

A go-with is easier to find than a match, but I can't guarantee I'll have that, either.

Don't Ask

"How do I know it's real?"

How do I know your check isn't bad?

"Be honest!"

When was the last time you beat your wife/abused your child?

"How do I know I'll get the same diamond back?"

You don't.

Have you hugged your jeweler today?

Apology Accepted

I've observed another quirk in consumer psychology: the Sorry Syndrome. This one's so deep, I'm afraid I'll offend. Well, that's never stopped me before, so here it is.

When people come in to have a battery replaced for a cheap watch, they often feel compelled to apologize for it. It's just a work watch, a knockaround watch, I really do have a good watch...

It makes for an awkward moment in the conversation and I really don't need to know that. I get 7 bucks for a battery no matter what the watch cost and I won't judge you a lesser person than if you were wearing one of my much more respectable Seiko watches.

The Old Switcheroo

People hate to leave their diamonds. I hear so many stories of switched diamonds that it's impossible for even a fraction of them to be true. Sharp practice is one thing, felony theft is another. How many in your profession are criminals? Are you? If you feel uneasy about a particular store, say a polite good-bye and go somewhere else. If you feel uneasy about every store, you've got a problem. You have to trust someone, sometime.

Literacy

On page 1 of the web site newsletter are two articles, one titled "Carats", explains the unit of weight for gemstones, and another titled "Carrots" (p. 165) is about a ring I made to resemble a carrot for a rabbit lover. Of course, I couldn't resist calling it a "one carrot engagement ring."

Once a month, I get statistics for my site which include the search terms that brought people to the site. In the last 3 months there were 10 searches for "one carrot diamonds". One more upscale request was for "3 carrot ring jewelry", and another asked plaintively "diamond rings what does carrot mean?"

I hope they read both articles.

Hard Bargaining

I generally don't bargain. I put the real prices on the stuff to begin with. But some people try to bargain and it's amusing how they go about it wrong. Here are some tips.

If you would bargain, first know what is a bargain. People inevitably try to bargain on the things that are already at bargain prices. Just asking for something off on everything isn't a winning strategy. You're better than everyone else?

Be ready to buy now, not maybe sometime next week or put it on layaway. You want something, money off. The store wants something in return: money now. When people ask if I can "do any better", and they're considering something I'd really like to sell, I tell them we'll talk when they're ready. They're never ready.

Pick something relatively expensive for the store. In a jewelry store, a few hundred bucks isn't enough to get the juices flowing. Five hundred is a good place to start. A thousand is better.

Don't whine about the sales tax. I've got my own taxes to pay, why should I pay yours, too? Besides, it's an irritating amateur move.

Don't shoot yourself in the foot. Something at a fair price is better than nothing but an inflated ego.

Finger Lickin' Bad

I asked you before not to lick your finger to remove a too-tight ring before you hand it to me (p. 57). You might also refrain from licking your thumb to count money. If the new bills you just printed stick together, give them to me and I will lick my thumb to count them.

However, I will excuse this unsanitary practice for counting hundred dollar bills.

The Glass is Half Full

Here's another quirk of you rascally consumers: The Glass is Half Empty Syndrome.

If the item of interest is more expensive than a similar one nearby, people always ask why it's so expensive.

It isn't. The other piece has a low price, for whatever reason. The one you want has a normal price. Your glass is half full, not half empty.

I'm damned if I do and damned if I don't.

String Theory

Please don't bring in a string or strip of paper for me to size someone's ring. One ring size is 2.5 mm or 1/10th inch in length. I need to know the ring size down to a quarter size. That's 25 thousandths of an inch. You can't get that precision with string.

Thinking Inside the Box

From time to time you ask me to sell you an empty box to use for jewelry you had that you're giving as a gift or - gasp! - bought somewhere else.

I really hate to sell my boxes because they have my store name inside and God only knows what you'll put in them.

I now have boxes for sale with no name in them. Bracelet folder, $2.50, ring box, red suede, $4.00. Earring box, quilted red velvet, $4.00, pendant, same, $5.00.

Thinking Outside the Box

For some reason, people bring in jewelry to be repaired in boxes that they want me to preserve, protect, and return.

Jewelry fits in little kraft job envelopes, with names in alphabetical order. Boxes don't fit in little envelopes. Besides, I have enough stuff to keep track of. Please take your boxes home with you when you drop off repairs.

Out of the Mouths of Babes

Here's a new one to add to the long list of cockamamie consumer behavior: the Out of the Mouths of Babes syndrome.

People often bring their ornamental adviser along to pick out a gift: the clueless husband with a daughter, the boyfriend with the sister of the girlfriend.

But sometimes people bring in a small child to help them pick out their gift. Of the course, the kid is even more clueless than the parent, an understandable age-related phenomenon.

Then the parent talks the child into agreeing with what the parent wants. I think it's a way of the parent convincing him/herself that the choice was right. I guess if it's wrong, it can subconsciously be blamed on the child.

If you missed the other syndromes in past newsletters, you're still guilty of them. Ignorance is no excuse.

Dollars and Sense

For some reason some people want to give me checks made out to cash rather than to the store.

I don't think people really know what the benefit of a check made out to cash is, but they think it's good for me. While I appreciate the sentiment, it doesn't help me. I'm just going to deposit the check in my bank so I can pay my bills, so it might as well be made out to Joseph's Jewelry.

A check you made out to cash can be cashed at your bank without appearing on a bank statement and so would be unknown to the taxman, if one were so inclined. But such a check is a bearer instrument: if it's stolen or lost, anyone can cash it. Banks discourage this practice, and so do I.

A similar sentiment is expressed by people who ask for a discount for cash. Cash doesn't bounce, is credited the same day by the bank, and there's no fee like a charge (the requested discount is always far more than the charge fee), but I'm just going to put it in the bank anyway.

If you really want to help, you can just buy more stuff. I accept money in any form.

Wrap Rage

6000 people go to emergency rooms each year with injuries caused by trying cut open those sealed-in-heavy-plastic packages that let you see stuff but not steal stuff.

It's made people so mad the industry has had to give it a name: wrap rage.

Amazon has started a "frustration-free packaging" program, getting some toy and electronic manufacturers to ship their products in low-tech cardboard boxes.

Joseph's has long had frustration-free packaging. Here are the directions for opening all those holiday gifts you're going to buy here.

A. Locate seam in gift wrap

B. Insert finger

C. Rip

Jerk

A guy came into the store and asked for a watch battery like the dead one he showed me. He kept interrupting the conversation by asking how much the battery would cost.

$3, I said. (Batteries installed are $7, to go are $3, tax included.) "Why are all you guys so expensive!" he asked. "I can get the same battery for $1.13 at the supermarket, but they're out of them."

I explained that I have every battery, and some of them cost me a lot more than that one, but I just sell them all for the same price to keep life simple. Out the door he went, no doubt burning a couple dollars worth of gas to find his battery at the right price. A principled stand.

Jerkette

A young woman came into the store and asked where I cleaned jewelry. I knew immediately that she wanted me to clean her engagement ring and didn't want it out of her sight.

The ultrasonic cleaner is in the bathroom, I told her. It's in the bathroom in the back of the store because that's where the sink is. (Cleaning is a wet business and near the sink is where wet belongs.)

She then asked if she could accompany me to the bathroom while I cleaned her ring. Never mind that I had two customers in the store at the time. I should drop everything and take her in the back and hope she wouldn't swipe the jewelry laying on the bench for repair on the way.

I told her that if she was uncomfortable, it made me uncomfortable, and I declined. She fled the store.

One of the joys of retail is you get to deal with every type of neurotic customer who is always right. I must say that after over 35 years in the business, I'm getting a little cranky about it.

If you can't bear to let your diamond out of your sight, you can buy one of my little sonic cleaners and do it yourself. But you can't go to the bathroom with me.

Yakety-Yak

We kindly appreciate your turning off that #!)$!@ cell phone.

Thank you so much.

Yakety-yak. Don't talk back, hang up. I like the phone that grows out of your ear. It looks like you've been assimilated to the Borg.

Second in annoyance is waiting for women to rummage around in their pocketbooks to find something. See *Ladies* next page.

The Ninny Factor

The two little kids leaning against the showcase are obviously not real (they haven't moved in years) but the melted ice cream on the rug next to them looks very convincing. (A dog once licked it.)

Occasionally people call to my attention that someone spilled ice cream on the rug, but they get the joke after a bit.

But one time a woman picked up the ice cream and brought it over to me telling me that someone had spilled ice cream on the rug. She didn't seem to notice that the ice cream didn't drip off the spoon.

I was telling this amazing tale to a guy and I concluded with "and you wonder why the country's in a mess." That sparked an outburst which I cut off when he got to "politicians."

And you wonder why the country's in a mess.

Don't Make Me Krazy

I often have to repair jewelry that customers have attempted to glue back together with krazy glue. I have to repair it because it didn't work. Hey, one drop holds a ton, why not?

Super glue is rated at 4000 pounds per square inch tensile strength. But the area you're trying to glue is maybe a few square millimeters. (■ 2 sq. mm, actual size.) 4000 pounds per square inch is 6.2 pounds per square millimeter. So it would take only about 12 pounds of pressure to break the glue. That's why it doesn't work.

Then I have to get the glue off before I repair it. This is accomplished by either soaking in acetone or burning it off. Either way is another aggravation I don't need.

So do me a favor and don't try to glue your broken jewelry back together.

HGE

People bring in jewelry they think is gold because it's marked "18K". But they ignore the letters "HGE" after the "18K". "HGE" stands for "Heavy Gold Electroplate". Translation: genuine metal.

Ladies

Please locate the watch that needs a battery, the broken jewelry, or the repair slip in your handbag before you come to the store. I estimate that I spend about 50 hours a year waiting for women to rummage through their handbags to find stuff.

You might try tying the item to a brick, which should be quickly found in even the most capacious and disorganized bag. (Is that a bag, or did you steal second base?)

Gentlemen

Please don't tuck your wife's or girlfriend's broken jewelry into your wallet to transport it to the store. The application of posterior pressure is generally deleterious to the repair process.

Remember those handbags for men in the 1970's? (Archie Bunker's son-in-law, Meathead, carried one.) I promise to keep a straight face.

Heavy Handed

One reason I don't believe you when you tell me your ring size is that you think it's the same for your right and left hand fingers.

If you're right-handed, your right hand fingers are usually a half-size larger. The reverse is true if you're left-handed. Some people have a full size difference.

This is so common that when I was puzzled by a man whose left and right ring fingers measured the same, he explained that he was ambidextrous.

Let's make up a cool scientific name for it. Ask your friends if they have chiral hypertrophy.

The Wrong Stuff

Please don't improvise a ring guard by wrapping thread, lots of thread, or adhesive tape around your ring. It takes me longer to remove it than to size your ring.

Batteries Included, Please

From time to time, people bring in their watch for a battery and, when I open the case, there's no old battery inside. There's a zillion different sizes of batteries and when I don't have the old battery, I have to figure out which one fits by trial and error, which is tedious. So please don't monkey around with your watch before bringing it in to have the battery changed.

It's Unavoidable

The State of New Jersey charges you sales tax. Unfortunately, It makes me collect it from you. I'm often asked if the sales tax goes away if the customer pays cash. It does not.

Such a customer is either asking for a 7% discount for the convenience of cash or, worse, suborning the crime of tax evasion by asking me to do the sale off the books.

Cash is convenient, not magical. Just about all the money, in whatever form, is deposited in the bank so I can write the checks to pay my bills. Just about all merchandise is shipped to the store and paid for by check. I also give myself a paycheck (That's why I can collect Social Security).

The advantages of cash are same day clearance at the bank, saving the 2-3% a charge costs me, and, of course, cash doesn't bounce.

Sure, I like cash. But not enough to give 2 to 4 times the charge fee off. Besides, if I were going to cheat on your taxes I sure wouldn't tell you about it.

Cheer up! Taxes are better than that other thing you can't avoid.

271   ## A Poser

When you figure this one out you'll understand appraisals.

The goal of an appraisal is to state the market price to replace lost jewelry. Most things most of the time sell at the market price, because that's how the market price is determined. If everybody's diamond appraises for 50% more than was paid, how much more than average should the average diamond cost?

See *Inflation* on p 176.

Sanitation Dept.

Please take out those diamond or gemstone earrings you never take out and clean them. They look horrible. The ear yuck underneath the stones makes them look dead.

I know when you knead the meatloaf, you get hamburger underneath your ring. I don't quite understand how ear stuff gets underneath earrings, but it does.

A toothbrush and elbow grease will do it. Or bring them in and I'll clean them in my ultrasonic cleaner.

It's Google Time

It always restores my faith in the absurdity of life when I get my web site statistics with a list of search terms that brought people to the site. The newsletters were posted in the site as PDF downloads, giving plenty of ammunition for googling.

I started the *It's Google Time* series in the newsletters in 2005. I ran articles until 2011. In August of that year there were 554 downloads of the *Selling Your Gold* pamphlet from the web site, the one I hand out at the store (p. 216).

From then on almost all the searches that brought people to the web site were about selling gold due to the run-up in price, so I discontinued the series, save for an outlier in 2014

Below are the best of the series in chronological order.

how can i not make the mistake of buying a fake diamond
go to a real store

big diamond that are not fake but cheap
Big and fake will probably look better than big and cheap.

a diamond as big as the ritz bathroom
Huh?

Cockamamie jewelry
For a cockamamie person?

how to get diamonds out of peanut butter
Use your tongue. Or see *But Was it Crunchy or Creamy* on p. 81.

Dummy buying diamond
I'll rename my diamond book *Diamonds for Dummies*

An appraisal for the diamond as big as the ritz
It was an interesting story.

Eat leather.com
You check it out.

lick fingers count money
I'll excuse this unsanitary practice for hundred dollar bills. (See *Finger Lickin' Bad* on p. 60)

Soldered collar ring wife
Huh?

Don't know the ring size of girlfriend
I don't think you'll find it on the Internet.

Is diamondaura better than cubic zirconia? (See *Luxe et Veritas* on p.93)
It is cubic zirconia.

What is a jewelry box?
It's a box you put jewelry in.

Removing jewelry odor
How'd you stink it up in the first place?

Jewelry box with aliens
Huh?

Are the summer changes good or bad in the last 20 years
Huh?

How much is 1 karat diamond at tiffany's
More than at Joseph's

Old folk cures for what ails you
A web site article *Attention Winos* about the Greeks believing that wearing amethyst while imbibing would prevent drunkeness adds "Of course, they also believed that Windex would cure whatever ails you", a reference to the 2002 movie My Big Fat Greek Wedding.

diamond static electricity
There are anti-static floor mats with a diamond pattern on them.

explained in one page
What needed to be explained in one page isn't in the query, but the description of Ornamentally Incorrect on the site states "In It's the Economy, Stupid, economics is handily explained in one page, so you can throw out that dense econ 101 textbook you never understood."

zirconia from your pets ashes
It's diamonds they make from your or your pet's ashes, since we are carbon-based life-forms. There is only 1 mg of zirconium in the human body (.005 carat). (see *A Human is Forever* on p. 28)

symbolism in a diamond as big as the ritz
The article "A Diamond as Big as the Ritz" (p. 58) is mentioned in the book description but this is a course in jewelry, not literature. (Maybe I'll take it up some dark and stormy night.) By the way, that diamond is as big as the Ritz-Carlton Hotel in the 1922 F. Scott Fitzgerald fable.

what to write in a jewellery newsletter
Hey! This stuff is ©opyrighted.

what is the right price to receive for a pennyweight of 14 carat gold.
The highest price

free activities for a once upon a dime book

The comic book *Once Upon a Dime* is free from the New York Fed. I think the activities in the comic involve money. (p. 100)

prospectus klondike 1897

A footnote crediting Scrooge McDuck as technical consultant for the Fed's comic book project mentioned that McDuck discovered the "Goose Egg Nugget" in the Klondike in 1896. I doubt there was a prospectus for the Klondike gold rush, although crackpot gold tout Glenn Beck might have one.

what is the price of 14 karat gold right now

More or less than it was when it changed one minute ago.

how to write an effective jewelry news-letter

Behold!

accidental salting with gold jewellery

Huh?

dog's ashes into diamonds cheap

Lifegem will squeeze your or your pet's ashes into a diamond, not so cheap. $3500 for a ¼ carat, $20,000 for a 1 carat.

buy big cheap diamonds paypal

Big diamonds aren't cheap no matter how you pay for them.

If you bleach fake diamond do they turn black

I guess it depends on how cheap that fake diamond is. Cubic zirconia won't.

Analyses of existing jewelry box

Sounds very literate, whatever it means.

200 word introduction of jewelry box

For a term paper on jewelry boxes?

The money in the shoe holiday

Another occasion to buy jewelry! When is it?

Shoes with weed on them

What have you been smoking?

Buying diamond at 1/2 appraisal good deal

There is a web site article called *A Poser* slyly debunking exactly that. (p. 64)

fake snakebites shop

Cobras give real snakebites. But "snakebite" was in the *Snake Shoe*s article. (p. 28)

cheap tick

Click It or Tick It was an article about pulling out the stem on your watch to save the battery. Maybe the searcher was looking for cheap tickets.

only 4 she jewelery

Beats me.

how much is a ten karat diamond cost

If literacy is correlated with income, you can't afford it.

Winos Shoes

Snake Shoes (p. 28) was an article about a cobra guarding gem-encrusted shoes in a department store window and *Attention Winos* (p. 26) about how the index of the top 100 wines went up even more than gold.

I was mystified why anyone would search for "winos shoes," so I tried it myself. There really are shoes called "winos", slip-on sneakers called winos because drunks buy them because they're cheap. Evidently they're now mainstream fashion, at about 15 bucks.

how do i prevent my imitation jewelry turning black

Buy real jewelry

how many karats of gold make an ounce?

What percent of a liquid is in a gallon?

how many pennyweights to an ounce in 18 karat gold

How much high-test gas is in a gallon?

oxymoron in the diamond as big as the ritz

You'll find it in the larger half of the book.

what is price paid for 22 pennyweight of 14k gold

22 times the price for 1 pennyweight.

do diamonds turn black over time

No, but they do get dirty.

can you weigh gold using a postal scale that weighs in grams

Yes!

is there value in 24 karat gold tableware

Maybe Louis XIV had it, but I don't think they make it. Too soft. Your butter knife would bend, not the butter. It's 24 karat gold-plated and it has no value.

cockamamie jewelry photos

Is it the jewelry cockamamie or who's wearing it?

how to remove tarnish from crowns

Your valet will do it, Your Majesty.

why are diamond rings so much cheap-er at kmart than sears

Sears owns Kmart. I guess Sears has the upscale price.

if you go into the city of thieves it does not matter how pure you are you'll come out a thief
That one's heavy. There was an article in the Spring newsletter titled *Burglars Strike Lightning* (p. 169) about thieves who stole the platinum tips from lightning rods atop Notre Dame cathedral in Paris in 1921.

spring coughing
There was an article about a thief who swallowed a ring and coughed it up in front of the cops.

underwear colors spring summer 2010
There was an article titled *Underwear Dept.* (p. 128) about the latest Victorias Secret diamond bra and the newsletter was *Spring/Summer 2010*.

selling your melted gold
Why'd you melt it? Sounds fishy.

summer ounces population 2010
Huh?

what is bigger a 10 carrot gold or a 14 carrot gold?
A 14 carrot gold.

how to refine 14 karat gold back into 24 karat gold
With lots of really nasty chemicals. Don't lick your fingers when you're done.

newsletter box
It's the box you store my past newsletters in. You should buy the book of the newsletters instead. It fits nicely on the coffee table.

i want to know if what i have that looks like a gold chain thats stamped with germany on it is real gold
Sie haben nach Deutschland zu kommen, um herauszufinden. Enjoy your trip.

jewelry cost more than gold because
Unlike you, the people that make it, ship it, insure it, and sell it get a paycheck.

how much are diamonds worth per pennyweight
A 1 pennyweight diamond would be 7.78 carats. A 1 carat diamond at $7000 would be $54,425 per dwt. Save your pennies.

postal scale to weigh your gold
You've got an avoirdupois ounce. You want a troy ounce. Divide by 1.0971429.

are gold karats valued the same in england as in the usa
They buy their ounces with pounds, their carats are karats, and they put extra letters in their jewellery. They talk funny, too.

flipping jewelry for profit.
Let me know when you figure out how to do that.

juweliers aankoop verkoop gouden juwelen portugal
I don't know about jewelers buying and selling gold jewelry in Portugal, but hop on a plane from Holland (or South Africa) to Pompton Lakes and we'll talk about it in sign language.

aqua regia vs jewelry
Gold is tested for karat by rubbing it across a black basalt stone to get a streak of the metal and then putting a drop of aqua regia on the streak to see if it dissolves. If it does, the aqua regia wins; if not, the jewelry wins. This is the origin of the phrase "acid test". Aqua regia is Latin for noble liquid, so named because it dissolves gold. (See *Noble Liquid* on p. 162)

do old european cut diamonds have a small hole on bottom?
If they had a hole in the bottom, the diamond would drain out. The black hole you see in the center of old European and old mine cut diamonds is caused by a flat on the bottom, rather than a point. Light drains out rather than being reflected back to the eye so it looks black. (p. 196)

how many pieces of jewelry make an ounce of gold
Your guess is as good as mine.

16 karat gold 32 karat diamond ring
16 karat is dental gold. A 32 carat diamond sold for $7.6 million in 2009. Maybe it's .32 carat.

16 karat diamond heart necklace
What's with the all the 16 karats?

25 karat ring
See 32 karat diamond above. Or do you mean it's 104.17% gold?

contemporary poison ring needle
There was an article about poison rings featuring Cesare Borgia's key ring with a poisoned needle (p. 193) Who do you want to kill?

aluminum foil gold dust companies in germany
Gute Reise.

how many gold carrots are there to a ounce of gold
What's up, Doc?

David v. Goliath et al.

Illigitimi Non Carborundum![1], Hab SoSII' Quch![2]

From time to time, it becomes necessary for the small enterprise to engage in an attitudinal adjustment dialogue with its larger business partners. Sharing this dialogue with 1400 people in the public forum of a newsletter helps level the field.

1. Fake Latin: Don't let the bastards wear you down. 2. Klingon: Your mother has a smooth forehead.

272

The Debtor Strikes Back

From time to time I report on credit card issues, how they sock it to you and me. But occasionally you can get even. I'm in pretty good shape on my credit card interest rates, except for one bad card. I don't use it any more. I just want to pay it off.

One day, the bad card sent me some loan checks. Usually they're a high interest rip-off, but this time they were offering 3.99% for the life of the loan on balance transfers.

I figured out a way to stick it to them with their own offer. I paid off the balance on the bad card with a check from a good card, then paid back the good card with the bad card's good check, lowering the interest rate from bad to good on the bad card.

If I had done it in reverse, paying the good card with the bad card, then transferring it back, it wouldn't have worked because credit cards apply all payments to the segment of your balance with the lowest interest rate first. I would have been back at square one.

The two legs of the transaction have to be done in different billing cycles of the bad card. If you pay it down then borrow it back in the same cycle, the two transactions will cancel each other and you'll be back where you started.

In this case, I was able to pay the bad card by the due date with the good card's check, then pay back the good card just after the closing date of the bad card (I called them to find this out) with the bad card's good check. For the sake of elegance, I did this in the 5 day window between the closing date of the bad card and the due date of the good card, staying in the same billing cycle of the good card, so the balance didn't change.

I hope you took notes. There will be a test (essay), starting with "Which card was first?"

Pay to the Order of

Have you noticed that all your credit cards want you to make the check out to "Cardmember Services" or something similar?

If you have umpteen credit cards like I do, you wouldn't be able to keep track of who got what if you did that.

Make the check out to whatever name is on the card. Trust me, they'll cash it. They just want your money. You could make it out to Alfred E. Newman and they would cash it with a what-me-worry? shrug.

I once switched checks mailed to two suppliers. One sent it back, but the other deposited it and it cleared. Banks don't check the payee on all those checks deposited by large institutions. As long as the payment coupon is included with your payment, it will go through.

Of course, the banks keep buying each other up, so the names keep changing, and some credit cards have two names on them. But this has a bright side: when the last bank swallows up the next to last bank, you'll just have one check to mail to Wilmington, made out to Karl Marx Kapital.

Life is Like a Box of Chocolates

My Capital One card promises no telemarketing. One day in comes email spam from Capital One. Something about ordering Godiva chocolates with their card. As far as I'm concerned, spam is the same as telemarketing.

So I emailed them about their no telemarketing promise. I also emailed Godiva: I don't like chocolate-covered spam and they shouldn't cooperate in making it. Lady Godiva replied, asking for the details, etc.

Her investigation revealed that it was done through a third-party spammer, she's sorry to have offended and, as a thank you for my cooperation she sent me a box of Godiva chocolates. I ate them. Delicious.

Comic Figure Gets Huge Award!

From a cease and desist letter:

...UFS [United Feature Syndicate] will not grant you permission to use any DILBERT® images or other copyrighted images. Additionally, your communication to our client has made it clear that you have been utilizing the DILBERT® name for your "Dilbert Points" system without license from UFS. This use of the DILBERT® name is an infringement and dilution of our client's rights and constitutes unfair competition under federal and state laws.

Email to Scott Adams:

Subject: Dilbert points for Dilbert

He hath taken his name in vain, sayeth the lawyer.

Sorry to bother you with this, but it strikes to the heart of everything I think you stand for.

I write newsletters for my jewelry store and occasionally I award corporate malefactors "Dilbert points" for their actions. For example, the bank that charged me to deposit cash and American Express, which charged me to send me a statement telling me how much they charged me, each got 100 Dilbert points.

I'm doing a composite newsletter and I thought it would be cool to have a little snapshot of Dilbert for the reprints of these articles. So I went on your web site and applied for permission. The next thing I know, your lawyers are all over me for the Dilbert points business with a bunch of cease and desist legal Mickey Mouse (ssh...don't tell Walt). And here I thought Dilbert would be honored! 1 million Dilbert points to...Dilbert! (And 1000 shyster points to his lawyers.)

Aside from the legal issues – I can't afford to fight you even if I'm right – I would like to know how you and Dilbert feel about this. This is for the record. My next newsletter will report the details and outcome of this incident.

Scott Adams did not reply to this email. I ceased and desisted and promised not to take the name of the unmentionable fictional person in vain again, and his lawyers let me off the hook.

I will be awarding dumbbells from now on. Threats to squash the little guy with ruin-your-life legal bills work. I'm glad it didn't come to awarding Kafka points. (Ssh...don't tell Franz)

Roborevenge

Robocalls, all day every day. I just look at the caller id and pick up the phone and hang it up. On one robocall I couldn't make it go away by hanging up; the recorded message kept going no matter what. I had customers and I needed to make a phone call, so I pressed 1 and when the robohuman answered I turned the air blue with the creative insults I heaped upon him. Then he hung up.

I figured that might be a good tactic so after I hung up on one call, I pulled it up on the caller id and picked up the phone which automatically dialed the number. Surprise! A recorded message gave me instructions on how to be removed from the call list. I tried it again with another call and, even simpler, I just had to press 1 to make them promise to go away, with another to press 2.

If you want to get into the annoyance business yourself, Call-Em-All LLC will set you up: "We believe everyone has something important to say."

The FTC held a Robochallenge contest for the best way to block illegal robocalls. Two winners tied for the $50,000 prize. Unfortunately, neither of the solutions entailed my favorite, melting the phone of the robocaller.

Then the FTC announced a Zap Rachel (from Cardholder Services) contest for the Def Con 22 Hacking Conference in Las Vegas in August, 2014.

The FTC was so pleased with the results that it released this Zap Rachel design on the T-shirts the staff wore during the Def Con Conference.

ZAP RACHEL

I wish they would zap Ashley from the loan department. She won't go away no matter how many times I opt out.

Pocket Change

I transferred a lot of higher interest credit card debt to Bank of America in 2004 with their 7.9% balance transfer offer. I finally paid it off this April [2011], mailing a check for the entire $261.16 remaining balance the day after the bill came.

I thought that would be the end of it, but in came another statement with a balance of $1.50. The statement closing date was April 13, and the payment was posted on April 21, so there should have been only 7 days interest. That works out to 40¢.

But there was no interest charged on the statement. The $1.50 was listed as a mini-mum interest charge fee. If it had been listed as interest, it would have been 26.33% apr, a violation of the balance transfer agreement.

I called Bank of America and explained this to them and they waived the fee, I'm sure as nuisance avoidance. After all, it's only pocket change.

It's may be pocket change, but it's my pocket. (For another episode of this bank behaving badly, see *Short Shorts* on p.71.)

This attempt to suck the last drop of blood from the consumer probably works most of the time: it's pocket change so people just pay it to be done with it.

Wikileaks is threatening to release lots of incriminating Bank of America docu-ments. Bank of America took the masterly step of registering 300 domain names with all its executives' names followed by "sucks" and similar to pre-empt anticipated bad publicity.

Piggy Bank

Businesses as well as consumers are being nickeled and dimed to death by new

or increased bank fees. Of course cus-tomers have to pay for in-creased busi-ness costs in higher prices. But my bank, First Union, has gone too far. They charg-ed me to deposit cash! Any cash deposited over a certain amount per month incurs a fee.

Now, it seems to me that if you're in the banking business, counting money is your job, and the more of it you have to count, the happier you should be.

You know they wouldn't dare try this with personal checking accounts. If they did, one night there would be a mob of angry consumers, with torches and whatever garden tools would serve as weapons, bent on rough justice.

Furthermore, charging to take cash is unAmerican! Joe McCarthy is turning in his grave. And there may be a constitution-al issue here. Is it legal to charge for legally tendered legal tender?

First Union seems determined to live up to its initials. 100 D****** points to First Union Bank.

[First Union is now Walkovia, excuse me, Wachovia. Too bad. "Piggy Bank" is a perfect knockoff of First Union's logo style. Wachovia died in the Great Reces-sion and was bought by Wells Fargo].

Hang Down Your Head Hal Leonard

Hang down your head and cry. Hang down your head Hal Leonard, you won't get a piece of the pie.

I wrote an article for *Ornamentally Incorrect* that extensively quoted the lyrics of *The Merry Minuet*, a 1959 Kingston Trio song (*They're rioting in Africa...*). It's copyrighted material and I figured I'd play it safe and apply for permission to quote it, so I contacted the Hal Leonard Company, which seems to own the rights to every song ever written.

Their online form wants to know how many copies will be in the initial print run. But that book was print on demand. If someone ordered it from Amazon, a big high tech machine cranked one out. That way, I didn't have to print up a thousand copies, like I did with my diamond book.

So I emailed the company. They didn't grasp the print on demand concept and still wanted to know how many copies would be printed. So I filled out the online form for 1000 copies. A notice said it would be three weeks, since they were so busy.

I gave up after 5 weeks. I pulled the song lyrics and wrote another article in its place. At seven weeks, I still hadn't heard back.

Adios farewell, Hal Leonard. I guess you don't give a damn about a greenback dollar. You wanted me to ride forever, but I'll be the man who never returned. So have a scotch and soda, Hal Leonard, here's some mud in your eye.

Short Shorts

(Wolf whistle)

(Spoken) Ooh man, dig that crazy chick.

Who wears short shorts
We wear short shorts
They're such short shorts
We like short shorts
Who wears short shorts
We wear short shorts

I was on hold with Bank of America and instead of the usual schmaltzy muzak playing was this raucous 1958 hit by the Royal Teens, first thing in the morning.

I had gotten a letter from Bank of America saying they would almost double the interest rate on my credit card balance unless I rejected those new terms. If I did that they would close the account and the interest rate would stay the same until the balance was paid off.

There was a number to call to reject the terms. I called the general customer service number instead because (a) I wanted to speak to a human, and (b) they wanted me to use the other number.

I figured I would just close the account and be done with them. It sends a stronger message than just rejecting the the terms. The outcome would be the same.

But it turns out there's a new wrinkle you should be aware of. If you just close the account, they can raise the interest rate in the future. You have to reject the terms to lock in your current rate.

Bank of America was bailed out with $20 billion of your money plus $118 billion in guarantees against losses in bad assets. They flunked the stress test, too. Their grade was -34 billion.

So with interest rates at all-time lows, what do they do? They thank you for giving them your money by raising the interest rate when they loan it back to you.

I emailed Bank of America asking for comment on this article. They responded first with an inanity, then with a non sequitur, and then with silence.

As the venerable sage Bart Simpson would say: Hey Bank of America — eat my short shorts.

Due Date

All my bills say "payment due by..." or similar except for my electric bill. It says "payment due upon receipt." They think this will scare people into thinking that if the bill doesn't go out in the next 10 minutes, the lights will go out.

It's so irritating I make sure I wait a week or more before I write the check, even though I pay all the other bills in the next 10 minutes. Due upon receipt means when I get around to it.

Once is happenstance
Twice is coincidence
Three times is enemy action

— Auric Goldfinger

They Did It to Me Again

In the Spring '08 newsletter I told you to get out your reading glasses because after I changed my listing from **bold** to fine print I was left out of the yellow pages altogether.

I called Idearc, the phone company's phone book company and they said they would give me a free bold listing for '09 as penance. They even sent me a letter to that effect.

So when the new phone book came out in March, I checked my listing and I was still missing in action. Two years in a row!

Another, even angrier, phone call — press this or that button, muzak on hold, speak to an oh-so-polite functionary...you know the drill. Same promise, but now two years of bold listing. But this time I will head off trouble by calling them in the fall, before the listings close.

But the phone still rings, so I guess you've found me some other way. Maybe the yellow pages isn't so necessary in the age of Google.

Anyhow, I'm still in the white pages, so get out your reading glasses.

Bulletin From the Department of Good and Evil

I am altering the deal. Pray I do not alter it any further. — Darth Vader

Thanks for transferring all that money from your other credit cards to Chase with our special offer. The low interest rate we gave you will never change, like we promised. But we hope you didn't figure the usual minimum payment in your budget. We just raised it 2½ times. We can do that because we can do anything we want whenever we want for any or no reason. We sent you a notice about that, remember? It was in the fine print.

Ok. Close the account, go to hell, goodbye. That way you'll lock in the old minimum payment, right? Wrong. It doesn't matter. You can't opt out. You're stuck.

Chase sent a notice to hundreds of thousands of Chase cardholders [in 2009] raising the minimum payment from 2% to 5%, without the usual option to reject the new terms, close the account and keep the old terms.

You transferred money from other cards to park your debt at 4%. You paid a 3% fee to do it but you're saving 10% so it pays for itself in a few months. You were paying the standard 2% on the other cards so your payment didn't change. But now, instead of paying, say, $200 a month, you have to come up with $500. What does that do to your budget?

Chase initially tried to charge an extra $10 a month service charge on all the low-interest balance transfer accounts, a sneaky way to raise the interest rate without raising the interest rate, but New York Attorney General Andrew Cuomo made them back down and refund the money.

So they increased the minimum payment instead.

If you plead poverty, they may or may not transfer you to someone in some country who will ask you intrusive questions about your finances so you can prove you're too poor to make those payments and then may or may not give you a lower fixed payment, a payment that will not go down as the balance declines.

Outrageous, sleazy, immoral, unfair, unethical. It's all those, but this crosses the line into **Evil**. This will force many people into default, and they know it. Then they'll jack up the interest rate to an astounding 30% plus penalty fees. Chase is trying to dump its low interest accounts ahead of new rules that go into effect in 2010.

Chase got $25 billion of your money last year but paid it back this June [2009]. But they still need to come up with a couple of billion to buy back warrants the company issued to the government when it got your money. The warrants allow the Treasury to buy the bank's stock at a fixed price any time in the next 10 years. That way if the stock goes up you'll make a few bucks for risking your money.

Bailed out banks are hot to buy back their warrants (cheap, of course) so they can get out of the TARP* (bank welfare) program. That way they're out from under government restrictions on, among other things, executive pay.

Chase CEO Jamie Dimon said that the government should cancel half the warrants "out of fairness". Dimon made $35.7 million in 2008, or $1,298,181 for each 1% Chase stock declined. What a rip-off. I would have run the company into the ground for the 1%.

Chase did this to over 1 million people. Some of them had transferred a lot of money with their low interest offer to consolidate debt and now find it impossible to make the new minimum payment. If banks can do this, they can do anything. Maybe they'll make the payment 10% or 100%. Who will stop them? There is no prohibition against this in the new credit card rules that went into effect in 2010. Perhaps the new Consumer Financial Protection Bureau will prohibit this abuse.

Chase was sued and they settled in 2012 for $100 million, only 45% of the fees they charged to people to transfer their balances. Oops! Forgot the lawyers' bill. $25 million. Roast in hell Jamie.

* I know, it's hard to keep all your bailouts straight. TARP, the Troubled Asset Relief Program, was part of the Emergency Economic Stabilization Act of 2008, enacted in October, 2008 under President Bush. That was when Bush's Treasury Secretary Hank Paulson wrote $700 billion to bail out the banks on the back of an envelope, gave it to Congress and they freaked out, but finally passed it. $387 billion was ultimately given out to banks, AIG, and the car companies. $204 billion

has been paid back and $189 billion is still owed. $28 billion has been paid in interest. The worst case assumption is that we'll lose $50 billion, the best case that we'll break even or turn a profit. Not too bad considering. (ProPublica.org keeps track of every dollar of all the bailouts.) Update: ProPublica reports that we made a profit of $46.3 billion on the TARP, Fannie Mae, Freddie Mac, auto company and other bailouts as of December 1, 2014.

The Government auctioned the Chase warrants Dec.10, 2009 for $936 million.

Don't confuse TARP with the $787 billion stimulus passed in March of 2009. That's the one that paved Greenwood Lake Turnpike. I guess they ran out of money before they got further down the road to miserably potholed Ringwood Ave.

Swipe a Credit Card

The Buck Stops Here! That was the famous sign on Harry Truman's desk in the White House. Visa, Mastercard, American Express, and Discover could use some Truman lessons.

You may not know it, but the merchant also pays a percentage fee when you pull out the plastic. And when nothing happens when your card is "swiped" through the machine, the numbers have to be punched in manually. And guess what? The store gets charged twice as much. It has something to do with not getting all the information that's on the magnetic strip on the back of the card into the computer.

In other words, when their product fails, I have to pay. Now I understand that extra costs have to be passed along in higher fees, but there's something about charging me directly each time their inferior product fails that sticks in my craw.

One day I decided to confront Visa with this. After some doing I was able to obtain the phone number of Visa International. The food chain is: Visa, card processor, issuing bank, lowly merchant. I found myself talking to someone who was absolutely astounded to be talking to a mere store. When I put it to him that they should make more durable cards and they should pay for it, he said that Visa doesn't actually make the cards.

Bzzz! Wrong answer! Your name's on it and you're responsible. The buck stops with you. Visa, I charge your account 100 Truman Bucks.

**Clip out this Truman Buck and send it
in with your next credit card payment.**

Foreclosure Dept.

Bank of America is foreclosing on a commercial building in Boynton Beach, Florida.The principal tenant of the building is a Bank of America branch. Maybe they can scoop up the bulding in a short sale and make up for the loss by lowering their own rent.

A Naples, Florida couple bought a foreclosed house from Bank of America and paid cash — no mortgage. But that didn't deter Bank of America from foreclosing on the house again. A lawyer got the foreclosure dismissed.

The couple got a judgement against the bank for $2534 for attorney's fees. When the bank didn't pay after five months, the couple went to court and got a writ of execution, which allowed them to sieze assets of the bank.

They showed up at a local branch with their attorney, sheriff's deputies, and a moving company truck to foreclose on the forecloser. "I'm either leaving the building with a whole bunch of furniture, or a check or cash or something," the attorney said.

Within an hour, the time usually allotted by the Sheriff's Office to come up with the money or have property hauled away, Bank of America cut a check for $5772.88 to cover the attorney's fees judgment, $685 billed by the Sheriff's Department, including the movers, and other costs.

There's No Business Like Show Business

A Night at the Opera

On April 17, 1906, the great Italian opera tenor Enrico Caruso sang the part of Don José in Bizet's Carmen at the Mission Opera House in San Francisco. He went to bed that night at the Palace Hotel.

At 5:12 in the morning of April 18, he had a rude awakening: the San Francisco earthquake.

"I put on my trousers. Oh, first I put on my shirt. I did not take time to look for anything except my jewelry. I snatched up my watch, my diamond pin, and my rings. Then I did what you call—skiddoo.," he told the New York Globe afterward.

Caruso ran out of the hotel and into the street and huddled with other refugees. After an hour with no further tremors he went back into the hotel only to be forced to flee again from another aftershock.

His valet, Martino, went back to Caruso's room and packed his belongings into trunks and dragged them down the stairs one at a time and out to the street.

Four Chinamen attempted to take one of his trunks. "I put my hand in my hip pocket and drew a revolver. You give me my trunk or I will shoot you," he said. But only the timely arrival of a soldier made them relinquish the trunk.

Caruso had rescued a framed photograph of President Theodore Roosevelt with a personal dedication which he used as a carte d'entrée. "When they saw the picture of the President, they would do anything for me."

Caruso had to pay $300 to a horse wagon driver to have himself and his trunks driven to the home of friends, Amy and Arthur Bachmann, in the Pacific Heights neighborhood. Caruso could not be persuaded to stay indoors and spent that night under a tree in the Bachmann's yard.

The next morning he got a ride to the Oakland Ferry and then got on a train to New York, both with the help of the Roosevelt photograph.

Note. Caruso gave two interviews, one in May to the New York Globe, and one in July to The Sketch, a London weekly. They differ. In the Globe account he was staying on the third floor and in the Sketch account, his valet dragged his trunks down six flights of stairs. In The Sketch account he uses "skiddoo" to describe the policeman shooing off the trunk thieves, spends the night outdoors in Union Square, doesn't mention the Bachmanns, and pays the horse wagon to take him to the Oakland Ferry. I have preferentially used the Globe account since it is closer in time to the event.

The Monkey House Trial

On November 16, 1906, 7 months after the earthquake, Enrico Caruso was arrested for "annoying" a woman in the Monkey House in the Central Park Zoo.

A plain-clothes policeman, James J. Kane, who was assigned to watch for men who annoy women in the zoo, observed a well-dressed man standing close to a woman in front of a monkey cage. According to Kane, the woman moved back from the man, called him a loafer, and threatened to have him arrested.

Kane then placed the man under arrest. The woman, who had a child along, reluctantly went along to the police station in the Arsenal in Central Park.

The man protested against his arrest: "I am Enrico Caruso, tenor of the Metropolitan Opera." I don't care who you are" replied the desk sergeant. "This officer says he saw you annoy this woman. He says you annoyed her more than once." "Three or four times," said the woman.

The woman gave her name as Hannah Graham and said, reluctantly, that she lived at 1756 Bathgate Avenue in the Bronx.

There being no cells at the Arsenal, Kane took Caruso to the East 67th street station. Caruso was searched before being taken away. The woman was told to appear in the Yorkville Police Court before 9:00 the next morning.

Caruso was arraigned at the 67th street station and then ordered to a cell to be locked up. Caruso wept and pleaded to be allowed to go and had to be pushed into a cell.

After he calmed down, Caruso sent a note to Heinrich Conreid, director of the Metropolitan Opera., who posted the $500 bail by pledging his house as security. Caruso made it back to the Savoy Hotel by midnight. He had been arrested at 4:50 P.M. He then discovered that an $800 black pearl scarf pin he had bought in Paris was missing.

"A canvass of the building from cellar to skylight by squads or reporters" found no one named Graham living there or known there at the Bathgate Avenue address given by Hannah Graham according to the New York Times on November 17.

Caruso's celebrity and the tawdry nature of the accusation was a sensation in the press with coverage of every conceivable angle of the case, including the antics of Knocko, the monkey who witnessed the affair front and center from his cage.

On November 22, Caruso's trial began. Oddly, the complainant was listed as Kane, not Graham, and Graham was never produced by the prosecution.

Kane took the stand and accused Caruso of molesting five other women in the monkey house before Graham. But under cross examination, it was pointed out that if that were the case, Sergeant Kane would have had plenty of cause to arrest Caruso in the 45 minutes he said he watched him before he molested Graham, and why would he watch idly as these women were molested?

Caruso took the stand and, through an interpreter, denied everything.

Conreid, Caruso's attorney, and the New York Herald reported receiving unsolicited letters from men arrested for molesting women in Central Park who were let off after paying off the policeman and "victim". William Devery. Former New York city police chief told the New York World that he thought Caruso's arrest was a shakedown.

Deputy Police Commissioner William Mathot claimed that other prominent men, including a bishop, had been arrested but the cases kept quiet to avoid embarrassing their families. This provoked a storm of demands for an investigation that only subsided after Mathot was dismissed.

After three days, Caruso was convicted and fined $10, the maximum allowed.

The Caruso affair stirred up interest in the monkey house at the zoo and the crowds of people must have overstimulated Knocko. He fell ill and was sent to the Central Park animal hospital, where he died the next day. A newspaper article reported that he was to be sent to a taxidermist to be stuffed and put on display at the American Museum of Natural History.

A one man play, Caruso and the Monkey House Trial starring Ignacio Jarquin opened in 2011. The audience is the jury and votes on guilt or innocence with a different ending depending on the result.

272 My Little Chickadee

"The Defendant is charged with violation of Section 949 of the Penal Law in that on September 13th, 1928, at 11:35 P.M., at 755 Seventh Avenue, the Earl Carroll Theatre, he did carry a bird in his pocket and took the same from his pocket and permitted the bird to fly upon the stage and cause said bird to fall to the floor so as to produce torture."

This is from the transcript of The People Of The City Of New York vs. William C. Fields — W.C. Fields. Fields pleaded not guilty to torturing the bird.

Officer Harry Moran, attached to the Humane Society, brought the complaint. He testified that Fields took "a bird from his pocket, known as a canary" put it to the chin of a man seated in a chair and released the bird which flew into the air and struck the scenery, fell to the floor, struggled to get up then flew offstage.

This was from a sketch in which Fields played a bungling dentist trying to find the mouth of a man with an enormous bush of a beard. The gag was that a canary concealed in Fields' hand appeared to fly out of the beard. The bird would fly out over the audience and then backstage.

Moran then went backstage and arrested Fields. Moran and his partner took Fields and the bird in a cage to the West 47th St. station. Fields posted $500 bail and was arraigned the following morning at the Seventh District Magistrates' Court. The trial began immediately after.

When asked by Field's attorney why he arrested him instead of issuing a summons, Moran said "The Code reads, 'summons or arrest,' and I placed him under arrest."

The bird in its cage was introduced into evidence. The judge noted "The bird evidently is dead now" and asked Moran when it had died. Moran said that he had noticed the bird gasping and took a cab to a veterinary hospital and the bird died on the way.

Both Moran and his partner Jacob Jacobs each testified that he had seen the bird hit the scenery and fall to the floor.

The property manager of the theater in charge taking care of the birds testified that there were a number of birds used in the act and that they were well cared for and this was the first one they had lost. He said he had witnessed the bird flying out of the beard and said it did not hit the scenery. He also said that Moran's partner Jacobs had dropped the cage with the bird in it outside the theater. Jacobs had earlier denied that he had dropped the cage.

Then another witness who had been at the theater also testified that the bird did not hit the scenery. He had gone along to the station house with Fields. He said that Moran had originally charged Fields with torturing a sparrow, which Moran had earlier denied.

He testified that the officers had posed for photographers outside the police station. Photographers in those days used flash powder in an open tray which produced thick acrid smoke and the witness said that the smoke from the flash had blown into the bird cage being held up for the photo.

"There is not a scintilla of proof that the bird was tortured," the judge said. He recounted testimony that the birds were well cared for, that none had ever had any problems, that the cage was dropped, and that smoke had blown into its cage. He also chastised Moran for arresting Fields rather than just issuing a summons.

"The bird did not die from any act on the part of this Defendant, William C. Fields, nor did the bird suffer any torture at his hands, whatsoever. Therefore, I find the Defendant not guilty, and he is acquitted," the judge ruled.

272   Special Effects

Ben Hur: A Tale of the Christ was an 1880 novel by Lew Wallace, a lawyer, Major General in the Civil War, and Governor of the New Mexico Territory.

In the book, Judah Ben Hur is wrongfully convicted of trying to assassinate a Roman governor and is made a galley slave by his Roman boyhood friend Messala, now a soldier.

Ben Hur rescues his Roman ship captain in battle and is given his freedom.

He returns to Jerusalem and becomes a charioteer. He defeats Messala in the famous chariot race by nudging his wheel into Messala's causing his chariot to break up and Messala to be trampled.

Later, Ben Hur witnesses the crucifixion and converts to Christianity.

The book became a best-seller, so gripping that President Garfield wrote Wallace a thank-you note and made him ambassador to Turkey and Ulysses S. Grant read it in thirty hours straight.

Producers clamored to stage Ben Hur as a play. Wallace refused. He did not want Christ portrayed by a mortal actor. But he accepted the idea that Jesus be represented by a beam of light and a voice.

The play was staged in 1899 with spectacular effects. The chariot race was done with real chariots pulled by live horses. The horses galloped on treadmills and electric rollers spun the wheels of the chariots. A cyclorama background revolving in the opposite direction gave the illusion of great speed and electric fans made clouds of dust.

The seven act play was a hit, running for 21 years altogether and was seen by 20 million people

Messala was played by Thomas S. Hart who went on to star in silent cowboy movies.

The 1959 movie starring Charleton Heston was a remake of a 1925 silent. The urban legend that a stunt man was killed by being run over by a chariot in the race is false.

BEN·HUR DRIVES SHEIK ILDERIM'S "STARS OF THE DESERT" TO VICTORY IN THE ANTIOCH CIRCUS, DEFEATING HIS ARCH ENEMY MESSALA

Gaiety Girls

"The Latest fad of women, delicate little paintings on the shoulders when in evening dress, was started by the Gaiety Girls, who now set the London styles. Two of them appeared at a supper party given by a spendthrift young earl at the Lyric club dressed in extreme decollete gowns. And on each shoulder was a delicately painted, small but gorgeous butterfly. The work was exquisitely done by a prominent water color artist."

— This article, titled *The Butterfly Fad* appeared in the *Carbon County Sentinel*, Gebo, Montana, April 5, 1901.

Gaiety Girls were showgirls who appeared in musical comedies at the Gaiety Theatre in London.

The extravagant shows were produced by George Edwardes. The eponymous *A Gaiety Girl* premiered at The Prince of Wales Theatre in 1893 and led to a series of hit "Girl" shows such as *The Shop Girl*, *My Girl*, and *The Circus Girl* at the Gaiety.

Gaiety Girls were respectable and admired. London fashion designers costumed them and this publicized their fashions much as red carpet movie galas do today. Consider that Gaiety Girl fashions were known even in a place as remote from London as Gebo, Montana.

Edwardes arranged for the Gaiety Girls to eat at Romano's Restaurant on the Strand, London's theatre district, at half-price which made the restaurant the place to see.

The Gaiety girls attracted "Stagedoor Johnnies", wealthy gentlemen who waited outside the stage entrance of a theatre hoping for a dinner date with a showgirl, many of whom then married into society or even the peerage.

One Stagedoor Johnny was George Charles Wentworth-Fitzwilliam, the 20 year old grandson of the 6th Earl Fitzwilliam. In 1886, he saw Daisy Evelyn Lyster (stage name Eva Raines) in *Little Jack Sheppard*, a burlesque about a thief famous for spec-tacular prison escapes in the early 18th century at the Gaiety Theatre.

The third time Fitzwilliam met her at the stage door, she announced that the show was closing and she would be going to Glasgow to appear in an operetta. Fitzwilliam followed her to Scotland and after seeing her performance in *The Beggar Student,* he proposed. But marrying a showgirl could imperil succession to the Earldom and Fitzwilliam aspired to join The Blues, Queen Victoria's household cavalry guards. The Queen had explicitly stated that no officer in her household guards would be eligible if he married an actress.

In Scotland at that time was marriage by "mutual consent." After a 22 day residency period a couple had but to proclaim that they took each other as husband and wife. George and Evelyn thus quietly returned to London as a married couple.

In 1888, George received his commission in the Blues and a son, George James, nicknamed Toby, was born. Worried about the legality of their Scottish marriage, they arranged a secret ceremony. Although the minister was sworn to secrecy, an elderly church usher who knew the family witnessed the ceremony and word of the marriage soon spread over London.

George was forced to resign his commission in the Blues and his family disowned him, suggesting divorce as the remedy, which the couple refused. But after two years, the Fitzwilliams relented and the couple and young Toby were accepted at Wentworth Woodhouse, the Fitzwilliams' estate in Yorkshire, the largest private house in England, 250,000 square feet with a room for every day of the year and Toby was treated as the eldest son of a Fitzwilliam.

George was back in the family fold, being made High Sheriff of Northamptonshire in 1894 and Mayor of Peterborough in 1900. In 1904, a second son, Thomas William Wentworth-Fitzwilliam was born.

Toby's 21st birthday in 1909 was celebrated with a lavish party with hundreds of guests. Toby was declared the heir to the estate and titles by Debretts Peerage.

Evelyn died in 1925. Her husband George died in 1935, having never become the Earl Fitzwilliam which title had gone to a cousin. The cousin was killed in a plane crash in

1948 and George's second cousin, who had no children, became the ninth Earl Fitzwilliam.

In 1951, Toby, then 63, brought a "friendly" suit against his younger brother to clarify whether the irregular Scottish marriage of his parents would prevent him from inheriting the title and the $3 million estate. After 19 days, the judge ruled in favor of his younger brother Tom. In 1952, the ninth Earl died and Tom became the tenth Earl. Toby died in 1955. Tom died in 1979 without children and the title expired with him.

The Fitzwilliam fortune was made in coal mining, with 70 collieries in the Yorkshire coal fields that surrounded the estate. They were noted for treating their workers well in an era and an industry that was infamous for brutal exploitation.

In 1946 Britain nationalized the coal mines and Manny Shinwell, the Minister for Fuel and Power of the Labour government decided to mine the coal on the Fitzwilliam estate in what was widely seen as an act of class warfare. The grounds were despoiled almost up to the doors of the great house and mining under the house caused it to subside.

Wentworth Woodhouse was bought in 1999 by London architect Clifford Newbold for £1.5 million. He sued the Coal Authority for £100 million for funds to restore the house, now sagging so badly the door to "the original Thomas Crapper* loo" couldn't be opened. The courts have ruled in favor of Newbold and ordered a study in 2014 to determine damages in a trial in to be held in 2016.

The mansion opened for tours in 2015 and is on the market for $11.1 million. But it needs $42 million in repairs.

The Gaiety Theatre was torn down to widen the Strand in 1903 but was rebuilt in the district the same year. In 1939, the Gaiety closed, it being too expensive to remodel it to code. The interior furnishings were sold off and the empty building was damaged by German bombs in World War II.

The hulk was bought with the intention of restoration but this turned out to be not feasible and the building was torn down. A hotel being built on the site went bankrupt in 2008 and at the end of 2012 it was finished as apartments and a luxury hotel.

*See Waste Management on page 246.

Daisy Evelyn Lyster as showgirl Eva Raines

Let's Rock And Roll

On the next 3 pages are articles from the fifties music themed newsletter. It was great fun – you should have seen all the people coming in with underlined or highlighted newsletters.

I left out some announcements that wouldn't be relevant here and the order of the articles is different from the original for formatting reasons. The newsletters are 8 ½ x 11 inches, and this book is 9 x 6.

A few notes:

It helps to be old. the Fifties were Sixty years ago and counting. But If you're an old fuddy-duddy, read All Shook Up on p. 84 first.

Products advertised are not for sale here. 1999 was long ago, gold was $255 and prices of those products are guaranteed to be more today.

I didn't have a digital camera then, so the newsletter is a bit primitive compared to recent ones.

The answers are on page 82. I initially put them upside-down to make it harder for you to cheat, but you seemed so upright, I relented. But if you do cheat, I'll put the answers to the movie issue upside-down. (See page 92.)

Start the music!

Your Hit Parade

Guess who sells the most jewelry? Tiffany? Cartier? Joseph's? Wrong! It's Walmart. Walmart sold almost 2 billion dollars worth of jewelry last year.

Here's the top ten:

1. Walmart
2. Zales
3. Sterling
4. Sears
5. J.C. Penney
6. Service Merchandise (America's Leading Jeweler™, now in chapter 11)
7. Finlay (Leases space in department stores).
8. QVC
9. Tiffany
10. Kmart

Costco was #21, Military base exchanges were #25, T.J. Maxx was #28, and Fortunoff was #30.

Walmart?

Rip Van Seiko

I've told you about the Seiko kinetic watches before. They're the no-battery quartz watches. Normal arm movement in wearing the watch generates electricity, which is stored in the watch. Wear it for one day, it'll keep ticking for a couple of weeks.

Well, there's a new kind of kinetic: the Autorelay. This watch will keep time for **four years** after you put it on the dresser. If the watch senses that it hasn't jiggled for three days, it goes into hibernation. The hands stop, but the brain keeps track of time.

So you can get your high school graduation present, go off to college for four years, come back home, and when dad yells "get a job", just give the watch a few shakes. The hands will reset to the correct time so you won't be late on your first day.

I have two models in stock. Men's only at this time.

Shell It Out

Remember wampum? It's a redskin to paleface word for money in a bad movie.

Actually, wampum is the shell of the Quahog clam. Its mother-of-pearl has purple swirls and it really was used as money by the Indians. (See p. 107.)

It comes from old Cape Cod, where you can still find it set in silver jewelry.

Uh '00

Everyday, it's a'getting closer; coming faster than a roller coaster.

That's right, the millennium is nigh. But don't get all shook up. Joseph's has squashed the Y2K bug.

After you've rocked around the clock to bring in Y2K, your repairs won't be scrapped because they're 100 years old and anything you buy on January 2nd will be dated 1/2/00, and not the twelfth of never.

Joseph's custom wetware computer and digital printer will get the year right.

I'm working on the legibility problem.

Bad Hair Day

Just another note on human behavior. In the last newsletter I told you how everyone who tries to adjust their watchband does it from the wrong end, in defiance of the laws of chance.

This time it's about hair. Whenever I ask people with long hair (mostly females, sorry if I'm politically incorrect) to turn around so I can put a chain around their neck to see how it looks, they instinctively pull up their hair to get it out of the way. This is necessary, but their timing is wrong. With one hand holding the hair, I can't get my arms around to put on the chain. So I always have to tell them to drop the hair, which causes them to turn around for an explanation, which is not always understood the first time. Then we start over. Turn around. Now the hair.

Great Balls Of Fire!

If you want to get your earth angel something to say that's amore, here's the stuff.

Diamonds for your April love

With my exceptionally brilliant diamonds. Sculptured open heart pendant with a .03 carat sparkler $99. Classic graduated diamond band ring .46 carat $750. Pink gold butterfly with pavé diamonds on a white gold chain $259.

Say love me tender with gold

Omega necklace, a heavy circle of burnished gold with a can't-come-open rocker lock. $399. Scalloped yellow gold necklace with subtle white and pink gold accents. $359.

Dedicated to the one I love

Have it engraved. $10 one line, $5 additional lines.

Devil or angel

The Jersey Devils charm $69. Blue agate angel cameo $99.

For Those Magic Moments

Does your watch weigh sixteen tons? This man's Seiko titanium no-battery quartz watch is light as a feather and water resistant to 100 meters, suitable for swimming or shallow diving. Wear it for a day, it won't run down for two weeks. $375.

The Great Pretender

Don't have $10,000 for diamond studs? CZ earrings, 1 carat size each, in a filigree basket with heavy backs. $69. Or I'll make them in any size you want.

Going To The Chapel

Wedding bands to say you belong to me. For her: hand-engraved 18 karat gold 6mm band. $395. For him: 5mm high-polish band with a platinum center section and 18 karat gold edges. $565.

Volare

Small heron in flight charm, purchase includes a contribution to the Audobon Society and presentation box. 14K gold $69. Sterling Silver $20.

Personality

Your name in gold. Extra thick. Available in a variety of styles and finishes. From $99 plus chain (usually $39). Allow a week to 10 days.

Entomology

- Colorful enamel butterflies, $29 and $59.
- Sterling enamel dragonfly pin, $79.
- To bee! That is the answer. 14 karat bee pin, formed from two opals, $259.

Cool Jool Tool

There's a new printer you can hook up to your computer to design jewelry: it prints in 3D! You design the jewelry on a CAD program and it gets printed as a ready to cast model. It's like an ink jet printer only it lays down thin layers of special plastic instead of ink to build up the model. Where the holes are supposed to be, it lays down an orange wax that is then dissolved out. Cost is $65,000.

How about a laser welding machine? You can hold a ring in your hands and weld platinum right next to a pearl. Talk about the magic touch! About $27,000.

Please round off donations to even thousands.

Go Stand In The Corner 'til You're 21

It seems that toddlers in the terrible twos stage make a beeline for the cards and finger them up. They instinctively know where to go to cause the maximum damage. I know it's tough to do business and keep track of the kid at the same time. But please, try to keep the little darling away from the cards.

But Was It Crunchy Or Creamy?

Soon after the first synthetic diamonds were made by General Electric in 1954, Robert Wentorf, one of the researchers, in a whimsical tour-de-force, made diamonds out of peanut butter.

The peanut, like you, is a carbon-based life-form (according to Mr. Spock) and diamonds are pure carbon. The result was tiny crystals of green diamonds. According to Wentorf, the green color was caused by nitrogen in the peanut butter.

You First, USA Last

In the last newsletter, in a section titled *USA First, You Last*, I gave a cautionary tale about how First USA, the largest credit card issuer in the country, will rip you off unless you watch them closely.

You must have listened. The New York Times reported in an article on August 25th [1999] that profits were bad at First USA. The stock of parent corporation Bank One plunged the same day.

Ain't that a shame!

Engraving

Keep engraving short and simple, otherwise it'll be too small to read. For some reason people always want to write the book of love on the back of a small disk. The problem is that the longer the line, the smaller the letters. If the letters are shrunk in width to fit them in, they also have to be shrunk in height. As you can see from the actual size example above, the letters can get pretty small.

Masonry

You may have noticed the brick hanging from a wooden stand on a corner of the showcase. The idea is not the brick, but the gold chain holding it up. It's a wheat chain, and if it'll hold that brick it'll hold your pendant. Made in the U.S.A. and guaranteed: if it breaks you get a new one, even if it's your fault. I once got a new wheat chain to replace one that had tangled with an arc welder and lost.

Deep Thought

*If you seek the unusual,
don't look in the usual places.*

Purple

No! It's not amethyst. This 1.42 carat oval purple tourmaline awaits your choice of setting. $230.

No! It's not amethyst. You'll find this 1.70 carat oval purple spinel much more brilliant than amethyst. $300.

Yes! It's amethyst. A ring with a rich deep purple oval amethyst with .24 carat of my exceptional diamonds on the sides. $475.

Purple people security alert! Spotted flying east from New Mexico was a one-eyed, one-horned flying purple people-eater!

That Old Black Magic

All black onyx is dyed black. Onyx is black and white banded agate. The generic material is a form of quartz called chalcedony (kal sed´eny). Black onyx comes out of the ground as gray chalcedony. It's then boiled in sugar and put in acid. The material is microscopically porous and the sugar gets into it and then the acid turns it black.

This is not new. Ancient Rome guy Pliny the Elder describes the process in his *Natural History*, completed in 77 A.D. But in those days they went to the honeycomb instead of the sugar bowl.

The Biggest

Crystal ball – 106¾ lbs. of flawless rock crystal quartz, over a foot in diameter.

Diamond – The Cullinan, discovered in 1905 in South Africa's Premier mine. It weighed 3106.75 carats or 1.37 lbs. It was cut into 105 finished stones, including the Cullinan I, the largest cut diamond. It is in the king's scepter of the British crown jewels.

Sapphire – The 423 carat Logan sapphire in the Smithsonian.

Go Stand In the Corner Til You're 50

If you liked Ike or went all the way with Adlai, wore dungarees and a D.A., if you were fortysomething when thirtysomething was must see TV, if you know who Snooky Lanson was, you should have noticed that the theme of this newsletter is fifties music.

$50 gift certificate to the first 2 people to come in with a list of all 30 references, song titles, lyrics, or other, to fifties music. No squares, please.

Searchin' Every Whichaway

For the chronologically challenged here are the 30 references to fifties music in the last newsletter.

1. Your Hit Parade
2. Get a Job
3. Everyday, it's a'getting closer....
4. All Shook Up
5. Rock Around the Clock
6. Twelfth of Never
7. The Magic Touch
8. Great Balls of Fire
9. Earth Angel
10. That's Amore
11. April Love
12. Love Me Tender
13. Dedicated to the One I Love
14. Devil or Angel
15. Those Magic Moments
16. Sixteen Tons
17. The Great Pretender
18. Going to the Chapel
19. You Belong to Me
20. Volare
21. Personality
22. Little Darling
23. Ain't That a Shame
24. That Old Black Magic
25. Honeycomb
26. Old Cape Cod
27. You Send Me (on engraved disk)
28. Book of Love
29. Flying Purple People Eater
30. Snooky Lanson.

Nobody got all 30 references. 5 people came in with lists containing 26 to 28 correct entries. Some people dug too deep, trying to make connections out of ordinary words. I'm not that devious. Most missed *Darling, You Send Me Love, Sam,* which was on the disk in the article about engraving. It was just a little too small to read. I'm a little bit devious, but it was an obvious place to be a little bit devious, and, anyway, you know you're supposed to read the fine print.

Everyone who tried got a little something, a discount, free repair, or a small item.

Royal Jewels

A long time ago, in a galaxy far, far away, this necklace was worn by a princess at a ceremony honoring the heroes who had liberated her subjects from the yoke of an evil empire. Her home had been destroyed and she wore this necklace that had been in the royal family for generations.

Princess Leia wore this necklace from the crown jewels of Alderaan at the awards ceremony at the end of *Star Wars Episode IV - A New Hope.* (That was the first Star Wars, released in 1977, the one in which Luke destroys the death star.)

The sterling silver necklace was made by Lapponia, a Finnish company and was puchased by George Lucas personally. The necklace was named "Planetary Valleys" and was produced from 1969-1981.

Squirmitis

"Paralysis of the posterior annex," that's the first symptom of "squirmitis," a malady caused by sitting through a double feature in a movie theater, especially if the movies are dogs, according to William R. Clay and George H. Siegel, Nutley, New Jersey cinema goers as reported in Time Magazine October 18, 1937.

Clay and Siegel were determined not to take this abuse sitting down and they formed the Anti Movie Double-Feature League of America. They ran a small ad in the Nutley Sun, picketed the theater and presented petitions signed by several hundred people to the manager and the theater agreed to stop showing double bills.

Word got out and letters poured in and the A.M.D.F.L. of A. took off, with 65 chapters the first month according to the Time article. The Literary Digest for November 27, 1937 says the League then had 3000 members.

According the the Digest, the members "gather signatures of persons who promise to boycott double-feature bills. Then the chapter presents its petitions to the local exhibitor. If the exhibitor is adamant, perhaps a picket line appears outside his theater with placards asking potential patrons not to encourage the theater to show two poor films instead of one good one."

Evidently dissatisfaction with double features had been percolating for some time. In 1936 Warner Brothers set out to "poll our patrons and find out whether they really want double features or whether they attend double bills only because there are so few theaters showing singles with shorts." 568,751 people of 725,824 polled were against double bills, 78%.

Meanwhile in Little Rock, Arkansas, The Society for the Booing of Commercial Advertisements in Motion Picture Theaters was formed. The members held theater parties to boo commercial ads shown with the movies.

"Debut party of the society was held last night in Little Rock's largest motion picture theater, where 30 charter members—men and women—sat together and emitted prolonged boos when commercial advertisements were thrown on the screen," according to the St. Petersburg Times (Florida) August 6, 1937.

272   The Magic Flute

French flute virtuoso Jean-Pierre Rampal (1922-2000) played a 14 karat gold flute.

In 1948, Rampal discovered an 18 karat gold flute at an antiques dealer. The dealer was going to sell it for the gold, unaware that the instrument had been made by French master Louis Lot, the Stradivarius of flutes, in 1869. With family help, Rampal was able to raise the funds to rescue the flute.

On his debut tour of the U.S. in 1958, he was presented with a 14 karat gold flute made like the Lot by the Haynes Flute Company of Boston. He retired the Lot flute to a bank vault in France and used the Haynes gold flute thereafter.

Georges Barrère (1876-1944), another French flutist, played a platinum flute made by Haynes in 1935, the first platinum flute made in the U.S. Made of 90% platinum, 10% iridium (the standard jewelry alloy), it cost $2,600 (over $45,000 adjusted for inflation) at $33 platinum and weighed in at 17.5 ounces. He traded in his gold flute bought in 1927 for $450 for a $650 credit on the platinum flute.

Rampal said of his Lot flute that the tone was "a little darker; the color is a little warmer..." Barrère said that the flute had "greater brilliancy of tone in the high register, a beautiful mellowness in the medium range, and a rich fullness in the lower tones."

Barrère played his silver, gold, and platinum flutes for scientists from Bell Telephone Laboratories in 1935 who swore that the platinum one was the best.

However, a 2001 dissertation for the Institute of Music Acoustics in Vienna using the same flute made from 7 different materials, including silver, various karats of gold, and platinum, played by professional musicians and with 110 test subjects "showed no evidence that the wall material has any appreciable effect on the sound color or dynamic range of the instrument."

Barrère commissioned a piece by avant-garde composer Edgard Varèse in 1936 called *Density 21.5*, the approximate density of platinum (in grams/cc). You can listen to it on YouTube. It's not exactly a catchy tune.

Jean-Pierre Rampal accompanied Miss Piggy singing *Lo, Hear The Gentle Lark* with his gold flute on the Muppet show in 1980. But when he attempted to converse with her in French, poseur Piggy claimed she had laryngitis, whispering "My vocal coach told me not to speak French. I'm not even supposed to eat French fries!"

All Shook Up

"We remarked with pain that the indecent foreign dance called the [Viennese] Waltz was introduced (we believe for the first time) at the English court on Friday last ... it is quite sufficient to cast one's eyes on the voluptuous intertwining of the limbs and close compression on the bodies in their dance, to see that it is indeed far removed from the modest reserve which has hitherto been considered distinctive of English females. So long as this obscene display was confined to prostitutes and adulteresses, we did not think it deserving of notice; but now that it is attempted to be forced on the respectable classes of society by the civil examples of their superiors, we feel it a duty to warn every parent against exposing his daughter to so fatal a contagion."
— From a report on the Prince Regent's grand ball, The Times of London, July, 1816

The American Federation of Musicians vowed never to play ragtime music at their national meeting in 1901. Ragtime was considered low music by some and was sometimes attacked with a whiff of racism.

The Commissioner of Docks in New York City forbade it in summer pier concerts and the Superintendent of Vacation Schools in New York would not allow ragtime in school music programs..

Thomas Preston Brooke, conductor of the Chicago Marine Band, made music history in 1902 by giving a ragtime only concert at the Cincinnati Zoo, which was so popular he gave two ragtime concerts a week after.

Brooke gave a passionate defense of ragtime in the Chicago Tribune in 1902, saying that ragtime was not a fad, that it "pleases the God-given sense of rhythm", and it will last "for centuries to come after we have been forgotten."

"Parisians Hiss New Ballet" "Russian Dancer's Latest offering 'The Consecration of Spring' a Failure." "Has to turn Up Lights." Manager of Theatre Takes This Means to Stop Hostile Demonstrations as Dance Goes On" headlined The New York Times June 8, 1913.

Igor Stravinsky's *The Rite of Spring* debuted in Paris on May 29, 1913. The boos started with the opening bars of a bassoon solo so unnaturally high in pitch the instrument was unrecognizable. When the curtain rose on dancers in pagan costume stomping rather than dancing there was laughter which escalated into an uproar that drowned out the music. "As a riot ensued, two factions in the audience attacked each other, then the orchestra, which kept playing under a hail of vegetables and other objects. Forty people were forcibly ejected," according to a contemporary account by The Guardian (London).

Life Magazine described King of Swing Benny Goodman as "The Pied Piper of the Panty-Waists" in a Speaking of Pictures article in the February 21, 1938 issue. An aside clarified panty-waists to mean adolescents. The article had pictures of youths in various stages of ecstasy listening to swing music. A lover of swing music is a "cat" and cats come in two subtypes: "jitterbugs" and "ickeys."

"A jitterbug is a cat whose reaction to swing is always intellectual, often physical..." as illustrated by a picture of a young man "who is so stirred that he cannot keep still even when sitting down."

"An ickey is a cat who is affected only emotionally by swing. Ickeys generally contort their faces into ecstatic expressions, emit low expressive noises."

Dancing to swing ("shag, truckin', Big Apple, Little Peach") has alarmed dance-hall proprietors "because the vigor of swing dancing causes dance hall floors to sag."

When Benny Goodman opened at the Paramount in New York on Jan. 26, "cats swarmed inside to dance and jitter madly in the aisles or, like this ickey, to remain ecstatic in their seats. Moved to religious fervor, she closes her eyes. opens her mouth, gives an unconscious shout and then, almost painfully, subsides."

Rock and roll is "the most brutal, ugly, degenerate, vicious form of expression it has been my displeasure to hear."

"It is sung, played and written for the most part by cretinous goons and by means of its almost imbecilic reiterations and sly, lewd—in plain fact dirty—lyrics, and as I said

before, it manages to be the martial music of every sideburned delinquent on the face of the earth."
— Frank Sinatra, in an Associated Press, article October,1957 excerpting an article in Western World (Paris).

"It's the greatest music ever, and it will continue to be so. I like it, and I'm sure many other persons feel the same way. I also admit it's the only thing I can do."
— Elvis Presley from the same article.

In a March 26, 1960 Timex special "Welcome Home Elvis" TV show, Sinatra and Elvis sang *Love Me Tender* as a duet.

"I too share your concern regarding this type of recording which is being distributed throughout the country and certainly appreciate your bringing it to my attention. It is repulsive to right-thinking people and can have serious effects on out young people."
— FBI director J. Edgar Hoover replying to a letter from a citizen who called rock and roll "filth." 1968.

"Rock gives children, on a silver platter, with all the public authority of the entertainment industry, everything their parents always used to tell them they had to wait for until they grew up and would understand later."
— Allan Bloom, *The Closing of the American Mind,* 1987.

"Quite honestly, hip-hop leaves me cold. But there are some people out there who think it's the meaning of life. I never really understood why somebody would want to have some gangster from L.A. poking his fingers in your face. As I say, it don't grab me. I mean, the rhythms are boring; they're all done on computers."
— Keith Richards of the Rolling Stones, 40th anniversary interview in Rolling Stone Magazine, May 3rd, 2007.

Gangsta Rap

Over 8,000 Juggalos came to the 13th annual Gathering of the Juggalos festival at the HogRock Campground in Cave-in-Rock, Illinois in August, 2012.

Juggalos (and Juggalettes) are fans of the hip-hop duo Insane Clown Posse and similar horrorcore (don't ask) music artists. The festival is put on by Insane Clown Posse's record label Psychopathic Records (also know as The Hatchet)

Insane Clown Posse used the occasion to let the Juggalos know that the FBI had classified them as a gang, saying "many Juggalos subsets exhibit gang-like behavior and engage in criminal activity and violence."

Violent J and Shaggy 2 Dope, Insane Clown Posse's members, said they have "retained legal counsel to investigate and pursue legal action including monetary compensation and/or other injunctive relief on behalf of their fan base."

Cave-in-Rock is a 55 foot wide riverside cave, now in Cave-in-Rock State Park.

Cave-in-Rock has a long history as an outlaw hangout from the 1790's to the 1870's. Early 19th century historians called it the "Ancient Colony of Horse-thieves, Counterfeiters and Robbers."

All the Time in the World

James Bond got married once, but it didn't last. His wife Tracy was killed in a drive-by machine-gun shooting after the wedding by archvillain Ernst Stavro Blofeld.

On Her Majesty's Secret Service was published in 1963, and the film was released in 1969, with George Lazenby as Bond and Diana Rigg as Tracy.Telly Savalas played Blofeld.

The most elusive prop from the movie is Tracy's wedding ring. The ring is formed from the words "All the Time in the World", from the Louis Armstrong song *We Have All The Time In The World*, entwined in white and yellow gold.

50 authorized replicas were made in 1970 and some rather unconvincing knockoffs are available on the web. The original ring, below in a close-up from the movie, has vanished into time.

Poor Old Dad

In the 1933 Disney cartoon *The Three Little Pigs,* an inside joke is the picture of the pigs' father hanging on the wall as a string of sausage links.

The original had the wolf coming to the door in a caricature Jewish peddler mask with a Yiddish accent. This was later redone with the wolf as a Fuller Brush man and television versions dubbed the wolf's voice to remove the Yiddish accent.

The tale of the three little pigs first appears in *The Nursery Rhymes of England* by James Orchard Halliwell-Phillipps in 1886 and the best known version is from *English Fairy Tales* by Joseph Jacobs published in 1890 which credits Halliwell-Phillipps as the source.

That's Life

In the October 15, 1945 Issue of Life (see p. 177), was a letter from Bessie Stewart praising the cover picture of her son, Jimmy, in the Sept. 24 issue. Life chronicled his homecoming to Indiana, Pa.

Jimmy Stewart was a bomber pilot. He flew more than 20 missions over Europe, including the harrowing October 14, 1943 mission over Schweinfurt attacking German ball bearing factories. He never talked much about it, appearing in the TV series *The World at War* as just "James Stewart, Squadron Commander."

Stewart enlisted as a private in 1941 and rose to colonel in four years, a rare accomplishment. He was promoted to Brigadier General in the Air Force reserve in 1959. Jimmy Stewart died in 1997 at 89.

John Wayne did not serve. He was re-classified from a 3-A family deferment to 1-A right before D-Day but Republic Studios got him a 2-A deferment, essential civilian activity — Wayne toured hospitals and bases in the South Pacific for 3 months in 1943 and 1944. It has been suggested that Wayne became superpatriot because of guilt that he didn't serve.

Ronald Reagan was classified for limited service because he was so nearsighted. He made training films during the war and never left the U.S.

Here's a partial list of those who did serve: Henry Fonda, Paul Newman, Charles Bronson, Tony Curtis, James Arness, his brother Peter Graves, Eddie Albert, Harry Belafonte, Ernest Borgnine, Kirk Douglas, Ed McMahon, Gene Autry, Tony Bennett, Lee Marvin, Mel Brooks, Raymond Burr (Perry Mason), Richard Burton, Clark Gable, Alec Guiness, James Doohan (Scotty on Star Trek), Desmond Llewelyn (Q in the Bond movies), Rod Serling (Twilight Zone), Robert Stack (Eliot Ness in The Untouchables), Sterling Hayden (General Jack D. Ripper in Dr. Strangelove), Charlton Heston....it goes on and on. Many were wounded and were awarded medals for bravery.

Audie Murphy was the most decorated soldier of World War II, winning the medal of honor. He became a movie star after the war, making 44 movies, mostly westerns (see *Hats Off* on p. 237) and played himself in *To Hell and Back* in 1955. He was killed in an airplane crash in 1971.

Waste Management

In 1982, Atari released a video game, E.T. The Extraterrestrial, based on the movie. It sold ok for a while, but too many were produced and the critics panned it.

In 1983, Atari buried 14 truckloads of unwanted inventory including the E.T. game in a landfill in Alamogordo, New Mexico.

On April 26, 2014, excavation of the landfill began as part of a documentary approved by the Alamogordo City Commission. In November, The first 100 games unearthed sold for $37,000 on Ebay, the highest for $1537. Games were sold to buyers in Canada, Germany and Sweden. A museum in Rome opened an exhibit on the project, including Alamogordo dirt. Proceeds went to the City of Alamogordo. (*Continued next page.*)

Atari consoles and more than 1300 games were excavated including *Centipedes*, *Warlords* and *Asteroids* as well as the E.T. game. Further auctions on Ebay will be held.

The documentary *Atari: Game Over* was released in November, 2014.

Alamogordo is a little over 2 hours by car from Roswell and 2 minutes by saucer.

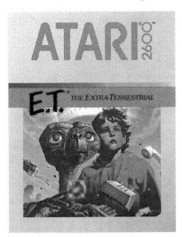

And Now a Word From Our Sponsor

A 1954 *I Love Lucy* episode involves a madcap chase of a "Bonus Buck" , a dollar with a winning serial number advertised in a newspaper contest. But those contests, common in the 1950's, were called "Lucky Buck" contests. I Love Lucy was sponsored by Phillip Morris and the contract forbade the use if the word "lucky". Lucky Strike, a competing cigarette brand, was often called just "Lucky".

A 1953 episode of Studio One dramatized a Rudyard Kipling novel *The Light that Failed* but was forced to change the title to *The Gathering Night* by the sponsor, General Electric.

In the Playhouse 90 drama *Judgement at Nuremberg* in 1959, the sponsor was the American Gas Association. In talk of Nazi gas chambers the word "gas" was actually edited out, resulting in the actors briefly moving their lips silently.

The 1956-57 show *Do You Trust Your Wife* hosted by ventriloquist Edgar Bergen was sponsored by L&M cigarettes. When a man was asked his wife's astrological sign he replied "Cancer." The sponsor made them reshoot the scene and change her sign to Aries.

General Motors would not allow Ford's Theatre to be named in a drama about the assassination of Lincoln and Ford agreed to sponsor a program only if the Chrysler Building were painted out of a New York City skyline backdrop.

Mugglemail

Listen up muggles! You can now send mail with stamps featuring the wizards of Hogwarts. The Post Office has issued a Harry Potter series of stamps. There are 20 different stamps including Harry, Hermione, Ron, Dumbledore, and Voldemort. There's even a stamp with the postowl but, being a muggle, you'll have to settle for snailmail via the postperson.

But philatelists are unhappy. There is a Citizens' Stamp Advisory Committee whose members are appointed by the Postmaster General that is supposed to sign off on new stamps. But the Post Office bypassed the committee with the Harry Potter stamps. "Harry Potter is not American. It's foreign, and it's so blatantly commercial it's off the charts," according to John Hotchner, former member of the committee and an ex-president of the American Philatelic Society.

The best selling commemorative stamp of all time was the 1993 Elvis stamp with 517 million. In 2009 a series of Simpsons stamps were released for the show's 20th anniversary. A billion stamps were printed, but only 318 million were sold, wasting $1.2 million in excess printing costs.

D'oh!

Here Comes the Judge

Judy Sheindlin, Judge Judy, was the highest paid TV star in 2013, taking in $47 million for her top rated syndicated daytime show according to TV Guide. Second was John Stewart of The Daily Show with $25-30 million. Matt Lauer was third with $22-25 million and Jay Leno and David Letterman tied at $20 million.

But radio beat TV: Rush Limbaugh gets $50 million a year from 2008-2016.

In January, 1898 an act at the Empire Theatre in Liverpool, England went badly wrong. As a pianist impersonating Paderewski played, a man in evening dress listened, absorbed in the music. But when the pianist started singing, the pained man picked up the piano with the pianist still sitting on the attached seat, still playing, and marched offstage in time to the music.

Unfortunately, the strongman stumbled and both piano and pianist went flying, causing considerable damage to both.

The pianist sued his partner in the act and won an award of £150 ($650) in January, 1900. The jury didn't believe the strongman's claim that a crease is the carpet caused the accident. The strongman appealed and the award was overturned.

The strongman was Eugen Sandow (1867-1925). Born Friedrich Muller in Konigsberg, in East Prussia (now Kaliningrad) he changed his name to avoid the Prussian draft.

He joined a circus as an acrobat. The circus went bankrupt in Brussels where Sandow met Louis Attila, a professional strongman who mentored him and the two eked out a living touring music halls.

They separated in 1889, with Attila settling in London and Sandow wandering around Europe ending up in Venice. Attila sent for Sandow later that year to come to London to challenge two strongmen, Sampson and Cyclops. Each night of their act, Sampson offered £100 to anyone who could duplicate the feats of strength of Cyclops and £500, a fortune at the time, to anyone who could perform Sampson's.

After Sampson announced his challenge on October 29, 1889 at the music hall of the Royal Aquarium, Attila rose and announced he had someone to take him up on it, amazing everyone, including Sampson.

Sampson hedged, saying the challenger would have to take on Cyclops first for £100, only then could he challenge the mighty Sampson. Attila demurred: the challenger had come all the way from Italy for the £500 contest. After consultations with theater management, it was agreed that Sandow would take on Cyclops that night and would return for the main event.

Sandow jumped on the stage wearing evening dress complete with monocle, which caused him to trip over weights and props on the stage to derisive laughter. But the laughter died when Sandow ripped off his suit, specially designed for this, revealing a Greek god physique in tights and Roman sandals.

Cyclops lifted a 150 pound dumbbell and then a 100 pound one over his head. Sandow lifted the 150 pound one and then lifted the 100 pound one twice. Then Cyclops lifted a 220 pound barbell over his head with two hands. Sandow then lifted it with one hand. For the final test, Cyclops lifted a 250 pound barbell lying on his back, which Sandow easily matched. The judges then ruled that the contest was over and Sandow had won.

But Sampson demanded that they start over again and keep at it until one man collapsed. The raucous audience was having none of it. The judges then proposed a final test. Cyclops lifted a 150 pound dumbbell with his right hand and a 100 pound kettlebell with his left overhead. Sandow bested the feat by lifting the dumbbell seven times over his head and the £100 was given to Sandow by the judges.

On November 2, Sandow returned to confront Sampson. The hall was so jammed that Sandow could not get in, finally entering late by breaking down the stage door.

Sampson bent iron pipes over his chest, legs and arms, then hammered them straight with his fists. Sandow, having never done this trick, was able to do it, but clumsily. The next feat was breaking a wire rope by expanding the chest, part of Sampson's routine which he did easily. Sandow was finally able to do it after the audience shouted out instructions to him.

Next was breaking a chain by flexing the bicep. Sampson offered one to Sandow, but he rejected it. Then Sandow produced his own chain. He had anticipated this test and had found Sampson's chain maker who supplied him with an identical chain, but with the proper fit, the key to the trick. He had arranged for the chain maker to be in the audience to verify that the chain was identical to Sampson's and Sandow passed the chain to the audience for examination. Sandow handily broke the chain.

After protestations by Sampson, the judges decided to award Sandow the £500 if he would perform some further feats of strength. Sandow picked up a man standing stiff with one hand, then performed some tricks with a 150 pound dumbbell.

Sampson stalked off the stage and the judges awarded the £500 prize to Sandow. Sampson left town and Sandow had to settle for £350 from the Aquarium management.

Sandow received offers to perform all over England and polished his act over the next four years.

In 1893, Sandow was enticed to go to America and while performing his act he was spotted by Florenz Ziegfield, later to become a famous Broadway impresario, who booked him into his father's nightclub, the Trocadero, which had been opened to get business from the nearby Chicago World's Fair.

Sandow was a hit and Ziegfield arranged for Sandow to tour the country with his act.

When Sandow returned to England, he founded a fitness empire with his Institute of Physical Culture, gymnasiums, a magazine, books, and exercise equipment he invented.

In 1901 Sandow organized the first bodybuilding competition in London (Sir Arthur Conan Doyle was a judge). He promoted exercise in schools, and traveled the world promoting the benefits of exercise.

Sandow died of a stroke in 1925. He had separated from his wife and she had him buried in an unmarked grave, forgotten for over 70 years until an admirer added a gravestone and plaque in 2002. In 2008, Sandow's great great grandson replaced it with a large pink sandstone with "Sandow" engraved vertically

Sandow today is revered by bodybuilders. The award for the Mr. Olympia contest is a statue of Sandow. Arnold Schwarzenegger won a Sandow in 1970.

There are many photos of Sandow online, often wearing only a fig leaf, including an 1894 Edison Kinetoscope of Sandow flexing his muscles.

It's a Small World

Its a world of laughter and a world of tears
Its a world of hopes and a world of fears
There's so much that we share that it's time we're aware
It's a small world after all

Those are lyrics from the most played song of all time, It's a Small World, with 50 million plays, composed by Disney staff for the 1964 World's Fair ride of the same name, "A salute to the children of the world" for the UNICEF pavilion.

Men are from Mars, Women are from Venus

My wife watches a TV show called *Say Yes to the Dress*. It's about women choosing wedding gowns and bridesmaid dresses in a bridal store with tears and rapture — and the occasional bleep.

That a show like that even exists is incomprehensible, let alone that someone would actually watch it.

But at least it doesn't interfere with World War II in Color on the Military channel.

The Sidewalks of New York

East Side, West Side, all around the town
The tots sang "ring-a-rosie," "London
Bridge is falling down"
Boys and girls together, me and Mamie
O'Rourke
Tripped the light fantastic
On the sidewalks of New York

This is the chorus to The Sidewalks of New York. One day in 1894, buck-and-wing vaudeville dancer and amateur composer Charles B. Lawlor walked into a hat store humming a tune, a waltz. He told his friend James W. Blake, who worked at the store, that he wanted to make it a song about New York. Blake wrote out the lyrics in a half hour.

The song was first sung by popular vaudeville comedienne and singer Lottie Gilson at the Old London Theatre in the Bowery and was an instant hit, the audience joining in singing the chorus. She went on to perform it at vaudeville houses for years.

Blake and Lawlor sold the rights to their song for $5000, which they split.

The song became a Tin Pan Alley staple, was identified with Jimmy Walker who rose from "The Sidewalks of New York" to become Mayor in 1926 and was the theme song for the 1928 presidential campaign of Governor Al Smith.

Blake lost his job as a velvet and velour salesman in the Depression and by 1933 was flat broke at 70. He was forced out of his small apartment in the Bronx along with his blind brother and 74 year old sister, whom he had been supporting.

Walking the cold sidewalks of New York in winter they saw the offices of the New York Herald Tribune. Blake had once been interviewed by the paper and he went in on a chance and told his sad story. The paper notified the Emergency Unemployment Relief Committee (see *Keeping Up With the Smiths* on p. 238) which agreed to help. But Al Smith read the story in the paper and immediately made arrangements to take care of Blake and his family.

Blake died 2 years later in 1935.

Blake put all his childhood friends in his song.

Boys and girls together we would sing
and waltz
While Tony played the organ on the
sidewalks of New York

That's where Johnny Casey, little Jimmy
Crowe
Jakey Krause, the baker, who always had
the dough
Pretty Nellie Shannon with a dude as light
as cork
She first picked up the waltz step on the
sidewalks of New York

The Sidewalks of New York was the parade to the post song for the Belmont Stakes horse race until 1996, when it was changed to *New York, New York*. The Belmont Stakes is the third jewel in racing's Triple Crown, following the Kentucky Derby and the Preakness Stakes. Eight horses since the song was changed failed to win the Belmont after winning the first two races until 2015 when American Pharoah did it, breaking the curse of Mamie O'Rourke. Her ghost finally gave up waiting to hear her song again.

It's Hard to Grow Old Alone

Darling, I am growing old,
Silver threads among the gold,
Shine upon my brow today,
Life is fading fast away.
But, my darling, you will be,
Always young and fair to me,
Yes, my darling, you will be
Always young and fair to me.

These are lyrics from Silver threads Among the Gold, one of the most famous romantic ballads of all time, published in 1873. The lyrics were written by Eben E. Rexford and the music by Hart Pease Danks (1834-1903), a composer, singer, and songwriter.

Rexford (1848-1916), an author and poet, was working his way through college as a writer when he got a request for song lyrics from Danks at $3 each. He submitted 9 songs and received $18, but didn't know which 6 songs had been accepted.

Rexford first heard his song by chance when it was sung by Oneida Indians in a concert in Shiocten, Wisconsin.

Danks prospered for a while, but separated from his wife. Silver Threads Among the Gold sold over 3 million copies, but Danks had sold the rights and he died penniless in 1903. His wife Harriet died also poor in a Brooklyn rooming house in 1924.

Danks wrote over 1000 songs and was inducted into the Songwriters Hall of Fame in 1970. *(Continued next page.)*

Danks was kneeling by his bed in a Philadelphia rooming house when Death embraced him. He was holding a copy of *Silver Threads Among the Gold* in his hand and had written on it "It's hard to grow old alone."

Cliffhanger

Before Hollywood, was Coytesville, a neighborhood in Fort Lee, New Jersey perched high above the Hudson on the Palisades cliffs.

Movie making started there in 1907 and early studios set up shop there, turning Coytesville into the movie capital of the world.

The Perils of Pauline, a 20 part serial, was shot in Coytesville in 1914. Each episode ended with the heroine, played by Pearl White, in a precarious situation to entice viewers to bite their nails until she was rescued in the next episode. One episode ended with her literally hanging from a cliff after a mishap during a balloon flight.

From this comes the expression "cliffhanger."

The Scream

Well I saw the thing comin' out of the sky
It had the one long horn, one big eye
I commenced to shakin' and I said "ooh-eee"
It looks like a purple people eater to me
— The Purple People Eater, written and sung by Sheb Wooley

Sheb Wooley was an actor who appeared in many westerns before starting a recording career that peaked with Purple People Eater, which hit #1 on the pop charts in 1958.

But it was the "ooh-eee" that was Wooley's ticket to immortality.

In the 1951 movie Distant Drums, a soldier is attacked by an alligator while his troop is wading in the Everglades escaping Seminole Indians in 1840. He gives out a short piercing scream.

That scream became the stock scream sound effect, used in over 300 films. Star Wars sound designer Ben Burtt tracked down the original scream to a reel labeled "man being eaten by alligator". Burtt named it the "Wilhelm Scream" after Private Wilhelm, a character in the 1953 film *The Charge at Feather River* who screams after being shot with an arrow.

Sheb Wooley voiced the scream for Distant Drums, although it sounds more like the classic "aaargh!!" than "ooh-eee."

The Wilhelm Scream was used in all the Star Wars movies, the Indiana Jones movies, Reservoir Dogs, Toy Story, Spider Man, Beauty and the Beast, Batman Returns, and my favorite, Them!, the 1954 horror movie about giant ants I saw as a kid.

Popcorn Profits

Early movie theaters tried to emulate stage theaters with splendid lobbies and carpets to appeal to a high class clientele. They didn't want the detritus of snacks despoiling the décor..

That changed with the Depression. A Dallas theater chain put popcorn in all but the 5 more upscale of their 85 locations. Profits went up in the popcorn theaters but declined in the ones without.

Popcorn was highly profitable. One popcorn magnate advised "Find a good place to sell popcorn and build a movie theatre there."

A 1915 ad in Photoplay Magazine touted the Butter-Kist Corn Popper:

"Pop Corn profits $508 ($11,684 in 2015 dollars) in 28 days! Just stand and take in the money while eager folks crowd around and watch the way this Butter-Kist Popper *runs itself!*" The machine cost $150 ($3450)

Today, a $6 box of movie popcorn only costs 60¢ to produce. $6 is 26¢ in 1915 dollars but popcorn then cost maybe a nickel.

17 billion quarts of popcorn are eaten in the U.S. each year, 53 quarts per capita, according to Scientific American, May 2015.

Deep Thought

We pay actors so much because we need them to tell us who we are.

91

Cinerama

Let's go to the movies. The next 6 pages are from the movie newsletter, Holiday '05. Since you didn't cheat on the rock and roll newsletter, the answers are printed right-side up on p. 98.

In and Out

Sulfur in the air causes silver to tarnish. The sulfur combines with the silver and forms silver sulfide, which is black. Liquid silver cleaners contain a chemical that reverses the reaction and turns the silver sulfide back into silver. It does this instantly.

But a long soak in silver cleaner will turn your jewelry black. If it doesn't do it within a minute, it isn't going to do it, so a quick dip will suffice. Be sure to flush thoroughly with water to get all the chemical off.

Avoid dipping hollow silver pieces, such as earrings. Even if they look completely sealed, there will be small holes at the seams (otherwise the piece would explode when heated for soldering) and some of the liquid may get inside. If you don't get all the chemical out it will bleed out over time and leave black streaks. Dip a corner of a paper towel in the liquid and rub it over the piece without getting the liquid inside. Then rinse off thoroughly.

Marathon Man

I'm at the store 7 days a week, although on Mondays and Tuesdays I only come in for a few hours in the afternoon.

But starting Monday, December 12th, I'll be there for the duration, until 8:00 every weekday evening, as well as normal Saturday and Sunday hours. Every year it seems like I'm working eight days a week. Needless to say, the remains of the day are devoted to the big sleep.

Christmas Eve Saturday, I'll stay until the last desperado (always a guy) comes in, but about 6:00 is the limit. Then it's home for the holidays.

If you start your Christmas shopping around 4:00, it won't be mission impossible, and you'll miss rush hour.

A Dollar and a Dream

If I had a dollar for every time the jewelry would be bought "when I win the lottery" I wouldn't have to buy lottery tickets.

It's my turn to win. You can win next week.

Blast From the Past

You know zircon as the brilliant blue December birthstone (although zircon also occurs in other colors — I have green and orange zircons).

But for geologists, zircons are a trove of information about the earth. Zircons contain trace amounts of uranium, which decays to lead at a known rate. Since lead atoms are too large to be taken up in the atomic structure of zircon during formation, all the lead must have come from the decay of the uranium. These little time bandits can be dated to within 1 percent.

Tiny zircon crystals, the size of a grain of sand, found in the Jack Hills, a remote area 500 miles north of Perth in western Australia, have been dated at 4.4 billion years old. This is far older than the oldest known rocks. Zircons are very durable, able to survive the breakdown of the rock in which they formed.

This implies that since the earth formed 4.5 billion years ago as a fiery, molten mass it must have cooled down much more quickly than the 500 million years previously thought.

Moreover, analysis of oxygen isotopes in the structure of the zircons (zircon consists of zirconium, silicon, and oxygen) indicates that they could only have formed in the presence liquid water, and therefore a cool earth.

Since the shining of the sun was 30% less than it is today, this means there had to be a lot of greenhouse gases in the early atmosphere to have liquid water and prevent a "snowball earth"

Hydrolith*

Those Greeks are at it again, making up our words.

"Crystal" comes from the Greek *krystallos* (derived from *kryos*, frost) the name for quartz. The Greeks believed that clear quartz, or rock crystal, was permanently frozen water.

* Just showing off. I made up this word. It's from the Greek roots for water and stone.

Market Share

In 2004, number one Walmart captured 4.3% of the U. S. jewelry market. Joseph's standing was .00003%.

Come on, show me the color of money.

Luxe et Veritas

In the last newsletter [Fall '05] I reported to you about DiamondAura, featured in a full page ad in Discover magazine.

There was insufficient technical information to for me to tell what it was. I speculated that since the jewelry offered was set in silver and a tennis bracelet with 14 carats of DiamondAura was only $200, it had to be cubic zirconia, like "Diamond Essence" which I exposed in the Spring '03 newsletter. (That ad was stupid enough to give numerical values for brilliance and fire, refractive index and dispersion, the only match being cubic zirconia.)

The DiamondAura ad was so irritatingly bogus it inspired a gemologist colleague of mine to call the company. Brandishing her credentials as a Phd scientist and gemologist, she was able to get the company to admit that "DiamondAura" was actually cubic zirconia. That being the case, the ad crosses the line from hype to fraud. Liar, liar!

The ad states that DiamondAura has "even more fire and brilliance than mined diamonds.", "in purely scientific measurement terms, the refractory characteristics of DiamondAura are actually superior to a diamond.", and "it is just like a diamond in almost every way."

These statements are false. Although cubic zirconia does have more fire (dispersion of light into colors) than diamond, it has far less brilliance, both scientifically (measured by refractive index) and visually, and the hardness and toughness are far inferior to diamond. And it is sold in stores.

DiamondAura is offered by a company that seems to be three companies that share the same address in an office building in a Minneapolis suburb. One company is the name on the ad, another a "consulting and training certification company", and the third a boiler room (excuse me, "call center").

But they run that expensive ad every month, so I guess some fools rush in in a leap of faith to buy the stuff. Nobody would buy it if they said it was cz. The sting is the pulp fiction they made up make you think it's something special.

What's In Your Wallet?

In the last newsletter, I explained (with a curse in Klingon) how your credit card charges me for your free miles. Nothing like spending other people's money.

I'm not the only one who thinks this is outrageous. A guy who owns some furniture stores didn't like it, either and he sued. This attracted the attention of some really big companies and they piled on.

Merchant credit card fees are much higher in the U.S. than in any other country, amounting to a $20 billion hidden tax on merchants and consumers, costing the average family $232 a year in higher prices.

There are now more than 30 antitrust lawsuits, alleging collusion and price fixing of fees, against Visa and Mastercard and a panel of federal judges is considering consolidating them into one large class action suit.

May the Force be with you.

Tea for Two

You may detect, mixed with the avuncular smell of pipe tobacco, a whiff of that pine stuff you clean your floor with.

That would be the tea I brew, lapsang souchong. It smells like that because it's smoked with pine chips. Once you get past the smell, it has a bracing smoky flavor. I drink it neat.

But it's not for everyone. In fact, most people can't stand it. My wife has nicknamed it "terrible tea" and I play along by taking a sip and enthusiastically exclaiming: "Aaah! That's terrible!"

For the intrepid palate, I offer a trial bag of lapsang so you can brew up your own cup of Joe.

Cold Warrior

Actress Paulette Goddard (1910-1990) was quite the jewelry collector. During the McCarthy era she said that if anyone accused her of being a communist, she'd hit him with her diamond bracelets.

While-U-Wait

- Watch batteries, straps, and pins
- Watchband adjustment
- Spring rings (the round locks)
- Ring guards and other things that can be done with pliers
- Gem identification
- Check your diamond
- Jewelry purchasing

Dumb and Dumber

Here are the most interesting searches that brought people to the web site in September [2005]. The first two are self-explanatory. The third is inexplicable.

"how can i not make the mistake of buying a fake diamond"

"big diamond that are not fake but cheap"

"a diamond as big as the ritz bathroom"

A Fake by any Other Name

Maybe it's a typo, but it's too good to pass up. An infomercial-type article in a trade magazine heralds the launch of a famous name sterling silver jewelry collection "accented with gemstones, diamonds, mother-of-pearl or precious resin."

I want to say one word to you - just one word. Plastics.

Final Cut

A diamond is faceted by putting it in a clamp and pressing it against a spinning cast iron wheel charged with oil and diamond dust.

Unlike other gemstones, the cutting of which requires the facets to be ground several times with progressively finer abrasives to achieve a final polish, diamonds are cut and polished on the wheel simultaneously.

There is no diamond dust in the polishing residue as might be expected from a grinding process. Analysis of the residue indicates that the surface of the diamond is converted to graphite, which then flakes off. The facet surfaces are smooth down to the nanometer level.

Out of Africa

The sole source of tanzanite is a three mile long strip near Mt. Kilimanjaro in Tanzania. In August, 2005 a 16,839 carat (6.6 pounds) tanzanite was found 860 feet down. The tanzanite rough is the size of a brick and is the largest ever found.

Tanzanite was first discovered by a Masai tribesman in 1967 and was named and first sold by Tiffany.

My Name is Joe

The store is Joseph's, because Joe's Jewelry sounds like it's in the back of Joe's Diner. But I'm Joe. I told you that two years ago, but it didn't take.

Close Encounters of the Canine Kind

We've had doggie jewelry, doggie jewelry with matching people jewelry, doggie waste management, and the dog that ate the pearl.

And now – the squeamish should avert their eyes – doggie people jewelry.

I made a silver pendant from a coyote claw brought in by a customer. I've never met a coyote and, judging by the size of that claw, I don't want to. Not my idea of beauty and the beast.

Warm Front

One plus for global warming is that as the ice in Siberia melts, more tusks from long frozen mammoths are being found. Trade in elephant ivory was banned in 1990, and the only legal source of ivory is from mammoths. Mammoths became extinct at the end of the last ice age, 11,000 years ago.

Deep Thought
The point of having money is to not have to worry about having money.

Deadlines

I will not be going to my watchmaker after Thanksgiving. That means you have to bring in that dead watch you want to wear for the holidays right now.

Jewelry repairs will slow down after Thanksgiving. After Dec. 15, I'll take in simple repairs only. After Dec. 20, happy New Year.

Reefer Madness

The largest concentration of platinum ore in the world is the Merensky Reef in South Africa, a thin vein of ore stretching 150 miles. It is named for Hans Merensky, the South African geologist who discovered it in 1924.

With platinum over $900 an ounce, they must be digging like mad.

Two Thumbs Down

To the Borough of Pompton Lakes for killing a parking space across from the store. It was fine for the 18 years I've been here. What's the problem now?

Not Guilty!

My monthly web site statistics list the search terms that people used that brought them to the site. Occasionally, someone searches by my name.

When I google myself, the first listing is of a Connecticut lawyer of the same name who was disciplined for using an obscene gesture in court.

That was in 1996, and it's still the top listing for my name. A Google is forever.

Hey Joe! Get your head screwed on right and stop embarrassing me or I'll turn you in to that other Joe Mirsky, Assistant U.S. Attorney.

Bottom   **Top**

Hearts and Arrows

Joseph's specializes in ideal cut round diamonds. The ideal cut business means that the angles and relative sizes of the facets are mathematically correct for maximum brilliance and fire (the breaking of white light into colors by the diamond).

But while we're at it we may as well get a perfectly symmetrical diamond, too. All the opposing facets line up exactly with each other, to go the last mile to perfection.

The photos above are of an ideal cut diamond seen through a special "hearts and arrows" viewer. The viewer is a simple instrument, just a lens and a colored plastic cylinder. The plastic colors some facets to form the hearts and arrows patterns. If the alignment of the facets is off just a little, the patterns will be skewed.

Come in to the store and see it in person and in living color (red).

When the Saints Go Marching In

I can order a medal for any saint you want, from Andrew to Thomas, but there's too many of them to stock. (I do have the most popular, St. Christopher.) Also available are communion, baptism, and miraculous medals.

There is an extensive catalog of religious jewelry, available in as little as one day, a miracle from St. Fedex

Three Seasons

Every spring, people notice that they haven't gotten a newsletter for quite a while and ask when they'll get the next one

There are three newsletters a year: the Spring/Summer issue in May, the Fall issue in September, and the Holiday issue in November.

That leaves a large gap between the Holiday and Spring/Summer issues. If I did the Spring/Summer newsletter earlier, it would be a Spring newsletter, and I'd have to do a Summer newsletter. I don't have 4 newsletters a year in me.

So for now it's hasta la vista, baby but come spring, I'll be back.

Popularity

If you type "jewelry newsletter" in Google, my web site is actually number one, top of the first page, out of 15,300,000 results. Why, I'm almost famous. Why anyone would search for "jewelry newsletter" is another story.

If you search for "jewelry box" I come in 17th, behind 16 sites that actually sell jewelry boxes. "jewelry box" is far and away the most popular search term that brings people to the site. Maybe they think *The Jewelry Box Newsletter* is a newsletter about jewelry boxes.

You've Got Mail

A woman brought an antique bracelet she had recently bought with two square sapphires missing. A quick look under the microscope showed gas bubbles in the remaining stones, proving that the sapphires were synthetic. She was told that the sapphires were natural.

I took a picture of the stones through the microscope showing the gas bubbles and emailed it to her as a PDF (Acrobat) file.

I also did this for a woman whose "white gold" bracelet had brass showing underneath where it was worn.

If you have something that checks out strange or bogus, I will take a photo of it through the microscope while you wait and email it to you, no charge. A camera store can make prints from the file, too.

But if this cinema verite inspires you legal eagles to sue, keep me out of the paper chase.

Diamond	Black Onyx	Garnet

Chips

How a chip on a gemstone looks can be an important clue to its identity. Most gemstones have a conchoidal, or shell-shaped fracture with a vitreous (glassy) luster like the garnet on the right.

Black onyx, center, composed of microscopic crystals of quartz, has a conchoidal fracture with a waxy luster and diamond has a distinctive "staircase" fracture.

Splash

Don't dunk your water-resistant watch until you check the depth. Watches rated for 30 meters, (3 atmospheres), which are most water-resistant watches, can only take a splash.

It sounds like 30 meters (100 feet) means you can go swimming with it, but it ain't so. That's a static pressure rating. It's like the gas mileage sticker on a new car. You wish.

If you want to shower or swim with your watch, you'll need one that's rated for at least 50 meters (5 atmospheres). If you want to go into the deep, you need at least a 100 meter (10 atmospheres) watch; 200 meters is a diving watch.

If your watch just says "water-resistant" on the back, it's probably only rated for 30 meters.

The Hunt for Red October is Over

This is a remake with a different star. Blinding red tourmaline ring in 14 karat white gold. Tourmaline, .89 carat, diamonds, .49 carat total. $1000.

Tourmaline is the birthstone for October. See it in color on the web.

The Color Purple

Purple spinel, oval, 1.70 carat. $300
Purple tourmaline, oval, 1.42 carat. $230.
Amethyst, pear shape, 9x7mm. $36.
Purple of Cassius

Nanoparticles of gold are red in color. This is because the particles are smaller than the wavelength of light, so the visual rules of engagement change. 17th century German chemist Andreas Cassius discovered a a deep purple solution containing very fine gold particles. When put into glass it turns it ruby red.

The Doctor is In

Joseph's is open on Sunday, from 12-4. (Except July and August – give me a break!).

Avoid the madding crowds and come on Sunday. Plenty of parking, with no tickets. And Sunday is dress-down day: unshaven, hair in rollers, ok (deodorant would be appreciated).

Besides, if I have to work on Sunday, you have to shop on Sunday.

The Doctor is Out

Many of you have fingers that wax and wane, making ring sizing difficult. But when the discussion turns to why it happens – weather, salt, medicine...– I have no advice to give you. That would be a medical opinion. I only give ornamental opinions. You need to see a doctor, not a jeweler.

Take two aspirin to make the swelling in your fingers go down and call me in the morning.

Sanitation Dept.

There's stubborn white stuff that forms underneath your rings and kills the shine of your diamonds. No amount of ultrasonic cleaning gets it off. This stuff is evidently not water-soluble.

The solution is a solution: equal parts of water, ammonia, and Wisk. Soak overnight (no pearls!), then have at it with a toothbrush and jewelry cleaner.

Better yet, get one of my little sonic cleaners and use it frequently and you won't suffer from whiteout. An ounce of prevention...

E.T. Phone Home

This is for the extraterritorials, customers who have moved away but still get the newsletter in South Carolina, Florida, Virginia, New York, Maryland, Pennsylvania, and Washington.

Send me an email once in a while to let me know you're alive. Go on the web site and click the contact link at the top of any page.

Go ahead, make my day.

Papillon!

Colorful butterfly ring with orange, green, yellow, and pink sapphires, .35 carat total. Diamonds, .07 carat total. In 14 karat white gold. $389. See it in color on the web.

Heist

The "hold-up of the century" took place on August 3, 1949 when three robbers stopped the Begum and the Aga Khan outside their home in the French Riviera. The thieves got away with 200 million old French Francs worth of jewelry, about 4.4 million dollars today.

Stocking Stuffer

You can get a last-minute little gift and stop me from bugging you to clean your jewelry at the same time.

Check out my mini sonic cleaner on the front counter. It's cute, and has a small footprint, only about 4"x 5", perfect for the kitchen, so she can clean her ring after she kneads the meatloaf with it.

It plugs in or runs on batteries and comes with a small jar of cleaning solution concentrate (I have the refill). It's 25 bucks, batteries not included (of course). It takes four AAA's.

You can test-drive my demo model with your engagement ring. It really works, as you will see from the crud lying in the bottom.

Two Thumbs Up

To anyone who gets all 40 movie titles and 6 movie quotes scattered throughout this newsletter.

"Three Seasons" (1999) is a movie title, but it's pretty obscure (In Vietnamese with English subtitles) so it doesn't count.

There's one movie not yet released, which doesn't count, but a pat on the back to anyone who spots it. (Hint: you'll get the big chill from this southern movie.)

The End

Answers to Movie Contest

The unreleased movie is "Whiteout", starring Reese Witherspoon. It is due to be released in December, 2005. It takes place in Antarctica.

Everybody should have gotten *In and Out.*. Some of it was filmed in Pompton Lakes. It was a big deal.

"Reefer Madness", the cult classic anti-marijuana propaganda film, was tough to work in, but irresistible.

Page	Quote	Movie	Year
93	May the Force be with you	Star Wars	1973
94	....Plastics	The Graduate	1967
95	I'll be back	The Terminator	1984
95	Hasta la vista, baby	Terminator 2	1991
97	E.T. phone home	E.T. The Extraterrestrial	1982
97	Go ahead, make my day	Sudden Impact	1983

Page	Movie	Year
92	In and Out	1997
92	Marathon Man	1976
92	Eight Days a Week	1997
92	Remains of the Day	1993
92	The Big Sleep	1946
92	Home for the Holidays	1995
92	Mission Impossible	1996
92	Rush Hour	2001
92	Blast from the Past	1999
92	Time Bandits	1981
92	The Shining	1980
92	The Color of Money	1986
93	Liar Liar	1997
93	Boiler Room	2000
93	Fools Rush In	1997
93	Leap of Faith	1992
93	The Sting	1973
93	Pulp Fiction	1994
93	Other People's Money	1991
93	My Name Is Joe	1998

Page	Movie	Year
94	Dumb and Dumber	1994
94	Final Cut	2004
94	Out of Africa	1985
94	Beauty and the Beast	1991
94	Ice Age	2002
94	Reefer Madness	1938
95	The Last Mile	1992
95	In Living color	1998
95	Almost Famous	2000
95	You've Got Mail	1998
95	Legal Eagles	1986
95	Paper Chase	1973
96	The Deep	1977
96	Splash	1984
96	The Hunt for Red October	1990
96	The Color Purple	1985
96	Rules of Engagement	2000
97	Papillon	1973
97	Heist	2001
97	The Big Chill	1983

It's the Economy, Stupid

Passing the Buck

I've been in business for over 35 years, so I do know something about the economy. Here's how the economy works.

You have your inbucks and your outbucks. Everyone's inbucks are someone else's outbucks and vice-versa. In other words, everyone keeps passing the buck and the buck never stops.

Inbucks have to be more than outbucks to pay the bills. If they're not, you have to get some loanbucks, which increases your outbucks, which means you need more inbucks. Or you can buy less stuff, reducing your outbucks and everyone else's inbucks.

If inbucks are more than outbucks, you can buy more stuff, giving more inbucks to everybody else. If you have a lot more inbucks, you have luxbucks — go ahead, treat yourself, you deserve it. Even more than that — congratulations! You won the rat race! Of course, you'll have to put those extra bucks in the bank, which turns them into bankbucks.

One bankbuck is worth 10 of your bucks, since the bank only has to keep 10% of your bucks on hand in case someone (but not everyone) wants his bucks back, and can lend the rest — talk about printing money! This is how the economy grows so everyone can have more bucks.

70% of the economy is retail, people buying stuff, it is said. Actually, it's 100%, since if you don't buy stuff, the people who make stuff and grow stuff won't have any inbucks and the government won't have any taxbucks to buy government stuff with. This is called trickle-up economics.

It's your patriotic duty to shop, so come on in and pass the buck.

Some of your outbucks become government inbucks, also known as taxbucks. People with big bucks are supposed to pay a higher percentage of their inbucks than people with small bucks. This is called progressive taxation.[1] If taxes are too low, the government won't have enough inbucks, too high, and people won't be able to pay them, or will find a way to avoid them for the same result. If you diagram this to find the point of maximum taxbucks, you will get a bell-shaped curve.

The question is, who gets to sit on the peak of the curve? The big bucks people have managed to push the small bucks people up the tax hill. This is why Warren Buffet's secretary paid 30% of her 60,000 inbucks and he paid 17.7% of his 46 million inbucks in taxbucks (2008). This diagram is called the Laugher Curve[2] because the people who drew it are laughing all the way to the bank.

Taxbucks are always less than government outbucks. This is called the deficit. This will continue until the pig gets lost in the smoke and flies into the mirrors.

Government outbucks can be divided into three categories: govbucks, daddybucks, and warbucks.

Govbucks are used to run the government: maintain the New Orleans levees, send men into space, collect taxbucks, pay congressmen, keep Wall Street from running amok, etc. Daddybucks are used to take care of the poor, the sick, and the old.[1] (Thanks Medicare!) Warbucks are shipped to the Middle East and burned for fuel due to the high price of oil.

And there you have it: economics in a nutshell.

1. "From each according to his ability, to each according to his needs!" — Karl Marx, Critique of the Gotha Program, 1875. In other words, you are your brother's keeper. A Sept. 13, 1987 Boston Globe poll found that almost half the population thought this phrase was in the Constitution.

2. Google "Laffer Curve".

Paper Profit

A spike in cotton prices in 2010 pushed up the cost of printing a buck to 9.6 cents from about 6 cents in a normal year.

Ordinary paper is made from wood pulp. Money paper is 75% cotton and 25% linen.

So the profit the Fed makes from printing a buck went down from 94% to 90.4%. It should happen to me.

Message to the 99%

"It is not good that the mass of our people should be forced to live a hand-to-mouth existence. There is no incentive in work that produces nothing for the future. The saving ability of our people must not be curtailed."
— The Literary Digest, January 8, 1910, quoting "a Cincinnati dispatch to the New York American" by Alexander MacDonald, president of Standard Oil of Kentucky and a millionaire.

Passing the Buck

Since we're passing the buck, the word "buck" for dollar comes from buckskin, deer hide, that the colonials used to trade with the Indians.

Conrad Weiser, a German immigrant to England and then to America spent a year as a youth with the Mohawk Indians and learned their language. He became an interpreter and negotiator for the Pennsylvania colony and later one of the founders of Reading and Berks County, Pennsylvania.

He recounts addressing Indians in his journal in 1748:

"Whiskey shall be sold to You for 5 Bucks in your Town, & if a Trader offers to sell Whiskey to You and will not let you have it at that Price, you may take it from him & drink it for nothing."

and

"Here is one of the Traders who you know to be a very sober & honest Man; he has been robbed of the value of 300 Bucks, & you all know by whom; let, therefore, Satisfaction be made to the Trader."

273 Depression Gold

On March 6, 1933, two days after his inauguration, President Roosevelt declared a bank holiday, closing all banks in the country. Since 1929, 20% of banks, over 6000, had failed, wiping out $2.5 billion ($45.7 billion today) in savings. The Emergency Banking Relief Act was passed on March 9, 1933. The act provided for the reopening of banks closed by Roosevelt's bank holiday on March 13.

It stopped bank runs by allowing the Federal Reserve to give unlimited money to reopened banks, creating de facto 100% deposit insurance. It also authorized the Secretary of the Treasury to require that gold be turned in for currency at $20.67 an ounce. Large gold outflows had reduced the money supply, intensifying the depression.

On April 5, President Roosevelt issued Executive Order 6102 requiring that all gold be turned in. There was one prosecution under the order. Frederick Barber Campbell, an elderly well-connected New York attorney had 27 bars of gold worth $200,754 ($3.67 million today) at Chase National Bank. Chase had agreed to store the bars for a fee and return them on demand. After Executive Order 6102, Chase refused to give Campbell back his gold.

Campbell sued Chase. The next day, a federal prosecutor indicted Campbell for failing to turn in his gold. A judge ruled that the order was technically invalid since it was signed by the President instead of the Secretary of the Treasury as required.

A new order was issued signed by Treasury Secretary Henry Morgenthau. The prosecution was dropped, but Campbell lost his gold and the legality of the government to seize gold was upheld.

Once Upon a Dime

That's the title of one of the 10 comic books* available from the Federal Reserve Bank of New York.

Once Upon a Dime is a fable about the growth of the economy of an island kingdom from barter to a modern system.

The New York Fed has been publishing monetary manga since the 1950's. Other titles include *A Penny Saved, The Story of Monetary Policy,* and *The Story of Foreign Trade and Exchange.* The comics are free up to 35 copies.

After you've read the comic book, you might want to see those stacks of gold bars the Fed stashes in the basement in person.

You can tour the gold vault at the New York Fed. Tours are given Monday through Friday, except bank holidays, at one hour intervals from 9:30 a.m. until 3:30 p.m. (except for a lunch break at 12:30).

The tour is free, but space is limited so you have to make reservations in advance, which you can do online.

* Technical consultant on the comic book project was Scrooge McDuck. His financial acumen and intimate knowledge of the genre made him invaluable. McDuck also knows gold: he discovered the "Goose Egg Nugget" in the Yukon Gold rush in 1896.

Oops!

When you take the Fed tour you'll see over $200 billion worth of mostly other countries' gold. To transfer gold from one country to another, they just move it to another vault. The Fed stores it for free, but charges $1.75 a bar to move it (2008).

"Gold stackers" work in teams hoisting 27.4 lb. Bars ($440,000 at $1100 gold) and wear $500 lightweight magnesium shoe covers just in case. Plenty of dings in the floor attest to the oops factor.

Leak Through Economics

Extensive research has determined that shit runs downhill.

"There are two ideas of government. There are those who believe that if you just legislate to make the well-to-do prosperous, that their prosperity will leak through on those below. The Democratic idea has been that if you legislate to make the masses prosperous their prosperity will find its way up and through every class that rests upon it."
— William Jennings Bryan, "Cross of Gold" speech July 9, 1896, at the Democratic National Convention in Chicago.

"The money was all appropriated for the top in the hopes that it would trickle down to the needy. Mr. Hoover didn't know that money trickled up. Give it to the people at the bottom and the people at the top will have it before night, anyhow. But it will at least have passed through the poor fellow's hands."
— Humorist Will Rogers in an article in the St. Petersburg Times, Nov 26, 1932.

"...there are two theories of prosperity and of well-being: The first theory is that if we make the rich richer, somehow they will let a part of their prosperity trickle down to the rest of us. The second theory...that if we make the average of mankind comfortable and secure, their prosperity will rise upward, just as yeast rises up, through the ranks."
— Franklin Delano Roosevelt, Campaign Address at Detroit, Michigan, October 2, 1932

"Federal revenue is lower today than it would have been without the tax cuts. There's really no dispute among economists about that."
— Alan Viard, senior economist at the Council of Economic Advisers during Bush's first term, as quoted in the Washington Post on October 17, 2006.

"As a matter of principle, we do not think tax cuts pay for themselves."
— Robert Carroll, deputy assistant secretary for tax analysis at the U.S. Treasury Department during Bush's second term, as quoted in the Washington Post October 17, 2006.

"As a general rule, I do not believe that tax cuts pay for themselves."
— Henry Paulson, Bush's Secretary of the Treasury, at his Senate Finance Committee confirmation hearing June 27, 2006.

"Kansas Governor Sam Brownback and his state legislature have embarked on a wonderful natural experiment. Once again we are testing the question: Can tax cuts pay for themselves? The answer — yet again — is a resounding no."
"...one cannot credibly argue that tax cuts increase revenue or even pay for themselves. They didn't for Ronald Reagan. They don't for Sam Brownback. They won't for the next politician who tries..."
— Forbes July 15, 2014.

"There's no evidence whatsoever that the Bush tax cuts actually diminished revenue. They increased revenue, because of the vibrancy of these tax cuts in the economy."
— Senator Mitch McConnell quoted in *Talking Points Memo*, July 13, 2010,

Gold Bug

Edgar Allan Poe submitted a short story to the Philadelphia Dollar Newspaper for a writing contest. He won the grand prize and *The Gold-Bug* was published in three installments in 1843.

The story is set on Sullivan's Island in South Carolina. The plot involves a man bitten by a gold-colored bug which leads him to Captain Kidd's buried treasure after decrypting a message written in cipher.

In 1896, William McKinley was elected president campaigning on the gold standard. (See *In Gold We Trust* on p 110.) His opponent was William Jennings Bry-

an, who favored bimetallism, free coinage of silver along with gold. At the Democratic Convention, Bryan gave his famous "Cross of Gold" speech.

McKinley supporters started calling themselves "gold bugs", sporting brass lapel pins in the shape of a bug. This one has pictures of McKinley (left) and his vice president Garret Hobart. Bet you didn't know we had a vice president named Garret Hobart.

You can see Garret Hobart in person. He was from Paterson and after he died in 1899, a bronze statue of him was erected in front of city hall.

The Smell of Money

In Canada, plastic money isn't just your credit card. The new Canadian $100 bill is made from polymer, aka plastic. Plastic money is harder to counterfeit than paper money. It costs twice as much to make but lasts 2½ times longer. And it's recyclable.

But it melts in the heat. A man put his bonus of 8 hundred dollar bills in a can too close to a radiator and the bills shriveled up. The serial numbers were still legible but banks wouldn't exchange them. His mom had to go to the Bank of Canada (the central bank) to exchange them.

People swear the new bills smell like maple syrup. Although it would be a great marketing ploy for the producer of 80% of the world's maple syrup, Bank of Canada denies that any scent was added.

A year's correspondence between the Bank of Canada and the public, obtained by the press through Canada's Access to Information Act, found the maple scent belief so pervasive that some people complained that the bills had lost their maple scent.

Botanists point out that the maple leaf on the bill is from the wrong kind of maple tree. Instead of one of the 13 indigenous maple species, the leaf is from the invasive Norway maple.

The native sugar maple is the leaf on the Canadian flag. Perhaps the botanists are wrong about the leaf on the money and it's the leaf of the sugar maple. That would explain the smell. Or maybe not.

Norway Maple   Flag Maple   Sugar Maple

Goldwater

There's a little gold dissolved in seawater. Not much, only 10 parts per trillion. At that concentration you would have to filter 662 cubic miles of water to win an ounce of gold.

But the oceans are vast, weighing 1.245 billion billion tons. So that infinitesimal bit of gold adds up to 12.45 million tons. That's $388 trillion at $1100 gold.

Collecting it is the trick. (See *Goldwater* on p. 181)

Representation Without Taxation

"Tax reform means 'don't tax you, don't tax me. Tax the fellow behind that tree.'"
— Louisiana Senator Russell B. Long (1918-2003), the Senate's tax expert at the time, characterizing the politics of tax reform in 1975.

According to etymologist Barry Popik, "The line is borrowed from a children's song, where a child implores Mister Bear to 'don't catch me...catch that fellow behind that tree.'"

This seems to imply that Long did the borrowing but the saying precedes him. A June 4, 1932 article in the Literary Digest titled "The Locust Swarm of Lobbyists" begins with "Congress, Congress, don't tax me, tax that fellow behind the tree."

More More Money than You Could Ever Spend

Remember that greedy little fellow Richard Grasso? He's the guy who was forced out as head of the New York Stock Exchange, a non-profit corporation, in 2003 after his buddies on the board gave him $140 million in deferred compensation on top of his $11 million a year regular paycheck. Not content, he sued to get another $48 million he was owed.

Just the interest on all that money would provide deluxe health insurance for 600 families. (5% interest, $1400 a month.)

His defenders say he earned it by doing great things for the NYSE. This is the usual argument for giving the CEO too much money.

But this does not address the point at issue. The point is not how great the accomplishment, but what great accomplishments are worth.

Here's the answer: nothing anybody ever did is worth that much money.

Besides, what's the difference if you get less more money than you could ever spend or more more money than you could ever spend? Do you think all the CEOs would quit to go flip burgers if all they could get was a measly million a year?

After all, they're just salarymen. If they need that kind of money, let them go out and start their own businesses so they can keep it all. (Hint: it's not so easy.)

Here's a better incentive: succeed or be fired.

Less More Money Than You Could Ever Spend

On the last day of January, 1905, James Hazen Hyde, 28, son and heir of the founder of the Equitable Life Assurance Society, gave one of the most sumptuous balls of the Gilded Age.

It was a costume ball with an 18th century theme held in the ballroom of society's watering hole, Sherry's Restaurant in New York. Six hundred costumed guests were entertained by the Metropolitan Opera Orchestra and a specially commissioned one act play performed by famous French actress Gabrielle Réjane. The guests feasted on three meals until 7 the next morning.

The ball was reported in all the papers. This gave James Alexander, Equitable's president, the excuse he needed to try to gain control of the company from Hyde, who was vice-president but had inherited a controlling interest. He accused Hyde of spending $200,000, ($5.2 million in 2015 at 26X inflation) on the ball and charging it to the company. Alexander was joined by Robber Baron board members E.H. Harriman, Henry Clay Frick, and J.P. Morgan.

The charge was false — Hyde had paid for the ball himself and it had cost probably $50,000. But the press reported Alexander's charge as fact and it caused a sensation and public outrage. The New York times ran 115 articles on the scandal in one year.

The New York State Legislature investigated the insurance industry, calling executives of New York Life, Equitable, and Mutual Life before the Anderson committee. Their testimony revealed conflict of interest transactions, large payments to politicians and unconscionable salaries for themselves. It came to be known as the Wall Street Scandal of 1905.

Hyde was forced to resign and left for France. He served as an ambulance driver in World War I. He returned in 1941 and died in New York in 1959.

An article in the February 5, 1911 issue of the Literary Digest quotes the New York Evening Post noting "an epidemic of lowering of the big salaries of the industrial and financial world." "Because of the public agitation respecting the high cost of insurance management in the United States and the unpleasant disclosures attending the Armstrong investigation in 1905."

The new president of the Steel Trust [U.S. Steel] found his salary reduced to $50,000 ($1.3 million in 2015) from the $100,000 of his predecessor. Equitable's president when he assumed office after Alexander resigned in 1905 asked that the $100,000 salary Alexander had been receiving be cut to $80,000.

The Post article goes on: "With the possible exceptions of one or two banks and trust companies, there is not a financial institution on Wall Street which reimburses its president at a higher salary than $50,000 a year."

Today the Equitable is a subsidiary of AXA, a French insurance company and CEO compensation is not available. Compensation for New York Life and Mutual Life (now MONY) CEOs are also not available.

In 2014, U.S. Steel president Mario Longhi made $542,763 in 1911 dollars. Prudential CEO John Strangfeld earned $727,796, and MetLife's Steven A. Kandarian took in $600,329.

JP Morgan Chase chief Jamie Dimon beat them all with $822,368. (See *Bulletin From the Department of Good and Evil* on p. 72.)

Moneybags

Carthage, near modern Tunis in North Africa, used money sealed in small leather bags around 450 B.C.

They made most coins of cheap metal and a few of silver. Coins, including the fakes, were sealed in a leather bag by the government and declared to have a face value as if all were silver. The bags were worthless if the seal was broken.

This system lasted about 50 years, until Carthaginian conquests in Spain yielded more silver from Spanish mines.

You know Carthage from its most famous son, Hannibal, who marched his army with elephants over the alps in the Second Punic* War (218-201 B.C.) to attack the Romans. The Romans utterly destroyed Carthage in 146 B.C. in the Third Punic War.

* "Punic" comes the the Latin "Poenicus", referring to the Phoencians (from modern Lebanon) who founded Carthage in 814 B.C.

103

Message to the 1%

"... the great bulk of the personal property of the States, especially of the class denominated 'securities,' including stocks, bonds, notes, mortgages, and such like, has escaped taxation. With a very few exceptions the great fortunes in this country are invested in such securities."

— Ex-president Benjamin Harrison in a speech, *Obligations of Wealth,* given to the Union League, Chicago, Feb. 22 1898.

Passing the Buck

Although I love it when you give me cash, I hate it when give it to me helter skelter. Bills need to be face up and all oriented the same, with the top of the Founding Father's head on the right (lefties may reverse this).

Excess cash from banks is returned to the Fed and until recently bills had to be oriented the same way. But new bill counting machines can count the money every which way, at 74,000 bills an hour. The machine spits out worn or counterfeit bills, too. The New York Fed counts your money at its East Rutherford facility.

But I would still appreciate it if you would give me your tidy sums tidy.

By the way, an average of 90% of bills have traces of cocaine on them with the highest at 95% in Washington D.C. and the lowest at 77% in clean-living Salt Lake City.

Bankers' Hours

Back in the pre everything 24/7 era, banks would only be open weekdays from 9 to 3, and maybe Saturday morning. I asked the branch manager of my bank what they did after 3:00. "That's when we play with the money", he said.

What's in Your Wallet?

"It is nothing less than a crime to withdraw money uselessly from banking and business channels by carrying unnecessarily large amounts in the pocket,"

This is from The Literary Digest, October 9, 1920, quoting an article in Forbes.

The article goes on to say a survey by a manufacturer employing 400 workmen showed they carried an average of $28, a week's pay at the time, and that "If everybody in America were to carry around twenty-eight dollars it would represent a sum greater than all the gold in the land. It would more than equal half the total currency in circulation in the United States."

Among other pernicious economic effects of carrying too much cash, "It reduces the banks' ability to furnish credit to the industrial and business world."

$28 adjusted for inflation would be $331 in 2015. Evidently people have mended their ways. Now they put $7 watch batteries on the plastic. (59¢ in 1920 dollars.)

273   Pennyweights

Precious metals are weighed in grams and pennyweights. Grams you know about, sort of. But what"s a pennyweight?

Well, it's not the weight of our penny. Pennyweights are a unit in the Troy system, named for Troyes, France where it is said to have originated. There are 20 pennyweights to the troy ounce (about 10% larger than the ounce you know about), and 12 troy ounces to the troy pound.

But it is the weight of the silver penny first minted by King Offa of Mercia, a powerful 8th century Anglo-Saxon king who ruled most of England south of modern Yorkshire.

Around 785, Offa had minted a silver penny weighing 24 grains (of barleycorn) or one pennyweight. The English silver penny was the only coin in use for 500 years, and was worth a day's labor for a peasant. The penny was cut in half (ha'penny) or in fourths (farthing).

Pennyweight is abbreviated *dwt.*, the "d" standing for the roman silver coin, the *denarius*. This is also the origin of the "d" used for nails. The 10d or ten penny nail cost 10 pennies for a hundred nails.

Penny Weights

So how many pennyweights would a penny weigh if pennies were weighed in pennyweights? It depends on the date on the penny. Prior to 1982, a penny weighed 1.99 pennyweights, from 1982, 1.67 pennyweights.

In 1982 the penny changed from 95% copper, 5% zinc to 97.5% zinc, 2.5% copper. In other words, the penny is now copper plated zinc. Take a file to the edge of a penny and you'll see.

What was that business about the fall of the Roman Empire and debasing the currency?

Master of the Mint

The English pound was defined as a troy pound (12 troy ounces) of sterling silver (92.5% silver), hence the Pound Sterling. There were 240 silver pennies or 20 shillings of 12 pence in a pound.

England was on the silver standard until Isaac Newton (the one who invented gravity) accidentally put England on the gold standard in 1717.

By the 1690's, silver coins in England were in bad shape. They were hammered coins, blanks put between two dies and struck with a hammer. Such coins were irregular and without uniform edges. Due to clipping, slicing off pieces around the edge, most coins were 30-50% below weight. Also, an estimated 20% of coins were counterfeit.

Although milled coins, coins with a reeded edge like our quarter, had been produced since 1662, they were hoarded. Silver coins circulated by tale, by the piece, it being too inconvenient to weigh them in the course of everyday commerce, unlike gold coins which were weighed. This is Gresham's Law, bad money drives out good.

Also, in 1663 a milled 22 karat gold coin, the guinea[1], was issued equal to a pound. The guinea fluctuated in value with the price of gold, but in 1698 it was fixed at 21 shillings, 6 pence. This valued gold at 15.5 times silver. But in Europe the ratio was 15 to 1. The result was a massive outflow of silver to Europe where it was used to buy gold and a flow of gold into England to buy more silver.

Isaac Newton was made Warden of the Mint in 1696. Ordinarily, The Warden's job was a sinecure, kind of like chairman of the board requiring a few public appearances. The day-to-day operations of the Mint were handled by the Master of the Mint, the CEO.

But the Master, Thomas Neale, rarely showed up and Newton took over and threw himself into his duties with vigor, increasing production 10 times and relentlessly going after counterfeiters.

There was a public debate about what to do about the dire state of the money with the worthies of the age, including the philosopher John Locke and architect Christopher Wren, weighing in.

In 1696, the government instituted the Great Recoinage in which hammered coins were recalled and new milled coins, some with the Latin motto *Decus et Tutamen*, "an ornament and a safeguard", inscribed on the edge were issued.

Newton oversaw the the Great Recoinage, completing it in 3 years.

Newton was appointed Master of the Mint in 1699 upon the death of Neale. As Master, Newton was paid for each coin struck and he became wealthy, earning the modern equivalent of a million dollars a year.

The great recoinage didn't stem the flow of silver out of England since gold was still overvalued relative to silver.

In 1717 Newton proposed reducing the guinea 6 pence to 21 shillings as a first step. This was accepted, but there was no further action. This set the silver/gold ratio at 15.28/1, still above the 15/1 in Europe and silver continued to flow out of England.

Finally, in 1816, England abandoned silver as the basis for the pound and there was another Great Recoinage. The guinea was discontinued and a new, slightly lighter coin, the sovereign, with the value of 1 pound was issued. New silver coins were struck for small transactions.

In 1983, England reintroduced the Latin motto in the edge of the 1 pound coin.

1. Gold at that time came from the Guinea coast of Africa, which became the British colony of the Gold Coast, now Ghana.

Modern British Pound

273   The Trial of the Pyx

Since 1249, English coins have been tested to make sure they contain the correct amount of gold or silver.

Coins selected at random are put in a "pyx", Greek for box, and tested against a plate of known purity.

In 1710, Newton's coins were found to be below standard when tested against the trial plate of 1707. Newton performed his own assays and determined that the

1707 test plate was .9210 fine and so 22 karat coins at .9166 were mistakenly determined to be substandard. The 1707 plate was withdrawn from use. An 1837 assay gave .917 fineness for the 1707 plate, Both differences are tiny amounts, 4 parts per thousand and 4 parts per ten thousand, and are impressive for the technology of their times..

The Trial of the Pyx is still performed today, once a year at the Hall of the Worshipful Company of Goldsmiths, under the supervision of the Queen's Remembrancer, resplendent in wig and tricorne hat.

A jury of financial leaders and at least 6 assayers from the Worshipful Company of Goldsmiths test randomly selected coins in sealed bags of 50 of each denomination over two months.

The jury then reconvenes and presents its verdict to the Queen's Remembrancer, the Master of the Royal Mint and the Chancellor or deputy of the Exchequer.

Portion of the 1707 trial plate

Change for a Buck

Take out a dollar bill and look at the back. The eagle with the arrows and olive branch should be familiar. But what's with the pyramid with the spooky eye above it? It's the reverse of the Great Seal of the United States. The eagle is the obverse.

Charles Thomson (1728-1824) was one of the Founding Fathers and secretary of the Continental Congress. In 1782, the Congress asked him to design a Great Seal.

Three different committees had been fooling around with designs since 1776, but they weren't so hot. Thomson used elements of the three committees plus his own ideas and came up with a design in a week and it was approved the same day, June 20, 1782. Thomson provided only detailed verbal descriptions. He explained the symbolism of the reverse of the seal: "The pyramid signifies Strength and Duration: The Eye over it & the Motto allude to the many signal interpositions of providence in favour of the American cause. The date underneath is that of the Declaration of Independence and the words under it signify the beginning of the new American Æra, which commences from that date."

The "Eye of Providence" is the all seeing eye of God. Annuit Coeptus is translated by the State Department as "He [God] has favored our undertakings". Novus Ordo Seclorum means "A New Order of the Ages."

The State Department actually uses the seal, like a notary public, on treaties so a die was cut that September from Thomson's description of the obverse side. The first drawings of the Great Seal weren't published until 1786. The first document impressed with the seal was one by the Continental Congress giving George Washington the authority to negotiate with the British on the exchange of prisoners in September, 1782. A die has never been made of the reverse side.

But the great seal didn't get on the back of the buck until 1935. Below is a picture of the dollar before the Great Seal. In 1934, Secretary of Agriculture Henry Wallace was perusing a history of the Great Seal while waiting in the State Department. He was struck by the fact that the reverse of the Seal had never been used.

He suggested to President Roosevelt that a coin be struck with both sides of the Seal.

Roosevelt preferred the seal to be put on the dollar instead. Both Wallace and Roosevelt were Masons and were struck by the all-seeing eye, which is a Masonic symbol. However, "The Great Seal of the United States is not a Masonic emblem, nor does it contain hidden Masonic symbols," according to the Masonic Service Association of North America.

Wampum

If you vacation in Cape Cod, you'll see inexpensive jewelry with white and purple mother-of-pearl set in silver. It is made from the shell of the quahog clam which has white and purple colors lining the inside of the shell. It's called wampum jewelry. Wampum sound familiar? It's that redskin to paleface word for money in old movies.

Wampum, Indian ceremonial beads later used as money, was originally woven into belts presented to commemorate important occasions and rites of passage such as engagement and marriage.

The Hiawatha belt of 6574 beads commemorates the formation of the Iroquois Confederacy, the union of 5 (later 6) tribes in New York and Canada sometime between 1450 and 1600. A wampum belt commemorates a treaty between a Catholic convert chief of the Mi'kmaq and the Vatican in 1610.

Wampum was made from two types of shell. White beads were made from whelk shells and purple from the shell of the quahog clam. The beads were cylinders about 1/4 inch long and 1/8 inch in diameter. Wampum was strung and sold by the hand length and the fathom, 6 feet, approximately 360 beads. The purple quahog beads were worth twice the white beads.

With European contact came metal tools that helped the Indians make more and better wampum beads. In 1622, a Dutch trader named Jacques Elekens seized a Pequot Indian chief named Tatobem in retaliation for Pequot raids and threatened to kill him unless he received a "heavy ransom." 140 fathoms of wampum, 50,000 beads, were given by the Pequots but Tatobem was killed anyway and his body given back to the tribe. A horrified Dutch West India Company recalled Elekens.

But this incident caused the Dutch to realize the value of wampum to the Indians. They obtained wampum from the coastal tribes who produced it in exchange for trade goods: blankets. cloth, tools, guns and gunpowder. They then used the wampum to buy beaver pelts from inland tribes which were much valued in Europe for hats. The British followed suit and wampum became New World currency. In 1637, wampum became legal tender in Massachusetts.

There were problems with quality early. In 1641, only 17 years after its founding, the New Netherland colony, Dutch settlements from New Amsterdam (Manhattan), up the Hudson to Fort Orange (Albany), found it necessary to pass an ordinance devaluing poorly made wampum. There were counterfeiting problems, too. White wampum would be dyed with huckleberry juice to pass it off as the higher priced purple wampum. This was easily detected by spitting on it to see if the color would rub off.

During the 1650's wampum drastically declined in value relative to beaver due to oversupply in New Netherland, dropping 25% by 1657.

By the 1660's wampum was demonetized in favor of coin in the British colonies but still used in the Dutch colonies which were dependent on the beaver trade and this was the only payment the Indians would accept. Wampum was used in the fur trade into the 19th century.

Conrad Weiser, Indian Interpreter and negotiator for the Pennsylvania Colony (see *Passing the Buck* on p. 100), mentions wampum many times in his journal of 1748:

Hired a Canoe; paid 1,000 Black Wampum [purple] *for the loan of it...*

...I desired of them to send a Couple of Canoes to fetch down the Goods from Chartier's old Town...I gave them a String of Wampum to enforce my Request

In 1789 the Campbell family set up a factory to manufacture wampum in what is now Park Ridge, N.J. By 1830, wampum had declined as currency for the fur trade. The Campbells made hair pipes, long shell tapered beads made into breastplates and other ornaments for the plains Indians into the 1890's.

Carl Linnaeus (1707-1778) the Swedish scientist who invented the system of classifying plants and animals was aware of wampum being used as money. In 1758, he named the quahog clam *mercenaria mercenaria*, Latin for wages.

A quahog clam dredged up off Iceland recently claims the record as the oldest animal with 405 annual growth rings.

Going for the Gold

In 1929, several families leased prime land at the southwest corner of Beverly Drive and Little Santa Monica Boulevard in Beverly Hills for 95 years to First National Bank of Beverly Hills. The rent was $2000 a month. A dollar was defined as a "United States of America gold coin composed of 25.8 grains of gold .900 fine,"* At $20.67 an ounce, the rent was 100 $20 gold coins or 96.76 ounces of pure gold a month.

On April 5, 1933, President Roosevelt issued executive order 6102, requiring everyone to turn in all gold coins, gold bullion, and gold certificates for $20.67 per troy ounce in other coins or currency. Small amounts were permitted to be held as well as collector coins and gold for use in industry. The gold had to be turned in to the Federal Reserve by May 1.

On June 5, 1933, a joint resolution of congress voided clauses in contracts requiring payment in gold. This "gold clause" prohibition was only repealed in 1977 at the instigation of gold bug Senator Jesse Helms. Contracts after that date could specify payment in gold. But contracts before that date could not reactivate a gold clause — too much water under the bridge.

Time passed and the First National Bank of Beverly Hills was gone and by the 1970's, the lease was owned by the Triangle Corporation, which continued to pay the heirs of the original land owners $2000 a month, but not in gold, since the gold clause of the contract had been voided in 1933.

In 1977, Triangle subleased the property to a bank for 35 years at $27,000 a month. In 1981, Triangle sold the lease to its tenant, the bank, for $4,225,000 and the bank became the new lessee under the 1929 lease, paying $2000 a month.

Both Triangle and the bank were aware that the gold clause in the original lease might become enforceable if the transfer were ruled a new lease with a new party. The bank's lawyers rated it possible but a long shot. Triangle refused a provision by the bank that would require it to compensate the bank if it would have to pay in gold, but the bank went ahead and signed anyway.

In 1986, one of the property owners read of a case in which the transfer of a long-term lease was ruled a novation, a new lease, and reactivated a gold clause in the contract. in 1991, the owners sued to reactivate the gold clause in the lease. They lost the first round but won on appeal in 1995.

On the day of the ruling, gold was $376.75 and the rent went up to over $36,000 a month. At $1100 gold, it would be over $106,000 a month. $2000 adjusted for inflation since 1929 would be $27,820 in 2015.

* 1 troy ounce = 480 grains. 25.8 x 20 x .9 = 464.4 grains. 464.4 ÷ 480 = .9675 oz. per $20 coin.

Goldman Sacks Gold Man

Well, they should. Listen up gold bugs. If Goldman can't get gold right what chance does a drossman like you have?

On March 28, 2012, Goldman Sachs released its forecast for gold prices: $1785 in three months, $1840 in six months, and $1940 in 12 months. Prices below are the London P.M. fix.

Gold fell below $1400 just 6 days after the March 2013 forecast, below $1300 June 20, broke $1200 June 28, rebounded above $1300 in July, then fell back into $1200's in November.

	Actual	Forecast
6/28/12	$1,559	$1,785
9/28/12	$1,776	$1,840
3/28/13	$1,598	$1,940

Deficits for Dummies

"...the crisis they [deficit scolds] predicted keeps not happening. Far from fleeing U.S. debt, investors have continued to pile in, driving interest rates to historical lows."
— Paul Krugman in the New York Times, November 25, 2012

"Despite the Administration's inflationary money policies and its huge program of spending and borrowing, the Government's credit does not suffer, as is proved by the acid test of the market for its securities."
— The Literary Digest, June 16, 1934

Leverage

Congratulations! You paid down your credit cards by $91 billion last year [2009]. Economists call it deleveraging and they worry about it. They worry about it when you leverage, too.

Double Eagle

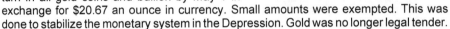

Designed by the sculptor Augustus St. Gaudens and considered the most beautiful American coin ever issued, this double eagle (the $10 coin was an eagle) $20 gold piece was struck from 1907 to 1933.

On April 5, 1933, President Roosevelt signed Executive Order 6102, requiring everyone to turn in all gold coins and bullion by May 1 in exchange for $20.67 an ounce in currency. Small amounts were exempted. This was done to stabilize the monetary system in the Depression. Gold was no longer legal tender.

The Mint had struck 445,500 1933 $20 gold pieces and they were melted down except for two that were presented to the Smithsonian's numismatic collection.

But a number of the coins were stolen, probably by a Mint cashier who switched the 1933 coins with ones of earlier dates.

Some of the coins made their way to a Philadelphia jeweler, Israel Switt, who sold them to collectors. In 1944, the Secret Service traced 10 of the coins to Switt who acknowledged selling 9 of them but could not be prosecuted because too much time had passed and the statute of limitations applied. The 9 coins were tracked down and confiscated by the Secret Service between 1944 and 1952. Three lawsuits contesting the confiscations failed.

In 1944 King Farouk of Egypt, who collected everything, bought a 1933 Double Eagle and applied for an export license which was mistakenly granted days before the discovery of the theft from the Mint.

In 1952, Farouk was deposed and his possessions, including the 1933 coin, were put up for auction by Sotheby's in 1954. The U.S. Government requested the coin from Egypt which said it would comply. But the coin vanished before the auction.

In 1996 the coin surfaced when British coin dealer Stephen Fenton was arrested in New York by Secret Service agents in a sting operation and the coin was confiscated and stored in a vault in the World Trade Center.

Fenton swore that it was Farouk's coin. The charges were dropped and Fenton sued the Government to recover the coin, arguing that it was legally exported. The Government settled with Fenton in July, 2001, agreeing that the coin would revert to the Treasury and would be auctioned and the proceeds would be split with Fenton. The coin was moved to Fort Knox 2 months before 9/11. On July 30, 2002, the Farouk Double Eagle was auctioned by Sotheby's in 9 minutes, bought by an anonymous buyer for $7,590,000 plus $20, the face value of the coin, for the Mint to declare the coin legal tender so it could be sold. This is the record for a U.S. Coin.

In 2003, Joan Langbord, the daughter of Israel Switt, discovered 10 more 1933 Double Eagles in a bank safe deposit box in Philadelphia. She took them to the Treasury to authenticate them and the Secret Service seized them as illegal, and sent them to Ft. Knox for safekeeping. Langbord sued the government retaining the same lawyer who represented Fenton.

On July 20, 2011 the jury returned a unanimous verdict after 5 hours of deliberation, siding with the government that since the coins were never issued, they were stolen.

Penny Foolish

It cost the Mint 1.7¢ to make a penny in 2014. And that's for a fake penny, zinc with a schmear of copper on top. Real pennies, all copper, went out after 1982. A real penny would cost 1.9¢ just for the copper (at $2.75/lb.).

The Mint estimates that there are 140 billion pennies in circulation.

Pound Wise

The wily Brits make their penny from copper-plated steel (since 1992). Steel costs 1/3 the price of zinc. I don't know if rusty pennies are a problem, though.

Beware the Ides of April

Studies of insurance claims show a consistent spike in claims of lost jewelry at tax time.

McKinley campaign poster showing him held aloft standing on a "Sound Money" gold coin by men of all classes (See *Gold Bug* on p. 101.)

In Gold We Trust

Money backed by gold! Hard money! How macho! Without getting in the middle of all the crackpot discussions about gold and the gold standard (99% of the Google-verse is crackpot on this), I'll give you two reasons why it would be a problem.

1. There ain't enough of it. Let's do the math. The money supply is $11.98 trillion according to the Fed July 16, 2015 and 258,641,878.074 troy ounces of gold are stashed in the basement of the New York Fed, Fort Knox, West Point, and various mints. That works out to about $285 billion at $1100 gold, or about 2.4% of the money supply. Under the gold standard, 40% of the money supply had to backed by gold. All the gold in the world would only add up to $7 trillion.

2. Where do you think money comes from? The Fed Fairy, right? Wrong! Banks create money.

I'm sure you're shocked!, shocked! to learn this. We have a fractional reserve banking system. Banks only have to keep 10% of deposits on hand and can loan out the rest. (See *Passing the Buck* on p. 99.)

So if you deposit $100 in a bank, the bank only has to keep $10 and can loan out $90, which gets deposited in another bank and so on. The upshot is that your $100 deposit results in $900 in new money — out of thin air.

That's how the economy grows. Money is created to loan to new business ventures. It works because not everyone wants to pull out his* money at the same time — a run on the bank — and because the FDIC insures bank deposits. It's not new. It's why banks run out of money in a run on the bank, even in ancient Rome. (See *Oeconomia Est O Asine!* on p. 128.)

Gold can't grow to back up an expanding money supply and a gold standard is incompatible with how a modern economy works. (See *Wall Street Closed!* next page.)

And the gold standard was an international system. You can't set it up in just one country. If you did, all the gold would flow out to pay for imports as the dollars we used to pay for them were redeemed for gold, and none would come in as payment for exports. In fact, with our $540 billion trade deficit (2012), all our gold would be gone in less than a year. (See *New Gold Rush* on p. 115.)

"Gold will not replace fiat currencies; the Gold Standard will not return."

"Nostalgia for a supposed golden age of the Gold Standard, coupled with concerns about governments' ability to manipulate fiat currencies, occasionally gives rise to calls for, or predictions of, a return to gold as the underlying basis for the international monetary system. This is not possible. Gold's relative scarcity means that it could only ever replace a fiat currency on a fractional basis. Even that is unlikely, as a legacy of history."

This is from a January, 2013 report from the Official Monetary and Financial Institutions Forum (OMFIF) ("Bringing together central banks and sovereign wealth funds") commissioned by the World Gold Council ("The market development organisation of the gold industry and voice of authority for gold.") If a World Gold Council study tells you it ain't gonna happen, it ain't gonna happen.

A 1981 Gold Commission appointed by President Reagan at the instigation of gold bugs Rep. Ron Paul (yes, that Ron Paul) and Senator Jesse Helms concluded in a 227 page report exhaustively detailing every aspect of gold and the history of the gold standard that "restoring a gold standard does not appear to be a fruitful method for dealing with the continuing problem of inflation."

In January 2012, a University of Chicago poll of 40 distinguished economics scholars "geographically diverse, and to include Democrats, Republicans and Independents as well as older and younger scholars" asked if "the price-stability and employment outcomes would be better for the average American" if the dollar were tied to gold. All of them disagreed, some with amazement that the question would be asked at all.

None of this puts a dent in the gold bugs. Capitalist Fool Steve Forbes wrote an article in his namesake magazine May 8, 2013 titled *Advance Look: What The New Gold Standard Will Look Like*.

To state the obvious, if the gold standard had worked, we would still be on it.

* See *Gender Bender* on p. 235.

273   **Wall Street Closed!**

The Federal reserve Act of 1913 states the purpose of the organization as "to furnish an elastic currency" and "to afford means of rediscounting commercial paper," accept short-term corporate promissory notes banks took for loans at a discount (with interest) as well as government bonds as backing for issuing new currency. This allowed the money supply to expand to accommodate increased economic activity. However, gold was still required to back 40% of the money supply.

"When gold exports began on a large scale a year ago, thus reducing the banks' lending power, the Reserve banks saved the member banks from the necessity of reducing their loans by purchasing Government bonds in the open market, thus releasing credit enough to replenish the reserves."
— The Literary Digest September 22, 1928.

This illustrates the problem of tying the money supply to gold. Counteracting the shrinking money supply by buying bonds as gold flowed out when exports exceeded imports was called "sterilization." The reverse, sterilizing gold inflows by selling bonds to mop up increased money, was also done. Sterilization violated "the rules of the game" of the gold standard. Gold outflows reduced the money supply and caused lower prices which increased ex-

ports which brought in more gold. Inflows caused prices to rise, damping exports and gold inflows. The situation was thus self-correcting if countries would bear the price and employment volatility. Of course, they could not.

In the summer of 1914, on the cusp of World War I, British and French investors were selling American securities for dollars to be converted into gold. The dollar was depressed on the prospect of this outflow of gold and it would have caused a depression due to the contraction of the money supply and might have forced the U.S. off the gold standard. It might also have caused a run on banks caused by customers spooked by the shortage of money.

The Federal Reserve wasn't up and running yet so, alone among nations, the U.S. had no central bank to counteract that. Treasury Secretary William McAdoo prevented the liquidation of $4 billion ($94 billion in 2015 dollars) in railroad stocks and bonds held by foreigners by closing the New York Stock Exchange for four months, from July 31 to December 12, a bold and unprecedented move.* He then allowed banks to issue emergency currency authorized after the Panic of 1907 and made a show of armored trucks bringing gold and emergency currency to the New York subtreasury building across from the Stock Exchange on Wall Street.

McAdoo then got Congress to create the Bureau of War Risk Insurance that provided government backed insurance for wartime shipments of U.S. agricultural products, cotton especially, that helped reverse the gold outflow. He also helped establish the U.S. Shipping Board. (See *The Biggest Bootlegger* on p. 4.)

He is credited with establishing New York as the world financial center at the expense of London. McAdoo was President Wilson's son-in-law. He went on to become a Senator and died in 1941 at 77.

* Of course, the capitalist spirit could not be that easily repressed. An informal market sprang up on the curb on New Street behind the New York Stock Exchange building.

The Dismal Science

"Wall Street indexes predicted nine out of the last five recessions!"
— Nobel Prize economist Paul Samuelson in Newsweek, September 19, 1966

Passing the Buck

The U.S. Secret Service is well known for protecting the President. But the Secret Service is part of the Treasury Department and its original mission at its founding in 1865 was to find counterfeit currency. It was only tasked with protecting the President in 1901 after the assassination of President McKinley.

In 1938, a phony one dollar bill was passed at a cigar store in Manhattan, and the Secret Service opened case file 880. What was unusual was that someone had bothered to fake a one and that it was a laughably bad fake. It was printed on bad paper with fuzzy letters and George's eyes didn't match.

By December, 1939 there were 600 bogus bills in File 880. And the printing was growing worse., even misspelling George's name as "Wahsington", as the counterfeiter tried to touch up his plates.

The counterfeiter passed only 40 or 50 bills a month and never passed them in the same place twice, making it difficult to follow a trail.

By 1947, the Secret Service had collected more than $5000 of the fake singles. Yet after all that time, despite an intense manhunt with thousands of interviews and hundreds of thousands of fliers handed out, the counterfeiter remained uncaught.

In January, 1948 a group of small boys was found playing poker with the phony dollars by one of their fathers. They had found the counterfeits and a few printing plates in an empty lot near Broadway and 96th Street in Manhattan 10 days earlier. The father turned the bills in at the local police station, and a detective contacted the Secret Service.

The Secret Service interviewed the boys and located the empty lot where they had found the fake money. They learned from people who lived in the area that there had been a fire in the top floor of a tenement overlooking the lot.

Firemen had tossed possessions of the occupant down into the lot. The occupant had not been home at the time of the fire, although his dog was and had succumbed to smoke inhalation.

The Secret Service went up to the apartment and found the printing press, plates and a pile of the famous fakes. They also found Mr. 880 himself, an affable, toothless 73 year old man, Edward Mueller, an Austrian immigrant whose real name was Emerich Juettner.

Mueller quit his job as an apartment super after his wife died and became a junkman. He just printed enough dollars to make ends meet. He never passed his bills at the same place twice, not to avoid being caught, but to limit the harm to the small businesses where he passed them.

His son and daughter were unaware of their father's financial situation and would have been willing to help him, but Mueller had an independent streak.

Mueller was convicted of counterfeiting and sentenced to a year and a day in jail but he was paroled after 4 months to live with his daughter. He also had to pay a real one dollar fine.

A movie was made from the case in 1950, *Mr. 880*, starring Burt Lancaster as the Secret Service agent and Edmund Gwenn (Kris Kringle in *Miracle on 34th Street*) as Mueller.

The Divine Miss M Dumps Bucks for Gold

Bette Midler demanded her $600,000 fee for a European tour in July, 1978 be paid in South African gold coins.

The dollar was falling, oil prices were rising and gold was soaring. (Sound familiar?) Gold was $180 an ounce then. Her timing was good if she held on to it for a while. A year later it was $281 and it peaked 6 months after that at $850 on January 21, 1980.

It's The Stupid Economy

"I could end the deficit in five minutes. You just pass a law that says that any time there's a deficit of more than three percent of GDP, all sitting members of Congress are ineligible for re-election."
— Warren Buffet

Deep Thought

If the results are wrong, the rules are wrong.

A Scandal of Extravagance

That's what the New York Press, a Republican paper, called the $1.5 billion projected appropriation of Congress to run the government in 1901. That would be $41.67 billion in 2014 dollars.

"Patriotism does not mean extravagance" opined the Cleveland Leader, noting that only a few years ago the government was spending only $1 million a day. ($9.96 billion a year in 2014).

"But as long as Congress continues to pass pension bills just because they are pension bills, to squander money on river and harbor improvements, and generally to use the Government and its treasury as agencies for the advancement of the political and personal fortunes of its members, and as long as the President signs practically every bill that is sent to him, we may expect that 'the tide' will continue to rise", according to the Indianapolis News, an independent paper."

But the Philadelphia Inquirer, a Republican paper, says the large appropriation means the country is growing and "if this money goes for public improvements men are put at work, and the men who work do not complain...if we have become a billion-dollar country, so much the better. Let us hope that shortly we will become a two-billion dollar country."

From the Literary Digest February 23, 1901.

The 2014 budget was $3.506 trillion, or about $126.2 billion in 1901 dollars, 84 times more extravagant.

Silverwear

U.S. coins from 1964 on back were 90% silver. A dollar face value of coins had .723 ounce of pure silver. 10 dimes, 4 quarters, or 2 half dollars had .723 troy ounce of silver. Silver dollars had .773 ounces.

But a $1000 face value bag of circulated coins contains only about 715 ounces of silver instead of 723 ounces. Silver is soft and the coins wear down jungling around in your pocket.

Silver coinage was discontinued after 1964 because the Silver Purchase Act of 1934 required the treasury to redeem silver certificates for silver coin at the mint silver price of $1.29 an ounce. So at a market price above that, it pays people to redeem silver certificates for coin and sell the coins to be melted. At $1.38 it would pay to sell coins already in circulation. Silver hit $1.29 an ounce in 1963 and $1.38 in 1966.

In 1961, President Kennedy halted sales of silver. The Silver Purchase Act was repealed in 1963 and the Coinage Act of 1965 discontinued silver coins.

Minimum Wage

Here's $886 a month. Live on it. I thought so. Ok, here's your raise: $1247. Oops. Forgot the payroll deductions. Shame!

Deep Thought

It's not about the rules, but who gets to make the rules.

Damned if You Do, Damned if You don't

The modern currency float has its problems. There is no magical monetary cure, monetary policy is a policy area almost uniquely crowded with trade-offs and lesser evils.

If you want a classical gold standard, you get chronic deflation punctuated by depressions, as the U.S. did between 1873 and 1934.

If you want a regime of managed currencies tethered to gold, you get regulations and controls, as the U.S. got from 1934 through 1971.

If you let the currency float, you get chronic inflation punctuated by bubbles, the American lot since 1971.

System 1 is incompatible with democracy, because voters won't accept the pain inherent in a gold standard.

System 2 is incompatible with the free market economics I favor.

That leaves me with System 3 as the worst option except for all the others.

— David Frum, Frum Forum, August 15, 2011

Pennywise

I reported to you before that pennies went from copper to copper plated zinc in 1983. But that wasn't the first fake penny.

1943 pennies were made from steel with a coating of zinc. That was because of a wartime shortage of copper, a strategic metal. (About 40 1943 copper pennies were made by accident when copper blanks were left in the press hopper. In 2010 the only known copper cent from the Denver mint sold for $1.7 million.)

In 1974, as the value of copper in the penny approached a penny, the Mint decided to switch to aluminum. 1,579,324 aluminum pennies were struck, but the Mint changed its mind before they were released into circulation.

Vending machine companies said that the new pennies would cause problems and pediatricians objected because aluminum doesn't show up well in X-rays and kids who swallow pennies would be at risk.

All the aluminum pennies were to have been destroyed, but 16 of them were loaned to members of Congress and Treasury officials and most were not returned. One was donated to the Smithsonian by a congressional staffer but 12 of the pennies are unaccounted for and are illegal to own.

Today it costs the Mint 1.7¢ to make a penny, including the cost of production and distribution. (The metal in a penny is worth .53¢.) It costs more than a nickel to make a nickel, too, but the Mint makes up for it with dimes and quarters. In 2009 the Mint made $777.6 million in coins and made a profit of $427.8 million.

The difference between the cost to produce a coin and its face value is called seigniorage and it seems to be a big deal for economists. One web site lists 37 scholarly papers on the topic.

Fool's Gold

In March, 2008 the news broke that the Ethiopian Central bank had bought a load of fake gold. The Ethiopian bank sent gold bars to South Africa and they bounced.

It turns out they were gold-plated steel. The bars were 400 troy ounce "London Good Delivery Bars" (see next page). Those are the gold bars you see stacked up in movies; they're the standard bars used for bank-to-bank transactions.

They also found another batch of fake gold that had been lying in the bank's vault for several years, having been confiscated from smugglers.

A 400 troy ounce bar weighs 27.4 pounds. A steel bar the same size would only weigh about 11 pounds. There's no way this radical difference in weight would not be noticed by workers handling the bars, so it had to have been an inside job. That's why national bank officials and the chemists who assayed the bars were arrested along with the supplier of the bars.

That's what happens when you cheap out making fake stuff. If you want to do it right, use tungsten, which has almost the same density as gold, and coat it with a layer of gold about 1/16" thick. That way it will pass the heft and x-ray tests.

It would cost about $350 for the tungsten and $2900 for the gold cladding, but would be worth $480,000 if you could foist it off on Ethiopia. Nice profit, but you'd better get a really big torch. Tungsten melts at 6200° F.

The Smell of Money

The African country of Benin has inaugurated a new series of coins, *Fameuses Plantes du Monde,* Famous Plants of the World. The coins are scratch and sniff: If you rub the the plant on the coin, it will emit its characteristic aroma.

The first in the series is cannabis sativa, also known as marijuana. The silver-plated 100 franc (20¢) coin features a raised green pot leaf. The mintage is limited to 2500 coins and comes encapsulated with a certificate of authenticity. The scent is good for about forty rubs before its gone.

But you can't get high by sniffing the coin. The aroma is a miracle of modern chemistry and comes with a certificate listing the amount of allergens in the formula, signed by the perfumer who developed it.

This would be the perfect coin to use in the marijuana vending machines coming soon to Colorado.

New Gold Rush

59 bars Leaving Every Hour
New Gold Rush: Out of U.S.

That was the headline in a Life Magazine article December 12, 1960. Those 59 bars weighed 27.4 pounds each* and were worth $823,000 ($6.6 million 2015 dollars.)

Although President Roosevelt took the U.S. off the gold standard in 1933, gold was still used for international settlements.* The Bretton Woods Conference in 1944 set up fixed exchange rates to the dollar for other currencies and the dollar was pegged to gold at $35 an ounce. So if we imported more than we exported, gold went out as foreigners redeemed dollars for gold. (Actually, it was just moved from one vault to another in the basement of the New York Fed. See *Once Upon a Dime* on p. 100)

The U.S. bestrode the world as an economic colossus after World War II, with half the world's gold reserves and the ruined countries of Europe clamoring for our cars, steel, and machines to rebuild.

The problem in 1960 wasn't the trade deficit: we had a $5 billion surplus. It was that our troops stationed around the world, foreign aid, and private investment in overseas business resulted in a $3.2 billion balance of payments deficit ($25.6 billion in 2015 dollars).

Gold continued to flow out of the U.S. until by 1971 there was only half the gold there was in 1960 and foreign banks held a lot more dollars than we had gold. President Nixon on August 15, 1971 issued an executive order ending convertibility of the dollar to gold, thus ending the Bretton Woods system and ushering in the era of floating currencies. This is called the Nixon Shock.

But at least no one could steal our gold. The Life article details the formidable defenses of Fort Knox — alarms, machine gun pillboxes, electrified fences, poison gas, bombproof roofs, and patrols so efficient "that a GI who once drove a golf ball off the adjacent course found 12 muzzles at his throat and had to be hospitalized for shock."

But the Fort Knox defenses didn't reckon with Goldfinger who was able to almost pull off the greatest heist of all time with a plot to poison the troops at fort Knox with aerial spray and bust into the vault with an atomic bomb. Fortunately, James Bond was able to foil the plot. (See *Atomic Secret* on p. 228.) Goldfinger was published in 1959, before the Life article.

The model for Goldfinger was Charles Engelhard who founded Engelhard, a company headquartered in Carteret, New Jersey. Now a diverse chemical company, Engelhard started as supplier of precious metals after Engelhard inherited a small metal shop from his father.

After the war, he went to South Africa to make his fortune in gold. The British government, which controlled South African affairs, prohibited the export of gold without government permission, which was hard to get.

But it was legal to export certain items made from gold. Engelhard hit upon making religious statues and other items from gold, exporting them to Hong Kong, then melting them back into gold bullion bars to sell on the world market.

Engelhard was a friend of Ian Fleming, the creator of James Bond, and Engelhard became the model for Goldfinger, who smuggled gold by making the body panels of his 1937 Rolls-Royce from it.

* Those would have been London Good Delivery Bars. See below.

Good Delivery

Those gold bars you see stacked up in bank vaults in movies are 400 ounce "London Good Delivery Bars." This is the gold bar that is used in international gold transactions.

The bars must meet the specifications of the London Bullion Markets Association. The bar must be at least 99.5% pure, must weigh between 350 and 430 troy ounces*, be stamped with the exact weight, a serial number, year of manufacture, and the mark of one of the 60 refineries approved by the association.

The bars must also look good.They must be free of surface pits or shrinkage because "A poor bar appearance might, on the other hand, suggest that standards of refining or assaying are less than desired," according to the LBMA rules (39 pages of them).

A 400 ounce gold bar is worth $440,000 at $1100 gold.

* A troy ounce is 9.6% larger than the the ounce you know, the avoirdupois ounce. See *Selling Your Gold* on p. 216.

Passing the Buck

The Treasury is making fewer bucks. 1,856,000,000 dollar bills were printed in 2010, a modern low. Production has ranged from about 2 to 5 billion since 1980.

The average dollar bill now lasts 42 months, up from 18 months 20 years ago. New equipment at the Fed can tell the difference between a rumpled bill and a torn one, so fewer are being destroyed. They are also passed less often as credit card purchases have soared, so there's less wear and tear.

It's all about the Benjamins. More hundreds were printed than singles last year for the first time. There are $7 billion out there in hundreds, two thirds held overseas.

The Bureau of Engraving and Printing makes your money in Washington and Fort Worth, Texas. You can tour either facility. Go to the Bureau's whimsically named web site, moneyfactory.gov for info.

They have a gift shop, too. There is a series of Chinese lucky number bills. The "Lucky Lion" is a 10 dollar bill with with a serial number beginning with 8888. 8 is an especially auspicious number for the Chinese*. It comes on a red presentation card and costs $28.88. But hurry, only 8888 of them are for sale.

By the way, "This note is legal tender good for all debts, public and private" printed on our money applies only to debts, so you can't legally make the stewardess take cash for your drink.

You can make me take cash, though.

* Many airline flight numbers to China have all eights. In 2003, a man sold an all eights phone number for $270,723 in Chengdu. The opening ceremony of the Summer Olympics in Beijing began on 8/8/08 at 8 seconds and 8 minutes past 8.

The True Value of Gold

Baron Nathan Mayer Rothschild (1777-1836), founder of the Rothschild dynasty, knew a thing or two about gold — his company smuggled gold coins across the English Channel to finance Wellington's defeat of Napoleon at Waterloo in 1815.

When asked about gold he replied "I only know of two men who really understand the true value of gold – an obscure clerk in the basement vault of the Banque de Paris and one of the directors of the Bank of England. Unfortunately, they disagree."

Lowering The Flag On The British Empire

The price of gold is fixed twice a day by a few large trading firms in London. This provides a twice daily snapshot of gold prices. Jewelry manufacturers and wholesalers use the afternoon fix, or "second London", which conveniently comes in at 10 o'clock Eastern time, as a daily base for prices, rather than the minute-to-minute fluctuations of the "spot" market.

On September 12, 1919, the first London gold fix pegged gold at $20.67. That's about $284 today. From then until 2004, representatives of 5 firms sat in the offices of the venerable NM Rothschild & Sons, which had chaired the proceeding since its inception. Each member had a little Union Jack flag, which was lowered when agreement had been reached. When all flags were lowered, the price was fixed.

No more. Rothschild, which smuggled gold to Wellington to help defeat Napoleon at Waterloo, quit the commodities business in May. 2004.

Now it's done in a conference call among 5 banks: Barclays, Deutsche Bank, HSBC Bank, Societe Generale, and Scotia Mocatta, the Bank of Nova Scotia's bullion division. If one of the traders disagrees, he must say "flag" and his company name. When agreement is reached, the chair, which rotates among the members, says "There are no flags, and we're fixed."

And so has the flag been lowered on another tradition of the British Empire.

Sunday School

Benjamin Franklin relates a story told to him by Indian interpreter Conrad Weiser (see *Passing the Buck* on p. 100) in *Remarks Concerning the Savages of North America* (1784).

Weiser tells of an Indian friend who, offering to sell his beaver pelts on a Sunday, was told by a trader that he couldn't conduct business on the Sabbath because this was the day they meet to learn good things.

The Indian tagged along with the trader to church services. He perceived that the angry man in black who spoke was angry at him being there so he left.

After the service he accosted the merchant again and asked if he would give more than four shillings a pound for his beaver. No, the trader said. Three and sixpence.

The Indian then asked other traders and they all told him three and sixpence. "This made clear to me that my Suspicion was right; and whatever they pretended of meeting to learn Good Things, the real purpose was to consult how to cheat Indians on the Price of Beaver."

Spreading the Wealth

"From each according to his ability, to each according to his needs!"— Karl Marx, Critique of the Gotha Program, 1875.*

Now that's Communism! Indians of the Pacific Northwest and Canada practiced it in the form of the Potlatch, ceremonies with feasting, singing, dancing, and giving away wealth. The status of a family was determined by how much they gave to other families.

Potlatches were banned in Canada in 1884 and in the U.S. in 1883 at the urging of missionaries as uncivilized and contrary to "Christian capitalist" values.

An Indian chief said to Franz Boas (1858-1942), the father of anthropology:

"We will dance when our laws command us to dance, and we will feast when our hearts desire to feast. Do we ask the white man, 'Do as the Indian does?' It is a strict law that bids us dance. It is a strict law that bids us distribute our property among our friends and neighbors. It is a good law. Let the white man observe his law; we shall observe ours. And now, if you come to forbid us dance, be gone. If not, you will be welcome to us."

The potlatch bans ended in 1934 in the U.S. and 1951 in Canada.

Potlatches continue to be important in the lives of the Northwest Indians, held for weddings, anniversaries, graduation, etc., costing up to $10,000 with a year of planning for a family or clan.

The Word "potlatch" is from Chinook Jargon, pidgin trade language of the Pacific Northwest Indians. ("High muckety muck" is also from Chinook Jargon.)

*As noted in a footnote in *Passing the Buck* on p. 99, a poll found that almost half the population thought this phrase was in the Constitution.

Guinea-Pig Market Up

A 1935 article in the Literary Digest with that title says that the cost of guinea pigs needed for medical research more than doubled, from 36¢ to 84¢ ($14.63 in 2015).

The United States Public Health Service uses 12,000 a year and will now raise its own. Not only that, but the cabbage they eat has gone up a cent a pound. (Cabbage prices at that time were around 3¢ a pound) The Service uses 50 tons a year to feed its guinea pigs.

Guinea pigs for medical research today cost $65-113 depending on weight, more if you need just one sex. Pet guinea pigs are $35.

Cabbage prices haven't gone up since 1935. Cabbage today is around 50¢ a pound, or 3¢ in 1935 dollars.

I had a guinea pig once. His name was Phineas. He was married to Toots. They ate anything vegetable, plywood included. The fabulous mating warble of the male guinea pig is among the most awesome sounds in nature.

Beard Tax

In 1697, Russian Tsar Peter the Great made an 18 month grand tour of Europe. He came back determined to modernize old-fashioned Russian customs.

In 1705 he ordered all men to shave their beards, adopting the clean-shaven European style of the time. Anyone who wanted to keep his beard had to pay a tax, a kopeck for peasants and up to 100 rubles for nobility and merchants. Orthodox priests were exempt.

Those who paid were issued a beard token, silver for nobility, copper for peasants. The Russian eagle was on one side and an image of a bearded face on the other with an inscription. The one above says "The money has been taken."

Beard tax tokens are collectible as coins.

Alien Superhero is an Alien!

Go back to the original 1938 Superman comic. The skyline of Metropolis suspiciously resembles Toronto. That's because Joe Shuster, who drew Superman was originally from Toronto. (Co-creator Jerry Siegel was from Cleveland)

To celebrate Superman's Canadian heritage, The Royal Canadian Mint has issued 7 Superman coins for his 75th birthday. 1 coin is 14 karat gold, 5 coins are fine silver and one is base metal. All but one of the coins are in color, one with Superman's S shield, the rest and picturing Superman in various iconic poses.

One silver coin has a hologram with Superman creating a sonic boom as he flies over Metropolis.

The base metal coin shows Superman then (1938) and now as the coin is tilted, below.

The coins feature the inscription "75 years of superman" written in Kryptonese and all have limited mintage except the now and then coin.

Siegel and Shuster sold the rights to Superman for $130 and a 10 year contract to create Superman stories.

Joe Shuster drew kinky sadomasochistic scenes for fetish comics anonymously in the 1950's. (The scantily clad women and muscled men look like Lois Lane and Superman.)

Hearing that a Superman movie was planned, Shuster put a curse on the movie in a lengthy press release in 1975. (Look what happened to Christopher Reeve!) The movie premiered in 1978.

Siegel and Shuster were awarded lifetime annuities of $20,000, subsequently raised to $30,000, in 1977. Joe Shuster died in 1992 at 78 and Jerry Siegel in 1996 at 81 without having shared in the fortune that Superman made for others.

The original 1938 check from Detective Comics to Siegel and Shuster for $412 with a line item "Superman 130.00" sold at auction for $160,000 in 2012.

Black Friday

No, it's not good business the day after Thanksgiving. That went away with the Great Recession. And it's not the start of the Great Depression, either. The 1929 stock market crash was Black Thursday.

During the Civil War, President Lincoln suspended the payment of gold for paper money, issuing Legal Tender Notes — greenback dollars, fiat money. The gold standard wasn't reestablished until 1879.

Shortly after President Grant took office in 1869, Robber Barons Jay Gould and James Fisk tried to corner the gold market.

Grant's brother-in-law was a financier named Abel Corbin. Gould and Fisk approached Corbin to recommend the appointment of Daniel Butterfield as Assistant Treasurer of the United States, which Grant did. In this position he would oversee the gold sales of the Treasury.

Gould gave Butterfield $10,000 (his salary was $8,000) and Butterfield agreed to tip him off when the government would sell gold. Corbin also arranged for Gould and Fisk to visit Grant socially, inviting him aboard Fisk's yacht. They tried to convince Grant that a high gold price was good for the country and so the Treasury should refrain from selling gold.

Gould and Fisk then began buying large amounts of gold, pushing up the price. Gold was then quoted in how many greenback dollars would buy $100 in gold coins.The price of gold went up from 130 greenbacks to 162.

Corbin's wife, Grant's sister, wrote a letter to Grant's wife about Corbin's interest in gold and Grant realized he was being manipulated. He ordered the Treasury to sell $4 million of gold, which it did on Friday, September 24, 1869. The price plummeted to 133 greenbacks in minutes. This was Black Friday.

Corbin was kept out of the loop on the gold sale but knew something was up and he tipped off Gould. Gould was able to secretly sell their entire position above 150 greenbacks without telling Fisk so Fisk's behavior wouldn't tip his hand.

Fisk thought he was ruined, but Gould revealed they had made $12 million. They gave $2 million to lawyers to tie up litigation and split the rest.

Stocks plunged by 20% and export grain crops by 50%, since international trade was settled in gold. Corbin was ruined and Butterfield was forced to resign.

Below is a photograph of the blackboard of the New York Gold Room taken on Black Friday detailing the times and prices of trades. It was used as evidence in Congressional hearings in 1870. You can buy it as a framed print.

The Goldfather

At least 50% of Italy's 28,000 cash-for-gold stores are Mafia owned according to an Italian anti-money-laundering watchdog In 2012. Most of the scrap gold is illegally smuggled into Switzerland.

In November, 2012, Italian police seized $207 million worth of gold bars in raids on 259 houses and shops.

The caption reads "This is a photograph of the Bulletin Board in the Gold Room at N.Y. Sept. 24, 1870 the Black Friday of the Gold Panic — It was produced in evidence before the Committee of Banking and currency. JA Garfield" Garfield, then an Ohio Representative, was chairman of the committee. The words below Garfield's signature are cut off but probably say "Chairman of the committee" or similar.

Financial Mystery

On January, 21 1980, when gold peaked at $850*, you could buy the Dow at 873 for a little more than an ounce of gold. On August 26, 1999 gold bottomed at $253 and it would have cost 44 ounces of gold to buy the Dow at 11,198.

At gold's all-time high of $1895 on September 5, 2011, the Dow was 11,240 or about 6 ounces of gold. As I write this on July 22, 2015, it would take 16 ounces of gold at $1093 to buy the Dow at 17,829.

I have no idea what, if anything, this means. But it sounds like something the Fed should be worried about, doesn't it?

* $2457 adjusted for inflation to 2015.

Close Shave

"A question of grave importance is being discussed vigorously in the local barbers' unions," reported the Baltimore Morning Herald April 3, 1900, about whether customers in Wheeling, West Virginia who come in for just a shave should be charged an extra 5 cents to also shave their necks. Several weeks of discussions in secret sessions of the union produced no agreement.

The barbers explained the problem as "in latter days the pride of a man has increased and he expects to be shaved and have his neck cleared of its shrubbery—all for the price of a shave."

...no business which depends for existence on paying less than living wages to its workers has any right to continue in this country.

— President Franklin Roosevelt, Statement on the National Industrial Recovery Act, June 16, 1933

Can't pay your bills with your McJob? Get financial advice from the boss. McDonalds has a brochure for its employees, *Practical Money Skills,* that has a budget journal to help you figure it out.

The brochure is "brought to you by Visa Inc. and Wealth Watchers International ("to help people spend less money than they make.") The chart below is recreated from the brochure to make the type larger.

Let's do the math. $2060 take home pay would be $13.88 an hour ($2387 gross) for two forty hour a week jobs according to Bloomberg. McDonalds pay for its crew is $7.88 according to Glassdoor.

McDonalds CEO Don Thompson was paid $13.8 million in 2013, $6900 an hour (40 hour week with a 2 week paid vacation.*)

As for that $20 a month for health insurance, McDonalds cheapest health insurance plan was $56 a month and the coverage "pretty terrible", according to a 2010 CNN article.

Sample Monthly Budget

Monthly Net Income

Income (1st job)	$ 1,105
Income (2nd job)	$ 955
Other Income	
Monthly Net Income Total	$ 2060

Monthly Expenses

Savings	$ 100
Mortgage/Rent	$ 600
Car Payment	$ 150
Car/Home insurance	$ 100
Health Insurance	$ 20
Heating	$ 50
Cable/Phone	$ 100
Electric	$ 90
Other	$ 100
Monthly Expenses Total	$1,310

Monthly Spending Money .... $ 750
(Monthly Net Income Total minus Monthly Expenses Total)

Daily Spending Money Goal .... $ 25
(Monthly Spending Money divided by 30)*

*the average of 30 days in a month is used to simplify your budget

---

* "After three years of employment, crew that have averaged 30 hours per week in the prior 12 months are eligible for 5 days of paid vacation. For each year of employment after that, employees will earn an extra day until a total of 10 days are accumulated."

Exemplary Employers – McDonald's

"In 2008, McDonald's partnered with Visa, Inc., the world's largest retail electronic payments network, to launch the country's largest employer-based financial literacy program. The "McDonald's Practical Money Skills" program is being made available to more than 500,000 restaurant-level employees throughout the majority of McDonald's 14,000 U.S. restaurants. This program is designed to empower employees with free, comprehensive money management tools and is part of the company's ongoing commitment to provide a wide-range of benefits to its employees. This program is especially beneficial to its employees during these turbulent financial times."

— Wealth Watchers web site 2014. "The mission of Wealth Watchers Inc. is to build viable communities by expanding the knowledge of low-to-moderate income individuals for the purpose of understanding the importance of basic finance and the accumulation of wealth."

Of course, you're making up the difference between a living dead wage and a barely living wage. 52% of fast food worker families are collecting public assistance, more than twice the average for all workers: Medicaid, the Children's Health Insurance Program, Earned Income Tax Credit, heating assistance, food stamps(!), and the Temporary Assistance for Needy Families program. This amounts to a $7 billion a year taxpayer subsidy to fast food companies. (A 2013 congressional report found that a single 300 employee Walmart store in Wisconsin cost taxpayers over $1 million a year.)

McDonald's has a dedicated corporate help line for employees called McResources that steers desperate workers to various public assistance programs.

I go to McDonald's once or twice a year, usually when my wife is away. I happened to go on Labor Day, 2014. I wished the server, a young girl, a happy labor day and asked if she at least got time-and-a-half for laboring on Labor's day. She did not.

Passing the Buck

On December 28, 1898, a Monroe head $100 silver certificate sent to the Philadelphia subtreasury[1] aroused the suspicion of a clerk when the red Treasury seal smeared under his damp thumb. The clerk took the bill to Washington where Treasury experts initially passed it as genuine but finally declared it counterfeit when it separated into two pieces when soaked in water[2]. Even though Monroe's cheekbones and hair over the ear weren't right, the counterfeit was so good that the Treasury had to recall the entire issue, $27 million and the new head of the Secret Service, John Wilkie, was directed by the Secretary of the Treasury to spend all his time on the investigation.

Genuine Monroe

Illustration from *Ten Million or Ten Years* by Secret Service chief John Wilkie in Frank Leslie's Popular Monthly, September, 1900.

Wilkie assigned the case to his best detective, William Burns. By asking around the trade, Burns determined which engravers had the necessary skills and had ordered certain materials. This led him to Arthur Taylor and Baldwin Bredell, engravers in Philadelphia.

The Secret Service watched the top floor of a building at Ninth and Filbert streets for over a year. One day Taylor and Bredell took a train to Lancaster, shadowed by a Secret Service operative. They visited a large cigar factory there owned by William Jacobs and a tobacco warehouse a block away run by W.L. Kendig.

When informed of this, Wilkie investigated and found that cigars made there had counterfeit revenue stamps on the boxes. But it was decided to continue the investigation until there was enough evidence to also tie Taylor and Bredell to the counterfeit hundred.

Jacobs and Kendig went to lunch together at noon, leaving the warehouse unoccupied. One day detective Burns broke a window in the warehouse with a baseball and boosted a small boy he had brought along from Philadelphia through the broken window. The boy went around to the front and opened a spring door from the inside. Burns went in and found 27 tons of blue paper used to make the counterfeit stamps, enough for 400 million cigars[3]. When Jacobs and Kendig returned they found a weeping boy who said he would pay for the glass if they would let him in to recover his ball, They did and forgave the broken window.

A night reconnaissance up a fire escape by Burns found all the windows at the Philadelphia engraving shop locked. Taylor and Bredell employed an office boy. Burns rented a costume and an agent bumped into the boy on the street and gave him fifty cents to take the package to a hotel and give it to Burns, posing as a theater man, who asked the boy if he'd like to be an extra in a play. The delighted boy was taken to another room where he changed into the costume, then to see an agent posing as the theater manager. Burns took the boy's keys from his pocket, and "whirled away" in a waiting carriage to the Yale Lock Company nearby, had the office key duplicated, then "whirled back".[4]

The next night Burns went into the engraver's offices for a look. Burns visited the offices at noon when Taylor and Bredell were away for lunch and also nights. He was able to make a key for a locker and in it found a plate for a counterfeit Lincoln-head hundred almost completed.

Finally, on April 18, 1899, Taylor and Bredell were arrested. Even though they were caught red-handed, they declined to make a statement. Opening a drawer, Burns found the Lincoln-head plate and also a genuine bill used to make the plate. Unbeknownst to the counterfeiters, the Secret Service had intercepted a letter from Jacobs to Taylor which they were able to open undetected in spite of elaborate safeguards. In the letter were two Lincoln hundreds. When Burns asked where the second hundred Jacobs had sent them was, and also told them he had arrested two lawyers named Ingham and Newitt who had been hired by Jacobs and Kendig to pay $500 a month to a Secret Service agent for information, who played along, they decided to confess.

Bredell went to a clever hiding place and extracted the other hundred along with a counterfeit fifty. Bredell told Burns that the plates for the fifty were hidden in the foundation of his house across the Delaware in Camden, New Jersey. Along with the plates, the Secret Service also found a machine used to number the counterfeit Monroes.

Taylor then told how they became counterfeiters. In 1896, an intermediary for Jacobs offered Taylor $25,000[5] (almost $700,000 in 2014) to engrave the plate for the counterfeit cigar stamps. When he accepted, he was introduced to Jacobs and Kendig who set him up along with Bredell in the Philadelphia shop. Jacobs and Kendig suggested counterfeiting money to Taylor in 1897. Taylor and Kendig toured the Bureau of Engraving and Printing many times, noting how the process was done.

That night Burns and Wilkie along with a secret service party took the train to Lancaster and entered the tobacco warehouse with keys found at Taylor and Bredell's shop and spent the night. Early the next morning Kendig was arrested when he came to the warehouse. He recognized Burns, even though he had never seen him. A crooked revenue agent had warned him that the the feds were nosing around and had provided a description of Burns.

But Jacobs had been up with a sick child and went to the cigar factory without first going to the warehouse as was his custom. Burns went to the cigar factory and posed as a buyer in order to be led to Jacobs without alerting him so that he could perhaps escape. Jacobs also recognized Burns from the description provided. Jacobs attempted to bribe Burns — he pointed to a $14,000 deposit he was making out on his desk and offered to double it in ten minutes.

Burns found the die rolls for printing the counterfeit revenue stamps in a drawer, but Jacobs insisted on a deal for the Monroe plates, which Burns refused. Burns then went back to the warehouse where Kendig was handcuffed to an agent and threatened to arrest his father. Kendig then led Burns to a hiding place behind some bricks in a wall and turned over the plates to the counterfeit hundred.

Taylor and Bredell were taken to Moyamensing prison in Philadelphia to await trial. A few months after that, a counterfeit twenty was found in circulation. Burns knew that Taylor and Bredell had made it — in prison! Burns visited them in prison and showed them the fake twenty and asked who could have made it. When they professed ignorance, Burns angrily told them how they had made it and circulated it. This elicited an account of how a lawyer, John Semple, had seen a newspaper article about the counterfeiters that also told how William Brockway, the "King of the Counterfeiters", had been given immunity several times for turning over counterfeit plates, although he was finally put in prison and was then serving a ten year sentence.

Semple told Taylor and Bredell about Brockway and they agreed to let him represent them. Semple visited Brockway in prison and he said that Taylor and Bredell would have been let go in return for the plates if they hadn't already been surrendered. Semple then suggested to Taylor and Bredell that they get out on bond and make another counterfeit note with the idea of negotiating leniency in exchange for the new plates. But the bond was too high so they figured out a way to print the counterfeits in prison.

But then they told Burns that they had printed the twenties before they were arrested and had thrown the plates in the Delaware river, which Burns pointed out contradicted their scheme to turn them over for leniency. After Burns threatened to put Taylor's mother and brother in prison as accomplices, the counterfeiters confessed that they still had the plates which were secreted in the grave of Taylor's father. Burns and Wilkie went to the cemetery and dug them up.

Relatives brought steel plates and other supplies to Taylor and Bredell. They were able to sensitize a steel plate and capture an image of a twenty without a camera by laying it on the plate under a piece of glass and exposing it to light, an old wet plate process. They then engraved the plate by tracing the image, taking turns at night under a black cloth with an oil lamp for light. They were able to completely bleach out one dollar bills so they didn't have to split them and they printed the fakes on them with an improvised press that worked like a clothes wringer. Semple smuggled in $150 in ones, paid for by Bredell's wife.

Taylor's brother Harry passed the twenties. He was caught and arrested. Semple was also arrested as were Ellery Ingham a former United States Attorney and Harvey Newitt, his former assistant and law partner, the lawyers who had thought they were bribing a Secret Service agent to provide information about the what the Service knew.

Taylor and Bredell were sentenced to seven years less the three years already served and were sent to the Atlanta Federal Penitentiary. Kendig and Jacobs were sentenced to twelve years, but were pardoned by President Roosevelt in 1905 after having served five years. Semple was tried once with a hung jury and acquitted in a second trial. In great pain from rheumatism, he shot himself in the heart in 1915. Ingham and Newitt were sentenced to 2½ years.

William Burns went on to found the William J. Burns International Detective Agency

and was appointed Director of the Bureau of Investigation, the predecessor to the FBI, in 1921. Burns was fired in 1924 when his mentor, Attorney General Harry M. Daugherty, was caught up in the Teapot Dome scandal and was cashiered. He retired to Sarasota, Florida and died in 1932. Burns was succeeded by his young deputy, J. Edgar Hoover. The William J. Burns International Detective Agency was acquired by Securitas Security Services in 2000, which had bought Pinkerton the year before.

King of the Counterfeiters William Brockway (real name William Spencer) was released early in January,1904 after he took the poor convict oath attesting that he could not pay his $1000 fine. He was arrested in 1905 in Brooklyn after detectives saw him buying fine quality paper at stationers, which he

William J. Burns

vigorously protested according to an article in the New York Times August 29, 1905, which also said "He is believed to have considerable money." Brockway died at a niece's house in New Haven, Connecticut in 1920 after a gas valve was accidentally left open. He was 98.

1. Government funds were held in the Treasury and subtreasuries independently of the banking system since there was no central bank at that time.

2. Burns' account says the Monroes were made from one dollar bills mostly bleached of ink, split, and glued together split sides out, so the bills were printed on blank genuine government paper. But the January, 1901 edition of Dickerman's United States Treasury Counterfeit Detector says the fakes "are printed on two pieces of paper, between which red and blue silk thread in imitation of distributed fibre is placed."

3. This is from an article in the Reading Eagle (Pa.) April 21, 1899. The Eagle also says that 2 million cigars were seized. That would be enough to cheat the government out of $6000 ($167,000 in 2014) at the $3 per thousand tax rate. Production was 1-1.5 million cigars a week with 500-600 employees according the article.

4. The primary source for this article is *Great Cases of Detective Burns,* by Dana Gatlin which appeared in McClure's, March, 1911. Wilkie also wrote an account of the affair titled *Ten Million or Ten Years* in Frank Leslie's Popular Monthly, September, 1900. In his account, the boy's keys were taken to the basement of the hotel where a duplicate was filed by a waiting locksmith in four minutes. Since Burns was the one who actually did it, I have used his version.

5. $25,000 according to Gatlin, but $3000 in the Eagle article, which sounds more likely.

Big Money

The island of Yap in the Carolines in the Western Pacific is known for its huge stone money that looks like millstones, ranging from a few inches to 12 feet in diameter.

Called *Rai* the stones were quarried with shell tools from a type of shimmering limestone on Palau, 250 miles away and carried on rafts towed by outrigger sail canoes.

In 1874, David O'Keefe* from Georgia who had been shipwrecked on Yap provided iron tools for the Yapese to quarry the stones and ships to transport them back to Yap where he traded them for commodities such as coconut meat. The stones grew from a maximum of 4 feet to 12 feet. But the new stones were considered less valuable by the Yapese since they were easier to get, a debased currency, if you will.

The large stones were not moved around, everyone knew who owned them, and were used only for large transactions.

Yap was a Spanish colony with the Philippines from the 17th century until 1899 when Spain sold the Carolines to Germany after being defeated in the Spanish-American war.

Japan occupied the Carolines in 1914 after declaring war on Germany and after Germany's defeat in World War I received a League of Nations mandate to govern the Carolines along with other Pacific islands.

The Japanese garrisoned Yap during World War II but it was bypassed by the U.S. Island hopping strategy. After the war, Yap was occupied by the U.S. and is now part of Federated States of Micronesia.

According to an article in Life Magazine April 25, 1949, "Told that U.S. money is now legal tender in Yap, a chief remarked "First Spanish money no good, then German money no good, now Japanese money no good. Yap money always good!'"

* A 1954 movie *His Majesty O'Keefe* starring Burt Lancaster portrayed O'Keefe's adventures.

Money Laundering

In 1912, the Bureau of Engraving and Printing installed money laundering machines. 30% of notes returned to the Treasury by banks were not worn, but simply dirty and the machine could process 40,000 bills a day according the the Bureau of Engraving and Printing, Since it cost 1.3¢ to print a new bill and only .3¢ to wash an old one, the savings were considerable,

The machine was a large Rube Goldberg contraption weighing 800 pounds. The bills were sandwiched between two endless cloth belts which were run over a series of rollers that could be raised and lowered into a hundred gallon tank of water with special soap. Then the bills went into a rinsing tank and finally were run over gas-heated drums which dried and ironed them. A girl fed the bills in one end of the machine and another girl collected the bills at the other end.

Another advantage of this money laundering was that with all the extra counting of bills coming in and going out, more counterfeits were detected. The supervisor of the operation, Miss Thomas, was quoted by The Michigan Manufacturer and Financial Record, October 9, 1915:

"A counterfeit hasn't a chance to escape us. From the time the bank's packages are opened by the counters to be verified to the time the money leaves this division finally, it is watched by expert eyes."

"It is a remarkable sight to watch sixty expert counters, who average 20,000 notes daily, run lightly through a bunch of bills and stop short suddenly when they come to a counterfeit in their hands. They identify these notes, almost perfect as they are, by the 'feel' of the paper."

Money laundering was discontinued in 1918 "due to problems with paper content and feel", according to the Bureau of Engraving and Printing.

Pin Money

Pins were quite expensive in 14th century England, so much so that their sale was restricted to 2 days a year lest women wreck the household budget. Money allotted by the husband for this purpose is the origin of the term "pin money", although today it means the opposite of the original.

In 1543 Parliament under Henry VIII passed an *Acte for the true making of pynnes* setting quality standards and a price cap of 6 shillings 8 pence a thousand. It was repealed 3 years later because due to the law "there hath been scarcitee of pynnes within this realme"

Deep Thought

It is always the big thief who shouts the loudest about the little thief.

— Hazen Pingree, Detroit Mayor 1889-1897, Michigan Governor 1897-1901

Fort Knox

That's where the gold is, Before the Depression, gold was money — gold coins freely circulated and paper money could be redeemed for gold.

In 1933 Roosevelt and the New Deal Congress made it illegal to own gold other than in jewelry. All gold was required to be turned in for dollars at $20.67 an ounce*. Even contracts that specified payment in gold were voided. That left the government with a lot of gold and no place to put it.

In 1936 the U.S. Treasury built the United States Bullion Depository at Fort Knox, Kentucky, a military base. The first gold shipment of $200 million of $10.6 billion arrived by train from Philadelphia, preceded by an empty decoy train, on January 13, 1937. The gold was sent registered mail under the protection of the Postal Inspection Service. It took 500 rail cars to carry the gold.

During World War II, Fort Knox gold peaked at 649.6 million troy ounces. As of May 31, 2015 there were 147.34 million ounces, worth $162 billion at $1100 gold.

The basement gold vault has a 22 ton door. No one person has the combination. Different people have to contribute partial combinations to open the door.

There are fences and guards of the United States Mint Police, of course. But you'll have to get through the 30,000 soldiers at Fort Knox first. (See *New Gold Rush* on p. 115.)

*Private ownership of gold was restored in 1974.

Audit the Fed!

We must audit the FED.
Open those books and let the record be read.
Audit the FED.
No more cover up. Let's get the truth out instead.
— Steve Dore, "Songs of Liberty, Freedom, sound money and common sense, politics, patriotism"

Gold crank Rep. Ron Paul called for checking the gold of the Federal Reserve in 2012 campaigning. (He also wants us to be the only country without a central bank: End the Fed.)

The Fed complied. In 2012 the Treasury went down in the basement of the New York Fed where 34,021 of our gold bars are stored and drilled 367 bars to collect samples for assay. The results revealed that in 3 of the tests the gold was more pure than advertised. So extrapolating we have 27 more ounces of gold than we thought, $29,700 at $1100 gold.

But a 1977 test of the gold at Fort Knox by the General Accounting Office found, after a couple of assays of the same samples, that the gold was within the tolerance allowed, but below what was listed in inventory records. The result was a decrease in value of the gold by $158.77.

An audit of the Denver Mint at the same time showed the gold was up to snuff.

You can make sure the Fed gold is all there yourself. As noted in *Once Upon a Dime* on p. 100, you can tour the gold vaults of the New York Fed. Tripadvisor web site reports 95 out of 132 reviews of the tour were excellent or very good. Be prepared for airport-style security.

As of May 31, 2015, we had $14.7 billion worth of gold at the New York Fed and $285 billion total at $1100 gold. But the Treasury books its gold at $42.22, the official gold price the last time we had an official gold price, raised from $35 in 1973. The Treasury has monthly updates. Google *Status Report of U.S. Treasury-Owned Gold*.

Trickle Down Economics

Old Leave It to Beaver episodes got you nostalgic for the placid and prosperous Eisenhower era? Hold on to your wallet. Here are the 1952-53 tax rates. Wow! 92%!

Taxable income after deductions. 23 brackets consolidated to 13. Figures in 2015 dollars, adjusted for 8.93X inflation. Rates apply successively to each portion of income.

Tax %	From $	To $
22.2	0	17,860
24.6	17,860	35,720
29 - 34	35,720	71,440
38 - 42	71,440	107,160
48 - 53	107,160	142,880
56 - 59	142,880	178,600
62 - 66	178,600	232,180
67 - 68	232,180	339,340
72 - 75	339,340	446,500
77 - 80	446,500	625,100
83 - 85	625,100	803,700
88 - 91	803,700	1,786,000
92	1,786,000	—

Rates went down a bit by 1965, ranging from 14 - 70%. In 1982 it was 0 - 50%, in 1988, 15 - 28%, and in 1993 15 - 39.6%

In 1913, the first year of the income tax, rates started at 1.0% for the first $478,000 and topped out at 7.0% for incomes above $11 million, both figures in 2015 dollars, adjusted for 23.9X inflation.

Herbert Hoover signed the Revenue Act of 1932, the largest peacetime tax increase in U.S. history, raising rates from1.5-25% to 4-63% — in the middle of the Depression!

2015 Tax Rates

Tax %	From $	To $
10	0	9,225
15	9,225	37,450
25	37,450	90,750
28	90,750	189,300
33	189,300	411,500
35	411,500	413,200
39.6	413,200	—

The top rate reverted to 39.6%, the rate in 2000, from 35% when the Bush tax cuts expired at the end of 2012 after a 2 year extension and a big fight in Congress.

Off the Chart

Elliott wave junctures, fibonacci retracements, relative strength index, death cross, momentum oscillator, bounded oscillator Hindenberg omen…This is the gibberish that chartists use to predict the price of gold, silver, stocks… whatever. No one has ever been able to predict the price of gold, silver, stocks or whatever (see *Goldman Sacks Gold Man* on p. 108), although some say women's skirt lengths can predict the stock market. (See *The Moral Gown* on p. 258.)

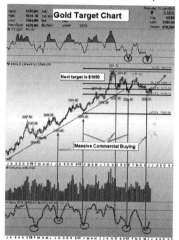

Made in China

Mr. John P. Young, managing editor of the San Francisco Chronicle, who has had close observation of California's Chinese residents for thirty years, thinks that the commercial future to which the plunderers of China are looking forward may not prove so rosy as they anticipate. Indeed, he predicts that China's population of 400,000,000, when awakened and introduced to Western civilization, instead of clamoring for European and American products, will begin to produce these articles themselves, not for their own use, but for us and at such ruinous prices that the labor market of the world will suffer a terrible blow.
— The literary Digest, Dec. 23, 1899

Deep Thought

"It is difficult to get a man to understand something when his salary depends upon his not understanding it" — Upton Sinclair

Silver Shoes on the Yellow Brick Road

We're off to see the Wizard
The Wonderful Wizard of Oz.
We hear he is a Whiz of a Wiz,
If ever a Wiz there was.
— Winston Churchill, *Their Finest Hour*, quoting a song popular with Australian troops in North Africa in 1941.

In *The Wonderful Wizard of Oz,* the children's book by L. Frank Baum published in 1900, Dorothy didn't wear ruby slippers. When her house landed on the Wicked Witch of the East, all Dorothy saw were two feet sticking out from under the house "shod in silver shoes with pointed toes."

When MGM made the famous 1939 movie, the silver shoes became ruby slippers, the better to stand out in the vivid new technicolor film.

A modern interpretation of the Wizard of Oz is that it was an allegory on the economic troubles of the time, the Panic of 1893 and the ensuing severe depression, the free silver movement, the gold standard.

The Panic of 1893 caused a spike in unemployment as high as 18%, and higher in industrial states. Baum witnessed the march of Coxey's Army in 1894. Thousands of unemployed men from all over the country set out for Washington in some 40 groups. Coxey's Army, its popular nickname, (Coxey called his group the Commonweal of Christ and styled himself as its commander) was the only one that made it the whole way.

Jacob Coxey was a wealthy businessman who owned a sand quarry in Massilon, Ohio. Outraged by the unemployment caused by the depression, he organized a march that reached Washington on April 30, 1894. To counteract the drastic shrinkage of the gold and money supply in the panic and to put people to work, he demanded the issuance of $500 million in paper money to pay for a public works program (Coxey's infant son was named Legal Tender Coxey).

Coxey arrived in Washington with 500 men and when he attempted to give a speech on the grounds of the Capitol, he was arrested for walking on the grass. (President Grover Cleveland was unsympathetic. See *The Proper Role of Government* on p. 153).

His speech was later read into the Congressional Record. Fifty years to the day later, on April 30th, 1944 Coxey finally was allowed to deliver his speech from the steps of the Capitol.

One of the lines from the speech, quoting an unnamed Senator, is eerily prescient today: "that for a quarter of a century the rich have been growing richer, the poor poorer, and that by the close of the present century the middle class will have disappeared as the struggle for existence becomes fierce and relentless."

It wasn't until 1964 that a political interpretation of the Wizard of Oz was first put forth by high school teacher Henry Littlefield who wrote an essay, *The Wizard of Oz: Parable on Populism*, that was published in the *American Quarterly.*

In the essay, Dorothy represents everyman, the silver shoes the silverite movement, the yellow brick road the gold standard, the lion William Jennings Bryan, the winged monkeys the plains Indians, the scarecrow Midwestern farmers, and the tin woodman Eastern laborers.

Some of the subsequent interpretations go a little far. One posits that Oz stands for the abbreviation for ounce, i.e. of gold. However, Baum in an interview said he got Oz from the O-Z label on a file cabinet. Although Baum wrote the lyrics for the adult musical version of his book, *The Wizard of Oz,* which premiered in Chicago in 1902, and which had references and jokes about the politics of the time, there is no evidence that Baum intended his book to be a political allegory.

Illustration of Dorothy holding the silver shoes by W. W. Denslow in The Wonderful Wizard of Oz

The Great Recession

Oeconomia est, O Asine!*

The current economic crisis has parallels with the panic of 33. That's 33, not '33.

In 32, a company in Alexandria, Egypt lost three spice ships in a hurricane in the Red Sea, and the value of ostrich feathers and ivory, its other businesses, fell. A dye house specializing in imperial purple headquartered in Tyre, in Phoenicia, went bankrupt due to a strike and embezzlement of a manager.

A large Roman bank had loaned money to both companies and there was a run on the bank by their depositors. Rumors spread on the Via Sacra (the Roman Wall Street) that a larger bank, Pettius Brothers was also involved.

Pettius Brothers had loaned a lot of money to the Belgae up in north Gaul. Troubles with the ornery Belgae caused the government to suspend business activity and Pettius Brothers couldn't collect on their loans and became insolvent. Both banks failed on the same day.

Emperor Tiberius had ordered that all senators invest a third of their money in land in Italy to support declining Italian agriculture. The deadline to do this was almost up and senators scrambled to find the money to invest.

Publius Spinther, a wealthy noble, had deposited 30 million sesterces (a sesterce would buy 2 loaves of bread) in his bank, Balbus & Ollius, two years before and now needed his money, which they couldn't come up with, and they closed two days later, registering bankruptcy with the praetor (magistrate).

Banks in Corinth, Carthage, Byzantium, and Lyons next failed and the survivors on the Via Sacra suspended payment to their depositors. Runs on banks all over Italy caused them to call their loans, abandoning their profitable XII% interest rate. Debtors had their property auctioned off by the praetor for a song, reducing many wealthy Romans to paupers.

Gracchus, the praetor, saw disaster looming and went to the Senate, which, after a hurried debate, dispatched a messenger to Emperor Tiberius at his retreat in Capri. After an ulcerous four day wait, a runner returned with a letter from the Emperor.

Tiberius suspended the investment decree and made available 100 million sesterces from the imperial treasury to bail out the banks, which would loan debtors at no interest for 3 years (providing double the amount of collateral was put up).

Soon normal lending resumed, ending the panic of 33.

* Ass (the animal).

Fairy Toll

Even the Tooth Fairy has been hit by the Great Recession. Results from a Visa survey show a decline in money left under the pillow since 2010. In 2011, it's an average of $2.60 per tooth, down from $3 last year.

It varied by region with the East the worst, down 38%. The South was down 21%, the Midwest 3%. The West actually went up a dime to $2.80.

Even the number of kids stiffed by the Tooth Fairy went up from 6% to 10%.

Underwear Dept.

Victoria's Secret has unveiled its 2010 diamond bra, the Harlequin Fantasy Bra.

2350 white, champagne and cognac diamonds criss-cross the "Very Sexy Plunge Multi-way bra" with a 16 carat heart-shaped champagne diamond dangling from the center.150 carats total, $3 million.

This is the recession bra. Last year's Black Diamond Fantasy Miracle Bra was 1500 carats for $5 million.

No one has actually bought any of the Victoria's Secret diamond bras.

Oeconomia est, O Asine!

You'd think that in the age of the Internet it wouldn't be hard to come up with the Latin translation of "It's the economy, stupid".

Googlius Rex was no help. There are a number of Latin to English sites and all were perfectly useless. And darned if I could find a native speaker. I called Mel Brooks, the 2000 year old man, but he said he had forgotten all his Latin. Well, it was a long time ago.

I participate in a forum for the software I use to bring you this newsletter and also the web site. I posted a call for anyone who could help me with Latin. The forum is headquartered in England. A man from Wales was able to contact a friend in Yorkshire who is a Latin scholar and she provided the translation.

Asine, ass or donkey, was the colloquial first century Latin word for a stupid person. Our word asinine is derived from it.

Brother, Can You Spare a Dime?

Sure. A quarter, even. If you need to feed the meter and don't have change I will donate the tariff. But then you have to feel guilty and buy something.

It's the Economy, Stupid*

Let me remind you that credit is the life-blood of business, the lifeblood of prices and jobs.

It is just as important that business keep out of government as that government keep out of business.

Prosperity cannot be restored by raids upon the public Treasury.

With impressive proof on all sides of magnificent progress, no one can rightly deny the fundamental correctness of our economic system.

Economic depression cannot be cured by legislative action or executive pro-nouncement. Economic wounds must be healed by the action of the cells of the economic body - the producers and con-sumers themselves.

— Herbert Hoover

* "The Economy, Stupid" was on a sign in Bill Clinton's Little Rock campaign office during the 1992 campaign intended to remind the staff to stay on message.

Spreading the Wealth

It is not very unreasonable that the rich should contribute to the public expense, not only in proportion to their revenue, but something more than in that proportion.
— Adam Smith, The Wealth of Nations, 1776.

The income tax was instituted in 1913 following the ratification of the 16th amendment and was progressive – the wealthy paid more.

The 16th amendment[1] was passed be-cause the Constitution had originally re-quired that direct taxes, as opposed to an indirect tax like a sales tax, be levied in proportion to each state's population.[2]

In 1895, the Supreme Court struck down a law imposing a 2% tax on incomes over $4000 ($114,000 in 2014 dollars), holding that it was a direct tax and violated the constitutional requirement of apportion-ment by population.

In 1909, progressives proposed attach-ing an income tax to a tariff bill. Conserva-tives pushed instead for a constitutional amendment thinking it would never pass but the strategy boomeranged.

1. The Congress shall have power to lay and collect taxes on incomes, from whatever source derived, without apportionment among the sev-eral States, and without regard to any census or enumeration.

2. Article I, sections 2 and 9.

Irrational Exuberance

Alan Greenspan, the Chairman of the Federal Reserve from 1987 to 2006, believed that markets would regulate themselves and acted accordingly. He championed deregulation of banks. We all know how that worked out.

He was grilled by Henry Waxman, chair-man of the Congressional Committee for Oversight and Government Reform in October, 2008 and admitted that he had been wrong in this view. "I found a flaw in the model that I perceived as the critical functioning structure that defines how the world works." Translation: Those Wall Street moochers didn't behave like they were supposed to.

Ask a cop how people do regulating themselves. Duh! I refer you to the *Deep Thought* on page 137: *Wisdom is knowing when smart people say dumb things.*

Requiem for the Middle Class

"There's class warfare, all right, but it's my class, the rich class, that's making war, and we're winning." Warren Buffet — The New York Times, November 26, 2006.

"The World is dividing into two blocs - the Plutonomy and the rest. The U.S., UK, and Canada are the key Plutonomies - economies powered by the wealthy. Continental Europe (ex-Italy) and Japan are in the egalitarian bloc."

This is from leaked Citigroup internal memos from 2005 and 2006. *Plutonomy: Buying luxury, Explaining Global Imbalances* and *Revisiting Plutonomy: The Rich Getting Richer* see the U.S. as a plutonomy, a society in which most of the wealth goes to an ever-shrinking minority, a race to the top.

According to the memos, the top 1% accounted For 20% of income*, 40% of financial wealth and 33% of net worth in the U.S. (more than the net worth of the bottom 95% of households put together) in 2001.

The memos reason that since the rich do most of the spending (they estimate that the top 20% did 60% of spending in 2005), investors should buy stocks of companies that sell to the rich. Citi put together a basket of "plutonomy stocks" of companies that cater to the wealthy. Tiffany, Coach, Porsche, Burberry, Sotheby's and Four Seasons Hotels are a few in the basket.

So what could go wrong? "At some point it is likely that labor will fight back against the rising profit share of the rich and there will be a political backlash against the rising wealth of the rich." That pesky one man one vote thing. But don't blame the messenger: "We should make clear that we have no normative view on whether plutonomies are good or bad. Our analysis is based on the facts, not what the society should look like."

(According to Deutsche Bank, 24% of luxury goods are bought by those middle-class Japanese egalitarians. The Japanese scrimp on other things to buy upscale status symbols. Since the 2011 earthquake and tsunami, they're in an austerity mindset and Japanese demand for luxury is expected to decline substantially for some time.)

Citigroup was bailed out in November 2008 with $50 billion and loan guarantees of over $300 billion. It paid it back by December, 2010, with a $12 billion profit to the taxpayers. Citigroup was kicked out of the Dow after the stock price fell to 97 cents in 2009. In 2011, a 10 to 1 reverse split instantly boosted the stock to over $40.

Legendary Marine Chesty Puller fed his troops from the bottom up, officers last. One Marine serving with him on Guadalcanal in 1942 groused that when he was with him in Nicaragua in the late 1920's the mules ate first, "and brother, them mules could eat!"

You'd think that those at the top of the financial heap would have learned this ancient lesson in leadership. Instead of agitating for lower taxes on their income, the wealthy should take care that they don't kill the goose that lays their golden nest egg so they'll still have a country to be rich in. I'm no dismal scientist, but it seems to me that everybody's income ultimately derives from the middle class and working stiffs buying stuff. We're the plankton in the economic food chain. If regular folks can't afford stuff, what will become of "plutonomy"? Indeed, what will become of us all?

* 24% by 2007. in 1915 it was 18%, rose to 23% by 1929, fell with the crash to 15%, then fell to under 10% from 1953 to the late 70's. Economists call this the "Great Compression". Ushered in by the New Deal, the rise of labor, and the GI Bill, it coincides with the golden era of the middle class in America. The subsequent rise in income inequality is called the "Great Divergence."

The Ninny Factor

Modern economic theories postulate that people are Homo Economicus, rationally acting in their own economic self-interest, balancing costs and benefits in light of the information they have.

Economics majors should be required to get a summer job in a store. Any business owner who deals with the public will tell you that, say, 20% of people are dingbats or doofuses, nincompoops or ninnies — "Keep your government hands off my Medicare." (See *The Ninny Factor* on p. 142)

Maybe that's why modern economic theories can't get us out of this mess because that includes 20% of the people who are trying to get us out of this mess, and the people who listen to the ninnies who got us into this mess.

Update on p. 236.

Where Have You Gone Ferdinand Pecora?

Remember those big-shot bankers being grilled on TV in January, 2010? That was the first hearing of The Financial Crisis Inquiry Commission that was set up as part of the Fraud Enforcement and Recovery Act of 2009. Its job was to find the dumb things that ruined the country and the dummies who did them.

This is actually round 2. We're having it because we forgot about round 1. Let's hope the second commission is as successful as the first one.

On April 11, 1932, the Senate Committee on Banking and Currency (now Banking, Housing, and Urban Affairs) opened hearings on the 1929 Wall Street Crash. Herbert Hoover was president and the Senate was controlled by Republicans.

The hearings dragged on for months to little effect as a series of ineffectual committee counsel allowed witnesses to dodge questions about stock manipulation, margin selling, stock pools, and other practices. After the latest counsel resigned in frustration, five others turned down the job but the last recommended Ferdinand Pecora, Assistant District Attorney for New York County.

Hired in January 1933 (at $255 a month) at the age of 51, Pecora was asked to write a report on the hearings but found there was nothing to write. Pecora asked for another month of hearings and new subpoenas.

The cigar-smoking, Sicilian-born Pecora was a relentless prosecutor and he forged ahead with the hearings, grilling the financial aristocracy like "banksters".

Against the backdrop of fresh bank runs and closures, Pecora cross-examined Charles Mitchell, Head of National City Bank (precursor to Citibank), about the risky securities it sold. Within six days he resigned.

JP "Jack" Morgan, son of Robber Baron JP Morgan, (the one with the bulbous red nose) was forced to disclose that he had paid no income tax in the previous three years and it came out that Chase Securities had financed "stock pools" to artifically inflate prices.

The hearings were a sensation. A senator accused Pecora of running a circus. As it happened, the Ringling Brothers circus was in town that June of 1933. A 21 (some say 27) inch tall midget named Lya Graf was spotted touring the Capitol. A reporter got her in to meet Morgan, saying "The smallest lady in the world wants to meet the richest man in the world!" Morgan shook her hand and when he sat down, a Ringling Brothers press agent picked her up and put her in Morgan's lap to the delight of photographers.

The hearings went on until June, 1934. Out of them came the Glass-Steagall Act of 1933*, The Securiities Act of 1933, and the Securities Exchange Act of 1934 that drastically changed the American financial system.

When President Roosevelt signed the Securities Exchange Act, he asked Pecora what kind of law it would be. "It will be a good or bad bill, Mr. President, depending upon the men who administer it", he answered.

Ferdinand Pecora was appointed one of the first commissioners of the SEC and later became a New York Supreme Court Judge. He wrote a book about the hearings, *Wall Street Under Oath*. Pecora died in 1971.

Lya Graf stayed with the circus for another two years, then returned to her native Germany. But she was Jewish — her real name was Furthmann. She was arrested in 1937 and sent to the Sachsenhausen concentration camp along with her family. In 1941 she and her parents were murdered in the gas chambers of Auschwitz .

*The Glass-Steagall Act created the Federal Deposit Insurance Corp. that guarantees your bank account, and separated commercial banks from investment banks and insurance companies. The act was partially repealed in 1999, an omen of the deregulation that led to the current financial unpleasantness. See *Rational Exuberance* on P.135

Treasure Hunt

Times are tough in Spain, too. Their budget is about $90 billion in the hole.

The good news is that they have $140 billion in gold and silver to cover it. The bad news is that it's at the bottom of the ocean.

When the Spanish blitzed the Incas and the Aztecs in the 16th century, they looted all the gold and silver and shipped it back to Spain. But a lot of the ships didn't make it. The Spanish government has ordered the navy to begin sonar surveys off the southern coast of Spain to locate the wrecks.

The First Bailout

Tis time, there must be a line of separation between honest men and knaves, between respectable Stockholders and dealers in the funds, and mere unprincipled Gamblers.

— Alexander Hamilton, March 2, 1792, writing about speculation that caused the Panic of 1792.

In the panic of 1792, stocks lost 25% in two weeks after the collapse of a speculative bubble in government bonds. Hamilton stemmed the panic by buying bonds, injecting liquidity into the financial system, foreshadowing modern practice.

In response to this, 24 stockbrokers gathered under a buttonwood tree at 68 Wall Street and signed an agreement establishing rules for trading stocks and bonds. This was the beginning of the New York Stock Exchange.

274 Message From the 1%

"I don't think the common person is getting it, Nobody understands why Obama is hurting them. We've got the message, But my college kid, the baby sitters, the nails ladies -- everybody who's got the right to vote -- they don't understand what's going on. I just think if you're lower income -- one, you're not as educated, two, they don't understand how it works, they don't understand how the systems work, they don't understand the impact." — Woman waiting in her Range Rover to get into a Romney fundraiser in Easthampton, Long Island as quoted in the Los Angeles Times July 8, 2012.

And for dessert — "Is there a V.I.P. entrance? We are V.I.P." asked a woman, also in a Range Rover, waiting in a 30 car line with the other V.I.P.'s to get into another Easthampton Romney fundraiser on the same day, as quoted in the New York Times.

Bulletin From the Department of Good and Evil

"The issue which has swept down the centuries and which will have to be fought sooner or later is the people versus the banks."

— Lord Acton (1834-1902) He was the one who said "Power tends to corrupt and absolute power corrupts absolutely," in a Letter to Cambridge ecclesiastical professor and later Church of England Bishop of London Mandell Creighton, 1887.

Joe's Bank &
FIRST NATIONAL JEWELRY

I lobbied intensely for the Jeweler Asset Protection Enterprise (JAPE) to be included in the bailout, but with no success, so I figured if I were a bank my odds might improve.

Announcing Joe's Bank and First National Jewelry!

Joe's Bank will lend you the money to buy jewelry from First National. Then Joe's Bank will bundle your loans and sell them as securities. Since your credit is so good, they should sell like hotcakes. The loan will just add a few extra bucks to your mortgage payment.

Then Joe's Bank will give a bridge* loan to First National until your loans are paid back. And if you buy so much you have trouble carrying it, a taxpayer will be available help you hold the bag.

As the CEO of Joe's Bank I'm especially looking forward to the $500,000 salary cap.

*It's in Brooklyn

I wouldn't presume to tell you how to run your business. That's because I don't know anything about your business.

But everybody knows all about retail.

People seem to think that spiffing up the town will end the Great Recession in Pompton Lakes. New sidewalks, quaint street lights — looking good! Shoppers on the way!

In the late 80's and early 90's, when the Pompton Lakes business district was thriving, Wanaque Avenue was dirty, the storefronts looked worse than today, there was no place to park, and traffic was so bad it took 10 minutes to cross the street. But business was good.

Business was good because the town was full of stores people wanted to shop in and people had money to spend. And so, shoppers came to town. Today, there are fewer stores, fundamental categories, such as clothing and gifts, are thinly populated, others are missing entirely, and people have less money to spend. And so, shoppers do not come.

Will a better ambience draw new merchants to open stores? Opening a store is a major big deal involving life savings or borrowed money, and lots of agita. The considerations are foot traffic, demographics (look at the cars), a diversity of other stores (and their answer to "How's business?"), rent, and parking, The ambience only matters if it is wonderful or terrible; in the middle it will neither attract nor deter merchants or customers.

Now, about that awesome-word title. Ultracrepidarianism means offering opinions and advice on matters outside of one's knowledge.

Roman author and naturalist Pliny the Elder (23-79 A.D.) tells a story about Apelles, a famous Greek painter of the late fourth century B.C. Apelles would put his paintings in public view and stand out of sight to listen to the comments. A shoemaker commented that a sandal on a figure in a painting was missing a loop. Then the shoemaker went on to criticize the leg wearing the sandal. Pliny writes that Apelles retorted "ne supra crepidam sutor judicaret." (The Latin translation from the Greek, I assume), literally "a shoemaker should not judge above the sandal." We would say "Stick to your knitting."

"Crepidam" is Latin for sandal (Greek "krepis"). Later Latin writers substituted "ultra" (beyond) for "supra" (above) in the Apelles quote. From that, William Hazlitt (1778-1830), an English essayist and critic coined "ultra-crepidarianism" and used it in a famously caustic 1819 letter to the editor of the Quarterly Review, the premier cultural and political journal of the day.

You probably know ultracrepidarianism in its common bilateral form, the political discussion.

Underwear Dept.

The Great Recession continues. Victoria's Secret's annual diamond bra has declined in price once again.

The 2010 Harlequin Fantasy Bra went for $3 million, down from the $5 million Black Diamond Fantasy Bra of 2009.

The 2011 Bombshell Fantasy Bra goes for a decidedly downmarket $2 million. The push up bra features 60 carats of diamonds and 82 carats of light blue sapphires and topaz all set in 18 karat white gold.The garment took 1500 hours of hand labor to make.

Them

Even though they know that the only thing that always goes up are home prices, people are always telling me that "they" say gold will go to $2000, $3000...whatever. So who are "they"?

If you got it from a TV ad, they're trying to sell you gold. What do you expect them to say?

If you heard it on the news, the odds of it coming true depends on the gravitas of the commentator.

If you got it off the Internet, you just stumbled into the wacky world of money becoming worthless, going back to the gold standard, and the collapse of civilization. (When that happens, your neighborhood warlord will take your gold away from you.)

But if you heard it in the beauty shop, it must be true.

Deep Thought
Bumper sticker slogans won't fix car wreck problems.

Debt for Dummies

"If Congress fails to raise the debt ceiling by $2.5 trillion that somehow the United States will go into default and we will lose the full faith and credit of the United States. That is simply not true."
— Minnesota Congresswoman Michele Bachmann July 13, 2011

The debt ceiling is raised to pay for stuff already bought. That's why there is a default, not paying the IOUs, if it isn't raised.

After months of posturing, Congress passed the debt ceiling increase on August 2, 2011. Three days later Standard & Poors downgraded the credit of the United States, saying that political brinksmanship had made governance and policymaking less stable, less effective, and less predictable.

"The Treasury has had to take extraordinary measures to allow the United States Government to continue to function normally as a result of the failure of the Congress to act. ....we must not imperil the full faith and credit of the United States Government and the soundness and strength of the American economy."
— George W. Bush June 25, 2002 in letters to Congressional leaders.

"The country now possesses the strongest credit in the world. The full consequences of a default — or even the serious prospect of a default — by the United States are impossible to predict and awesome to contemplate."
— Ronald Reagan, in a letter to Republican Senator Howard Baker, Senate majority leader, Nov. 16, 1983.

The debt ceiling was raised 18 times under President Reagan, 7 times under President Bush, and 5 times under President Obama. There have been 102 increases since 1917.

"As a very important source of strength and security, cherish public credit. One method of preserving it is, to use it as sparingly as possible; avoiding occasions of expense by cultivating peace, but remembering also that timely disbursements to prepare for danger frequently prevent much greater disbursements to repel it; avoiding likewise the accumulation of debt, not only by shunning occasions of expense, but by vigorous exertions in time of peace to discharge the debts, which unavoidable wars may have occasioned, not ungenerously throwing upon posterity the burthen, which we ourselves ought to bear."
— George Washington, Farewell Address, September 17,1796.

Debt for Dummies

"The War of the Rebellion brought new and extraordinary demands, and the debt went booming upward at the rate of more than a million and a half a day. On August 31, 1865, when the debt stood at its highest point, the outstanding principal was $2,844,549,626.56..."
— Handbook on Currency and Wealth, George Burnside Waldron, Funk and Wagnalls, 1896.

That's a little over $41 billion, $1171 per capita, adjusted for 14.49X inflation.

In 2015, the national debt was $58,437 per capita.

Gearing Up for the Next Crash

Since the start of the Great Recession, there has been a spike in Wall Street traders getting testosterone replacement therapy. 90% are in their 30's or 40's according to a doctor who gives the treatments.

Regaining your inner Gordon Gekko is the goal. "If you're going to be trading on Wall Street or dealing with large sums of money, you had better be confident. The man who is wishy-washy is not going to be successful," he said.

And between steaks you can nosh on Ruffles new manly potato chips. The ridges are twice as wide and deep so you can scoop up more manly amounts of dip. Choose from Sweet & Smokin' BBQ and Kickin' Jalapeno Ranch flavors.

Apocalypse Now

From a web site that rates gadgets, this is the lead-in to electronic gold testing machines:

"If you're planning to exist in a barren post-apocalyptic wasteland where food is scarce and gold is king, as I know many of you are, you had better make sure you have the capacity to test the purity of gold you encounter. Using your teeth just won't cut it. Which of these great gold purity testing electronic gadgets would you most want to trust your post-apocalyptic economy to?"

Irrational Exuberance

"Business Will be Fine in Nineteen-Twenty-Nine, This jingling product of one sloganwright's mind lightly expresses the conclusion which seems to be reached almost unanimously by the multitudinous authorities who have been engaged during recent weeks in predicting the business and industrial trend of the new year."
— The Literary Digest, January 19, 1929

"The depression in Wall Street will affect general prosperity only to the extent that the individual buying power of some stock speculators is impaired."
— November 9, 1929, quoting The New York Sun

"Unless all the economic experts are off their trolleys, the spring of 1930 will see a tremendous flood-tide of prosperity, because the slight depression of the fall of 1929 was due to lack of confidence rather than economic reasons."
— January 18, 1930, quoting The Emporia Gazette (Kansas).

Rational Exuberance

Financial Center's New Conservatism

"On Wall Street there are two principal kinds of bankers: commercial bankers and investment bankers. The commercial banks, such as Chase and National City, make loans, accept deposits, finance foreign credits, buy government and state bonds. They also usually have a trust department which executes wills and acts as trustee. The investment bankers, such as Morgan Stanley and Kuhn, Loeb underwrite and distribute new security issues for corporations. They also usually have a brokerage department which buys and sells securities."

"The Banking Act of 1933 made it illegal for one firm to act both as a commercial bank and investment banking house.* Until then the two were often combined. The 1929 crash exposed the dangers of these dual functions. With one hand banks were taking deposits. With the other hand they were financing new securities. When the businesses they were promoting failed, the depositors, security holders and the bank itself were in trouble."

"Today the very nature of Wall Street bankers has changed. In place of the speculators and market manipulators there are sound, deliberate investors who by choice and well as by law are more interested in government bonds than in a flier in the market. Their conservatism is reflected in their clothes, often imported from England, and in their offices, simple, high-ceilinged, fireplaced and deep in rugs."
— Life Magazine January 7, 1946

* This was the Glass-Steagall Act. Two sections that kept investment banks and commercial banks separate were repealed by the Gramm-Leach-Bliley Act in 1999 with bipartisan fanfare. This in itself didn't cause the Great Recession, but was a harbinger of the lax oversight that let slip the animal spirits of new banksters with new shenanigans to play havoc with other people's money, displacing those sound, deliberate investors, foretold at the time, below.

Rational Reluctance

"I think we will look back in 10 years' time and say we should not have done this, but we did because we forgot the lessons of the past, and that which is true in the 1930s is true in 2010. We have now decided in the name of modernization to forget the lessons of the past, of safety and of soundness."
— Senator Byron Dorgan (D-ND), November 4th, 1999, in debate on the Gramm-Leach-Bliley Act, also known as the Financial Services Modernization Act of 1999. (See footnote above.)

Message From the 1%

"If you destroy the leisure class you destroy civilization."
— J.P. Morgan Jr. testifying before the Senate Munitions committee*, February 4, 1936.

According to Morgan the leisure class are those who "can afford to hire a maid," "perhaps 30,000,000 families".

Unfortunately, there were then only 27,500,000 families of two or more persons in the U.S. according to the Columbia Daily Spectator February 7, 1936, citing census figures. The Spectator put the absolute minimum income to be able to afford a maid at $2500 ($42,550 in 2015). 20,000,000 families made less than that and "That leaves 7,500,000 families to save civilization."

*Special Committee on Investigation of the Munitions Industry headed by isolationist Senator Gerald Nye (R-North Dakota). The committee investigated allegations that greedy arms manufacturers pushed the U.S. into World War I and it contributed to U.S. isolationist policy between the wars. The Senate cut off funds to the committee after Nye overreached with an accusation that President Wilson had withheld information from Congress material to the declaration of war.

Work Ethic

"You work three jobs? Uniquely American, isn't it? I mean, that is fantastic that you're doing that."
— President George W. Bush to a divorced mother of three, Omaha, Nebraska, Feb. 4, 2005

274   Pocket Change

a 1996 law allows the Secretary of the Treasury to issue platinum coins in any denomination, unlike other coins whose denominations are specified by law.

This prompted some to suggest we could forestall the debt ceiling fight by minting a $1 trillion platinum coin and depositing it at the Fed. (The debt ceiling is raised to pay the bills for stuff already bought, not new spending.)

The idea of the platinum coin came from a 2009 article in the Wall Street Journal detailing how people took advantage of a free shipping offer from the U.S. Mint to buy $1 coins at face value. People bought the coins, in lots of 250, on a credit card that offered frequent flier miles. Then they deposited the coins in the bank and wrote a check to pay the credit card. Voila, free miles. People reported buying $10-15,000 in coins.

One fellow, "Mr. Pickles", bought $800,000 in coins, using several banks and credit cards. He said he had to bribe bank tellers with pizzas to deposit all those coins.

The Mint shut this practice down by processing the purchases as cash advances, which they literally are, rather than credit. Free miles were only for credit purchases.

Actually, I thought of this trick first. In The Debtor Strikes Back (p. 68) I showed you how to lower the interest rate on a credit card with the card's own balance transfer offer by paying off the balance with a loan check from another card, then paying off that card with the balance transfer offer of the first card.

Less More Money Than You Could Ever Spend

The Literary Digest January 27, 1934 reports in an article titled Vanishing Multi-Millionaire that tax return figures show a drop from 234 earning $1-1.5 million in 1929 to just 12 in 1932. The score for $5 million or over was 38-0. That, of course, was because of the Great Depression.

The number of million dollar earners peaked in 2007 at 392,220 and plunged to 236,883 in 2009 in the Great Recession. Those making $10 million and over fell from 18,394 to 8274 from 2007 to 2009 and $50 million from 151 in 2007 to 72 in 2009.

But a million bucks ain't what it used to be. $1 million in 1932 was worth $15.66 million in 2009 and $1 million in 2009 works out to about $64,000 in 1932.

H.R. Dept.

"The American people will not accept, and the House cannot pass, a bill that raises taxes on job creators"
— Speaker of the House John Boehner July 12, 2011.

I own a very small business, a Sub S corporation like many mom and pop operations. I only created one part-time job. But if I wanted to avoid higher taxes, I could invest in a tax deductible expense like new machinery or — gasp! — a new employee.

A caller on the Brian Lehrer Show July 12, 2011 summed it up with what should be obvious, saying, as an aside to the main discussion, that he was one of those small business "job creators" with 85-110 employees and in 35 years he had never hired or fired anyone because of taxes or tax rates. If business was good and he needed people to do the business, he hired them. If business was bad he would downsize by attrition or layoffs.

Consider that the unemployment rate in 1952 was 3% and the top tax rate was 92%. See Trickle Down Economics on p. 126.

Deep Thought

It is impossible to defeat an ignorant man in argument.

— William Gibbs McAdoo, Treasury Secretary 1913-18 (see Wall Street Closed on p. 111)

Politics!

Politics?

Hey! No talking politics in the store!

We're not in the store, we're in your living room. (Or, more likely, your bathroom.)

Resume

So who am I to give you my two cents? I only know what I read in the papers, same as you.

You can get two talking heads to learnedly contradict each other on any political subject. That's because they're trying to prove what they already believe *a priori**

The most blatant example of this is the late William F. Buckley's cri de coeur "A Conservative is a fellow who is standing athwart history yelling Stop!"

Wow! Wants to stop history! I don't think it worked. There's been a lot of history (and herstory, too, fellow) since 1955, over 60 years worth.

It's the same with think tanks. They come in two flavors: conservative and liberal. I picture them sitting up late at night getting tanked, thinking of ways to a prioritize all that history that didn't stop.

Why can't we have a think tank that thinks straight, not right or left? Factcheck.org is a good start.

I'm not a policy wonk, but I can spot *a priori* a mile away.

* That's a philosophy word. It means pulling it out of your ass because mommy and daddy beat it into your head.

Tell Me What You Want, What You Really Really Want

Conservatives. What do you want to conserve? The environment? Oops. That's conservationists.

Liberals. What do you want to liberalize? Freedom from government interference? Oops. That's libertarians.

Theory of Relativity

How do you know that politician who would ruin the country is left or right wing? Maybe he's in the center and you're out in left or right field.

Deep Thought
Wisdom is knowing when smart people say dumb things.

The Militant Moderate Manifesto

I am a Militant Moderate — be reasonable or else!

Here's the Militant Moderate credo:

The liberals exist to keep the Neanderthals from ruling the world.

The conservatives exist to keep the pointy-heads from ruling the world.

The liberals have the arts, education, and the media. The conservatives have business and the military. Sounds fair and balanced to me. For a Military Moderate Manifesto see note on p. 277.

Extremism in the defense of of moderation is no vice! Moderation in the pursuit of reasonableness is no virtue.

Moderates of the world unite!

Stem Cell Research

We'll see how you feel when you get that disease. Probably like Nancy felt when Ronnie got that disease. And hurry up. I hope it's just a cold I feel coming on.

You may choose from the following:

A. It's just cells they're going to kill anyway so it's ok.

B. It's a potential human, but they're going to kill it anyway, so it's the lesser of two evils.

C. It's a human and they shouldn't create it or kill it and when they find the cure, I'm going to turn it down and die.

Pro-Life

How do you feel about the 3 million Vietnamese we killed? (Why did we do that? I forget.)

Pro-Death

We have the death penalty because some people we can't live with. But there's been a problem killing the right people.

Gay Marriage

As long as they buy wedding bands, it's ok. Actually, it's none of my business. If your money's green, you're welcome in my store.* Live and let live. I don't understand how their family hurts your family. We have more important things to worry about.

*There are limits. I once refused to do business at a flea market with a guy wearing an SS pin.

Assisted Suicide

We'll see how you feel when you get that disease. When you've got to go, you've got to go. People have got death backwards. It's not the being there (there's no you there to know you're not here), it's the getting there.

Medical Marijuana

We'll see how you feel when you get that disease. If it didn't make you high, no one would care. Medicine is supposed to make you feel bad before it makes you feel good. One of the most laughable objections to it is that smoking it tars up your lungs, since you can eat it (remember Alice's brownies?) for the same effect.(it sends you to belly high).

It's a question of medical efficacy, not cultural phobia. Pot is a wussy drug compared to morphine, which is legal.

Health Insurance

"In the middle income class, a family may suddenly be stricken with a major illness, be staggered by a sickness bill of $200, $500 or more which may throw its modest budget out of line for years."

"At the moment, the whole subject of health insurance is highly controversial, is amazingly complicated by confusions, contradictions, disagreements, name-calling, internecine schisms and political jockeying."
— The Literary Digest January 30, 1937

We'll see how you feel when you get that disease. All talking heads who pontificate about health insurance should first be required to state what health insurance they have and what it costs them.* No one on Medicare or who works for any government with health insurance provided by taxpayers is allowed to comment.

National health insurance? Socialism! Social Security, socialized medicine for veterans and seniors, air traffic control, defense, education, mail delivery, police, garbage pickup, scientific research, and electricity in Tennessee are enough socialism! (Did I leave anything out?)

I know a couple for whom national health insurance isn't just socialism, it's communism! And their health insurance? It comes from the Veteran's Administration where the wife works as a nurse.

Another man I know who is against whatever socialism they're cooking up in Washington works at a state agency and gets health insurance courtesy of New Jersey taxpayers.

I'm haunted by a customer, solid middle class guy with a wife and kids, who had lost his job. Unemployed, he couldn't possibly afford the $1400 a month to COBRA his health insurance. And I've had desperate women sell their gold to buy medicine.

49.9 million people uninsured (2010 census) is why we had to have national health insurance. There's no going back, so stop the socialist name-calling and do whatever it takes to make it work, even if it makes Obama look good. We'll worry about what to call it later. (See the nomenclature dilemma in *Shirt-Waists are for Pantywaists* on p. 55.)

The New York Times August 24, 2009 profiled a 62 year old Georgia man, a quiet type, but who drove an hour to a town hall with his congressman to speak out against the health care proposals then gestating in Congress that would become the Affordable Care Act in March, 2010.

He said he feared a government takeover of health insurance and giving care to younger people first, making the elderly wait.

His wife had breast cancer and his employer-provided insurance paid for everything except for radiation treatments it considered experimental, leaving him with a $63,000 bill. Fortunately for them, the hospital wrote off the bill.

His employer pays his insurance premiums, but he has to pay $509 a month for his wife, which has been going up by 15% a year, while their deductibles have quadrupled. He realizes that if he loses his job, his wife's pre-existing condition might make her uninsurable.

He gets his information from Fox news, Rush Limbaugh, and the Drudge Report.

I'm sure the point of the Times article was to show that people can be convinced to vote against their own interests by partisan misinformation. (See *Truth to Tell* on p. 147.)

If you work for Uncle Sam, Doctor Sam will take care of you. The Federal Employees Health Benefits (FEHB) program lists 38 plans it approves. No fooling around with those exchanges, either: "If you are covered through the FEHB Program, you will not need a Marketplace plan." And the government will pay 72% of your premium.

Here are some of the benefits offered.
• Guaranteed coverage that your plan can't cancel *(Continued next page.)*

- No waiting periods, medical examinations or restrictions because of age or physical condition.
- Catastrophic protection against unusually large medical bills
- Continued group coverage into retirement or while you are receiving Workers' Compensation
- Continued group coverage for your family

The Affordable Care Act requires members of Congress and their staff to get health insurance from the exchanges. Most of them use DC Health Link, an exchange run by the District of Columbia. Over 600 plans are listed. The government still pays 72% of the premium.

The President and administration employees can still use the FEHB program.

* I'll lead off. I had to bend the rules to get a group plan for my business so I was the only active one in the group. It cost $382 a month (in 2007), about a third of the unaffordable cost to buy insurance as an individual. It was an HMO, so you had to hope that the only doctor who could cure that horrible disease you might get was in the book. Meds were 50% off, of what I don't know. But now I'm on Medicare (I told you I was an old guy), so you have pay for it. Thanks!

For Grownups of All Ages

On January 2, 2011, the House passed HR 2, *Repealing the Job-Killing Health Care Law Act,* introduced by Republican Majority Leader Eric Cantor.

Republicans claimed that the non-partisan Congressional Budget Office said that the Affordable Care Act* would result in the loss of 650,000 jobs.

Actually, the CBO said that the legislation would cause a small number people, one half percent, previously shackled to their jobs as the only way to get affordable health care, to retire or choose not to work.

Both Factcheck.org and Politifact called the job loss claim false.

Speaker John Boehner then one-upped Cantor by calling the health care law "job crushing."

The Senate blocked a vote on HR 2 on Feb. 5.

Cantor and Boehner were then spotted throwing spitballs at the President when Secret Service agents weren't looking.

* The "Obamacare" label was taken by opponents from a health care lobbyist's coinage of "-care" attached to each candidate's name in 2007 campaigning.

Freedom of Speech

I went to hear Noam Chomsky, the famous linguist and anti-war activist, speak at the University of Pennsylvania circa 1968. I was attending Penn after serving two years in Vietnam in the Air Force and I wanted to hear what he had to say.

Men walked up and down the aisles of the auditorium filming the audience. I involuntarily obscured my face with my hand. You know that expression "chilling effect"? That's what it means.

Right to Work

Employee's right to work. Makes it a Class A misdemeanor to require an individual to: (1) become or remain a member of a labor organization; (2) pay dues, fees, or other charges to a labor organization; or (3) pay to a charity or another third party an amount that represents dues, fees, or other charges required of members of a labor organization; as a condition of employment or continuation of employment.

— From Indiana HB 1001, signed into law by governor Mitch Daniels Feb. 1, 2012.

What a wimp! A macho governor would go all the way. Slavery — now that's business friendly!

Oh, right. The Henry Ford thing. We'll sell our stuff to the Chinese! They're slaves too? Oh, all right. Pay 'em $5 a day.

Deep Thought

If others tell you what is in your self-interest it is in their self-interest.

The Long and Short of It

"What happened to the Eighth Amendment [cruel and unusual punishment]? You really want us to go through these 2,700 pages?"
— Justice Antonin Scalia, March 28, 2012, the final day of oral arguments in National Federation of Independent Business v. Sebelius, which upheld the Obamacare individual mandate.

"In 2010, Congress enacted the Patient Protection and Affordable Care Act, 124 Stat. 119. The Act aims to increase the number of Americans covered by health insurance and decrease the cost of health care. The Act's 10 titles stretch over 900 pages ..."

— National Federation of Independent Business v. Sebelius, p.7.

Actually, you can read the act online, google Public Law 111-148 and you'll get a PDF of the law, all 906 pages.

So where did the 2700 page business come from? In order to pass some amendments to the act without a filibuster in the Senate, it had to be combined with a budget reconciliation bill, The Health Care and Education Reconciliation Act of 2010, that also had lots of other stuff in it like the Student Aid and Fiscal Responsibility Act attached as a rider.

I can understand opponents of Obamacare spreading the 2700 page lie, but you'd think Scalia would have known better, since the truth is written in his own 193 page document. Maybe not. He voted against the mandate.

Look at the law. The margins are 1½" on three sides and 2½" on one, 36 sq. inches, 62% of a page with 1" margins, so it would be 561 normal pages. And it's a law — everything has to be spelled out in detail with lots of annotations.

Mad Men

In a 2006 interview on All things Considered on NPR, Scott Sanders and Dennis Steele, the two most famous voices in political ads, demonstrated their talents, reading with menacing contempt.

Sanders: "Humpty Dumpty sat on a wall. He said he could put himself together again. But after wasting thousands of our tax dollars, all the king's horses and all the king's men, he failed us. Humpty Dumpty. Wrong on wall sitting. "

Steele: "London Bridge is falling down. Falling down, falling down. And who's the blame for withholding needed infrastructure funding? My fair lady. Take the key and lock her up. It's time for a change. "

Deep Thought
I believe that people would be alive today if there were a death penalty
— Nancy Reagan

Nut Country

Nelson Bunker Hunt* ran an ad in the Dallas Morning News on November 22, 1963. The ad headlined "Welcome Mr. Kennedy to Dallas", then went on to say "...we free-thinking and America-thinking citizens of Dallas still have, through a Constitution largely ignored by you, the right to adress our grievances, to question you, to disagree with you, and to criticize you. "

The ad went on to ask 12 questions such as:

• Why is Latin America turning either anti-American or Communistic, or both, despite increased U.S. foreign aid, State Department policy, and your own Ivy-Tower pronouncements?

• Why have you approved the sale of wheat and corn to our enemies when you know the Communist soldiers 'travel on their stomachs', just as ours do? Communist soldiers are daily killing and/or wounding American soldiers in South Viet Nam.

• Why did you host, salute and entertain Tito — Moscow's Trojan Horse — just a short time after our sworn enemy, Krushchev, embraced the Communist dictator as a great leader and hero of Communism?

• Why has Gus Hall, head of the U.S. Communist party praised almost every one of your policies and announced that the party will endorse and support your re-election in 1964?

• Why have you banned the showing of "Operation Abolition" — the movie by the House Committee on Unamerican Activites exposing Communism in America?

The ad concluded "Mr. Kennedy, as citizens of these United States of America, we DEMAND answers to these questions and we want them NOW." The ad was signed *The American Fact-Finding Committee*, "an unaffiliated and non-partisan group of citizens who wish truth."

Jack Kennedy read the ad in his hotel room that sunny morning of the last day of his life. "We're heading into nut country today", he said.

* See *Shootout at the Circle K Ranch* on p.170.

Propaganda Machine

"You want no Bolsheviki in your plant. The very thought of them makes shivers chase each other up and down your spine."

This is from an ad for Multigraph, an early office printing machine, in the January 25, 1919 Literary Digest. The ad goes on to explain that some methods used by management "are just the kind to turn intelligent, loyal honest workers into *Bolsheviki*." (Translation: join a union.)

This was the Red Scare era. The Soviet revolution had happened just 14 months earlier. The Bolsheviks* had signed a treaty with Germany ending Russian involvement in World War I and the Russian civil war was raging. U.S. and allied troops were sent to Russia in 1918 to restore the Eastern Front and defeat the Bolshevik army and Communism.

This was also the era of the rise of trade unions with strikes and labor unrest which was often conflated with Bolshevism. The Multigraph ad was part of a corporate effort to head off worker unrest by printing company newsletters "that tell your workers frankly what you're trying to accomplish and showing them you want their confidence and cooperation." "It will solve some of the labor problems that have worried you for months."

Multigraph had instituted a company union in 1918, an employee representation plan that was not a real union. Company unions were outlawed in 1935 by the National Labor Relations Act.

The Multigraph ad cleverly advanced anti-unionism and boosted its business at the same time by selling its machines to other companies.

* "Bolshevik" means majority in Russian. (Bolshoi means large.) The Bolsheviks won a fight over the editorial board of the party newspaper at the Second Party Congress in 1903 and claimed majority status thereafter. Menshevik means minority.

Freedom From Religion

When I went to elementary school in Pennsylvania, you had to take turns reading the Bible every morning (after the Lord's Prayer), at least 10 verses, by state law. You could choose between the New and Old Testaments, though, a concession to Jewish sensibilities, if not to Buddhists, Hindus, Moslems, Sikhs, etc.

The Supreme Court ruled in 1963 that this was an establishment of religion in violation of the First Amendment, since it takes place in a government facility (the school) and is conducted by government employees (the teachers).

The No Child Left Behind Act requires that schools that get funds allow prayer that is organized by the students out of class time, but on public property.

Your religion is none of my business, and I'd like to keep it that way. If you just wanted your kids to pray, you could get them up a minute earlier in the morning. But, of course, it's not about prayer, but the politics of religion.

Class Warfare

In one of the lavish party scenes in the 1974 movie *The Great Gatsby* with Robert Redford and Mia Farrow, the extras dressed as party guests started ordering around the extras dressed as waiters and waitresses between takes.

Message From the 1%

"We mean to have less of Government in business and more business in Government."

— Warren G. Harding

Message to the 1%

"There can be no effective control of corporations while their political activity remains. To put an end to it will be neither a short nor an easy task, but it can be done."

"I believe that the officers, and, especially, the directors, of corporations should be held personally responsible when any corporation breaks the law."

— Theodore Roosevelt, Osawatomie, Kansas, August 31, 1910

Mission Accomplished

"…major combat operations in Iraq have ended. In the battle of Iraq, the United States and our allies have prevailed."
— President George W. Bush aboard the aircraft carrier USS Abraham Lincoln May 1, 2003 with a Mission Accomplished banner behind him.

"To begin withdrawing before our commanders tell us we're ready would be dangerous for Iraq, for the region and for the United States. It would mean surrendering the future of Iraq to Al Qaida."

"It'd mean that we'd be risking mass killings on a horrific scale. It'd mean we'd allow the terrorists to establish a safe haven in Iraq to replace the one they lost in Afghanistan. It'd mean we'd be increasing the probability that American troops would have to return at some later date to confront an enemy that is even more dangerous."
— President Bush, White House news conference July 12, 2007.

President and CEO

Before you vote for the candidate who says successfully running a business is qualification to run the country, consider which presidents were most successful in business.

Herbert Hoover was a very successful mining engineer. He was worth $4 million in 1914, ($95 million in 2015). He was 40. (See *Message From the 1%* on p. 143.)

Warren Harding made a fortune in newspaper publishing. He sold his paper in 1923 for $550,000 ($7.6 million in 2015).

Jimmy Carter was a successful peanut farmer.

George H.W. Bush made money in the oil business with the connections of his father, Prescott Bush. George W. Bush didn't do so well with it.

The presidents who ran the largest organizations were Grant and Eisenhower.

Save Us From the Madness

"Have mercy upon us, oh God, and save us from the madness…Deliver us from the hypocrisy of attempting to sound reasonable while being unreasonable."
— Senate Chaplain Barry Black, prayer opening the Senate Session October 3, 2013, the third day of the 15 day government shutdown.

Deep Thought

Good principles make bad dogma

The Ninny Factor

Rep Robert Inglis (R-SC) reported that at a town hall meeting in Simpsonville in 2009, a man stood up and told him to "keep your government hands off my Medicare." Inglis said he politely explained "Actually, sir, your health care is being provided by the government, but he wasn't having any of it."

A 2011 Cornell University study showed that 44% of Social Security recipients, 40% of those on Medicare, 43% of people collecting unemployment benefits and 41% of veterans using the GI Bill say that they "have not used a government program."

Deficits for Dummies

George W. Bush's Treasury Secretary Paul O'Neill opposed a second round of tax cuts, saying to Vice President Cheney at a meeting of the Bush economic team in November, 2002 that they would cause unsustainable deficits and a fiscal crisis. The deficit then was already running at $158 billion.

"You know, Paul, Reagan proved deficits don't matter," Cheney replied "We won the midterms. This is our due."

O'Neill was fired a month later.

In fact, After a huge 1981 tax cut that slashed the top rate from 70% to 28%, Reagan then raised taxes 12 times during his two terms. Needless to say, this is easily verified. Tax increases are laws passed by Congress and signed by the President and are part of the public record.

Republican House Majority Leader Eric Cantor's press secretary Brad Dayspring denied that Reagan increased taxes, shouting from off camera "that just isn't true and I don't want to let that stand," during a 60 minutes interview Jan 1, 2012 with Cantor when Leslie Stahl brought it up.

Newspeak

"Political language…is designed to make lies sound truthful and murder respectable, and to give an appearance of solidity to pure wind."
— George Orwell, *Politics and the English Language* in Horizon, a British magazine, April, 1946.

Abstinence Only Sex Education
Teens will stop screwing. Ha!

Freedom from Religion
"Hold fast to the Bible. To the influence of this Book we are indebted for all the progress made in true civilization and to this we must look as our guide in the future."

"Leave the matter of religion to the family altar, the church, and the private school, supported entirely by private contributions. Keep the church and state forever separate."
— Ulysses S. Grant

Bye-Bye bin Laden
"God bless all the brave men and women in our military and our intelligence services who carried out a successful mission to bring Osama bin Laden to justice. We thank President Bush for having made the right calls to set up this victory."
— Sarah Palin May 2, 2011 Lakewood, Colorado

"We need to open the program today by congratulating President Obama. President Obama has done something extremely effective, and when he does, this needs to be pointed out."
— Rush Limbaugh May 2, 2011

"Thanks to George Bush, Because if Obama had gotten his way we wouldn't have gotten bin Laden, you know that."
— Sean Hannity Dec 9, 2011

"I do believe the President did a gutsy, good job on this"
— Bill O'Reilly May 3, 2011.

"So I don't know where he [bin Laden] is. Nor -- you know, I just don't spend that much time on him really, to be honest with you. I'm more worried about making sure that our soldiers are well supplied, that the strategy is clear, that the coalition is strong,…"
— President George W. Bush March 13, 2002

Sick Around the World
That's the title of a 2008 Frontline episode in which a correspondent with a bum shoulder went to 5 countries, The U.K., Japan, Germany, Taiwan, and Switzerland for treatment and reported on their health care systems. You can watch it online. It's an eye-opener
Nations with living standards comparable to ours spend a half to two thirds less per capita than we do and with better results, according to a Salon article March 9, 2009.

Bipartisanship
New York Times columnist Thomas Friedman took a trip down under in 2012.

"In New Zealand and Australia, you could almost fit their entire political spectrum — from conservatives to liberals — inside the U.S. Democratic Party."

A member of parliament from New Zealand's conservative National Party, once told a group of visiting American Fulbright scholars: "I will explain to you how our system works compared to yours: You have Democrats and Republicans. My Labor opponents would be Democrats. I am a member of the National Party, and we would be … Democrats as well."

Freedom From Religion
"Believing with you that religion is a matter which lies solely between man and his God, that he owes account to none other for his faith or his worship, that the legislative powers of government reach actions only, and not opinions, I contemplate with sovereign reverence that act of the whole American people which declared that their legislature should 'make no law respecting an establishment of religion, or prohibiting the free exercise thereof,' thus building a wall of separation between church and State."
— Thomas Jefferson, letter to the Danbury Baptists in Connecticut, Jan. 1, 1802

Message From the 1%
"If a man has not made a million dollars by the time he is forty, he is not worth much."
— Herbert Hoover

Message to the 1%
"We can have democracy in this country, or we can have great wealth concentrated in the hands of a few, but we can't have both."
— Justice Louis Brandeis (1856-1941), recounted in a eulogy by his friend Edward Keating in *Labor*, October 14, 1941.

Message to the 99%
"I Will Tell Off Your Boss for Free."
— Sign at an Occupy Wall Street demonstration.

Deep Thought
A fool and his money are soon elected — Will Rogers

Original Intent

The Supremes have decided that the force may be with you.

"A well regulated militia, being necessary to the security of a free State, the right of the people to keep and bear Arms, shall not be infringed." — Second Amendment.

"The right of the people to keep and bear arms shall not be infringed. A well regulated militia, composed of the body of the people, trained to arms, is the best and most natural defense of a free country..."
— James Madison, I Annals of Congress 434, June 8, 1789

Madison said in Federalist Paper 46 that a standing army could only have 25-30,000 men with the population of the country at that time, but that "To these would be opposed a militia amounting to near half a million of citizens with arms in their hands, officered by men chosen from among themselves, fighting for their common liberties, and united and conducted by governments possessing their affections and confidence. It may well be doubted, whether a militia thus circumstanced could ever be conquered by such a proportion of regular troops."

"What, Sir, is the use of a militia? It is to prevent the establishment of a standing army, the bane of liberty .... Whenever Governments mean to invade the rights and liberties of the people, they always attempt to destroy the militia, in order to raise an army upon their ruins."
— Rep. Elbridge Gerry of Massachusetts, spoken during floor debate over the Second Amendment, I Annals of Congress at 750, August 17, 1789

"A well regulated militia, composed of the body of the people, being the best security of a free state, the right of the people to keep and bear arms shall not be infringed; but no one religiously scrupulous of *bearing arms* shall be compelled to render *military service* in person." (Emphasis mine, see below.)
— Draft version of the Second Amendment sent by the House of Representatives to the United States Senate, August 24, 1789.

"In the absence of any evidence tending to show that possession or use of a 'shotgun having a barrel of less than eighteen inches in length' at this time has some reasonable relationship to the preservation or efficiency of a well regulated militia, we cannot say that the Second Amendment guarantees the right to keep and bear such an instrument. Certainly it is not within judicial notice that this weapon is any part of the ordinary military equipment or that its use could contribute to the common defense."
— United States v. Miller, Supreme Court decision 8-0, May 15, 1939

"The Second Amendment protects an individual right to possess a firearm unconnected with service in a militia, and to use that arm for traditionally lawful purposes, such as self-defense within the home."
— District of Columbia v. Heller, Supreme Court decision 5-4, June 26, 2008

The Second Amendment "has been the subject of one of the greatest pieces of fraud—I repeat the word 'fraud'—on the American public by special interest groups that I have ever seen in my lifetime."
— Warren E. Burger, conservative Chief Justice of the Supreme Court 1969-1986, MacNeil/Lehrer NewsHour, December 16, 1991.

The Heller decision states "The Amendment's prefatory clause announces a purpose, but does not limit or expand the scope of the second part, the operative clause." This, of course, is precisely the controversy about the Second Amendment. It's easy to win an argument if you assume the point at issue at the outset. This is called sophistry.

Do you remember your grammar school grammar? Or are you devoted to *forgetting* it? (*gerund*). Do you *refuse* to think about it? (*intransigent verb*). Is your head *spinning* yet? (*present participle*). All I remember is the admonition to never use a preposition to end a sentence with.

"A well-regulated militia being necessary to a free state" is a *nominative absolute*. A nominative absolute is a free-standing part of a sentence that modifies the whole sentence. The following examples only make sense if read as the nominative absolute part is the whole point of the other part. This is called strict construction.

The judge having ruled in our favor, we celebrated with a beer. (This Bud's for you.)

Common sense being necessary to the Supreme Court, Judge Judy should be nominated. (And speedy Justice Judy will decide three cases every half hour.)

Wisdom being necessary to the Justices, Yoda seek they should. (I feel a great disturbance in the Force.)

"To bear arms" means to serve in the military, see draft amendment above and also as noted in the Declaration if Independence: "He has constrained our fellow Citizens taken Captive on the high Seas to bear Arms against their Country,"

"The text is the law, and it is the text which must be observed."— Antonin Scalia, *A Matter of Interpretation*. Hmm...it says militia, it means militia.

So why did they put militias and the right to bear arms in the same sentence? Because you can't have B.Y.O.G. militias if the troops don't have guns to bring. Duh!

Anyhow, there are no more militias. The National Guard is not a militia. The Militia Act of 1903 consolidated the state militias into the present National Guard, which is formally part of the United States military.

It's not about guns. It's about what those slave-owning dead white guys said over 200 years ago in quaint English, from a vanished world of muskets and horses, quill pens and candles, about the balance of federal and state power.

Deep Thought
The Constitution, like the Bible, means whatever you want it to.

Proportional Response

"As President Obama indicated during the campaign, there are just a few gun related changes that we would like to make, and among them would be to re-institute the ban on the sale of assault weapons. I think that will have a positive impact in Mexico, at a minimum."
— Attorney General Eric Holder 2/25/2009

"Outrage tonight over claims the Obama administration is trying to weaken our rights under the Second Amendment. As we reported to you here yesterday, Attorney General Eric Holder is willing to sacrifice our gun ownership rights under the Constitution for the benefit of a foreign government, in this case Mexico. The attorney general, who apparently thinks we're a nation of cowards when it comes to race, seems to believe that we're also a nation of cowards and fools when it comes to our constitutional rights."
— Lou Dobbs on CNN 2/26/2009.

E Pluribus Unum

"When a company of New Jersey militia volunteers reported for duty to Washington at Valley Forge, the men initially declined to take an oath to 'the United States,' maintain-ing, 'Our Country is New Jersey.' Massachusetts Bay men, Virginians and others felt the same way. To the American of the 18th century, his state was his country, and his freedom was defended by his militia."
— Former Chief Justice Warren Burger, Parade Magazine, January 14, 1990

The Wild West

Ordinance No. 9, Tombstone, Arizona

"To Provide against Carrying of Deadly Weapons" (effective April 19, 1881).

Section 1. "It is hereby declared to be unlawful for any person to carry deadly weapons, concealed or otherwise [except the same be carried openly in sight, and in the hand] within the limits of the City of Tombstone.

Section 2: This prohibition does not extend to persons immediately leaving or entering the city, who, with good faith, and within reasonable time are proceeding to deposit, or take from the place of deposit such deadly weapon.

Section 3: All fire-arms of every description, and bowie knives and dirks, are included within the prohibition of this ordinance."

Weapons could be carried into town, but had to be checked at the Grand Hotel or the Sheriff's office.

In 1994, the Arizona state legislature passed a law allowing carrying concealed weapons, superseding the Tombstone Ordinance. In 2010, a new law allowed concealed carry without a permit.

Weapon of Convenience

You can bypass the metal detectors at the Texas State Legislature if you show a concealed carry permit, and many Texas lawmakers carry guns in their offices and even on the floor of the House or Senate.

Some journalists and lobbyists got the permits just to avoid the lines. They don't carry guns, they just carry the permits to speed their entry into the Capitol.

Own The Ultimate Weapon!

You have the right to bear arms.

Order your Acme atom bomb kit today! Militia membership included with purchase. Batteries not included. Some assembly required. Not sold in stores.

And remember — atom bombs don't kill people, people kill people.

— Ad in a gun magazine

Militant Immoderate

"I would remind you that extremism in the defense of liberty is no vice! And let me remind you also that moderation in the pursuit of justice is no virtue!"

— Senator Barry Goldwater, acceptance speech for the Republican presidential nomination, San Francisco, July 16, 1964.

"Dogmatic ideological parties tend to splinter the political and social fabric of a nation, lead to governmental crises and deadlocks, and stymie the compromises so often necessary to preserve freedom and achieve progress."

— Republican Michigan Governor George Romney in a letter to Barry Goldwater explaining why he did not endorse him, December 21, 1964.

Bundles for Congress

In January,1942, Congress voted pensions for itself along with other government employees. The country reacted not with howls of outrage, but with guffaws of laughter.

The Spokane, Washington Chamber of Commerce mounted a campaign of ridicule to get the Congressmen revoke their pensions.

The Chamber recruited the Spokane Athletic Round Table for the purpose (Bing Crosby was a member). The Round Table was famous for elaborate pranks. They came up with a Bundles for Congress campaign publicized in the Spokane Spokesman-Review.

The idea was a spoof of the recent Bundles for Britain campaign that sent care packages to Britons in the Blitz.

The Pittsburgh Post Gazette, February 5, 1942 summed up the sentiment: "What's the price of a bomber or two compared to the comfort of an ailing congressman who couldn't make the grade at election time? He's got to have aid."

Life Magazine March 2, 1942 showed pictures of some of the objects collected for Congressmen. "False teeth to help out hungry congressmen", an artificial leg with a sign "They haven't a leg to stand on!", onions with a sign "Let's all cry!", old tires and tubes, canes, crutches, umbrellas, and "old shoes, shirts, corset, long underwear, gloves, purse, hat, and wig."

The Round Table sent each member of Congress a "Coochie Bird", with a pinecone body and long bill with a tag that said "Here Comes Coochie" that told congressmen to "never worry about the war and taxes; get that pension first"; and "we're giving you the bird right now."

After collecting $3000 to truck 2000 packages of the oddball donations, the Round Table called off the drive and used the money to buy war bonds instead.

The Round Table's president Joe Albi told the New York Times on February 6, 1942 that "requests had poured in for the truck to be routed through everybody's home town," but that the organization knows when to end a joke and that the campaign had served its purpose in calling attention to the inappropriate Congressional pensions.

The joke worked. Congress repealed its pension two months after it passed it.

Today congressional pensions are about "2-3 times more generous than what a similarly-salaried executive could expect to receive upon retiring from the private sector," according to the National Taxpayers Union, as quoted by Snopes.

Diplomacy

"If I said to my wife, 'You have a face that would stop a thousand clocks,' that would be stupidity. But if I turned to her and said, 'Dear, when I behold you, time stands still,' that's diplomacy!"

— Everett Dirkson, Republican Senator from Illinois 1951-1969. The quote "A billion here, a billion there, pretty soon it begins to add up to real money", is ascribed to him.

Please read the next 3 articles, *The N Word, Truth to Tell,* and *The big Lie* in sequence.

274   The N Word

"Adolf Hitler, like Barack Obama, also ruled by dictate."
— Rush Limbaugh, Aug. 6, 2009

"I want to put it to you bluntly. What they are attempting to do in health care, particularly in treating the elderly, is not something like what the Nazis did. It is precisely what the Nazis did."
— Richard Land, keynote speaker for the 20th anniversary "God and Country Banquet" of the Christian Coalition of Florida, Sept. 26, 2009. Land is president of the Ethics and Religious Liberty Commission of the Southern Baptist Convention. He was appointed by George Bush to the U.S. Commission on International Religious Freedom, a federal agency.

"The secular socialist machine represents as great a threat to America as Nazi Germany or the Soviet Union once did."
— Newt Gingrich in his book, *To Save America.*

"George Soros admitted on TV to have collaborated with the Nazis."
— Anne Coulter, to Sean Hannity Oct 15, 2009.

Soros was 13 when the Nazis invaded Hungary in March, 1944. Soros' father, a Jew, paid a Christian Hungarian official to take in Soros as his godson. Soros had to accompany his phony godfather as he made his rounds confiscating property from Jews. Soros told this story on 60 Minutes.

"The Bush administration and the Nazi and Communist regimes all engaged in the politics of fear...Indeed the Bush adminstration has been able to improve on the techniques used by the Nazi and communist propaganda machines by drawing on the innovations of the advertising and marketing industries."
— George Soros, The Age of Fallibility, p. 84-85.

"It's Not Too Late for Father's Day!" Zazzle.com lists 457 items as "Nazi Obama Gifts": T-shirts, bags, bumper stickers, and a skateboard with pictures of Obama in a Nazi uniform at $59.95.

Godwin's Law: As an online discussion grows longer, the probability of a comparison involving Nazis or Hitler approaches 1.

Note: A Google search for "Bush Nazi" turned up assorted citizen wing-nuts and B-list celebrities, but no well-known commentators. An exhaustive lisiting of Bush/Nazi comparisons is at semiskimmed.net/bushhitler.html.

274   Truth to Tell

House proposal that Medicare pay for end of life counseling with a doctor, dropped from the final health care reform law,The Patient Protection and Affordable Care Act:

From Section 1233, "Voluntary Advance Care Planning Consultation," of HR 3962:

CONSTRUCTION.--The voluntary advance care planning consultation described in section 1861(hhh) of the Social Security Act, as added by subsection (a), shall be completely optional. Nothing in this section shall --

(1) require an individual to complete an advance directive, an order for life sustaining treatment, or other advance care planning document;

(2) require an individual to consent to restrictions on the amount, duration, or scope of medical benefits an individual is entitled to receive under this title; or

(3) encourage the promotion of suicide or assisted suicide.

"The America I know and love is not one in which my parents or my baby with Down Syndrome will have to stand in front of Obama's 'death panel' so his bureaucrats can decide, based on a subjective judgment of their 'level of productivity in society,' whether they are worthy of health care. Such a system is downright evil."
— Sarah Palin, in a message posted on Facebook Aug. 7, 2009.

"We should not have a government program that determines if you're going to pull the plug on grandma."
— Iowa Senator Chuck Grassley at a town hall meeting, August 12, 2009.

"...a spokesman said the Senator [Grassley] does not think the House provision would in fact give the government such authority in deciding when and how people die."
— The Washington Post, August 15, 2009

"...my husband has a pacemaker. And he was told last year when he got it that: If Obamacare health care passes, this would have to go to a committee, and, with all your other existing health problems, they will decide whether this pacemaker would be cost-effective. And I can almost guarantee you, you wouldn't get it."
— Dee Williams, a Florida retiree, in a panel discussion moderated by Gwen Ifil on the PBS NewsHour, April 13, 2010

"If you don't stop Medicare, one of these days you and I are going to spend our sunset years telling our children and our children's children what it once was like in America when men were free."
— Ronald Reagan, from a 1961 LP record recorded for the AMA. 3000 copies of "Ronald Reagan Speaks Out Against Socialized Medicine " were distributed across the country for use in Operation Coffeecup, coffee-klatches organized by the Women's Auxiliary of the AMA. The Reagan record was played at the gatherings.

Medicare was signed into law on July 30, 1965 by President Johnson in Independence, Missouri, with President Harry Truman attending. President Johnson enrolled President Truman as the first Medicare beneficiary and presented him with the first Medicare card. Truman had proposed a national health care program in 1945.

The Big Lie
"In the big lie there is always a certain force of credibility; because the broad masses of a nation are always more easily corrupted in the deeper strata of their emotional nature than consciously or voluntarily; and thus in the primitive simplicity of their minds they more readily fall victim to the big lie than the small lie, since they themselves often tell small lies in little matters but would be ashamed to resort to large-scale falsehoods.

It would never come into their heads to fabricate colossal untruths, and they would not believe that others could have the impudence to distort the truth so infamously. Even though the facts which prove this to be so may be brought clearly to their minds, they will still doubt and waver and will continue to think that there may be some other explanation. For the grossly impudent lie always leaves traces behind it, even after it has been nailed down, a fact which is known to all expert liars in this world and to all who conspire together in the art of lying."
— Adolf Hitler, *Mein Kampf*, vol. I, ch. X

I Pledge Allegiance
At a signal from the principal the pupils, in ordered ranks, hands to the side, face the flag. Another signal is given; every pupil gives the flag the military salute—right hand lifted, palm downward, to a line with the forehead and close to it. Standing thus, all repeat together, slowly; *"I pledge allegiance to my flag and the republic for which it stands; one nation indivisible, with Liberty and Justice for all."* At the words "to my flag," the right hand is extended gracefully, palm upward, towards the flag, and remains in this gesture till the end of the affirmation; whereupon all hands immediately drop to the side. Then, still standing, as the instruments strike a cord, all will sing America—"My Country 'tis of Thee;" or "The Red, White, and Blue."
— The Public School Journal, October, 1892

This was part of the ceremony of the National School Celebration of Columbus Day, October 21, 1892 celebrating the 400th anniversary of the arrival of Christopher Columbus in the new world and timed to coincide with the opening of the World's Columbian Exposition (Chicago World's Fair). (Note the original wording of the Pledge of Allegiance, italicized.)

The description of the salute to the flag with extended arm was provided by Francis

Bellamy (1855-1931), author of the Pledge of Allegiance, in August, 1892. It was published in *The Youth's Companion*, a children's magazine, in September,1892. James Upham, editor of the magazine, had suggested the the salute to Bellamy.

Upham and Bellamy got President Benjamin Harrison to proclaim October 12, 1892 as Columbus Day. Schools across the country held flag raising ceremonies with the recitation of the Pledge and the salute.

An April 13, 1942 article in Life Magazine shows an assembly at Will Rogers High School in Tulsa, Oklahoma in the Bellamy salute with hands palm-up, correctly, but photos of school children show many of them saluting palm down which unfortunately resembled the fascist salute. The fascist salute originated independently and was not copied from the Bellamy salute. Congress amended the flag code in December, 1942 to substitute the hand-over-the-heart for the Bellamy salute.

Francis Bellamy was a Baptist minister and a Christian Socialist. He was dismissed from his Boston church in 1891 for his socialist sermons. Even today he is reviled as a socialist:

"...the Pledge was designed by an avowed socialist to encourage greater regimentation of society," according to Gene Healy, a vice-president of the libertarian Cato Institute in a 2003 article. After reviling Bellamy for being a socialist, he anachronistically reviles him for being a fascist:

"Bellamy's recommended ritual for honoring the flag had students all but goosestepping their way through the Pledge."

"Under God" was added to the Pledge in 1954 after President Eisenhower heard a sermon by Presbyterian pastor George MacPherson Docherty advocating it. The Ninth Circuit Court of Appeals ruled "Under God" constitutional under the Establishment Clause in 2010. The Massachusetts Supreme Court of ruled it constitutional under the Equal Protection Clause in 2014.

This May, 1942 photograph by famed Navy photographer Charles Fenno Jacobs shows schoolchildren in Southington, Connecticut in the salute with most hands palm down. This is a famous photo and is shown reversed on many web sites which makes it look like the children have their left hands raised. The one I used was reversed but the clearest. I flipped it in Photoshop.

Romney Flunks Make-up Exam

"I have said that when it comes to preventing Iran from obtaining a nuclear weapon, I will take no options off the table, and I mean what I say. That includes all elements of American power: A political effort aimed at isolating Iran, a diplomatic effort to sustain our coalition and ensure that the Iranian program is monitored, an economic effort that imposes crippling sanctions and, yes, a military effort to be prepared for any contingency.

Iran's leaders should understand that I do not have a policy of containment; I have a policy to prevent Iran from obtaining a nuclear weapon. And as I have made clear time and again during the course of my presidency, I will not hesitate to use force when it is necessary to defend the United States and its interests."
— President Obama, address to the American-Israel Public affairs Committee (AIPAC) Policy Conference Washington, D.C. March 4, 2012, 11:10 - 11:42 A.M.

"This is a president who has failed to put in place crippling sanctions against Iran. He's also failed to communicate that military options are on the table and in fact in our hand, and that it's unacceptable to America for Iran to have a nuclear weapon."
— Mitt Romney, Snellville Georgia, March 4, 2012, 1:09 P.M.

Sanctions choke off Iran oil output

Iran's oil production has fallen to a 10-year low and could drop to levels last seen during the Iran-Iraq war in the 1980s as sanctions over its nuclear programme disrupt an industry already suffering from years of underinvestment....

Tehran's oil output had already been in long-term decline as previous US sanctions deterred foreign oil companies from investing, starving Iran of the technology needed to boost its flagging production.
— Financial Times, March 14, 2012.

If you're going to make shit up, you've got to do better than this. Jabberjockey Mitt gyres and gimbles again, the slithy tove! In case time has marched on by the time you are reading this, Romney was the Republican candidate running against President Obama in 2012. "Severe conservative" Romney said that 47% of people are moochers, corporations are people, that as president he would create jobs and that government doesn't create jobs in the same evening, wanted to shoot Big Bird, and called for the repeal of Obama's health care law that was pretty much the same thing he set up as governor of Massachusetts. He lost. His father made more sense. See *Militant Immoderate* on p. 146.

Tabula Rasa

Get out a blank sheet of paper and write down your political views. Let me know if you get more than a page of platitudes and propaganda — keep the country safe, stop illegal immigration, end a war, start a war, tax that fellow behind the tree, etc.

That's about all you're going to get because you're not in the political business. Neither am I. That's why there's 28 pages of political business and 252 pages of other business.

But I have a pretty good crap detector.

Most crap has one of two characteristics: an attempt to prove an a priori belief or an argument assuming the point at issue.

The first leads to cherry-picking or distorting facts. The counter is to challenge the facts and ask their source. The second only works if the respondent buys into the argument and tries to counter the logic instead of the premise.

And do your homework. Don't just spout some talking point you heard somewhere. As you can see, I research everything I write in depth. I stick with reputable sources and cross-check everything. I burrow deep into old newspaper and magazine articles and book excerpts.

Discussing the new president with a long-time customer, I mentioned that he was the president of the Harvard Law Review. He indicated that this was a result of some sort of affirmative action program. If he had done his homework, he would have learned that the Review is an independent student organization. Half the editors are chosen for their grades and half by students in a writing competition. Obama was elected president of the Review by the 80 other student editors.

Oh, and everybody is as patriotic as you and loves freedom, capitalism, truth, justice, and the American way just as much as you do. Mom and apple pie, too

The War to End All Wars

"We began the war a year too soon. When we have secured a German peace we must begin at once a reorganization upon a broader and firmer basis than ever before. Establishments that produce raw materials essential to the Army must not only continue their work, but enter into it upon lines of increased energy, forming thus the kernel of economic Germany in preparing in the economic sense for the next war."

— Walther Rathenau, in the *Berlin Lokal Anzeiger* as quoted in The Literary Digest, January 13, 1917.

Walther Rathenau was a German industrialist, son of the founder of a large electrical engineering company. Although Jewish, he was an ardent German nationalist. He became Foreign Minister of the Weimar Republic. He was assassinated in 1922 by an anti-semitic secret organization, Organization Konsul. His two assassins committed suicide when cornered in a castle turret.

"Konsul" was called "the most sinister of all the German secret societies", in a Literary Digest article May 5, 1923 titled *Secret Orders and Murders in Germany*.

The article features a photo of uniformed men carrying a swastika flag captioned *A "Hitler-Guard" on the March. This German organization is said to be one of forty or fifty similar secret "bunds" who are the greatest present danger to Germany, Europe, and the peace of the world.*

The Rathenau assassination was commemorated annually by the Weimar Republic. Schools and streets were named for him. When the Nazis took power, they systematically erased all public traces of him while carrying out his *Deutschland über alles* policies. A memorial stone was placed on the grave of his assassins in 1933 by Hitler.

Show, Don't Tell

If Fox news has to tell you they're fair and balanced, they're not. They should have stuck with the Simpsons. Now that's fair and balanced: it socks it to everyone.

I like BBC radio. That Owen Bennett Jones takes no prisoners.

Popular Opinion

"'Republicans being against sex is not good,' GOP strategist Alex Castellanos told me mournfully. 'Sex is popular.'"

— Columnist Maureen Dowd, The New York Times February 26, 2012.

Organized Propaganda

"Washington has seldom seen so numerous, so industrious, or so insidious a lobby. The newspapers are being filled with paid advertisements calculated to mislead the judgement of public men not only, but also the public opinion of the country itself. There is every evidence that money without limit is being spent to sustain this lobby..."

— President Woodrow Wilson, statement to the press, May 26, 1913.

Hold Lobby Exists, But Of A New Kind
It's the Organized Propaganda, Say Senators, Justifying Wilson's Charges
— The New York Times, June 6, 1913.

Wilson charged lobbies with trying to influence the tariff bill of 1913. Tariffs, duties on imported goods, were the primary source of revenue for the government at that time, providing 44% of the budget in 1913.

There was a long list of dutiable goods with different rates and many exempt products. Sugar, cotton, liquor, wool, and many other interests were vitally interested in tariff rates.

Wilson made a special joint appearance before Congress in April and spoke before a packed House about the need for tariff reform. Press coverage of his lobbying charge resulted in the public demanding reform.

North Carolina Senator Lee Slater led a Judiciary subcommittee that found unparalleled lobbying influence seeking to undermine Wilson's tariff reforms, the first reduction of the tariff since the Civil War. The rationale was to give consumers a break and make business more competitive.

To make up for the lost revenue, the Underwood-Simmons Tariff Act also instituted the first income tax pursuant to the 16th Amendment just ratified that February (see *Spreading the Wealth* on p 129).

Big Brother is Tweeting You

The CIA opened a twitter account.

• We can neither confirm nor deny that this is our first tweet..

• No, we don't know your password, so we can't send it to you.

• Remember reports of unusual activity in the skies in the '50s? That was us.

• Knife skills are important! — Oops, that was from the Culinary Institute of America.

Silly Syllogism

The February, 2010 record snowstorms in the Northeast were proof enough to Sean Hannity that global warming was a hoax thought up by Al Gore.

Hmm. We had record snow. Snow is cold, therefore we had record cold so the world isn't getting warmer. You flunk logic 101.

We got buried in New Jersey, but it wasn't particularly cold. Doesn't global warming predict more precipitation and bigger storms, winter and summer?

People don't "believe" in global warming because they don't want to hear it for poltical or tempermental reasons. Of course, science is true whether you believe it or not. Since you don't want to have an ultracrepidarian opinion (p.133), here's your science lesson.

99% of carbon is carbon 12, 1% is carbon 13, with an extra neutron. Plants preferentially take up carbon 12. The carbon 12/13 ratio has increased .15% since the start of the industrial age, 5 times the natural variability of .03%, which is known from analyzing CO_2 from air bubbles in ice cores and the carbon in tree rings, which can be precisely dated. (Although enriched in carbon 12, tree rings still mirror the relative changes of carbon isotopes in the atmosphere.)

Fossil fuels are ancient plants, so an increase in the carbon 12/13 ratio in atmospheric CO_2 can only be explained by burning material enriched in carbon 12.

Also, radioactive carbon 14 is created by bombardment of nitrogen atoms in the atmosphere by cosmic rays. The amount is minuscule, only 1 carbon atom in a trillion, but enough so that there is some of it in every plant. This is the basis of carbon dating. The half-life of carbon 14 is about 5700 years. Coal, oil, and gas are so old, tens or hundreds of millions of years, that all the carbon 14 has long decayed away. The Carbon 14/12 ratio has been decreasing as would be expected from burning fossil fuels.

The formation of CO_2 consumes two atoms of oxygen, which has decreased by about .095% since the pre-industrial era.

CO_2 has a radiative forcing of 1.66 watts/m², a measure of its ability to trap heat from the sun, over half the 2.64 w/m² total for all greenhouse gases.

Believe it or not!

Back to the Future

The Georgia Railroad strike of 1909, the "Race Strike", began after the railroad replaced 10 white firemen paid $1.75 a day with 10 blacks paid $1.25. The white firemen's union struck, closing the railroad.

There was violence when the railroad attempted to break the strike with trains with black firemen. The railroad asked Governor Hoke Smith to call out the militia for protection, but he declined.

After two weeks, arbitration settled the strike with equal pay for all firemen. The union believed that equal pay would cause the railroad to preferentially hire whites, but black firemen remained.

An eerily prescient article about the strike was in the June 5, 1909 edition of The Literary Digest with the headline *New Kind of Race War in Georgia*.

"Whatever the immediate result of the strike of white firemen against the employment of Negro firemen on the Georgia Railroad, many keen observers see in it, as the New York Globe remarks, 'the first skirmish of a new kind of conflict between the white and colored races, a conflict that may bring new evils to both blacks and whites in the South.'"

Prescience

"I made the visit deliberately, in order to be in a position to give first-hand evidence of these things if ever, in the future, there develops a tendency to charge these allegations merely to 'propaganda.'"
— General Dwight D. Eisenhower, letter to General Marshall, April 15, 1945. Eisenhower had toured the Ohrdruf concentration camp near Gotha on April 12.

"In the councils of government, we must guard against the acquisition of unwarranted influence, whether sought or unsought, by the militaryindustrial complex. The potential for the disastrous rise of misplaced power exists and will persist.

We must never let the weight of this combination endanger our liberties or democratic processes. We should take nothing for granted. Only an alert and knowledgeable citizenry can compel the proper meshing of the huge industrial and military machinery of defense with our peaceful methods and goals, so that security and liberty may prosper together."
— Eisenhower, farewell address to the nation, January 17, 1961.

Word Barf

"If you can't explain what you're doing in plain English, you're probably doing something wrong."

This quote is from a celebrated memo to his staff by economist Alfred E. Kahn, then head of the Civil Aeronautics Board, in 1978.

This salvo in the war on bureaucratic gobbledygook was published in the Washington Post, got Kahn a marriage proposal from a Boston Globe columnist, a vote for a Nobel Prize from a Singapore newspaper, and a nomination for President from a Kansas City newspaper.

Shortly after the memo, Kahn was appointed to the Usage Panel of the American Heritage Dictionary, a position he held to his death in December, 2010 at 93.

Kahn was known as the "father of airline deregulation" and was President Carter's "Inflation Czar".

The cause of plain speaking has been taken up by Elizabeth Warren. Warren is a Harvard law professor, defender of the middle class (that's us!), special advisor to the President who set up the new Consumer Financial Protection Bureau, and was elected Senator from Massachusetts in 2012.

She characterized the legalese in consumer financial contracts for credit cards, mortgages, etc. as "word barf."

Deduct One Capitalist

That was the title of an article in Life Magazine Nov. 14, 1949 that told of the friend of one of the staff "a rich Wall Streeter, who is forever announcing that somebody ought to do something about the Communists. Outlaw 'em, jail 'em, get 'em out of Washington, send 'em back to Russia, etc. etc."

When he was asked to contribute to an anti-Communist candidate in a race the Communists were contesting, he hemmed and hawed and finally asked if if he could deduct it from his income tax.

"When the Communists take over Wall Street, we'll know why."

The First Law of Political Dynamics

The amount of energy necessary to refute bullshit is an order of magnitude bigger than to produce it.

— Computer programmer Alberto Brandolini

Anyone Got Raid?

Animal Planet has a variety of cutesy animal cams: kittens, penguins, wild birds, butterflies....you can watch the natural behavior of over 11 species live 24/7.

But you'll go from aaaw to eeew, with the newest addition: cockroach cam, cockroaches doing the roach thing in a roach motel kitchen. Cockroach cam is sponsored by Orkin exterminators, of course.

Cockroach cam should not be confused with C-SPAN. With just a 9% favorability rating, Congress ranked lower than cockroaches in a January, 2013 poll by Public Policy Polling.

Congress was rated for favorability against 26 different things. Head lice beat Congress 67-19, colonoscopies, 58-31, and Brussels sprouts, 69-23. Cockroaches edged out Congress 45 to 43.

On the plus side, Congress beat telemarketers 45-35, Lindsay Lohan 45-41, and trounced the ebola virus 53-25.

The Proper Role of Government

"...I do not believe that the power and duty of the general government ought to be extended to the relief of individual suffering which is in no manner properly related to the public service or benefit."

"...though the people support the government, the government should not support the people."

— Grover Cleveland, vetoing the Texas Seed Bill, which appropriated $10,000 ($245,000 in 2015) to help drought-stricken Texas farmers in 1887. Cleveland was a Democrat. Cleveland is the face on the thousand dollar bill.

Big Brother

"If you want to keep a secret, you must also hide it from yourself."

— George Orwell, 1984.

The leak about the NSA collecting metadata (who you called, not what you said) about your phone calls and emails has caused a spike in sales of 1984, George Orwell's 1949 dystopian novel of an all-controlling government where Big Brother knows everything you do, say, and think.

A June, 2013 Rasmussen poll found that 68% of people believe that the government is listening to their phone calls.

Big Brother knows you bought 1984, too.

Religion

Oy! Worse than politics.

I am a militant agnostic. It's unknown. It's unknowable*. What's for lunch?

How liberating! Now you don't have to worry about how many angels can dance on the head of a pin, if his holy book is holier than thine, have to do this, can't eat that.... No one knows, so why spin your wheels?

Acceptance of divine mystery is, I have heard, the hallmark of spiritual maturity. I just cut out the middlebeing and get my mystery directly. Occam's razor shaves God's beard.

Now that you don't have to worry about what it's all about, you're a naive realist, like your dog: it is what it is.

The fundamental mystery is that there is anything at all. To be or not to be. Let me know when you figure that one out.

Amen.

* Unknowable is the militant part:

Epistemology 101

Creationism is not worthy of comment, but if you feel compelled to debate people who have painted themselves into a logical corner with a priori beliefs, try this.

Evolution is just a theory, not a fact. Theories are explanations of facts, and can't logically become facts, except in a theory about theories. The fossils are the facts. Evolution is the explanation. Ask what facts support the biblical theory of creation. God said it doesn't count. (It's a circular argument.)

Irreducible complexity. There's no way to know if something is irreducibly complex and therefore could not have evolved incrementally. To assert it assumes the point at issue, that it can't be explained, which doesn't mean that only God could have done it. This is a logical fallacy called an argument from ignorance.

For people of the Flintstones school of paleontology, tell them to hop on their dinosaurs and go back to their caves.

God Only Knows

My town [West Milford] voted to allow holiday religious displays on public property, all comers allowed — the no establishment of religion thing.

The town put up the standard pagan "Holiday tree" in front of the municipal building with no religious ceremony. A resident pushed to have it officially called a "Christmas tree", but the town council declined.

A rabbi agreed. Instead of ecumenically christening it a Hanukkah bush, he asserted that it was a Christian symbol and put up a menorah, which he said was not a religious symbol but a universal symbol of freedom and light.

Then the Christians put up a nativity scene. The infidels trumped that with a 2 x 9 foot billboard with the three wise men, the nativity scene and Star of Bethlehem (6 pointed version) saying "*You KNOW it's a Myth. This Season Celebrate REASON!*" The billboard was promptly desecrated in the dead of night, either by an ill wind or sacreligionists unknown.

You never see agnostic billboards. Vigorously asserting that it can't be asserted comes off wimpy: *It May or May not be a Myth!*

God Only Knows sounds better.

Dobson, Falwell, Robertson, et al.

Gentlemen of the anal persuasion. Keep your religion in your pants.

Hmm....O'Reilly, Sharpton, Coulter, Limbaugh, Rosie O'Donnell, The Donald, and Congressman Joe Barton. (He's the asshole who apologized to BP for the oil spill fines.) 277

My Friends Across the Aisle

The Federalists opposed the Louisiana Purchase fearing it would dilute the power of the original 13 states. Of course they were denounced in papers friendly to Jefferson and his Democratic-Republican Party

The Gettysburg Gazette, August 5, 1803 calls out those darn Federalists "...for the systematic violations of truth which characterise the opponents of the administration." and for denouncing Robert Livingston, the minister to the Court of Napoleon in France, "solely to furnish an occasion to revile the President and to repress that sentiment of gratitude and admiration which an enlightened nation will ever pay to the successful execution of great talents."

Deep Thought
The Bible, like the Constitution, means whatever you want it to.

Not Many Crooks in Congress

So said David S. Barry, Sergeant-at-Arms of the Senate in an article titled *Over the Hill to Demagoguery* in New Outlook[1], February, 1933:

"Contrary, perhaps, to the popular belief, there are not many crooks in Congress, that is, out and out grafters, or those who are willing to be such; there are not many Senators or Representatives who sell their vote for money, and it is pretty well known who those few are; but there are many demagogues of the kind that will vote for legislation solely because they think that it will help their political and social fortunes." He cites as examples of this the passage of constitutional amendments providing for direct election of Senators[2], women's suffrage, and prohibition.

The three page article laments the decline of conservatives in Congress. Barry was a Republican and Congress was Republican until the new Democratic Congress swept in with the Roosevelt landslide of 1932 was seated March 3.

He fondly cites Senator Nelson Aldrich (1841-1915), Republican from Rhode Island, for whom Barry had worked, as sincerely believing that "the masses of the people were not capable of suggesting legislation, because they really did not know what was best for them." Barry notes that the Congressmen who also felt this way "are now too few to make their influence readily felt..."

Barry had been Sergeant-at-Arms for the Senate since 1919 and would have had to retire in March when a Democrat would have been appointed. Barry had arranged to publish a series of articles in the magazine after his retirement for $250 each ($4550 2015 equivalent). This article was scheduled to be published in the March issue, but somehow appeared in February.

There was immediate outrage in the Senate by both parties. Barry, 74, was grilled for hours:

"Who are these Senators and Representatives who have sold their votes for money?"

"I have not the slightest idea. I had no Senator in mind, and I do not know there is such a Senator."

"What, then, Mr. Barry, did you mean by that language?"

"My idea in writing that was to defend the Senate from the popular belief that that there are crooks and grafters here."

Barry was ousted from his job by a vote of 53-17 three weeks before he would have lost it anyway with the change to Democratic control, damned for faint praise. David Barry died three years later.

The Sergeant-at-Arms position paid $8000 a year ($145,600 2015 equivalent). Congress reduced its members' pay in 1932 due to the depression from $10,000 ($182,000) to $9000 ($163,800), to $8500 ($154,700) in 1933 and returned to $10,000 in 1935. Congressmen are paid $174,000 today. The Sergeant-at-Arms is paid $172,500.

1. The Outlook was a weekly magazine published in New York from 1870-1932, bought out of bankruptcy by Alfred E. Smith and published as New Outlook until 1935.

2. Senators were originally elected by state legislatures. The 17th amendment provided for the election of Senators by popular vote in 1913.

Friends and Enemies

I have no trouble with my enemies. I can take care of my enemies all right. But my damn friends, my god-damned friends, White, they're the ones who keep me walking the floor nights!

— Warren G. Harding, to Emporia Gazette editor William Allan White in 1923.

Deep Thought

It's not how high the taxes but if you get what you pay for.

Nothing has Changed

That the people justly view with alarm the reckless extravagance which pervades every department of the Federal Government; that a return to rigid economy and accountability is indispensable to arrest the systematic plunder of the public treasury by favored partisans; while the recent startling developments of frauds and corruptions at the Federal metropolis, show that an entire change of administration is imperatively demanded.

— Republican Party Platform of 1860.

Wind and Wisdom

"Such a prolonged display of bad temper and personal animosity, obstinacy, narrow-mindedness, and disregard for the public interest, with total defiance of the rules of orderly parliamentary procedure," the Literary Digest quotes the New York Times in article titled *The Filibuster At Its Worst*, March 19, 1927.

"We face the practical consequences of the Senate's enforced failure to pass certain measures necessary for the support of the Government. The most important. of these measures killed by the final filibuster was the second Deficiency Appropriation bill, carrying appropriations for the Army and Navy, World War veteran hospitalization, pensions, radio regulation and many other activities of the Government…the Administration is trying to meet the emergency by switching funds, and by a loan," says the Digest.

"'If the Senate can't vote, what good is it?' asks the Chicago Journal of Commerce, which adds: 'As the case stands now, a single Senator can block action by all the rest.'"

"We got wind where we had paid to get wisdom," said humorist Will Rogers.

277   Exactly the Reverse

- Conservative — a liberal who was mugged.
- Liberal — a conservative who lost health insurance.
- Strict construction — when the judge rules for you.
- Judicial activism — when the judge rules against you.
- Enemy — Someone who voted for the clueless jerk.
- Friend — Someone who voted against the clueless jerk.
- Capitalism — the exploitation of man by man.
- Socialism — exactly the reverse.

Deep Thought

Those who control the present control the future. Those who control the future control the past.
— George Orwell, 1984

The Telling Moment

Strange how there's something about someone you can't quite put your finger on, then with a word or gesture some essence of the person crystallizes.

I once worked in a small factory with a squat, coarse fellow. If he were in 1930's Germany he would have made the perfect Brownshirt.

One day he was telling me how he had applied to be a policeman but failed because "It was all politics". He said it as if, of course, everyone would know that it wasn't his fault. It was when he then stuffed his pipe with VIP brand tobacco that the picture of a small, inadequate, deeply insecure man came into sharp focus.

I have in-laws, a couple who are right-wing Bible-thumpers. I read The New York Times, and when they visit, the husband comments that it is a communist paper.

Of course, I go out of my way to leave the paper lying so he will see it. One time he picked up the society section and was so astounded by the marriage notices of gay couples that he read them out loud in disbelief.

Another time, he avidly read a lengthy article about Russia in the Soviet era detailing all sorts of bad Communist stuff and commented that he was surprised that this was in the Times.

Evidently his communist paper remarks weren't hyperbole. He really believed it was a Communist paper

Exactly the Reverse

I support them and give them food, and clothes, and cars, and houses. Who gives it to them? Does someone else give it to them? Do I know that I have—Who makes the game? Do I make the game, or do they make the game? Is there 30 owners, that created the league?
— Donald Sterling, Los Angeles Clippers basketball team owner who was forced to sell the team after he was recorded telling his mixed race black and Mexican mistress not to bring black people to his basketball games in 2014.

The mostly black Clippers fed Sterling $15 million in profit on $218 million in revenue in 2013.

Microsoft CEO Steve Ballmer bought the team for $2 billion from Sterling's wife after she had him declared incompetent.

Japan "was, indeed, a yellow peril, not only to Japan itself, but to the Far East. Dazzling as the progress of Japan has been, she has as much need of the Gospel and Christian teaching as Central Africa has, and possibly more."

Isabella Bird Bishop said this at a church congress in Newcastle, England, as quoted by the Literary Digest January 12, 1901. Bishop was a famous traveler to the orient and author of *Unbeaten Paths in Japan* and the first woman member of the Royal Geographical Society.

The Japanese were not amused. The *Kobe Chronicle* of November 15, 1900 reported:

"It puzzles us how a lady of Mrs. Bishop's observation can, after visiting not only the beaten but unbeaten tracts of Japan, believe that her own particular country exhibits under Christianity such immense moral superiority that any nation failing to profess the same religion is going straight to perdition, and is a 'peril,' yellow or white."

Christian missionaries "will receive better treatment on the whole in Japan than a Buddhist missionary would receive in England."

To compare Japan to the "savages of Central Africa, because she is not Christian...is a flight of imagination that may cause an inquiry from an agnostic Japanese as to whether veracity is included among the Christian virtues."

"There are Japanese who have visited Europe and America without being much impressed by the overwhelming moral superiority that ought to be evident in the West....We venture to say that there is no country in the world where life and property are more safe than in Japan; there are few civilized countries where there is less of that hopeless wretchedness which is the result among industrial nations of the wide gulf established between the rich and poor."

The Chronicle article goes on to say that the Chinese were far safer under the "heathen Japanese troops than among the Christian Occidentals." (Peking was then occupied by an 8 nation alliance to relieve the siege of the legation quarter by the anti-foreign Boxers.) But just 37 years later came the atrocities of the Japanese in China in the Rape of Nanking.

Isabella Bird (1831-1904) was the daughter of a Church of England minister. She was a world traveler, writing of her adventures in books and magazines.

In 1872, she traveled to Australia and Hawaii. She went to Colorado in 1873, traveling over 800 miles in the Rockies on horseback. She took up with Jim Nugent, Rocky Mountain Jim, a one-eyed outlaw, "A man any woman might love but no sane woman would marry," and her "dear desperado." The trip inspired her fourth and most famous book, *A Lady's Life in the Rocky Mountains.*

She married John Bishop, an Edinburgh doctor quite a few years her junior in 1880. Bishop died 6 years later.

Bird then went to India, Tibet, Persia, Kurdistan, Turkey, China, Korea, and Morocco, traveling into her seventies.

A Red-Headed Jew in Dogpatch

The secret of how to live without resentment or embarrassment in a world in which I was different from everyone else was to be indifferent to that difference.
— Al Capp

I have a friend who has red hair and a Jewish last name. He once lived in a tiny town in Arkansas adjacent to the military base where he worked.

He quickly became known to the locals as "The Red-Headed Jew from New York." At Christmas time he would get anonymous phone calls: a voice would say "we forgive you" and hang up. They meant forgive him for killing Christ.

I would have answered "that's mighty white of you."

Beware The Ides of April
Signs spotted at nationwide tax day Tea Party protests in 2011:
• Don't steal from Medicare to support socialized medicine
• Thank you Fox news for keeping us *infromed*
• Who needs oil I ride the bus
• This is America and our only *lanaguage* is English
• Get a brain! Morans
• Democrat ☐ Socialist ☐ Communist ☐ All of the Above ☒
• We came unarmed [this time]

Shaving Shovels

Foreign Laborers at the Hoosier limestone quarry in Bedford, Indiana had their wages cut from 15¢ to 12½¢ an hour in 1907. The men then marched off to the machine shop and had 2½ inches cut from their shovels. "They say short money, short shovels" according to the New York Times November 27, 1907.

The Daily Bulletin of the Manufacturers' Record, December 14, 1907 titled *Shaving Shovels* asks "were they actually doing 15-cents-an-hour shoveling before the reduction was made?" In a lengthy commentary the article states that employers have noticed that increased wages have led to decreased efficiency — why work as much if you can get the same money for working less?

And the cause of this decline in the work ethic? "Unfortunate twists that have been given latter-day elementary educational methods have apparently dwarfed, if not destroyed, the sense of responsibility, and consequently, the habit of reliability and dependability."

The victims of those unfortunate twists "by the hundreds of thousands, cajoled or compelled to remain in school during the years when they should be learning to perfect themselves in productive labor, in the only possible way, working for a wage, and deceived by educational occupations which are essentially play, are turned loose upon the world to make a living with the senses vibrant to the gong for recess or for closing."

"They naturally come to do as little work as possible without losing their jobs. They are shaving shovels. Presently they will find themselves without shovels to shave."

So put the kids to work in the schools:

"You say to somebody, you shouldn't go to work before you're what, 14, 16 years of age, fine, you're totally poor. You're in a school that is failing with a teacher that is failing. I've tried for years to have a very simple model. Most of these schools ought to get rid of the unionized janitors, have one master janitor and pay local students to take care of the school. The kids would actually do work, they would have cash, they would have pride in the schools, they'd begin the process of rising."

— Newt Gingrich as quoted in the New York Times, November 19, 2011.

Past and Future Tensions
Jihad

"In all corners of the earth Christianity and Mohammedanism are coming into collision, and the indications are that a struggle for the mastery is inevitable. The Moslems are burning with anxiety to see such a crisis and such a conflict; but Christianity does not seem to be in a condition to welcome the struggle, as, especially in Europe, it would be almost absolutely impossible to enthuse the masses for a religious contest to the same degree and extent in which this will be possible among the Mohammedan peoples."

— From a summary of "Christianity and Islam", an address by Dr. Martin Hartmann of the Oriental Seminary in Berlin in the Literary Digest January 21, 1899.

Diplomacy: Back to the Future

Floundering around for a Middle East policy? Can't reason with those ornery fundamentalists? Feel like you're wandering around in some foggy bottom?

Well, you didn't do your homework. It's been done before (or maybe since). You can find all the guidance you need in the voluminous papers of Federation policy toward the Klingons.

Hab SoSII' Quch! (Your mother has a smooth forehead!)

There is – no kidding – a Klingons for Christ web site. Sounds like an evangelical challenge.

Deep Thought

We are a rich Nation; we can afford to pay for security and prosperity without having to sacrifice our liberties in the bargain.

— President Roosevelt, Fireside Chat, April 14, 1938

Gentlemen Do Not Read Each Other's Mail

"It appears to have, for a long period of time and under many successive administrations, been an established practice, that the foreign correspondence of foreign ministers, passing thro' the general post office, should be sent to a department of the foreign office, before the forwarding of such correspondence according to its address. The postmaster general having had his attention called to the fact that there was no sufficient authority for the practice, has since June discontinued it all together."
— The Chatham Gleaner (Canada) September 7, 1844, quoting a House of Commons report.

"Gentlemen do not read each other's mail." This is a quote from U.S. Secretary of State Henry Stimson in 1929 when he withdrew funding from the Cipher Bureau, also know as the Black Chamber, forerunner to the NSA, that had been set up after World War I and was tasked with intercepting and deciphering messages from foreign diplomats.

"The National Security Agency monitored the phone conversations of 35 world leaders after being given the numbers by an official in another US government department, according to a classified document provided by whistleblower Edward Snowden," reported The Guardian October 4, 2013.

German Chancellor Angela Merkel was one of the 35 and she was pissed. She called President Obama to complain. "She unmistakably disapproves of and views as completely unacceptable such practices," said a spokesman.

"The president assured the chancellor that the United States is not monitoring and will not monitor the communications of the chancellor" said White House spokesman Jay Carney. However, when asked by the Guardian if the U.S had bugged her phone in the past "a top White House official declined to deny that it had."

The Republican Manifesto

"there is one point…the effort to place capital on an equal footing with, if not above, labor in the structure of government. It is assumed that labor is available only in connection with capital; that nobody labors unless somebody else, owning capital, somehow by the use of it induces him to labor.

Labor is prior to and independent of capital. Capital is only the fruit of labor, and could never have existed if labor had not first existed. Labor is the superior of capital, and deserves much the higher consideration."
— Abraham Lincoln, State of the Union Address, December 3, 1861

We pledge ourselves to:
Protect the right of labor to organize and to bargain collectively through representatives of its own choosing without interference from any source.
— Republican Party Platform of 1936

The Republican Party is firmly opposed to involving this Nation in foreign war.
— Republican Party Platform of 1940

We pledge prosecution of the war to total victory against our enemies…
— Republican Party Platform of 1944

We support the right of States to enact Right-to-Work laws and encourage them to do so to promote greater economic liberty. Ultimately, we support the enactment of a National Right-to-Work law to promote worker freedom and to promote greater economic liberty. We will aggressively enforce the recent decision by the Supreme Court barring the use of union dues for political purposes without the consent of the worker.
— Republican Party Platform of 2012

The S Word

Ours is the party which rebuilt a shattered economy, rescued our banking system, revived our agriculture, reinvigorated our industry, gave labor strength and security, and led the American people to the broadest prosperity in our history.
— Democratic Party Platform of 1948*

We charge that they [Democrats] work unceasingly to achieve their goal of national socialism.
— Republican Party Platform of 1952

* The platform of 1952 says essentially the same thing, but less concisely.

The S Word

He's a socialist!

Socialism: A way of organizing a society in which major industries are owned and controlled by the government rather than by individual people and companies.
— Merriam Webster Dictionary

The Fourth Estate

"The power that squelched a rabble-rouser can crush American quislings!"*

That was the banner on a full-page ad from Scripps-Howard newspapers in Life Magazine October 7, 1946. The ad showed a group of young people, perhaps collegians, listening intently to a presumably subversive agitator and shows the transition from the war against the Fascists to the war against the Communists with classic cold war rhetoric.

"Ugly whispers raced through Cleveland. Heard about the new party?"…"We'll put those foreign-born ——s in their place."…

A reporter for the Cleveland Press "shadowed a mysterious stranger who had been preaching a dangerous gospel of hate and racial bias — and collecting donations to finance his 'party'."

"Then the *Press* ripped off the mask! A series of four articles exposed the stranger as a professional rabble-rouser and apostle of sedition."

The articles were written by Eugene Segal beginning in July, 1945. They exposed Joe McWilliams as the rabble-rouser. McWilliams, dubbed Joe McNazi by Walter Winchell, ran for Congress from Yorkville, the German section of Manhattan, in 1940 with anti-Semitic harangues (see note). He was indicted for sedition with 29 others in 1944. *United States v. McWilliams* became known as the Great Sedition Trial. A mistrial was declared after the judge died and the matter was not pursued thereafter.

McWilliams became a fundraiser for the American Nationalist Party founded by isolationist and fascist apologist ex-senator Robert R. Reynolds in January, 1945. Reynolds had associations with unsavory neofascists of the period such as Gerald L.K. Smith, anti-Semite, white supremacist and founder of the America First Party.

The Segal articles had nation-wide circulation and exposed these connections and Reynolds disbanded the party in October, 1945.

Then the Life ad makes an effortless segue to the cold war:

"America has one weapon that can deal with either a local troublemaker or a national menace. That weapon is Public Opinion. The menace is the *Communist Fifth Column.*"

The ad then says that there is no problem with Russian Communists — it's none of our business.

"But your newspaper warns against the *international* Communists within our own country—men who call themselves Americans, but take their orders from Moscow. Men who serve foreign masters—yet spread their poison in our labor unions, political parties, schools, even our homes."

"Daily, your newspaper puts the finger on these traitors and their sometimes more dangerous 'fellow travelers'".

"An informed and unified Public Opinion is the ONLY force strong enough to protect America against these peddlers of subversive *foreign* ideals, these saboteurs of American democracy."

"Give light and the people will find their own way."

* Vidkun Quisling seized power in Norway during the German invasion in 1940 with Nazi backing and was Minister-President of Norway, collaborating with the Nazis. He was tried and executed by firing squad in October, 1945. His name has since become an eponym for traitor.

Yellow Journalism

Right-wingers really don't like the New York Times. At a forum at Ohio University May 21, 2012, Fox News chairman Roger Ailes called the Times "a cesspool of bias" and Times reporters "a bunch of lying scum." He accused the Associated Press of left wing bias and said comedian Jon Stewart admitted he was a socialist when he once told Ailes in a bar his vote would be for Socialist Norman Thomas (d. 1968) without laughing.

I was telling someone that I had stumbled across the factoid that the "legal tender for all debts public and private" business on our money only applies to debts (see *Passing the Buck* on p. 116) in an article in the Times and was treated to a lecture on how they had got "caught with their pants down." Of course, he doesn't read the Times. I would have believed that even if I had heard it on Fox.

The Smell of Politics

In a study titled *Assortative Mating on Ideology Could Operate Through Olfactory Cues*, The American Journal of Political Science had conservatives and liberals sniff each other's armpits.

146 people between 18 and 40 from "a large city in the northeast United States" rated their politics on a 1 to 7 scale from "strongly liberal" to "strongly conservative."

From them was chosen 21 people, 10 liberals and 11 conservatives, who had the strongest views. After washing in fragrance free soap and shampoo, a gauze pad was taped to each of their underarms.

"Participants wore these pads for 24 hours following a strict protocol which prohibited smoking, drinking, deodorants, perfumes, being around strong odours or candles, animals, eating strong-smelling foods or sleeping in a bed with any other sentient beings".

The pads were put into sterile vials and frozen. A week later they were thawed out and the other 125 participants sniffed the vials in random order (with a cleansing whiff of peppermint between samples). They rated the attractiveness of each on a 5 point scale.

Both conservatives and liberals liked the smell of their political bedfellows better, sometimes extremely so:

"In one particularly illustrative case, a participant asked the experimenter if she could take one of the vials home with her because she thought it was 'the best perfume I ever smelled'; the vial was from a male who shared an ideology similar to the evaluator. She was preceded by another respondent with an ideology opposite to the person who provided the exact same sample; this participant reported that the vial had 'gone rancid' and suggested it needed to be replaced."

"Smell signals," the researchers concluded "are an efficient evolutionary mechanism by which to enhance reproduction."

But then there's the conundrum of those literal odd bedfellows, Cajun liberal commentator James Carville and his wife Mary Matalin, Republican political consultant.

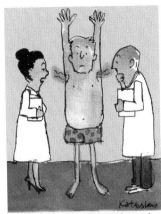

Image courtesy of Fiona Katauskas

In this cartoon by Australian artist Fiona Katauskas, the woman scientist says "His left armpit smells left wing & his right one smells conservative," and the man says "Must be what they call a 'Swinging Voter'."

Klanbake

In the 1924 Democratic convention in Madison Square Garden, former Treasury Secretary William McAdoo, a Southerner from Georgia, was endorsed by the Klan, which he did not repudiate. (See *Wall Street Closed* on p. 111.)

Mcadoo and Al Smith were the frontrunners. After 99 ballots in which neither won, both withdrew and a compromise candidate, John Davis, was chosen on the 103rd ballot, the longest nomination contest in U.S. history. The Klan issue was so contentious fistfights broke out on the floor between pro- and anti-Klan delegates.

The convention was dubbed the "Klanbake" when Klan delegates defeated a platform plank denouncing the Klan for violence. The next day, July 4, 20,000 Klansmen held a picnic in New Jersey in a field across the Hudson from the Garden, complete with white hoods and cross burnings.

Campaign Slogan

I don't know much about Americanism, but it's a damn good word with which to carry an election."
— Warren G. Harding

Deep Thought
Don't criticize others for what you hate in yourself.

The Bible, Like the Constitution, Means Whatever You Want it to

An ad in the Charleston Mercury, March 14, 1848, touts the book *A Defense of Negro Slavery as it Exists in the United States* by Matthew Estes of Columbus, Mississippi.

The 1846 book "is made up of profound thought and research upon a subject of deep import to mankind in general, and the Southern portion of the United States in particular. The writer has not confined himself to such a defence of slavery as it exists in the United States as will meet the arguments of the abolitionists of our own country, but has gone to the root of the matter and examined the subject like a philosopher upon its merits."*

It's all in the Bible, starting with the Tenth Commandment, not coveting thy neighbor's house, wife, ox, ass, or manservant or maidservant — meaning slaves.

There was lots of slavery all over the ancient world which was "fully known to Christ and his Apostles, and to all the early Christians; still we do not find in the New Testament a solitary word condemnatory of the institution of slavery."

But the real defense of slavery is that somebody has to do the dirty work, revealed in a quote from ex-Governor James Henry Hammond (who owned more than 300 slaves) "one of the very few authors who have taken the correct view of slavery," in a letter to the author:

"This idea that Slavery is so necessary to the performance of the drudgery so essential for the sustenance of mankind and the advance of civilization, is undoubtedly the fundamental ground on which the reason of the institution rests."

The Negro, of course, is conveniently suited for slavery. Chapter III of the book is titled *The African Race: Their Inferiority, and Fitness for the Condition of Slavery.*

At least in the TV series *Roots*, slavemaster George Ames (Vic Morrow) knew perfectly well that Negroes had the same capabilities as whites. He didn't have to justify his evil. He did it because he could.

* "...the decision of the subject has been placed upon the ground of reason alone. It was not deemed necessary to appeal to the passions in order to obtain a favorable verdict on this subject, as the intrinsic merits of the subject itself, when fairly presented, were thought fully sufficient to convince every candid inquirer after truth."

The Constitution, Like the Bible, Means Whatever You Want it to

In 1894, Edward Marshall wrote an article in the New York Press titled *Bread and Filth Cooked Together*, an exposé of basement tenement bakeries. The article described rats, cockroaches, poor ventilation and plumbing, and other unsanitary and unhealthful conditions. This was backed up by state factory inspectors.

The cellar bakers worked 12 or more hours 7 days a week, often sleeping in the bakery. Union bakers in more modern factories worked 10 hours 6 days.

The New York State Legislature unanimously passed the Bakeshop Act in 1895 setting sanitary standards and limiting hours to 60 a week and 10 a day.

In 1902, a Utica baker named Lochner was fined $50 for allowing a worker to exceed 60 hours. The case was appealed, with the help of a trade association, and wound up in the Supreme Court.

The Court invalidated the Bakeshop Act 5-4 on the grounds that it interfered with "liberty of contract", the right of the employee to negotiate hours with the employer, and that the act exceeded the permissible police power of the state.

This case ushered in the Lochner Era when labor laws were routinely invalidated.

The Lochner Era ended in 1937 with West Coast Hotel Co. v. Parrish when the Court upheld a Washington state minimum wage law for women 5-4.

Below is the what the Constitution means according to these two decisions.

"There is no reasonable ground, on the score of health, for interfering with the liberty of the person or the right of free contract, by determining the hours of labor, in the occupation of a baker." — Lochner

"In dealing with the relation of employer and employed, the legislature has necessarily a wide field of discretion in order that there may be suitable protection of health and safety." — Parrish

The final blow to Lochner came in United States v. Carolene Products in 1938 which upheld a law banning "filled milk", skim milk with ersatz cream added back, from interstate commerce, holding that government regulation of economic activity is entitled to a presumption of constitutionality.

Justice Harlan Stone in Footnote Four,

the most famous footnote in constitutional law, qualified that by saying legislation of any sort that affects "discrete and insular minorities" deserves "more searching judicial inquiry." This opened the door to subsequent civil rights legislation.

There is a libertarian revisionist literature that argues that Lochner was right, that after New Dealers and liberals made it a bogeyman "it became mostly futile to invoke Lochner's logic — that individual rights often trump government's powers to boss people around", according to George Will in the Washington Post, September 7, 2011.

Hey George, maybe you can negotiate the part time 60 hours at the bakery with the boss. The pay, too:

"Nevertheless, raising the minimum hourly wage for the 23rd time since 1938, from today's $7.25 to $10.10, is a nifty idea, if:

If you think government should prevent two consenting parties — an employer and a worker — from agreeing to an hourly wage that government disapproves."
— The Washington Post December 13, 2013

Wanted Dead or Alive

...no society can make a perpetual constitution, or even a perpetual law. The earth belongs always to the living generation...Every constitution, then, and every law, naturally expires at the end of nineteen years. If it be enforced longer, it is an act of force, and not of right.
— Thomas Jefferson, letter to James Madison, September 6,1789.

On every question of construction carry ourselves back to the time when the Constitution was adopted, recollect the spirit manifested in the debates and instead of trying what meaning may be squeezed out of the text or invented against it, conform to the probable one in which it was passed.
— Thomas Jefferson, letter to Supreme Court Justice William Johnson, June 12, 1823.

Jefferson wasn't wasn't in Philly for the Constitutional Convention in 1787. He was in Paris as Minister to France and did not participate in the debate.

After two months of debate, the Founding Fathers decided it would be more efficient to have a committee prepare a draft of the Constitution. Five people were appointed to the Committee of Detail to do this. After a week and a half the committee reported back to the convention.

Virginian Edmund Randolph wrote in the preamble of the report that the Constitution should have "essential principles only, lest the operations of government should be clogged by rendering those provisions permanent and unalterable, which ought to be accommodated to times and events."

"I have classes of little kids who come to the court, and they recite very proudly what they've been taught, 'The Constitution is a living document.' It isn't a living document! It's dead. Dead, dead, dead!"
— Justice Antonin Scalia speaking at Princeton University December 10, 2012.

Ability and Likeability

I rarely talk politics in the store — wouldn't be prudent — but somehow President Reagan came up in conversation with a fellow who said "He was a good president."

This guy wouldn't know a good one from a bad one and I doubt he could give an example of something Reagan did that made him a good president.

He liked him, so he was a good president and I think this is a common reaction. The reverse, too: if you hated him, he was a bad president.

I like Ike, Harry Truman, Franklin Roosevelt, Jack Kennedy, George H.W. Bush, Gerald Ford, Jimmy Carter and Bill Clinton. I hated George W. Bush and Richard Nixon.

Wikipedia has rankings of presidents from surveys of scholars by a number of organizations. Of the presidents I like, Ford, H.W. Bush, and Carter ranked low and the rest high. George W. Bush and Nixon ranked very low. Reagan ranked high.

As for Reagan, how could they tell he had Alzheimer's?

Deep Thought

The great enemy of the truth is very often not the lie, deliberate, contrived and dishonest, but the myth, persistent, persuasive and unrealistic.
— President John F. Kennedy

The Water Cure

"The water cure is an old Filipino method of mild torture. Nobody was seriously damaged whereas the Filipinos had inflicted incredible tortures on our people."
— Letter from President Theodore Roosevelt to German diplomat Speck von Sternberg July 19, 1902

"A man is thrown down on his back and three or four men sit or stand on his arms and legs and hold him down; and either a gun barrel or a rifle barrel or a carbine barrel or a stick as big as a belaying pin, -- that is, with an inch circumference, -- is simply thrust into his jaws and his jaws are thrust back, and, if possible, a wooden log or stone is put under his head or neck, so he can be held more firmly. In the case of very old men I have seen their teeth fall out, -- I mean when it was done a little roughly. He is simply held down and then water is poured onto his face down his throat and nose from a jar; and that is kept up until the man gives some sign or becomes unconscious. And, when he becomes unconscious, he is simply rolled aside and he is allowed to come to. In almost every case the men have been a little roughly handled. They were rolled aside rudely, so that water was expelled. A man suffers tremendously, there is no doubt about it. His sufferings must be that of a man who is drowning, but cannot drown. ... I did not stop it, because I had no right to.... Major Geary was about sixty yards away."
— Lieutenant Grover Flint; S. Doc. 331, 57 Congressional 1 Session (1903), page 1767-1768

"Another technique was waterboarding, a process of simulated drowning. No doubt the procedure was tough, but medical experts assured the CIA that it did no lasting harm."
— George W. Bush in his 2010 book *Decision Points*.

"From my experience -- and I speak as someone who has personally interrogated many terrorists and elicited important actionable intelligence -- I strongly believe that it is a mistake to use what has become known as the 'enhanced interrogation techniques,' a position shared by many professional operatives, including the CIA officers who were present at the initial phases of the Abu Zubaydah interrogation."
"These techniques, from an operational perspective, are ineffective, slow and unreliable, and as a result harmful to our efforts to defeat al Qaeda. (This is aside from the important additional considerations that they are un-American and harmful to our reputation and cause.)"
— Former FBI agent Ali Soufan in testimony before the Senate Judiciary Committee, May 13, 2009.

"Look, all that's been done to this country, and I heard about water being dropped on someone's face, and I never considered it torture. Even when I was laying there, I thought this is going to be no big deal. I go swimming. It's going to be like being in the tub. I do now want to say this: absolutely torture. Absolutely. I mean, that's drowning."
— Conservative extremist* talk show host Erich "Mancow" Muller, May 22, 2009. Muller had just been waterboarded on his radio show as a stunt. He lasted 6 seconds.

"The Committee makes the following findings and conclusions:
#1: The CIA's use of its enhanced interrogation techniques was not an effective means of acquiring intelligence or gaining cooperation from detainees."
"The waterboarding technique was physically harmful, inducing convulsions and vomiting. Abu Zubaydah, for example, became 'completely unresponsive, with bubbles rising through his nose, full mouth.' Internal CIA records describe the waterboarding of Khalid Shaykh Mohammad as evolving into a 'series of near drownings.'"
— Senate Select Committee on Intelligence, Committee Study of the Central Intelligence Agency's Detention and Interrogation Program, 2014

* "The idea that the U.S. will win the war in Iraq is plain wrong." — Ex-governor of Vermont Howard Dean, then head of the Democratic party, in an interview with WOAI radio in San Antonio, December 5, 2005.

"Howard Dean ought to be kicked out of America." "He ought to be tried for treason. He is the enemy." "These people want every boy to die. They're bloodthirsty animals. Howard Dean is a vile human being." — Erich Muller on Fox and Friends December 6, 2005.

Bijoux and Beyond

The Handwriting on the Window

Rough Diamonds are often found as octahedrons, two four-sided pyramids set base to base. Until the 14th century diamonds were set in jewelry as found.

The first primitive diamond cut was the point cut. By grinding with diamond dust at a slight angle to the natural faces the appearance of the diamond could be improved by removing irregularities.

There isn't much sparkle to these diamonds. They were worn for their magical powers and also because you could use them to scratch a message on anything.

Point cut diamond rings were called "Tower Rings" because they were used by people jailed in the Tower of London to scratch their names and messages on the walls and windows.

French king Francis I (reigned 1515-1547) wrote on a window at the Palace of Chambord in a place that would be seen by his mistress, the Duchess d'Etampes, *Women are often fickle; quite mad is he who trusts them.*

Sir Walter Raleigh scratched on a window pane *Fain would I climb, but that I fear to fall.* In reply Queen Elizabeth wrote *If thy heart fail thee, do not climb at all.*

Deep Throat

Diamonds are formed 120 miles under the earth. They then hang out down there until they're brought up by a passing volcano unrelated to their formation.

Now, don't go out to your neighborhood volcano and start digging. Diamonds are only brought up by a specific type of volcano, one that spews a rock called kimberlite or a related rock called lamproite.

The volcanoes are eroded flat over geologic time and their remaining cores, called pipes, become diamond mines. The diamonds that washed away as the volcano eroded are mined from ancient river gravels, now buried.

Some diamonds wash all the way to the sea and are vacuumed up by purpose-built ships, mainly off the coast of Namibia.

Carrots

The most unusual engagement ring I ever made was for a woman whose hobby was raising rabbits. She got a ring that looked like a carrot: a pear shaped orange sapphire for the carrot and 3 small marquise green tsavorite garnets for the leaves. A one carrot engagement ring!

Carats

The carat, the unit of weight for gems, is derived from the carob bean. The carob, or locust tree, grows in the Middle East. In ancient times, merchants found that dried carob beans were very uniform in weight. The modern carat is defined as 2/10ths of a gram. A dollar bill weighs 1 gram or 5 carats. That's only 20¢ a carat. Cheap!

Here Comes the Groom

Wedding bands for men are a recent innovation, only becoming popular in the 1940's and 50's.

A campaign in the 1920's by the jewelry industry to convince men to wear a groom's ring failed. It was not the manly thing to do then.

So unfamiliar was the notion of a man's wedding ring, that in 1944 a Catholic priest had to ask the Ecclesiastical Review whether it was permissible to bless the groom's ring as well as the bride's. (It was.)

But jewelers persisted and after the war it became a new tradition. Middle class gender roles were changing and middle class prosperity made it affordable. Only 15% of weddings were double-ring ceremonies before the Depression. By the late 1940's, it was 80%.

Humphrey Bogart got his first ring for his fourth wife, Lauren Bacall, in 1946.

And don't take the ring off. See below.

The Anti-Infidelity Ring

TheCheeky.com sells a wedding band with "I'M MARRIED" engraved large on the inside. It imprints your skin and your marital status is visible when you take it off. Titanium, $550.

The Kindest Cut

Yes, diamonds are expensive. But you can't blame the diamond cutters. The cost of cutting averages only 2% of the retail price of a diamond.

Diamond in the Rough

Pro golfer Sergio Garcia's tee shot at the third hole of the Bridgestone Invitational tournament in Akron, Ohio August 3, 2014, went off course and smacked the engagement ring of a spectator, knocking the diamond out. The diamond fell into the tall grass of the rough. Garcia gave the woman a signed ball and offered to replace the diamond if it couldn't be found. Fortunately, someone else in the gallery found it.

Photos of the empty diamond ring show a 4 prong setting with no distortion of the prongs. If the ball had hit with enough force to actually bend the prongs, it would have broken her finger. What probably happened is that one or more of the prong tips were worn and plinked off with the golf ball hit.

There are two lessons for you here. First, bring in your ring once a year or so the have the prongs checked. Second, Have your diamond set in 6 prongs. If one prong goes in a 4 prong setting, the diamond will fall out. If you lose 2 prong tips in a 6 prong setting, your diamond will still be there.

This is more critical for rings in which the diamond sits high up in the prongs rather than low settings like the old-fashioned engagement rings from the 20's through the 50's.

Garcia bogeyed the hole and finished second in the tournament.

Seeing Red

Red is the rarest color of diamond, with only about 20 known stones and only 3 weighing more than 5 carats

A 5 carat red diamond, the Kazanjian Red, is now on display at the American Museum of Natural History in New York.

A 35 carat dark rough opaque diamond was discovered at Lichtenburg, South Africa in 1927 during a diamond rush. A diamond broker paid 280 British pounds ($16,000 today) for it

It was sent to the Goudvis brothers in Amsterdam to be cut. After 7 months of study, a ruby-red 5.05 carat square emerald cut emerged as well as a smaller 1.43 carat reddish-orange stone.

With conflicting estimates of its value in Amsterdam, the stone was shown around New York but with no interest. Shortly after it arrived back in Amsterdam, a cable from Tiffany announced "Have customer for red stone." Back to it went across the Atlantic.

Tiffany's customer offered $100,000 ($1.2 million today). But the Goudvis brothers held out for $150,000 ($1.86 million today) and the customer withdrew the offer and the diamond was returned to Amsterdam.

At the outbreak of the war, the diamond was placed in a safe in Arnhem but was stolen by the Nazis in 1944 along with all the stock of Dutch diamond cutters. After the war the red diamond turned up in a salt mine in Bavaria, mistaken for a ruby by General McNarney, commander of U.S. Occupation forces in Germany,

The heirs of the Goudvis brothers sold the diamond. It changed hands several times then disappeared in 1970 into a private collection until it was bought by Kazanjian Brothers in 2007. See *Hail to the Chief* on p. 30

You've Got Mail

In 1958, Harry Winston, famed New York jeweler, donated the Hope diamond to the Smithsonian. Forget the Brink's truck and guards with tommy guns. He sent it registered mail in a plain brown box.

Diamond Oddities

Carbonado is a rough, porous black diamond that is only found in Brazil and the Central African Republic. Carbonado is not a single crystal like gem diamonds but a mass of microscopic diamond crystals. This makes It extremely tough and it is used for cutting tools.

Carbonado has never been found in diamond deposits. It contains hydrogen, unlike other diamonds, and the way nitrogen is incorporated into it is also different. It is thought by scientists that carbonado was formed by supernova explosions and landed on earth as asteroids.

Ballas diamonds are aggregates of microscopic diamond crystals that grew radially to form a sphere. They are extremely tough. They are of terrestial origin and are found only in Brazil and South Africa.

Ballas Diamond

Photo courtesy of Barbara Smigel

Robbery at Spring Mountain Ranch

On April 10, 1959, three men forced their way into the house on Spring Mountain Ranch near Las Vegas, yanked a large diamond ring off the hand of Vera Krupp and tied her up back-to-back with the ranch foreman. The men also stole $700,000 in cash.

The FBI turned its attention to John William Hagenson, a fugitive from a similar crime in California. They tracked him to Louisiana and arrested him.

Six weeks later, agents followed a lead about a man looking to sell a large diamond in Newark, New Jersey and arrested James Reves. The large center diamond was found sewn into his coat lining. This was the Krupp diamond, a 33.19 carat Asscher cut (a square emerald cut). The two baguette side stones from the ring were tracked to a jeweler in St. Louis. With all the stones recovered, the ring was recreated.

Vera Krupp was the second wife of Alfried Krupp, head of Krupp Works, munitions makers to Hitler. Alfried was convicted of war crimes in 1948 and sentenced to 12 years in prison, but was given an amnesty in 1951 with his property restored.

Vera Hossenfeldt was a gold-digger of the first water*. She left her first husband and emigrated to the United States in 1938 to marry a failed movie producer. She divorced the producer, became a citizen and married a doctor for whom she was working as a receptionist, husband number 3. She divorced that husband in Las Vegas and returned to Germany a few years after the war. She married Krupp in 1952. The Krupp diamond was her engagement ring.

Unhappy with her dreary life in Essen she returned to Las Vegas. She bought the ranch in 1955 and divorced Krupp in 1957.

She sold the ranch to Howard Hughes in 1967 and died a few months later in Los Angeles. The ranch became a state park in 1974. Her bedroom and closet full of expensive clothes are on display as they were when she lived there.

Richard Burton bought the Krupp diamond in 1968 at auction for $305,000 ($2 million in 2015) and gave it to his wife Elizabeth Taylor. It was one of her favorites. It was featured in a Here's Lucy show in 1970 and her toon wore it in the Simpsons in 1993.

Elizabeth thought it fitting that she would own the Krupp: "When it came up for auction in the late 1960s, I thought how perfect it would be if a nice Jewish girl like me were to own it." (Raised as a Christian Scientist, Taylor converted to Judaism in 1959 at 27.)

Elizabeth Taylor's jewelry was sold by Christie's in a series of auctions beginning in December, 2011. (See *Paper Profit* on p. 33)

*The phrase "of the first water" refers to diamonds of the best color looking like water. The phrase dates back to at least the early 17th century.

Waste Management

French company Veolia Environnement is sweeping streets in Britain and recovering from the street dust minute particles of platinum, palladium, and rhodium emitted in exhaust from catalytic converters

A pilot plant near Birmingham extracts £100,000 worth of precious metals from 44,000 tons of sweepings. But this is just a side effect. Street dust is primarily treated to remove toxic elements so it can be used in construction rather than burying it in a landfill. That way the dust can be sold rather than paying to bury it. This strategy only works where landfill costs are high, £100 a metric ton in England.

The company hopes to scale up its operations tenfold by opening other treatment plants and also treating sweeps from other companies and municipalities.

Beethoven's 10th, 11th, 12th

LifeGem, the company that will squeeze what's left of you (or your pet) after cremation into a diamond (see *A Human is Forever* on p. 28), made diamonds from Beethoven's hair.

This quintessential longhair's long hair was provided by a Westport, Connecticut autograph and memorabilia dealer who holds the Guinness World Record for the largest collection of famous locks, including Lincoln, Napoleon, Einstein, and (of course) Elvis.

3 diamonds were made from 10 strands (with extra carbon added). A .56 carat light blue diamond was listed on Ebay for $1 million but sold for $202,700 in September, 2007. Of the other two diamonds, one was given to the hair collector and the other kept by LifeGem.

Double Takes

Rock Show Boffo As Audience Gets Stoned!
The annual gem show was great.

Joe Sez Pinko Pearls Red, White, Blue
The cold war is over and we won! You can wear pink pearls from Red China and make a fashion statement, not a political statement.

O Christmas Plea
Why do I have to tell you every year not to bring in repairs at Christmas?

Christmas With All The Fixin's
Why do I have to tell you every year not to bring in repairs at Christmas?

Hot Studs For Birthday Babes
Birthstone earrings for sale.

For 2¢ Plain
Or 2½¢ with a white block to write on. Joseph's sells those handy little 2x3 inch ziplock plastic bags.

Heavenly Host And Tabby, Too
Blue agate cameo pendants: angels are just heavenly; lionize your little tigers with a cat cameo.

Ladies And Gentlemen [Watch ad]
For the gentleman (or the gentleman's gentleman) and the gentlewoman. These elegant timepieces whisper "old money". Buffy and Biff will never know you paid but a modest amount of new money for them.

Shopper To Get Purple Heart!
Not for combat in the mall zone, but to soothe the wounds of life with a display of good taste. Pendant, rich purple amethyst in a bed of diamonds. Looks like a million bucks but costs 2000 times less!

E.T. Phone Home
Extraterritorials, customers who have moved away but still get the newsletter, send me an email once in a while.

Teddy Bares All!
Except for a marcasite-studded bow-tie, that is. Sterling silver teddy bear pin. Also gold teddy charm and earrings. Ursis curses, I almost forgot the little teddy bear locket.

No Spin Zone
Fit your ring with a shank that opens to go over a large knuckle.

Fair and Balanced
The newsletter socks it to everyone equally.

Flip-Flop
Foot-in-mouthwear as neckwear: flip-flop charm.

Go Jump in the Lake
Water resistant watches for sale.

Hit the Road, Jill
Two time zone watch so you'll always know when the folks back home are asleep and you're not.

Break a Leg!
Crutch charm for the unlucky skier or lucky thespian.

Pour Vous
Miss Piggy charm for sale.

Thinking Inside the Box
Boxes without the store name for inferior stuff you bought somewhere else.

Live From New York
It's Saturday night and you need to know the price of gold. Check it on the web site, from a [upstate] New York refiner.

To Bee! That is the Answer.
Bee pin formed from two opals.

The Hunt for Red October is Over
Red tourmaline ring for October's girl.

Sometimes Mr. Right gets it wrong
I Want! I Want! I Want! wish list for him.

High Carbs
Larger diamond for sale; diamond prices going up.

Low Carbs
Small diamond earrings for sale.

Back to the Future
Tomorrow's heirlooms are here today: single source gemstones will be gone.

Man of the Cloth
I touch up your jewelry with a polishing cloth because it works.

When the Saints Go Marching In
Religious medals available in 1 day, a miracle from St. Fedex.

On With their Heads!
Boy's and girl's head charms for sale, includes attaching to charm bracelet.

Low Bandwidth Causes Time Out Error
Too narrow watch strap will pop off.

Name Dropper
Carol, you dropped your name necklace down between the showcases.

Evil Emporium Retains Title
Walmart sells the most jewelry, again.

The Legend of the Crystal Skulls

Dan Aykroyd founded Crystal Head Vodka. The liquor is quadruple distilled and triple filtered through Herkimer diamond (quartz) crystals.* (Sounds good, but I couldn't find any Google chemists who said that pouring booze over quartz does anything. Ditto for Double Cross Vodka filtered through diamond dust)

The vodka comes in a clear bottle shaped like a skull. A 750 ml bottle sells for about $45. You may be able to buy it cheaper though: 21,000 bottles of Crystal Head were stolen from a California warehouse in May, 2011.

Although Crystal Head is made in Canada, you can't buy it in Aykroyd's native Ontario. Canada has provincial monopoly liquor stores (except for Alberta). The Liquor Control Board of Ontario banned it as too gross. You can buy it in all the other provinces, though.

Ghostbuster Aykroyd nicely summed up the myths about crystal skulls in a 2010 interview with the Santa Fe Barman:

The story behind Crystal Head Vodka is one of positive spiritual energy. Thirteen of these polished skulls have been found on our planet. Eight are in the possession of individuals and institutions. Five are missing. Of the eight each one is unique. Some are green, orange, cloudy and crystal clear.

They are believed to be between 5,000 and 35,000 years old and appear to have been carved over a period of several hundred years – but they don't bear any tool marks. Their very construction defies common logic.

They are believed to offer spiritual power to those who hold or possess them.

Crystal skulls, carved from single quartz crystals, first appear on the market in the mid to late 19th century, bead size early and large ones later. Museums bought them as pre-Columbian Aztec or Maya artifacts.

Most museum crystal skulls trace back to French antiquities dealer Eugène Boban (1834-1908) who was active in Mexico City in the 1860's.

In 1992, a 10 inch milky quartz crystal skull was mailed to the Smithsonian with an unsigned letter stating that it was of ancient Aztec origin.

Smithsonian anthropologist and researcher Jane MacLaren Walsh along with a British Museum scientist investigated this skull and a large one in the British Museum that originated with Boban.

Examination under a scanning electron microscope revealed tool marks that could only have been caused by rotary wheels with hard abrasives, a technology unavailable in pre-Columbian Mesoamerica. A tiny residue in a cavity in the Smithsonian skull was identified by x-ray crystallography as carborundum, a synthetic abrasive invented in 1893.

No crystal skull has been authenticated as a pre-Columbian artifact and it is thought that all the crystal skulls are 19th or 20th century forgeries.

You can catch all the crystal skull myths in action, with aliens too, in the 2008 movie Indiana Jones and the Kingdom of the Crystal Skull.

*See *Mine Your Own Diamonds* on p. 195.

Smithsonian Skull

Burglars Strike Lightning

On March 3, 1921 burglars stole the lightning rods from the tops of the twin towers of the Cathedral of Notre Dame in Paris.

The motivation for this daring theft 300 feet up was the platinum tips on the 10 foot plus copper rods, about 16 ounces of it, worth $1200 at the time, about $15,000 adjusted for inflation, and $16,000 at $1000 platinum in 2015.

The thieves broke through 4 doors to gain access to the roofs of the twin towers of the cathedral. Then they sawed down the copper lightning rods and removed the platinum balls.

Stemwinder

I'll keep this speech short. You can't overwind a wind-up watch. Wind until you can't wind any more. But don't force it. If you do, you'll strip a gear or break the spring. That's what happens when a watch is "overwound."

Shootout at the Circle K Ranch

In early 1974 a shooting contest was held at the Circle K Ranch in Kaufman, Texas, 35 miles southeast of Dallas. The ranch belonged to the Hunt family, oil billionaires. Cowboys competed to be among the dozen to ride shotgun on three 707's bound for Zurich, Switzerland loaded with 40 million ounces of silver, almost 1400 tons.

The silver was owned by Nelson Bunker Hunt and his brother Herbert. They were sons of H.L. Hunt, who fathered 15 children in three families. H.L. Hunt had made his fortune in oil and was one of the richest men in America.

The Hunt brothers had inherited the apocalyptic world view and John Birch Society politics of their father. Nelson believed that the world-wide Communist conspiracy, abetted by the Eastern Liberal Establishment and the Rockefellers, threatened the world as he knew it and his fortune.

In 1973, his very lucrative oil field in Libya was nationalized by Moammar Gaddafi, who imposed a 51% royalty on the other oil companies, but let them keep their wells. Hunt blamed the State Department, the CIA, and the Rockefellers. This was also the period of high inflation and Hunt began looking for an investment that would preserve his wealth. He became obsessed with silver.

In 1973, the Hunt brothers started buying silver and by early 1974 they owned 55 million ounces, about 8% of the world supply. Silver went from $2-3 in 1973 to over $6 by the spring of 1974. They would have to pay a 5% tax to bring it back to Texas, and they feared govermment confiscation, so they decided to stash it in Switzerland.

Three chartered 707 jets flew from Dallas and landed at LaGuardia in the middle of the night. Armored trucks drove the silver from the New York Commodity Exhange warehouse in Manhattan and it was loaded into the planes watched by the cowboys armed with shotguns. But there had been a miscalculation when the planes and cowboys were hired. There was only room on the planes for 40 million ounces; they were 4 cowboys and one airplane short. The other 15 million ounces had to stay in warehouses in New Jersey and Chicago.

When the planes arrived in Zurich, armored trucks took the silver to 5 different warehouses. It had cost a fortune to move the silver and would cost $3 million a year to store it in Switzerland and the U.S. But the Hunt brothers were just getting started.

In 1979 the Hunts bought 43 million ounces of silver contracts to be delivered in the fall with two Saudi partners. In the fall of 1979, silver doubled in price from $8 to $16 in just two months. Then others started buying large amounts of silver.

The Chicago Board of Trade, one of the exchanges the Hunts used to buy silver, changed the rules by increasing the margin, the deposit required to buy a 5000 ounce silver contract for future delivery, and limited the number of contracts anyone could hold, requiring the selling of the excess by February, 1980. The New York Comex followed suit in January, 1980. But the Hunts bought even more silver futures contracts in London and the price of silver touched $50 on Jan. 17th, 1980.

On Jan. 21, the Comex limited trading to liquidation orders only and the next day silver fell to $34. In February, the Hunts took delivery of 26 million ounces of silver, bringing their holdings (with their Arab partners) to 155 million ounces.

In January and February alone, 22 million ounces of scrap silver came on the market as people lined up to sell their silver. ($50 in 1980 would have looked like $144 in 2015.) Interest rates rose as the Fed fought inflation of over 14%. The prime rate was 18.5% in March and hit 20% by April. By March 14, silver had fallen to $21.

As the price of silver fell, The Hunt's contracts were worth less and they had to come up with more margin, deposit money, to keep the 60 million ounces they had agreed to buy at a higher price. On March 25, the Hunts got a margin call for $135 million. They couldn't make it and their broker sold off $100 million worth of their silver futures.

On March 27 — Silver Thursday — silver opened at $15.80 and closed at $10.80. The Hunts were into the silver they had already bought for around $10, but they were well underwater in their futures contracts averaging $35. They owed $1.5 billion.

Fed Chairman Paul Volcker approved a bailout in which banks loaned the brothers $1.1 billion with $8 billion in collateral pledged. In 1988, a $135 million judgement related to his attempt to corner the silver market forced Nelson to file for personal bankruptcy.

Nelson was still around in 2011 at 85: "We are pleased to announce that Nelson Bunker Hunt of Texas will again serve as a member of the Council of The John Birch Society." (See *Nut Country* on p. 140.) Nelson Bunker Hunt died October 21, 2014 at 88.

Waiting for Goldot

Sometimes, when people come in to sell their gold, if I tell them gold has gone down they ask "should I wait?" They mean wait until gold goes back up.

This is wishful thinking. Even if it goes up, it's unlikely it will go up enough to make a difference. If you have $1000 and gold goes up 10%, which is a lot, you would have an extra $100. Maybe gold will go down 10% while you're waiting and you'll lose $100.

One fellow actually said he believed that gold would go up because all the ads exhorting you to buy gold said it would go up. ("Experts say gold will go to $5000!")

If you had waited for gold to go to $1000 after its $850 peak January 21,1980 (everyone was saying it would at the time), you would still be waiting.

Gold fell to $590 by the end of 1980 and languished between $260 and $500 until 2006, 26 years of waiting for Goldot.

Gold passed $850 at the end of 2009. But you forgot about inflation. $850 in 1980 was equivalent to $2457 in 2015. The peak price of $1895 (London P.M. fix) on September 6, 2011 ("I will not vote to raise the debt ceiling...") was equivalent to $656 in 1980.

You know that old saying, a bird in the hand…? Here's another one: nobody ever went broke taking a profit.

Diamonds Found in New Jersey!

Cape May diamonds are found in New Jersey (at Cape May, of course), but unfortunately they're not diamonds. They're quartz. They look like small clear pebbles.

One theory is that the quartz falls into the Delaware River in Pennsylvania near the Delaware Water Gap. It takes 1000 years for the quartz to be washed the 200 miles to the mouth of the Delaware Bay at Sunset Beach, Cape May, becoming rounded pebbles from tumbling all that time in the currents.

A World War I experimental concrete ship, the Atlantis, while being towed to be sunk as a breakwater at the entrance of the then new Cape May Canal in 1926 broke loose during a storm and washed a mile west, coming to rest off Sunset Beach. It is thought that the wreck diverts the quartz pebbles to Sunset Beach rather than being washed out to sea.

Another theory, from the New Jersey state geologist no less (I didn't know we had one) is that the quartz pebbles were in gravel deposited by retreating glaciers at the end of the last ice age.

Careful, or You'll Have to Leave It to Beaver!

In the November 13, 1958 episode, Beaver's Aunt Martha sends him a gold ring that once belonged to his namesake uncle,Theodore.

Beaver takes it to school against parental orders, figuring it's safe tied to his belt loop. The other kids convince him to try it on and it gets stuck on his finger and the school nurse has to cut it off.

You can avoid getting the big lecture Beaver got by getting on over to Joseph's while you can still get your ring off to have it sized. If not, you'll have to leave it to my brand new Becton-Dickenson "Beaver" ring cutter.

The Sound of One Hand Clapping

Part I (Fall 2000)

I sold an excellent sterling silver ring with a large opal, a nice heavy ring. A week later, the customer came in with the bottom of the ring bent out of shape. It seems that she had gone to a Broadway show and had applauded vigorously.

Silver is quite soft and even heavy pieces are easily bent.

Part II (Holiday 2008)

Another opal story. A ring with two opals was too large and when the woman wearing it applauded, it spun around to the bottom of her finger and smashed into the bottom of a ring on the other hand, shattering one of the opals.

Practice Zen applause.

Gold Mine

There are only a few grams per ton of gold in gold mine ore and extracting this low concentration is an arduous process.

But there are over 300 grams of gold in

a ton of old smartphones, about 10,000 phones, according to a spokesman for Sims Recycling Solutions, the world's largest electronic scrap recycler.

200 laptops or a ton of computer circuit boards would yield 5 troy ounces of gold, 155 grams.

According to the EPA, a million recycled cell phones would yield 35,000 pounds of copper, 772 pounds of silver, 75 pounds of gold, and 33 pounds of palladium without the bother of digging it out of the ground.

Noble Liquid

Gold is tested for karat by rubbing the item across a black basalt stone to get a streak and then putting a little drop of acid on the streak to see if it dissolves. This is the origin of the phrase "acid test".

The acid is called aqua regia, Latin for noble liquid, so named because it will dissolve gold. It is a mixture of nitric and hydrochloric acids. Aqua regia is formulated in a variety of proportions to dissolve different karats of gold. If the streak stays with 14 karat acid and dissolves in 18 karat acid, the gold is 14 karat. The streak from gold-plated costume jewelry dissolves in any of the acids.

Base metal turns green when aqua regia is put on it, gold does not. Silver turns a cream color.

Nobel Liquid

German Jewish physicists Max von Laue and James Franck had left their gold Nobel medals with Niels Bohr, the Danish Nobel-prize winning physicist, at his Institute of Theoretical Physics in Copenhagen to safeguard them from the Nazis.

When the Germans occupied Denmark in 1940, Bohr dissolved the 23 karat medals in a bottle of aqua regia and left it on a shelf in his laboratory, hiding in plain sight, and escaping the notice of the Nazis who occupied and searched the Institute.

Bohr escaped from Copenhagen to Sweden by boat, then was spirited out to England in a harrowing flight in a British airplane in 1943. He then went to the United States and worked on the Manhattan project, which developed the atomic bomb.

When Bohr returned in 1945 the bottle was still there. The gold was recovered and presented to the Nobel Foundation in Stock-

holm, and the Swedish Royal Mint struck new medals from the recovered gold for von Laue and Franck in 1950.

It Doesn't Tick. It Hums

Actual size

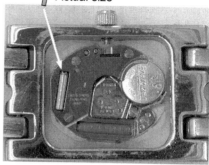

The quartz business of a quartz watch lives in the cylinder (arrow) shown in the top photo of a watch movement. In the bottom photo, I carefully cut away the cylinder to expose the heart of the watch, a quartz tuning fork. A gold circuit pattern is printed on it.

Quartz is piezoelectric. If you apply an electric current to it, it vibrates. The quartz tuning forks in quartz watches are designed to vibrate exactly 32,768 times per second (32K, one of those bits and bytes computer numbers), far above the human hearing range. Electronic circuitry steps that down to a once a second impulse sent to the tiny step motor that drives the hands.

Early electric watches, such as the Bulova Accutron, used a vibrating metal tuning fork that was directly coupled to the gears of the watch.

The first quartz watch was unveiled by Seiko in 1969. It cost $1250, then the price of a Toyota Corolla.

Benediction

May the Lord bless you and keep you: may the Lord cause his face to shine upon you and be gracious to you; may the Lord lift up his countenance upon you and grant you peace. (continued next page.)

This poetic verse from the Bible is heard at the conclusion of Jewish and Christian services everywhere.

Recently two ancient miniature silver scrolls discovered in 1979 in a tomb near Jerusalem were re-examined with modern computer imaging techniques. The heavily corroded and cracked scrolls have this verse, the Priestly Benediction, incised on them in archaic Hebrew.

From the type of script used, the scrolls have been dated around 600 B.C., the oldest known biblical verse.

It is thought that the scrolls were worn as amulets on a cord or carried in a pouch.

Submarine Treasure

On December 8, 1941*, ten hours after the attack on Pearl Harbor, the Japanese invaded the Philippines.

On December 23, General MacArthur ordered the evacuation of Manila and transferred his headquarters to the island of Corregidor at the entrance to Manila Bay. Corregidor had a tunnel complex built in solid rock by Army engineers.

Corregidor was pounded day and night by Japanese bombers. The island's anti-aircraft gunners took a toll on the Japanese, with at least 200 shot down, but their shells had a limit of 24,000 feet and the Japanese started to fly above that altitude. What was needed was a type of shell that could reach to 30,000 feet, the service ceiling of the bombers, but which was in short supply.

A submarine, the USS Trout, was ordered from Pearl Harbor to Corregidor with 3500 rounds of the high-altitude ammunition. She set sail on January 12, 1942, Lt. Cmdr. Frank Fenno commanding, and reached Corregidor on Feb. 3. Trout was met by a PT boat and guided through minefields in the dark.

After the shells were unloaded, the sub was too light and needed ballast. Fenno requested 25 tons of sand bags or crushed rock, but this was needed for defenses and could not be spared.

Anticipating the fall of Manila, large amounts of gold, silver, and other portable wealth had been transferred to the tunnels of Corregidor. 20 tons of gold and silver, 319 gold bars and 630 bags of a thousand Philippine silver pesos, were put aboard the Trout. This solved the sub's ballast problem and also kept the gold reserves

of the Philippines out of enemy hands.

Trout then set out on patrol in the East China Sea, following her orders. She sank a cargo ship and hit another after a near-miss by an enemy torpedo.

Trout arrived at Pearl Harbor March 3 and unloaded her precious ballast.

Trout took part in the Battle of Midway from June 3-6. Frank Fenno turned over command of Trout on June 17. On February 8, 1944 she was reported missing.

Frank Fenno went on to become a Rear Admiral in the Navy. He won the Distinguished Service Cross, the Navy Cross, the Silver Star, the Legion of Merit and the Bronze Star. He died on August 15, 1973 at 70 and is buried in Arlington National Cemetery.

President Roosevelt ordered MacArthur to Australia. He left on March 11, 1942 and flew to Australia from the southern Philippine island of Mindanao after a harrowing three day trip in a PT boat. Corregidor surrendered to the Japanese on May 6, 1942. and was recaptured February 26, 1945 after a ferocious 10 day battle.

*December 7, Hawaii time. The Philippines is on the other side of the international dateline.

First Strike

The first documented gold strike wasn't in California in 1848, it was in North Carolina in 1799.

A Hessian soldier, John Reed (Johannes Reith) who settled as a farmer in North Carolina after the Revolutionary War, found a 17 pound yellow rock in a creek on his farm. He used it as a door stop for three years. In 1802, he took it to a jeweler in Fayetteville who bought it for the asking price of $3.50. It was worth about $4700, given the gold price of $19.89/oz at the time.

The next year, Reed started mining for gold with three partners. They worked part-time during the fallow season and over 20 years unearthed $100,000 in gold.

Word spread and gold was found in other creeks in the area. Underground mining began in 1831. Reed died a wealthy man in 1845. The Reed mine closed in 1912.

Can I Borrow 6000 Tons of Silver?

That was the question asked by Col. Kenneth Nichols of Assistant Secretary of the Treasury Daniel Bell on August 3, 1942.

Col. Nichols was there on behalf of General Leslie Groves, head of the Manhattan Project that built the first atomic bomb. The silver was to be used for powerful electromagnets in calutrons[1], the devices that separated the rare (.7%) U-235 isotope of uranium needed for the bomb. The silver was needed because of the wartime shortage of copper.

"How many troy ounces is that?" Bell asked. Neither man knew how to convert tons to troy ounces. "What difference does it make how we express the quantity?" Said Nichols. "Young man, you may think of silver in tons, but the Treasury will always think of silver in troy ounces." Bell retorted.[2]

The silver was shipped in October, 1942 from the West Point Bullion Depository to plants in New Jersey where it was rolled into 3 inch strips 40 inches long. The strips were sent to Allis-Chalmers in Milwaukee where they were wound onto giant steel spools to form the magnets.

The magnets were shipped to Oak Ridge, Tennessee to a facility code-named Y-12.

The uranium was converted to uranium tetrachloride, zapped with an electric arc to ionize it, give it an electric charge, then the ion stream was accelerated into the magnetic field of the calutron which bent the slightly lighter U-235 isotope more than the heavier U-238, giving separate streams for collection.

Ultimately, 14,700 tons (429 million troy ounces) of silver were used in 1152 calutrons. It took 22,000 people working around the clock for a year to separate 110 pounds of 88% pure U-235 used in Little Boy[3], the bomb dropped on Hiroshima on August 6, 1945. Less than 1 gram of the uranium was converted to the energy that destroyed the city. (Now you know what $E=MC^2$ really means.)

After the war the silver was reclaimed and returned to West Point, the last of it in 1970. A few of the calutrons were used to separate isotopes of other elements, some used for medical treatment until then. Only .0036% of the $300 million of

silver was missing.

1. Coined from California University Cyclotron where it was developed by Nobel Prize winning physicist Ernest O. Lawrence.
2. 175,080,000 troy ounces.
3. Another 31 pounds of 50% enriched uranium was used.

Each section is a calutron with two beams

The Hole in the Wall Gang

A company in China knocked two holes in the Great Wall of China looking for gold.

300 feet of one of the oldest parts of the wall, built in the third century B.C. in Inner Mongolia, was irreparably damaged. This part of the wall is low and built of earth and stone, unlike the part of the 4000 mile wall tourists visit in Beijing.

Police are investigating the incident. Last year five miners went to jail for damaging another part of the wall in Inner Mongolia.

Don't Hold Your Breath

It won't do you any good anyway at 7 miles under the ocean. But you'll know the exact time you're crushed into oblivion.

The Bell & Ross "Hydromax" watch holds the Guiness Book of World Records title for water-resistance in a watch at 11,100 meters.

This beats the trunks off of Breitling's just introduced "Avenger Seawolf". You'll be wading at the shallow end of the pool at a mere 2 miles deep with this pansy watch, while your macho friends do some serious diving.

A proprietary clear fluoride oil fills the case of the Hydromax. An air bubble expands and contracts with pressure. The air bubble is kept out of the way in the back of the watch. A rubber disk behind the movement also cushions the innards. 2300 Euros.

Why 11,100? The deepest place on earth is the Marianas Trench at 10,994 meters ± 40 meters, so you're covered in any case.

The Great Diamond Hoax

In 1872, two Kentucky Prospectors, Philip Arnold and Jack Slack, brought a bag of uncut diamonds, rubies, and sapphires to the Bank of California in San Francisco. The bank president, William Ralston, was alerted to this bonanza.

Two San Francisco jewelers examined the stones and judged them to be natural and of excellent quality. Ralston said he would arrange financing for a mining venture if Arnold and Slack would show two of his men the site where the gems were found.

After a 36 hour train ride to the east and two days on mules, blindfolded, Ralston's men reached the site. They returned to San Francisco with 7000 carats of rubies and 1000 carats of diamonds.

Ralston's jewelers appraised the stones for $125,000. Ralston then sent the gems to his New York attorney, who took them to Charles Lewis Tiffany, founder of the prestigious store, who valued them at $150,000.

Next, Ralston hired a mining engineer to inspect the site. He, too, had to submit to a blindfolded journey. He reported that there were $5000 of gemstones per ton of ore and that a 20 man crew could recover $1 million a month.

Ralston was now convinced. He started a mining company with $2 million raised from 25 people, including Civil War general George McClellan. The story appeared in newspapers as far away as London, and a dozen other companies were formed to pursue these riches. Ralston and his investors bought out Arnold and Slack for $600,000. They took the money and vanished.

Meanwhile, a government geologist, Clarence King, became suspicious. King had led the Fortieth Parallel Survey in 1867, documenting, among other things, the geology of a 100 mile wide by 1000 mile long swath along the route of the transcontinental railroad. King knew the occurrence of rubies and diamonds in the same place, and on the surface, was unlikely.

King interviewed the mining engineer about his blindfolded trip to the gemstone site and concluded that it must lie within the Fortieth Parallel Survey area, in northwest Colorado Territory, now Moffat County, Colorado, He knew he had found the site when he saw a sign nailed to a tree claiming rights to a nearby water source signed by the mining engineer.

King found gemstones everywhere, many in obviously man-made crevices. One "rough" diamond had been partially faceted. It turned out that the diamonds were African rejects Arnold and Slack had bought in London for a song. Some of the rubies were garnets and others Burmese reject rubies. The sapphires were rejects from Ceylon.

Detectives tracked down Arnold in Kentucky, where he had bought a bank. Kentucky refused to extradite him, but he repaid $150,000 in return for immunity from further prosecution. Slack was never found. He had become an undertaker in New Mexico, where he died in 1896.

Ralston paid off his investors, but he and Tiffany were seen to be fools around the world. In 1875, Ralston's body was pulled from San Francisco Bay, a suicide.

It is still possible to find some of the salted stones at the site. Go to Maybell, Colorado and ask directions.

A Diamond Is Forever Wasn't Forever

The slogan "a diamond is forever" sounds like it's been around forever. However, it was created in 1948 by the N.W Ayers advertising agency on behalf of DeBeers, the South African company that is the world diamond monopoly.

It is arguably the most famous slogan ever created and the most successful advertising campaign in history.

It got you, didn't it?

Grand Slam In Diamonds

15 million years ago a meteor over a thousand yards across slammed into graphite bearing rock in Germany creating an estimated 79,000 tons of minute diamonds. The town of Nördlingen in Bavaria is built of stone that contains millions of tiny diamonds, all less than the size of the period at the end of this sentence.

The Popigal crater in Siberia was hit by a meteorite 36 million years ago and converted similar rock into even more diamonds.

War Gems

Gem materials have numerous industrial uses. On p. 199 is an article about a diamond window on a spacecraft that went to Venus. You're probably wearing industrial gems on your wrist: the quartz tuning fork that regulates your watch and the synthetic ruby "jewels" that are the bearings for the gears.

During World War II, there was a critical need for many natural gem materials: quartz for radio and radar, industrial diamonds for grinding and polishing and tourmaline for pressure gauges for submarines.

Tourmaline (October's birthstone), which comes in all colors, is piezoelectric: it develops an electric charge when subjected to pressure. Tourmaline was the material of choice for pressure gauges during the war.

While quartz was easily obtained from Brazil, the only suitable large crystals of tourmaline came from Madagascar, a French colony. 2000 pounds of Madagascar tourmaline were known to be in occupied France.

A remarkable man named Martin Ehrmann was sent to occupied France in 1944 to get the tourmaline out. He succeeded "under exceptionally difficult circumstances", although the details of the mission are, even now, unclear.

Ehrmann was born in 1904 in what is now Belarus. The family moved to Kiel, Germany around 1914. In 1921, Ehrmann, a teenager working on a German ship, got off in New York and set out to make a new life.

In 1928, he married the secretary to Dr. Ping Won Kuo, whose company imported Chinese jade into the U.S. Ehrmann became a salesman for the company and developed a a lifelong interest and expertise in mineralogy.

Ehrmann volunteered for the army in 1941, at age 37, and rose to become a Lt. Colonel and commander of the Ordnance Bomb Disposal School in Aberdeen, Md. by 1944. His expertise in mineralogy, world-wide contacts in this field, and perfect German, made him the ideal candidate for the tourmaline mission.

After the war, Ehrmann was a principal interviewer of German scientists for Operation Paperclip, the project that brought German rocket scientists, including Werner Von Braun, to the U.S.

Ehrmann was the preeminent American dealer in mineral specimens of his era and his legacy lives on in museums and collections around the world. He is fondly remembered for his charm and intrepidity in traveling the world in search of minerals. Ehrmann died in 1972.

Inflation

Many consumers believe that insurance appraisals for jewelry should value the jewelry at much more than would be paid to replace it.

All an inflated appraisal does is cause you to pay higher insurance premiums. Every appraisal course explicitly forbids inflated valuations as unethical.

From the web site of Jewelers of America, a trade organization:

"Intentionally over-valuing items on appraisals is considered illegal under Federal Trade Commission (FTC) guidelines and unethical by all nationally recognized appraisal organizations. The value assigned to the piece of jewelry should not be inflated beyond what is considered a fair retail selling price."

See *A Poser* on page 64.

Down the Drain

In January, 2009 a patron at a Phoenix diner lost her 7 carat diamond engagement ring when it slipped off her finger and fell into the toilet as she flushed it.

Opening the drain pipe outside the the restaurant and more flushing to push it down the line didn't work, so the rotorooter people were called in.

A video camera snaked into the pipe found the ring just a few feet down. The floor had to be jack-hammered and the pipe removed to recover the $78,000 diamond. The bill came to $6000 plus $1000 in tips. A 6 foot hole was left in the ladies room floor.

I hate to tell you this, but $11,000 a carat won't get you a great 7 carat diamond. Pretty yellow with lots of flaws.

Joseph's will size your ring so it won't slip off your finger for about 25 bucks.

That's Life

The cover story of the October 15, 1945 issue of Life Magazine is titled *Fall Jewelry*. On the cover is a model wearing a heavy choker necklace and a row of clunky bracelets.

"The current fashion for quantity and confusion in jewelry is related to the fact that necklines and sleeves are plain, hence often need adornment. But even this avalanche of jewelry is only a beginning. The costume jewelry trade, restricted by four years by scarcities, will soon have available tons of metals released from war contracts and thousands of artisans released from war plants and work on service medals. When jewelers really get going, women will be even more heavily weighted down than they are in the pictures on these pages and on the cover."

The war had ended just six weeks earlier with the surrender of Japan on September 2, 1945.

Baubles for Buddies to Barter

On April 16, 1943 (my birthday), the Ottowa Citizen had a small article about a half-ton shipment of junk jewelry, 17,157 pieces, on its way to the South Pacific to barter with the natives for work.

A Baubles for Buddies to Barter campaign by the San Francisco League for Service Men collected it in 10 days.

The Picture of the Week in the May 24, 1943 issue of Life Magazine was a photo of a heap of bangles, beads, earrings and brooches with what may be a pin of Vivien Leigh from Gone With the Wind wearing a large hat in the center.

"For cheap earrings and a glittering brooch, one native dug 32 foxholes for U.S. soldiers," the caption read.

El Dorado

"Over the Mountains of the Moon, Down the Valley of the Shadow, Ride, boldly ride ....If you seek for Eldorado!"
— From the poem *Eldorado* by Edgar Allan Poe

The tale of El Dorado, the legendary city of gold, comes from the Spanish explorers of South America in the 16th century.

The locals told a tale of a king of the Muisca people who covered his body with gold dust then boarded a raft in Lake Guatavita, near modern Bogata, Colombia.The king would dive into the lake, washing off the gold dust, then throw gold objects into the lake to appease the god who lived in it.

The Spanish called this chief "El Dorado", the gilded one, and from this sprang up the legend of a city of gold. Many fruitless expeditions were launched to find the mythical city of gold.

The Spanish tried to drain Lake Guatavita in 1548 using a bucket brigade. After 3 months of labor, the level of the lake had gone down by 9 feet and a small amount of gold was found.

In 1580 a Bogota businessman was able to lower the water level by 60 feet by cutting into the rim of the lake. 12,000 pesos worth of gold was found.

In 1898 a British company successfully drained the lake. Unfortunately, the 4 feet of mud at the bottom made exploration impossible and then the mud hardened up like concrete. Only £500 worth of gold was found and auctioned at Sotheby's. The company eventually went bankrupt.

Aur Cymraeg*

On April 26, 1923, Albert, Duke of York married Lady Elizabeth Bowes-Lyon in Westminster Abbey. Their wedding rings were made from a single nugget of gold from the Clogau mine in Wales.

Albert became King George VI and Elizabeth the Queen Mother.

Queen Elizabeth and Prince Philip married with Clogau gold wedding bands from the same nugget in 1947, as did Elizabeth's sister, Princess Margaret, and Antony Armstrong-Jones in 1960, Elizabeth's daughter Princess Anne and Captain Mark Phillips in 1973. The last of the original nugget was used for Princess Diana's ring, although Prince Charles' ring was also made from Clogau gold. Charles and Camilla also exchanged Clogau gold rings.

So will William and Kate have Clogau gold wedding rings? In 1986, Queen Elizabeth was presented with 1 kilo of Clogau gold (about 32 troy ounces) for her 60th birthday so there should be plenty left. Not a peep from the royals about it. Maybe they'll say after the wedding.

The Clogau mine started as a copper mine in Roman times, with gold being discovered in 1854. The mine was worked out in 1911 and operated intermittently until it was closed in 1998.

Welsh gold jewelry is made by the mine owners by adding a dab of Clogau gold from an existing stockpile to each piece. They expect to use it all by 2016.

* "Welsh Gold", in Welsh, I hope.

Rough and Ready

In the spring of 1849, Capt. A. A. Townsend, a Shellsburg, Wisconsin mining engineer, formed a company and set out for California and the gold rush.

He named his company Rough and Ready Mining Company after General Zachary "Old Rough and Ready" Taylor under whom he had served in the Mexican War and who had just become the 12th president.

Townsend set up camp in what is now Nevada County and named it Rough and Ready. They struck gold and the camp quickly became a town of 3000.

The federal government imposed a mining tax in 1850 and this riled up the Rough and Ready residents. On April 7, 1850, they voted to secede from the United States at a town meeting and became the Great Republic of Rough and Ready.

E.F. Brundage was elected president, a constitution was adopted and a Secretary of State and a marshall appointed.

But with the Fourth of July celebrations approaching, pangs of patriotism sapped the sovereign resolve. When the saloons in the neighboring town of Nevada City refused to sell liquor to the foreigners, another meeting was hastily called and rough and Ready rejoined the union.

Rough and Ready today has a population of about 1500 and celebrates Secession Day the last Sunday in June.

Foiled Again

An exhibition of diamonds at the Natural History Museum in London closed suddenly in November, 2005, 3 months early. Scotland Yard had received a tip that villains were plotting to steal the centerpiece of the exhibit, the 203 carat pear-shaped Millennium Star.

This was not an overreaction. In 2000, thieves were foiled in a spectacular robbery attempt at a diamond exhibition at the Millennium Dome in Greenwich.

After two failed armored car robberies by a London gang, police put the gang leader under surveillance instead of arresting him. He led them to the diamond exhibit, where he paid inordinate attention to the security. The rest of the gang was monitored and they, too, showed up at the diamond exhibit.

The night before the raid, the diamonds were switched for replicas and the next morning police were stationed undercover inside the dome.

At 9:30, a bulldozer crashed through the security fence and into the dome. The gang threw smoke grenades and broke through the armored glass with a nail gun and sledgehammers. Then the police, disguised as janitors, sprang into action, pulling out semi-automatic weapons.

They surrendered without a shot fired. Outside, the rest of the gang was arrested in their getaway speedboat, which was to have raced away down the Thames.

The robbers are still in jail.

Money Grows on Trees!

Researchers at Commonwealth Scientific and Industrial Research Organisation (CSIRO), Australia's national science agency have found that Eucalyptus trees that grow over gold deposits have minute amounts of gold in their leaves.

It's thought that the roots, which can grow as much as 130 feet deep, absorb gold particles. The gold is toxic to the plant so it tries to expel it through the leaves.

The particles are tiny, 1/10 the width of a hair. The gold is detected through x-ray analysis and the leaves of 500 trees would be needed to get enough for a wedding band.

Other trees and shrubs that grow over gold deposits also have gold in their leaves and this has great potential for simplifying and speeding up gold prospecting.

It's a Spinthariscope, Kemo Sabe

See genuine atoms split to smithereens inside this Kix Atomic Bomb Ring. For just 15¢ plus a Kix cereal boxtop the Lone Ranger Atomic Bomb Ring could have been yours in 1947.

The ring was advertised on the Lone Ranger radio show. It was also advertised in print, but came to be known as the Lone Ranger Atomic Bomb Ring. The contradiction of a 19th century cowboy selling a 20th century weapon was missed, maybe because the business end of the ring bomb looked like the Lone Ranger's silver bullet. (My wife actually had one as a kid.)

The red tail fin on the bomb could be removed to expose a secret message compartment. Then you could go into a dark room and look through a lens at the back and see a shower of light flashes.

The light flashes were caused by particles emitted by a radioactive element hitting a screen coated with zinc sulfide. This is called a spinthariscope.

The spinthariscope was invented by English scientist Sir William Crookes (1832-1919) in 1903. Crookes was experimenting in the dark with radium bromide, observing how it made a screen coated with zinc sulfide glow, when he accidently spilled some of the very costly radium on the screen. When he examined the screen under a microscope to locate even the smallest speck, he saw flashes of light rather than a uniform glow.

Crookes then built a small device with a speck of radium bromide on the tip of a needle, a zinc sulfide screen behind it, and a lens in front, all inside a brass tube. He named it a spinthariscope, from the Greek word for scintillation.

On May 15, 1903, Crookes showed his spinthariscope at a gala affair at the British Royal Society. It was a hit, and soon became the must-have toy for toffs.

The Lone Ranger spinthariscope used polonium 210, really bad stuff (remember that Russian guy who was poisoned with it?). But the alpha particles it emits don't penetrate the skin and the glass lens blocks them. (The problem comes when you eat it.) It has a half-life of only 138 days, so all the old Lone Ranger rings are dead now.

You can buy spinthariscopes today that use thorium or americium.

Mine Your Own Diamonds

You can mine your own diamonds at the Crater of Diamonds State Park in Murfreesboro, Arkansas.

In 1906 a farmer, John Wesley Huddleston, found 2 diamonds on his property. Illiterate but shrewd, he sold an option on his land for $36,000, big money at a time when a good mule cost $80, should it turn out to be a diamond mine.

It did, and the Arkansas Diamond Company was formed. But there were 40 adjacent acres of diamond bearing soil owned by another farmer who refused to sell.

He eventually sold a ¾ interest in his property to a man who promptly died and which was then bought by Austin Millar and his son who operated a successful diamond mining operation until the plant was destroyed by arson in 1919.

Various mining ventures worked the diamond field without much success until the Depression put an end to them in 1932.

During World War II, the government took over Crater of diamonds because of problems with DeBeers refusing to supply industrial diamond abrasive, a critical war material (see *Diamond Crooks Cop Plea* on p. 208). A contract was given to aviation pioneer Glenn Martin but the venture proved uneconomical. The property was returned to its owners after the war.

Between 1951 and 1972 various competing tourist attractions were opened. In 1970 all the land was consolidated and in 1972 the state of Arkansas bought the 80 acre diamond bearing site and 800 surrounding acres for $750,000 forming the Crater of Diamonds State Park.

Over 75,000 diamonds have been found since 1906. The most notable is the Uncle Sam diamond, found in 1924 and, at 40.23 carats, the largest diamond ever discovered in the United States. The Uncle Sam was cut into a 12.42 carat emerald cut, slightly yellow, but almost flawless. It was sold to an anonymous owner in 1971 for $150,000.

The Kahn Canary is a 4.25 carat yellow diamond discovered in 1977. It was set uncut in an 18 karat yellow gold and platinum ring from jewelry designer Henry Dunay in 1992 and loaned to Hillary Clinton for Bill Clinton's inauguration in 1993.

597 diamonds were found in 2010 with 23 diamonds over 1 carat. The Park released a list of the 7 largest diamonds:

- 4.89 carat grayish white
- 3.65 carat brown
- 3.17 carat yellow
- 2.93 carat yellow
- 2.70 carat white
- 2.44 carat brown
- 2.13 carat brown

Apache Tears

See the smooth black nuggets by the thousands laying here
Petrified but justified are these Apache tears
— Johnny Cash, Apache Tears

In 1870, General George Stoneman established a military outpost near present day Superior, Arizona in response to Apache raids.

Although there is no official record, legend has it that that winter U.S. Cavalry troops found a secret trail to the top of a mountain occupied by Apaches and attacked them at dawn. Outnumbered and surprised, 50 warriors were killed outright and the remaining 25 leaped off a cliff to their deaths rather than be captured.

Apache women gathered below the cliffs of what is now called Apache Leap Mountain and wept, their tears turning to black stones of mourning.

Apache tears are obsidian, black volcanic glass, and are found around Apache Leap Mountain and other areas in Arizona and New Mexico. The small lumps of obsidian are found embedded in perlite, a white porous material that is obsidian that has weathered.

Apache tears are sold as tumbled healing stones and set in jewelry.

Death by Gold

The Jivaro Indians of Ecuador were among the fiercest tribes in history. They were headhunters — and headshrinkers, too, the only headhunters to do this.

The Spanish established towns in Jivaro country in the mid 16th century and impressed the Indians into work in gold mines and taxed them on their gold trading.

In 1599, in response to a new tax, the Jivaro massed 20,000 warriors, attacked the town of Logrono at night and slaughtered 12,000 Spaniards. They executed the governor by pouring molten gold down his throat "in order that he might have his fill of gold".

Next they attacked Sevilla del Oro, filled with refugees from other towns. After fierce resistance, the Jivaro broke off the attack after killing 14,000.

The warlike Jivaro were the only tribe never conquered by the Spanish, despite many attempts.

Of course, there is a job placement company named *Jivaro Professional Headhunters*. They don't seem to have a psychiatric division, though.

Olden Goldie

A 2000 year old gold earring was recently found in an archeological excavation in a parking lot in the City of David section of Jerusalem.

The earring is made of gold with pearls and emeralds and is in pristine condition.

The City of David is a hilltop from which King David dedicated Jerusalem as his capital 3,000 years ago. The earring dates from around the time of Christ in the Roman period

Finds from the Roman period are rare in Jerusalem because the city was destroyed by the Romans in 70 A.D.

Goldwater

British chemist Edward Sonstadt discovered that there is gold dissolved in seawater in 1872.

In 1896, the pastor of a Baptist church in Middletown, Connecticut, the Rev. Prescott Ford Jernegan, approached jeweler Arthur Ryan claiming to have invented a method of extracting gold from seawater, revealed to him in a vision when recovering from typhoid fever.

The Gold Accumulator was a wooden box with holes in it to let in water. There was a pan with mercury mixed with a secret ingredient and a battery. The box was supposed to be lowered into the water, and the electrified mercury would extract gold from the seawater.

In February, 1897, Jernegan gave Ryan and a few colleagues instructions and then left to avoid the suspicion of impropriety. They then lowered the Gold Accumulator into the sea from a wharf in Providence, RI. They stayed the night in a shanty on the wharf.

The next morning, they raised the box out of the water and found gold flakes embedded in the mercury. The gold was assayed at $4.50 (that would be about ¼ ounce given the 1897 gold price of $18.98)

Jernegan, with an assistant, Charles Fisher, Ryan, and other investors formed The Electrolytic Marine Salts Company that year and they they leased a tidal grist mill in Lubec, Maine and put 240 accumulators in the inlet pond.

Enough gold came out of the accumulators to convince investors and shares in the company were floated. Jernegan publshed a prospectus, *A Sketch of a Commercially Profitable Process for the Extraction of Gold and Silver from Seawater*. The prospectus cited the work of Sonstadt and others and claimed $65 million of gold was in a cubic mile of seawater.*

Construction was begun on another plant nearby, a hive of activity employing 700 laborers.

Then Jernegan and his assistant disappeared in July, 1898, and the accumulators stopped producing gold. It turned out that the assistant, Fisher, Jernegan's boyhood friend, was a trained diver and had been salting the boxes with gold at night.

Jernegan and Fisher absconded with $200,000 each. Jernegan sailed to France under an assumed name. While living in Brussels, Belgium, Jernegan returned $75,000 to his investors. He later went to the Philippines to work as a schoolteacher and wrote a history of the Philippines in 1915. Fisher was never heard from again.

* Modern estimates of gold in seawater are 10-15 parts per trillion. At 10 ppt there would be 1 ounce of gold in 662 cubic miles of seawater. That would be about 2.9¢ per cubic mile at 1897 prices. See *Goldwater* on p 102 .

Ice Lathe

Gold chains are often "diamond cut", shaved with a diamond tool to give them a brilliant finish. Generally, chains are diamond cut on 4 sides. Smaller chains are cut on a machine that does all four sides at once. But larger chains are diamond cut on an ice lathe.

The chain is wound onto a cylinder, carefully positioned, and sprayed with water. A refrigeration unit inside the cylinder then freezes the water, locking the chain in position. The cylinder then rotates and a diamond tool shaves off a little gold. This has to be done four times to cut each side of the chain.

Considering the work that goes into it, the little extra you're charged for diamond cut chain is remarkable. The photo is courtesy of the company that makes that wonderfully strong wheat chain that has had a brick hanging from it for over 25 years in the display on the corner of one of the cases.

Silverpoint

Graphite for drawing began with the discovery in the 16th century of a large deposit in northwest England. This deposit was very pure and solid and could be sawn into blocks, still the only significant find of solid graphite.

At the time it was thought to be a form of lead and was called plumbago, Latin for lead ore. (Whence the lead in your pencil, which is actually a mixture of clay and graphite.)

Before graphite, fine drawing was done by the technique of metalpoint, a metal tip on a wooden stylus, with silver giving the best results. Paper or parchment was coated with powdered bone mixed with hide glue. This gives a slightly abrasive surface so that minute particles rub off from the silver point leaving a fine gray line.

The silver tarnishes to a mellow brown over time. The silverpoint technique gives a fine defined line and requires a light touch, with tonal differences built up laboriously with hatching.

Albrecht Durer, Rembrandt, Raphael, Jan van Eyck and Leonardo DaVinci are some of the artists who worked in silverpoint. Study of a Horse, above, is a silverpoint by Leonardo, circa 1490. Silverpoint declined after the discovery of graphite.

Silverpoint is still done by contemporary artists using a variety of surface preparations, sometimes just flat white latex paint. Silica (diatomaceous earth) in paint gives it the tooth to rub off particles of silver.

I tried it. I had an old can of white primer paint and I sprayed it on an index card. I took a fine sterling silver wire, heated it to soften it and put it in a pin vise. The result is the calligraphic masterpiece at right.

The Only Law Never Broken

It is ordained and established that none from henceforth shall use to multiply gold or silver nor use the craft of multiplication and if any the same do and be thereof attaint, that he shall incur the pain of felony.*

This *Act Against Multipliers* was passed in England in 1404, during the reign of Henry IV (1399-1413). To multiply gold and silver referred to alchemists transmuting base metal into gold or silver. It wouldn't do for someone to be richer than the king.

The act was repealed in 1689 after lobbying by Robert Boyle, one of the founders of modern chemistry (Boyle's Law). Boyle, along with his contemporary, Isaac Newton, was an alchemist, seeking to change base metal into gold. He wanted the act repealed because he thought he had found the secret.

Actually, minute amounts of gold have been made from mercury and platinum in nuclear reactors at great cost.

* They didn't fool around in the 15th century. "Pain of felony" meant the death penalty, no doubt painful.

Chryselephantine Sculpture

"Chryselephantine" is formed from the Greek words "chrysos", gold, and "elephantinos", ivory. It's an ancient sculptural technique of attaching ivory and sheets of gold to an inner wooden frame. The ivory was used to represent skin and gold for everything else.

The technique goes back to the second millennium B.C. A famous statue of a youth circa 1500. B.C. from the Minoan civilization was found in eastern Crete.

The best known examples of chryselephantine statues are of Athena, 40 feet high, which the Parthenon in Greece was designed to house in 438 B.C., and the 43 foot seated Zeus in the temple at Olympia, one of the seven wonders of the ancient world. Neither statue has survived.

A 16.5 inch chryselephantine statue of a mounted Napoleon entering Cairo in 1798 made by French artist Jean-Léon Gérôme (1824-1904) in 1897 is for sale for $198,000 at a New Orleans antiques dealer.

The Pearl of Allah

Wilburn Cobb, a San Francisco archaeologist, tells this story of the largest pearl in the world. The pearl is not like the pearls you know. It was formed in a giant clam, *Tridacna Gigas*, and is porcelaneous, like the dull interior surface of its shell, and doesn't have the luster of pearls from oysters and mussels with their iridescent shell linings. The pearl is 9.45 inches in length and weighs 14.1 pounds.

Cobb was visiting with Dyak villagers on the Phillippine island of Palawan in 1934 when he learned that a boy diving for conch shells had been trapped by a giant clam and had drowned. The boy and the clam were recovered and a giant pearl weighing 14 pounds was found inside the clam. Cobb wanted to buy the pearl but the Dyak chief refused, saying that it resembled a turbaned Mohammed and it would be sacreligeous to sell it.

Cobb returned to Manila. Two years later, he received a letter from the Dyak chief telling him of the discovery of an ancient burial ground of his people. Soon after he arrived to begin excavation of the site, he was told that the son of the Muslim religious leader was stricken with malaria. Cobb had atabrine with him, a better treatment than the quinine they were using, and he was able to cure the boy and was given the pearl.

In 1939, Cobb returned to the United States and had the pearl authenticated by the American Museum of Natural History in New York. He exhibited the pearl at Ripley's Believe it or not! Odditorium in Times Square with a price tag of $3.5 million.

30 years later, in 1969, Cobb wrote about the pearl for the Mensa (the high I.Q. club) Bulletin, hoping to no avail that Mensa would broker the sale of the pearl for $3.5 million for a commission. He claimed that while the pearl was being exhibited at Ripley's in 1939, a Chinese man, Mr. Lee, claimed that the pearl was the lost pearl of Lao Tzu, (b. 604 B.C.?) the founder of Taoism.

Lee said that Lao Tzu had disciples plant a jade carved with the faces of Buddha, Confucius, and himself in a clam as the nucleus for a pearl. The pearl was then transferred to ever larger clams as it grew. In 1750, the clam with the pearl inside was sent out of China for safekeeping in a boat that was lost in a storm off Palawan where it remained until discovered by the drowned diver. Cobb says that Lee offerred $3.5 million for the pearl, but Cobb refused and Lee left Ripley's and vanished.

Critics contend that this revised story 30 years after the fact was an attempt by Cobb to increase the value of the pearl he was trying to sell by conjuring up an awesome provenance. And why would he turn down his asking price?

Aside from being bogus on the face of it, this tale has technical problems. No one has ever cultured a pearl in a clam. It is unlikely it was done 2500 years ago. Giant clams live about 100 years, so generations of disciples would have had to attend to retransplanting the pearl. The final clam would have been old in 1750 and would have to live another184 years until its discovery in 1934. The original story has problems, too. Giant clams close their shells slowly, so it would be hard to be trapped by one.

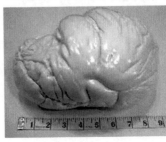

Wilburn Cobb died in 1980. The Pearl of Allah was purchased from his estate by Peter Hoffman and Victor Barbish for $200,000. Barbish took a loan from Colorado bar owner Joseph Bonicelli giving him an interest in the pearl as collateral. In 1990 Bonicelli sued Barbish to collect the loan. The court ruled that Hoffman, Barbish, and Bonicelli were equal partners in the pearl and ordered it sold and the proceeds split three ways. The order was never carried out.

Bonicelli died in 1998. Bonicelli's wife Eloise had been murdered in her house in 1975, but the case was never solved. In 2000, a local barber was caught on tape saying that he had arranged the murder and that he was paid $10,000 by Bonicelli. Bonicelli's estate, including his share of the pearl, had gone to his second wife and daughter. The children of his murdered first wife filed a wrongful death suit and were awarded $32.4 million in 2005, based on wild appraisals of the pearl of from $42-90 million. (The world's second largest pearl, the 5 pound Palawan Princess, failed to sell at auction in 2009 with an estimate of $300-400,000). The second wife and daughter appealed and the Pearl of Allah still sits in a Colorado Springs bank vault awaiting the outcome of the litigation.

Bahia Emerald

In September, 2010, Larry Biegler called the Los Angeles Sheriff's office claiming his large emerald worth $400 million had been stolen from a warehouse.

Detectives tracked the emerald to two businessmen in Eagle, Idaho who were trying to sell it. The men said that Biegler had put it up as collateral for $1 million in diamonds the men had paid Biegler for, but had not been delivered. The men had picked up the emerald in the warehouse.

Biegler said he had completed the diamond deal and that the rwo men had agreed to pay $80 million for the emerald. The men agreed to turn over the emerald to the Sheriff's deputies pending resolution of the matter.

But the emerald wasn't in Idaho, it was in secure storage in Las Vegas. The Los Angeles detectives went to Las Vegas and picked up the emerald, an 840 lb. rock with large emerald crystals embedded in it, and took it back to a Los Angeles Sheriff's Department evidence locker

The emerald conglomerate is called the Bahia Emerald from the Brazilian state where it was found in 2001.

According to Ken Conetto, a Brazlian gem dealer who owned the rights to the mine where it was found shipped it to him in San Jose, California in 2005 to find a buyer in exchange for a cut of the profits.

Conetto shipped the emerald to New Orleans to show a buyer but Hurricane Katrina flooded the bank vault in which it was stored and it spent weeks underwater. The deal fell through and the emerald was brought back to San Jose.

Conetto contacted Biegler to help him sell the emerald and they drove it to Los Angeles. Biegler said Conetto pledged the stone as collateral for a loan he didn't pay back and the emerald was his. Conetto says he never borrowed the money and he owned it.

At one point the emerald was listed on Ebay for a buy it now price of $75 million.

Anthony Thomas also claims the emerald. He says he paid $60,000 for it in 2001 but the Brazlians never shipped it to him. He has photos of him in Brazil next to the Bahia Emerald. But his house burned to the ground after someone left a pot of beans on the stove and his receipt for the emerald was destroyed.

A gemologist in Brazil appraised the stone for $372 million, but even the most impressive mineral specimens top out at a million or so according to a spokesman for the New York Museum of Natural History.

On January 29, 2014 Judge John A. Kronstadt of The Los Angeles County Superior Court rejected the claims of Anthony Thomas, round two will be decided in a future trial.

Missing Mass

Platinum is so impervious to corrosion that the International Prototype Kilogram was made from it in 1879 and adopted as the standard in 1889. It's a cylinder of a platinum iridium alloy that serves as the reference weight for the kilogram (2.2 pounds), the weight of 1 liter of water. It's kept locked up in Sevres, France under nested glass bell jars.

Official replicas were provided to other countries (the U.S. Has 4) and the copies are returned to France every 40 years to be compared against the original.

The third comparison, carried out between 1988 and 1992, found that the standard had lost 50 Millionths of a gram compared to the copies. (That's worth .17 cent.) It's a big deal to scientists because the units of force, energy, and pressure depend on the kilogram. Scientists haven't a clue what's going on. They haven't figured out where the missing mass of the universe went, either.

The Chiemsee Cauldron

In 2001, an amateur diver found a metal bowl on the bottom of the Chiemsee, a large lake in Bavaria, in southern Germany, near the Austrian border.

Dubbed the Chiemsee Cauldron, it is 24 pounds of 18 karat gold, 20" in diameter and 12" high. The cauldron is decorated with raised mythical figures in the Celtic tradition, similar to the 2000 year old silver Gundestrup Cauldron, discovered in a Danish peat bog in 1891.

The director of the Bavarian State Archaeological Collection examined the cauldron and determined that it was a 20th century forgery, possibly from the Nazi era, on the basis of the soldering technique.

A director of a long established Munich jewelry company said that the company's goldsmith told him before his death in the 1960's of a gold cauldron exceeding 10 kilos with figurative ornamentation that had been made over 14 years between 1925 and 1939. He said the cauldron had been commissioned by industrialist Albert Pietzsch, a member of the Nazi party and an early benefactor of Hitler. (When this came out, the German press promptly dubbed the cauldron "Hitler's bedpan".)

Speculation is that the cauldron was thrown in the lake so it wouldn't fall into the hands of the advancing Allies at the end of the war.

A Nazi provenance, which would have given ownership to the state of Bavaria, was not proven so the Cauldron was declared "discovered treasure" which gave the diver half ownership with the state.

The Cauldron was sold for 300,000 Euros to a Swiss investor who hyped it as a 2000 year old archaeological treasure worth hundreds of millions. A woman from Kazakhstan paid $1.5 million for a share of future earnings, then had buyers remorse and sued the Swiss businessman in 2006 and the Cauldron was confiscated by the Swiss authorities in 2007. A fraud trial began in October, 2010. Google lost track of it after that.

Chiemsee
Cauldron

Gundstrup
Cauldron

Boss Tweed Stickpin

William M. Tweed, Boss Tweed (1823-1878), the corpulent symbol of 19th century corruption in New York City, shamelessly sported a huge 10½ carat diamond stickpin that cost $15,500 in 1871 ($279,000 today).

The stickpin is prominent in political cartoons in Harpers Weekly by Thomas Nast skewering him. Jailed in 1876, Tweed escaped and fled to Spain where he was arrested by a customs official who recognized him from Nast's caricatures.

His jeweler was Thomas Kirkpatrick. As a boy Kirkpatrick worked for Ball, Black & Co., a leading 19th century jeweler. For years he took turns with another boy sleeping under the counter to guard against thieves. Kirkpatrick opened his own store in 1856.

"It was said that he was on friendly terms with more of the public men of the city than any other jeweler. The late "Boss" Tweed always bought his jewelry from Mr. Kirkpatrick."

— From his obituary in the New York Times, December 28, 1906.

Wrist Jewels

The jewels in a watch are tiny doughnuts of synthetic ruby. They serve as the bearings for the axles of the gears. Ruby is far harder than metal. If a gear rotates once a minute, it would turn over 5 million times in 10 years. If the gears rotated in holes in a metal plate, they would soon enlarge the holes and start to wobble.

Quartz watches have maybe 7 jewels, tops. Mechanical watches, with many more moving parts, up to 27 jewels.

The Dewey Diamond

On the night of July 2, 1834, a merchant ship captain, Samuel Dewey, rowed out to the USS Constitution in the Charleston Navy Yard in Boston and sawed off the figure-head of President Andrew Jackson under the bowsprit. He cut the head off from the nose up, leaving the mouth and chin behind.

While the Constitution was refitting, a new figurehead of Jackson was installed to replace a figure of Hercules that had been damaged in a collision. Jackson was so unpopular in Boston the commandant of the Navy Yard received death threats when word of the new figurehead got out. Dewey was an ardent Whig, the anti-Jackson party.

Dewey took the head to Washington intending to present it to President Jackson himself. But Jackson was ill and Dewey took it to Vice-President Martin Van Buren, who suggested he take it to the Secretary of the Navy, Mahlon Dickerson. Dickerson threatened to have Dewey arrested, but Dewey told him no jury in Boston would convict him of anything and Dickerson relented and took the head.

The head stayed in Dickerson's family and was finally reunited with its mouth and chin in 2010, documented in an episode of History Detectives.

Dewey became a ship broker, became wealthy, and took up mineralogy.

In 1854, a laborer, Benjamin Moore, discovered a large diamond while grading a street in Manchester, Virginia. (now part of Richmond). Moore took it to a jeweler who appraised the 23.75 carat stone at $4000 ($92,000 today). It was the largest diamond yet found in the United States.

Dewey had been collecting mineral specimens in Virginia and, hearing of the stone, he showed up to test it. He conducted scratch tests and put it in an iron furnace where it was held at red heat for over two hours. It emerged unscathed and he pronounced it a diamond.

According to an account in True Richmond Stories by Harry Kollatz, researched from contemporary newspaper articles, Dewey exhibited the diamond at 12¢ a look, then told Moore he'd sell the diamond in New York and split the proceeds but Moore never heard from Dewey again.

Dewey had the diamond cut in Boston for $1500. After cutting the diamond weighed 11.15 carats, was off-color and with a flaw. It was worth less than the cost to cut it, an 1890 account giving its value at $300-400.

Dewey had pledged the stone as collateral on a loan to J. Anglist, which he failed to redeem and, in turn, Anglist pledged it as collateral for a $6000 loan to John Morrissey. Anglist also defaulted and Morrissey became the owner of the Dewey Diamond.

Morrissey was a tough guy, an Irish immigrant who became the bare knuckle heavyweight boxing champion in 1858. He was a member of the Dead Rabbits gang in New York. He was nicknamed "Old Smoke" when he was pinned to the floor on burning coals from an over-turned stove in a fight, endured the pain, then got back up and beat his opponent senseless with smoke rising from the burning flesh on his back. He was a founder of Saratoga Race Track and became a New York State Senator and a U.S. Congressman. He died in 1878. No one knows the whereabouts of the Dewey Diamond today.

Samuel Dewey died in poverty in Philadelphia in 1899 at 92. His obituary in the New York Times says that "during a tramping tour through New Jersey Capt. Dewey picked up the biggest American ruby yet discovered" and that it is in the Academy of Natural Sciences in Philadelphia. I contacted the Academy and a curator responded that they may never have had it. He emailed me a photo of a ruby in matrix specimen from the William Vaux collection with a note that it had been purchased from "Col." Dewey for $5, which doesn't fit the "biggest American ruby yet discovered" description.

The Academy was given the mineral collection of William Vaux after his death in 1882. Both Dewey and Vaux lived in Philadelphia and must have known each other given the $5 ruby sale. I think the ruby was known to be in the Vaux collection and that is why the Times placed it at the Academy.

The Proceedings of the Academy from 1885 note that several people familiar with the Vaux collection noticed that a number of fine specimens were missing. Vaux had a nephew, George Vaux, also a mineralogist. The Mineralogical Record notes on its web site that George picked 25 fine specimens from his uncle's collection before it was given to the Academy. George Vaux died in 1927 and his collection was donated to Bryn Mawr College by his family in 1958.

I contacted Bryn Mawr, thinking the Dewey ruby must surely be there. They emailed me 10 photos of ruby specimens, but noted that they were all quite small, about 1 cm. These are mineral specimens, opaque rubies still encased in the host rock, not gems, and all from Sussex County.

Then the Academy sent me a photo of another New Jersey ruby specimen, though not ascribed to Dewey, much larger, 1.14" long X .4" wide. We both agree that this is the maybe Dewey ruby. It was probably considered insufficiently large or wonderful to be noted as such for posterity.

Actual size

Photo courtesy of the Academy of Natural Sciences

Gutter Ball

A senior GIA (Gemological Institute of America) gemologist reports that a client once sent in material with blue swirls that he thought was an opal. It turned out to be a piece of a bowling ball.

Subway Garnet

In August, 1885 a huge red garnet weighing 9 pounds 10 ounces and 7 inches in diameter was unearthed on West 35th st. near Broadway in Manhattan during excavation for a subway. Or maybe it was a sewer, but Subway Garnet sounds better.

Some accounts say the garnet was used as a doorstop in either a shop or the Department of Public Works. But eventually the garnet made its way to George Kunz (1856-1932), an eminent mineralogist. (You may have a pink gem named for him, kunzite).

Kunz gave the garnet to the New York Mineralogical Club which later donated it to the American Museum of Natural History. Many fine mineral specimens have come from Manhattan.

Quality Control

You may buy cultured black pearls with some confidence that you won't get stuck with crap.

Most cultured black pearls come from French Polynesia. In the late 1990's and early 2000's, new pearl farmers in French Polynesia flooded the market with low-quality black pearls. By 2001, black pearl prices had plunged by half. That prompted the government to impose stringent controls.

Every pearl is required to be inspected by a government office before it can be exported. Blemished pearls are rejected. The ones that pass this first step are then x-rayed to determine the thickness of the nacre*. Any pearl with less than a .8 mm nacre thickness over 20% of the surface is rejected. The pearls that pass are sealed for export and the rejects are crushed.

In July, 2005 a 132 lb. parcel of pearls destined for export to China was seized in Tahiti because half of the pearls were rejects. The good pearls were auctioned, the rejects destroyed and the offenders were given a stiff fine.

If diamonds were subject to this type of quality control, the department stores would be out of business.

*Cultured saltwater pearls are created by inserting a mother-of-pearl bead almost the size of the pearl into the oyster. The oyster coats the bead with nacre, the pearl substance.

Illegitimi Carborundum*

I don't expect you to clean the old gold rings you bring in to sell since you don't clean the rings you wear. So if the stones are so dirty I can't tell whether they're diamonds or not by looking, I'll tell by grinding.

A quick swipe of an abrasive wheel across the top will unmask the fake. It won't put a dent in a diamond but it will carve a groove in anything else.

If they're diamonds, I'll take them out and give them back to you or buy them if they're wonderful. If they're fake, further mayhem will remove them: bashing them to powder with a hammer.

* I hate to have to explain a joke, but this one is a little obscure. "Illegitimi non carborundum" is faux Latin for "don't let the bastards grind you down." You'll see it on T-shirts, mugs, keychains, etc. It was coined during World War II and was adopted by General Joseph "Vinegar Joe" Stilwell as his motto.

Up, Up, and Away!

The Supermen of America Club was founded in 1939 and ran for over 25 years. Members pledged to increase their strength and courage to aid the cause of justice.

1600 Supermen of America Club members were awarded a toy Superman ring in 1940. Only 20 rings are known to still exist and one was auctioned on Ebay in March, 2010 for $13,100.

Bijoux Macabre

I reported to you about the company that will take your "cremains" and squeeze you (or your ex-pet) into a diamond. (See *A Human is Forever* on p. 28)

Recent patent filings reveal progress in this macabre art. A patent was filed to recover elements other than carbon from remains and make other gems, such as garnet, spinel, and quartz.

Another patent describes combining calcium phosphate (from your bones and teeth, I suppose) and mixing it with glass. The glass (like lead crystal) is then put into laser drill holes in a real diamond. A company in Canada is doing this and selling the diamonds through funeral homes.

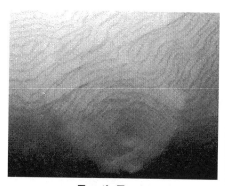

Tooth Test

The photo above shows why you can tell a real pearl from an imitation by drawing it across a tooth. The lines are actually ridges marking the borders of the layers of nacre, the pearl substance, laid down by the oyster. The ridges give a gritty feel on the tooth.

Imitation pearls are made by coating a glass bead with a lacquer containing tiny crystals of guanine extracted from fish scales. Guanine underneath the scales give fish, and imitation pearls, their iridesc-

ence. The surface of an imitation pearl is smooth and will flunk the tooth test.

This is not new. Godey's Lady's Book January, 1832 details the process:

"We can perfectly imitate the brilliancy and reflection of these natural pearls by means of a liquid termed essecnce of pearl and which is prepared by throwing into liquid ammonia the brilliant particles which are separated by friction and washing from the scales of a small river fish named the bleak."

The ammonia with pearly particles was blown into thin glass bulbs through the stringing holes and evaporated with heat resulting in a coating of the pearl essence inside the class bead. The bulbs were then filled with white wax.

Gold Filled

Gold filled sounds like there's gold on the inside, but actually the gold is on the outside. You can see the thin layer of gold that has peeled away from the base metal on this old gold filled bracelet.

The gold layer on gold filled jewelry, although thin, is much thicker than on gold plated jewelry. Gold plating is measured in millionths of an inch; the gold layer in gold filled jewelry is 500 to 1000 times thicker. That's why gold plating easily wears off and vanishes when heated during a repair. Gold filled jewelry is much more durable.

Gold filled jewelry is made by bonding the layer of gold to the underlying metal before fabricating the piece.

The piece above is marked "1/20 12K G.F." That means that 1/20th of the piece is 12 karat gold by weight. 12 karat gold is 50% gold so that works out to 2½% gold.

You'll also see 1/20th 14 karat gold filled and 1/20th or 1/10th 10 karat rolled gold plate. Rolled gold plate is the same as gold filled.

The Amber Room

Called the eighth wonder of of the world, the legendary Amber Room in the Catherine Palace Museum near St. Petersburg, Russia, is still missing. The 6 tons of intricately carved and inlaid amber panels backed with gold foil and inset with gemstone mosaics was created in Germany in the early 18th century and given to the Russian Czar Peter the Great by Prussian ruler Friederich Wilhelm I in 1716.

In June, 1941, the Germans invaded Russia and by September had encircled Leningrad (now St. Petersburg), beginning the 900 day siege of Leningrad. By November they had overrun the palace. The Russians had attempted to disguise the amber room by covering the panels with wallpaper, but, of course, the location of the famous room was known. The Germans dismantled the room, packing the amber panels and mosaics in crates, and shipped it to Konigsburg (now Kaliningrad), the Baltic port and capital of East Prussia, where it was reassembled in a museum in a castle and displayed for over two years. Allied bombs destroyed the castle in 1944, but notes from the museum curator indicated that the amber room had been packed up and stored before that. The curator and his wife died of typhus and never revealed the location of the amber room.

In the 50 years since the Amber Room was last seen, theories have been floated that it sank with the Gustloff, a crowded refugee ship torpedoed by a Russian submarine in January, 1945 in the Baltic Sea or was in an abandoned flooded salt mine near Gottingen.

In 1997, the son of an officer who had accompanied the shipment of the Amber Room was found trying to sell one of the mosaics, which was seized and returned to Russia.

Work was begun to re-create the Amber Room by the Soviet Government in 1979 by studying old black and white photographs. When lack of funds threatened to halt the project in the late 1990's, Germany's largest natural gas company, Ruhrgas, donated $3.5 million to complete the project.

And so, coming full circle, Germany, which built the Amber Room, gave it to Russia, stole it, then gave it back.

The reconstructed Amber Room opened to the public in May, 2003, just in time for the celebration of St. Petersburg's 300th anniversary.

A Diamond Bigger Than the Ritz

Scientists at Harvard recently announced the discovery of a star with a diamond core the size of our moon. 50 light years away, the star is a white dwarf, as our sun is likely to become (but not in the next 10 minutes).

When a star burns most of its hydrogen to helium, literally running out of gas, it collapses. This provides enough energy to fuse the helium to heavier elements, ending at carbon if it isn't too big (1.4 times the mass of the sun). At this stage the star heats up and swells to become a red giant (the earth is toast at this point). When it runs out of helium it collapses into a white dwarf. With nothing left to burn, it cools and the core, carbon, crystallizes into a gigantic diamond.

Scientists measured pulsations in the star's brightness caused by currents in its still gaseous outer layers. The time between pulsations got shorter over time as the core solidified and grew.

This diamond is calculated to weigh 10 billion trillion trillion carats.

Gold Found in New Jersey!

There's enough gold under your home to lower your property taxes from astronomical to merely outrageous.

Unfortunately, it's about 1800 miles under your feet, in the earth's core.

It is thought that the earth formed from the collision of planitesmals (dinky planets) that condensed from the flattened disc of dust and gas that surrounded the sun in the nascent solar system. Meteorites are leftovers from that time and their composition should mirror that of the earth.

But there's a lot more gold in meteorites than in the earth's crust, so the missing gold must have sunk to the earth's core when the young planet was in a molten state.

It is calculated that 99% of all the gold in the earth is in the core, enough to cover the earth 1½ feet deep. The gold we find was deposited by meteorites after the crust had cooled

Gem Identification

The refractive index of a gem is a measure of its ability to bend light. This measurement is is critical to gem identification. An instrument called a refractometer can precisely measure refractive index. A gem is placed on the glass of the instrument with a drop of contact liquid and light from a monochromatic yellow light source (not shown) enters the back of the instrument. Some of the light enters the stone and some is reflected off of it. This creates a dark/light boundary. The reflected light is directed onto a scale. The higher the refractive index, the higher up the scale is the dark/light boundary.

In this demonstration a golden tourmaline is used. Tourmaline belongs to a class of crystals that splits a beam of light which then takes two paths through the stone. Each ray has it's own refractive index. A polarizing filter fitted over the lens of the instrument can pick out each ray separately when rotated slightly. The low reading of 1.62 and the high reading of 1.64 are clearly seen in the photographs, right ,and conclusively identify the gem as tourmaline. The bottom left photo is the reading from an amethyst, quartz, at the low reading of 1.54 (the high reading is 1.55).

The limiting factor of the instrument is the refractive index of the contact liquid, which has to be higher than that of the gem. Unfortunately the only liquid that won't poison you or burst into flames has a refractive index of 1.81 and so limits the range of the instrument to that or below. This covers most gems but excludes diamond (2.417), zircon (1.96), and cubic zirconia (2.15-2.20 depending on composition).

Light and Magic

An indispensable instrument for the gemologist is the polariscope. By viewing a gemstone in polarized light its atomic structure and a clue to it's identity is revealed.

If you imagine a light wave coming toward you, it vibrates in all directions — up and down right and left and in between. A polarizing filter only lets the up and down or left and right vibrations through.

A polariscope has two polarizing filters, the black-rimmed discs in the photo below, with a light below the bottom one. The top filter can be rotated. When it is rotated so that it is at right angles to the bottom filter, neither the up and down waves or the right and left waves can get through and all the light is blocked.

Gemstones come in 2 optical types: singly refracting gems that don't split light into two paths, such as diamond, garnet and spinel, and doubly refracting gems that split light into two paths such as aquamarine, topaz, and tourmaline. When a doubly refracting gem is rotated between the crossed polarizers, it blinks light and dark. The gem crystal itself is acting as a polarizer, alternately being parallel and perpendicular to the instrument's filters. Singly refracting gems stay dark when rotated.

Gems that split light come in two types, uniaxial and biaxial. Uniaxial gems have one direction through the crystal in which light is not split, called the optic axis. Biaxial gems have two directions.

Near the optic axis, interference colors appear under the polariscope as the two rays recombine. With magnification provided by a glass rod with a ball on the end touched to the area with the interference colors, an optic figure will be seen. Uniaxial and biaxial gems have different optic figures. See the photos below. Quartz has a variant of the uniaxial figure, called a bullseye. The optic figures are quite colorful, whereas this book is not. *(Continued next page)*

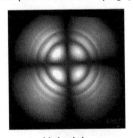
Uniaxial

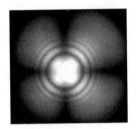
Quartz uniaxial

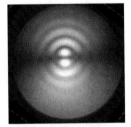
Biaxial

Polariscope

Because doubly refracting gems split light into two rays that take different paths through the stone, double images of anything inside the stone can be seen providing you are not looking down the optic axis. The mineral calcite does double images in spades.

The "Double Image" photos look at the text through a piece of calcite. The top image is as you see it. The bottom image is viewed through a polarizing filter. If the filter is rotated the image jumps back and forth between the two images shown in the top photo. It blocks one image and you see them one at a time. The gray areas in the letters are where the overlapping images interfere with each other. The cloudiness is in the calcite, a natural mineral.

Luxe et Veritas

You don't have to be a scientist to answer this question. If you coat something with diamond, is it more brilliant than a diamond? Duh.

I reported to you about a company peddling cubic zirconia (p. 93) and fake pearls (p. 215) with false claims and fancy names. Now it's "Zolastar", synthetic white sapphire coated with a film of diamond.

Zolastar has been "scientifically measured to be superior to a top quality diamond in all key optical characteristics" according to the ad copy. The ad does not tell how the measurements were made, or who made them as is customary for such radical claims.

Well, I scientifically measured the optical characteristics of zolastar with my scientific calculator. I calculated how light would be bent by the diamond layer and then by the sapphire core as it bounces around the stone. I diagrammed the results below. The arrows indicate the direction of light rays coming out of the stone for overhead light for the main facets. I had to tinker with the angles of the zolastar to get the best result. For the diamond, the light converges to the eye. For the zolastar, half the light is directed away from the eye, and there's no light coming from the sides of the stone.

I also calculated the dispersion, the breaking of light into colors like a prism, for two representative light paths. The higher the dispersion, the greater the difference in the angle of red and blue light as it exits the stone. In both cases, the zolastar scored lower than a diamond.

A company selling diamond-coated cubic zirconia, which should be more brilliant than diamond-coated sapphire, does not claim that it is more brilliant than diamond.

A diamond shines because it bends and concentrates incoming light and reflects it out the top of the stone without it leaking out the bottom. This ability is inherent in the material and is maximized by cutting it with the proper angles. Due to the laws of optics, when the light is bent by the diamond, then enters the sapphire, it is bent the opposite, and wrong, way. This changes the angles of entering and exiting light to the detriment of brilliance.

This is fraud by this company again.

The ad also has the company's trademark factual errors. It states that sapphire has a hardness of 8.5. Actually, the hardness is 9. And the ad refers to cubic zirconium (the metal). It should be cubic zirconia (the oxide).

I'll leave you with the best line of the ad. "Don't Kiss Her Until You Wipe the Tears From Her Eyes."

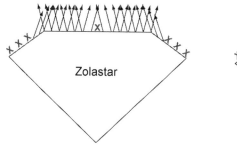

Zolastar

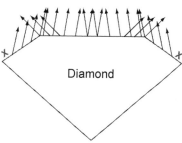

Diamond

Sanitation Dept.

The mission of a diamond is to shine. Dirty diamonds don't shine. Most diamonds are never really clean, even if you think they're clean. I'm going to inflict a physics lesson on you to explain why clean diamonds shine and dirty ones don't.

Diamonds shine more than other gems because they have a very high *refractive index*. The refractive index is the ratio of the speed of light in air to the speed of light in the gem. Light slows down from 186,000 miles per second in the air to about 77,000 miles per second when it enters a diamond, giving a refractive index of 2.417. The higher the refractive index of a material, the smaller the *critical angle*. The critical angle is an escape window for light. In order to shine, a diamond has to reflect incoming light from the bottom facets back out the top of the diamond to your eye. Any light that hits one of the bottom facets inside the critical angle isn't reflected — it leaks out the bottom of the diamond.

Diamond has a chemical affinity for grease and oil and so, in the course of everyday living, your diamond will quickly become coated with oily dirt, soap residue, etc. The refractive index business operates at the boundary between two materials: diamond/air when the diamond is clean, and diamond/grease when it isn't. The refractive index of grease is about 1.5. The effective refractive index of a diamond coated with grease is 2.417÷1.5 = 1.61, about that of topaz. The critical angle, the window for light to escape, increases by about 50%. So when your diamond is coated with oily dirt, more light leaks out the bottom and the diamond loses brilliance.

A thick coating of oily dirt on the bottom of a diamond is very tenacious and difficult to remove. Preventive maintenance is the cure. I suggest you get one of those home ultrasonic cleaners. They start at around $25. Ignore any directions about a 5 or 15 minute cleaning time. 45 minutes should do it, more if the diamond is caked with dirt.

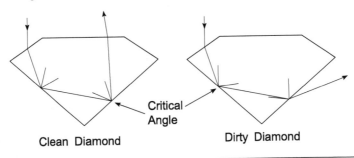

Clean Diamond   Critical Angle   Dirty Diamond

A Ring to Die For

A poison ring is a ring with a top that opens on a hinge, to reveal a hidden compartment, like a locket. Although notorious as poison rings, they were actually used to hold various keepsakes, such as a lock of hair. In the movie *Casablanca* there is a ring that conceals a Cross of Lorraine, the Free French symbol. Today, urn rings hold ashes of the deceased.

It is reported that Pope Alexander VI (1431-1503), one of the notorious Borgia Popes, had a key ring, a ring with a functioning key on top. The Pope would ask someone to open a cabinet with it and in the process, a needle in the key ring coated with poison would prick the victim's finger.

His son Cesare Borgia had a signet ring with a secret compartment that could have been used to carry poison.

Hannibal, the Carthaginian general who crossed the alps to invade Italy with elephants in 218 B.C., took poison in 182 B.C. to avoid being captured by the Romans. It is said that he carried the poison in a ring he wore.

If you search for poison ring you will turn up myriad web sites selling a Pope Alexander VI casket ring. It features a rectangular amethyst colored crystal set in the lid of a coffin that forms the top of the ring.

There is an account that describes Alexander's key ring as being used to open a casket. But casket is also an old word for chest or box. the dictionary gives one meaning of "casket" as "a small chest or box, as for jewels."

Nailhead

Fisheye

Dull Diamonds

I've been telling you over the years how the cut, the correct angles and relative sizes of the facets, is what makes a diamond shine. The angle that forms the bottom cone of a diamond is the most critical, a few degrees off and it kills the shine.

Above are photos of (top left) a diamond cut too steeply on the bottom, called a nailhead, and (top right) too shallow, a fisheye.

The nailhead is completely dark in the center. This is because the too-steep bottom angle causes the light to come out the top of the diamond angled away from the eye. You'll be able to spot a nailhead easily, even in tiny diamonds. (Go ahead, look at your ring now.)

The white ring just inside the table, the large stop sign shaped facet, in the fisheye is a reflection of the girdle, the edge of the diamond, and is the smoking gun for a shallow diamond. Fisheyes look lifeless, because the light leaks out the bottom of the diamond instead of being reflected by the bottom facets to return to the eye as brilliance.

Bottom right is an ideal cut diamond. The small light colored circle in the center is a reflection of the table. If you look closely, you'll see its octagonal shape. Its size and lightness is an indication that the bottom angle is correct. This diamond is brilliant because the maximum light that enters the diamond is reflected back to the eye.

Eye of the Beholder

People often freeze up when asked to look at a colored stone or diamond. They think it takes a "trained eye". Or they think they don't know how it's supposed to look.

This is the mind's eye refusing to look. Use your eyes. If it looks good, it is good. Colored stones and diamonds are supposed to be beautiful. And you can judge beauty as well as anyone.

Down the Drain

A sewage treatment plant in Suwa Japan has more gold than the world's best gold mines.

Machining and electroplating businesses nearby are thought to be the source of the gold in wastewater. 1700 grams (3.75 lbs.) of gold per ton of incinerated sewage sludge have been recovered.

The Hishikari gold mine, one of the world's top mines only gets 40 grams per ton. South African gold mines yield 4-9 grams per ton.

No Fooling

People have been reporting to me that they've read articles or seen on TV that jewelers can't tell the difference between a diamond and moissanite, the new imitation.

At arm's length, it can be difficult to tell. Moissanite is as brilliant as diamond. But a quick inspection under the microscope reveals the fake.

Moissanite belongs to a class of crystals that show double images of anything in the stone or of the back facet edges (see *Light and Magic* on p. 191). Diamond does not do this. However, in moissanite there is one direction through the stone that does not show doubling (the optic axis) and the stones are cut with this direction face-up. So it is necessary to look at the stone from an angle. The right picture below shows strong double images of the culet (point), facet edges, and inclusions in a moissanite.

Also, moissanite has distinctive needle inclusions that are never seen in diamond. The left photo shows these needles.

There are instruments that can separate diamond from moissanite by measuring the electrical conductivity of the gem, but the double image business and the needles are easily seen and this is enough to make a positive identification.

Moissanite is named for French chemist Henri Moissan, who discovered natural silicon carbide grains in Meteor Crater, near Winslow, Arizona in 1893. They were made by the impact of the meteor, 50,000 years ago. This topic is covered in greater detail in my book, *Consumer Guide to Diamonds*.

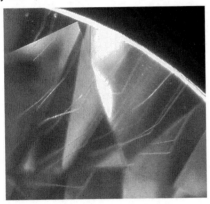

Below: double images of facet junctions and inclusions are circled. Left: distinctive needle inclusions.

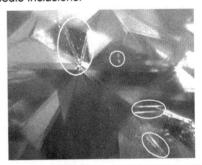

Mine Your Own Diamonds

Well, not really. They're Herkimer diamonds, perfectly formed crystals of clear quartz. They're from the area around Herkimer, New York, 80 miles northwest of Albany.

Pockets in 500 million year old limestone were infiltrated by water with dissolved silica, quartz. Quartz doesn't stick to limestone, so instead of a becoming embedded in rock, the crystals complete their development into perfect doubly terminated crystals with 18 sides. They are found loose in the pockets.

There are four dig 'em yourself sites in the area: Herkimer Diamond Mines, Ace of Diamonds Mine, Crystal Grove Diamond Mine and Campground, and Diamond Acres. Hand tools only, which you can rent at the sites.

Crystal Head vodka is filtered through Herkimer diamonds. (See *The Legend of the Crystal Skulls* on p. 169.)

actual size
3/8" X 1/4"

Vintage Jewelry

Forget about granny's old ring you inherited or the Victorian jewelry you see on the Antiques Roadshow. That's new stuff. Archaeologists recently found the oldest ornaments ever in a cave in South Africa. The tiny snail shell beads are 70,000 years old.

Old Mine Diamond

The picture below left shows what is called an old mine diamond. As you can see it's pretty crude. It looks like it was hacked out by Conan the Barbarian.

A mathematical analysis of the optimum angles and proportions of a diamond to achieve maximum brilliance and fire by a Belgian named Marcel Tolkowsky in 1919 paved the way for the modern cut diamond in the 1920's.

Before that, diamonds looked like this. The black hole in the center of the diamond is a large flat on the bottom instead of a point (called the culet). The three black spots on the left are a reflections of it in the too-steep crown (top part of a diamond).

As you can see, the diamond is squarish, rather than round, although this diamond is more asymmetrical than most old miners.

Old mine diamonds do not have very good brilliance due to their poor proportions, and are valued as recut candidates.

An old European diamond is like an old mine diamond except that it is round. Old European diamonds have the same defects as old mine diamonds: large culet, shallow bottom, tiny table facet, and very steep crown, yielding poor brilliance.

An old mine or old European diamond can be recut to improve brilliance, but you can expect 25-30% weight loss in the process as the diamond is rounded and the culet is closed up.

Old Mine Cut

This one is more asymmetrical than most. The black hole in the center is the large culet, which is typical. The black areas at the left are reflections of the culet due to the very steep crown.

Old European Cut

This diamond has the typical very small table and large culet. The facets have been outlined for clarity. There is a chip at the lower left.

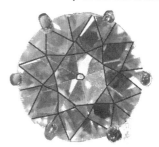

Speak No Evil

People often ask me if a a gemstone is precious or semi-precious and I don't know how to respond.

The traditional precious stones are diamond, ruby, emerald, and sapphire. And the traditional semi-precious stones are everything else. But these terms have come to mean less and less as lower qualities of "precious" stones have flooded the market.

Is a lifeless diamond so full of cracks that it would have once been crushed for industrial abrasive a "precious" stone? or a cloudy emerald, opaque ruby, or blue sapphire so dark it looks black?

Also, some "semi-precious" stones are certainly expensive enough. Tanzanite, tsavorite garnet, alexandrite, and Paraiba tourmaline (vivid blue and green tourmalines from Paraiba, Brazil, now mined out). would qualify as "precious" on the basis of cost.

Some gems that department store ads lump together as "semi-precious", such as black onyx and carnelian are really ornamental materials; they sell by the pound and occur in sizes large enough to be carved into ornaments.

As you can see, "precious" and "semi-precious" have little meaning and they are not used within the jewelry trade.

You are hereby officially forbidden to use the terms "precious" and "semi-precious".

Trigons!

No, trigons are not Star Trek aliens. They're natural features on the surface of a rough diamond.

The pictures of diamonds above show naturals with trigons. A natural is the original surface of the rough diamond that wasn't ground away during polishing, to save weight. Naturals are usually on the girdle (edge) of a diamond, and are not considered a defect if they are small and don't intrude into the stone. Often a stone will have two naturals on opposite sides of the girdle, an indication that the cutter was trying to maximize the diameter of the diamond.

Naturals usually look like a shiny irregular facets with angular striations that are related to the underlying atomic structure of the diamond crystal.

But occasionally a natural will show ghostly little triangles: trigons. The typical structure of a rough diamond is two four-sided pyramids set base-to-base, called an octahedron. Trigons occur on the triangular faces of the pyramids, with the point of the trigon facing the base of the pyramid.

The right photo shows a large natural on and extending below the girdle of a round diamond. It sports a single trigon.

The diamond in the left photograph is a rectangular princess-cut. The natural is on the bottom end facet, just below the girdle. The natural is actually recessed, like a flat-bottomed crater, perhaps a few hundredths of a millimeter deep. The ragged edge is its border. It shows a forest of trigons.

The natural surfaces of the rough diamonds you are looking at are least 1 billion years old.

Rule Titania

Rutile, the "titania" gem. carat $9.95
More Brilliant Than Diamonds

"Rutile", not an imitation diamond but a man-made "Gem" in a class by itself. It is clear in color and has much more brilliance than a diamond.

Men's gold mounting $12.99 addl ladies gold tiffany style setting $9.99 addl

This is from an advertisement in The Billboard from August 9, 1952 by a wholesale jeweler in Chicago.

Rutile, synthetic titanium dioxide, was first produced in 1948 and enjoyed a vogue as a diamond imitation until about 1955 when it was superseded by strontium titanate (sold as Fabulite), then YAG (yttrium aluminum garnet), GGG (gadolinium gallium garnet), and cubic zirconia in the late 1970's.

Actually, rutile does have more brilliance than diamond. But it has a yellow tinge and extreme dispersion — showing rainbow colors, and It is very soft.

The Billboard from that era billed itself as "The Amusement Industry's Leading Newsweekly." It's the precursor to today's Billboard magazine devoted to the music industry.The Billboard was founded in 1894.

Back issues of The Billboard are available for viewing online and are worth the trip for the articles and ads showing the sheer eclectic diversity of every conceivable aspect of entertainment.

There are 110 pages in this issue. Page 63 is titled *Rinks and Skaters* and features articles about the roller rink business with ads for roller skate wheels, coatings for roller rinks, portable maple rink floors, and skating tights.

Drive-in theaters, television, radio, night clubs, music, burlesque, magic, arenas and auditoriums, ice shows, fairs, expositions, circuses, movies, carnivals, parks, resorts, pools, vending machines, jukeboxes, bingo, pinball machines and more, as well as entertainment politics are covered in depth. And obituaries: "Final Curtain."

There was an ad for Eisenhower and Stevenson buttons with "attractive sepia brown finish". (Truman was president. Adlai didn't go all the way in 1952.) And there was an ad for WGAL television in Lancaster, Pa., right down the Lincoln Highway from my house.

How It's Done — Ring Sizing

Most rings are sized by cutting and soldering. For gold, the solder is the same karat as the ring so the joint is invisible when filed and polished. Since, for example, 14 karat gold is about 58% gold, the other 42% allows plenty of leeway to add stuff to lower the melting point so the solder melts before the ring.

To make a ring smaller, the appropriate length is sawed out of the bottom of the ring with a jeweler's saw, which looks like a small coping saw. The gap is then closed by pushing the ring together and a small square of sheet solder is wedged in the gap. The ring is then dipped in liquid flux to prevent blackening of the metal which would interfere with the solder flow. Heated to 1485° (for 14k) with a small oxygen torch, the solder melts and flows into the joint. The excess solder is then filed away and, when polished, the seam is invisible.

To make a ring larger, the ring is sawed at the bottom and spread apart. A piece of gold of the appropriate length, a little wider than the ring, is wedged in the gap. After fluxing, a clipping of solder is laid over each joint and the ring is heated from below to pull the solder through the joint. The piece is then filed flush with the ring and polished. (See next page)

The trick in ring sizing is to get a good fit, with no gaps, between the pieces being joined. Otherwise, when the ring is polished, the seam will show as a line, or small pits in the solder will show up as a dotted line.

If the bottom of the ring is thick and the ring hasn't been sized before, I can size a ring down without solder. I roll out the piece of gold I cut out of the ring to about .0005" thick and wedge it in the joint. Since it is so thin it melts just before the ring, even though both have the same melting point. This is the best joint since it's all the same metal fused together. This is best for sizing down; I can sometimes do it for sizing up also, but it's tricky.

14 karat white gold solder tends to show the seam as a gray line so I use 19 karat white gold solder which gives an invisible joint. Silver solders contain less silver than sterling. Sterling, at 92.5% silver does not allow enough leeway to mix in anything else to lower the melting point, so the silver content is lowered. Silver conducts heat so rapidly that sizing stone rings can be a problem, especially if the ring is heavy or if the stone is heat sensitive. Sometimes it is not feasible to size silver stone rings.

Seamless wedding bands are stretched on a machine that looks like a ring measuring stick split lengthwise into six segments. The ring is put on the stick and a lever forces a ram down the middle of the segments and expands the ring uniformly.

This doesn't work with two piece rings, i.e. white and yellow gold, or hand-made rings that are soldered together. The force applied by the machine is considerable and would crack any soldered seams.

Plain bands can be squeezed smaller by this machine by a disc that forces the ring into a cup-shaped die. But any pattern on the ring would be obliterated.

Eternity rings, with diamonds all around can only be sized by adding or removing a piece with a diamond. Invisible-set rings, multiple square stones set edge to edge in rows with no metal between them, have to be sized at the factory. The stones pop out at the slightest provocation, and you can't get them back in.

It Doesn't Work That Way

People often ask if I can "thicken" the bottom of a ring that is so thin it bends. They have in mind molding more gold onto the ring like clay.

The only way to make the bottom of a ring thicker is to saw off the bottom, curve a strip of gold stock and solder it to the top, creating a new and thicker bottom.

This is called reshanking a ring. The new shank has to be filed down to blend with the part of the ring to which it is soldered and so can't be thicker than the original sides of the ring.

This is How a Ring is Made larger.

1. The ring is sawed at the bottom and spread out. A piece of gold stock is cut to the precise size needed, curved, and filed so it fits with no gaps.

2. The ring is dipped in flux and small squares of solder are laid across the joints.

3. The ring is fired with a torch and the solder flows (at 1500°) and is drawn into the joints.

4. The added piece is filed flush with the ring, sanded with rubber cylinders containing coarse and fine abrasives using a flexible shaft machine, then polished on a buffing machine. Since the solder itself is 14 karat gold, the added piece blends into the ring.

This ring was sized up a little over 3 sizes by adding a piece of gold 8 mm long x 2 mm wide x 1.5 mm thick (▬▬ actual size).

All this takes time and skill and it's not done while you wait, no matter how paranoid you are about your diamond.

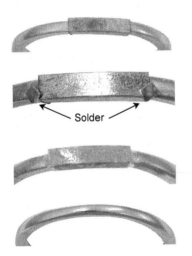

Solder

Alien Ship Brings Ice To Venus!

If you think the weather gets bad on earth, try it on Venus. The 1978 Pioneer Venus probe did, and survived an 865° heat wave, corrosive atmosphere, and pressure 94 times that of earth.

Peering out through a 13.5 carat diamond window, Pioneer looked at infra-red radiation.

The diamond window, about the size of a quarter, was cut from one of only two pieces of rough diamond that could be found that met the specifications, free of nitrogen impurities, which would block infrared light, and internal strain.

Cutting the diamond was equally difficult: the two sides had to be perfectly flat and parallel.

And so, a 13.5 carat diamond still sits on Venus.

Zeppelin Hunts Diamonds

Zeppelins didn't die with the Hindenberg. DeBeers is using a zeppelin, filled with helium, not hydrogen, to prospect for diamonds in Botswana. A cigar-shaped zeppelin has a rigid internal frame; a blimp is a floppy bag of gas.

Diamonds are found in the eroded cores of certain ancient volcanoes. The diamonds form 120 miles down and are brought up quickly when the volcano erupts. The volcano erodes over geologic time, with diamonds accumulating in ancient riverbeds and even washing all the way to the sea. The volcano cores become diamond mines, the diamonds encased in rock called kimberlite.

Diamond-bearing kimberlites are rare. There are 6500 known kimberlites in the world of which less than 50 can be commercially mined. The kimberlites can be detected from the air by minute changes in gravity with very sensitive equipment.

The vibrations of aircraft are too much for the equipment, but a zeppelin solves the problem.

The diamond-hunting missions are flown at night. The cooler temperatures improve results. The zeppelin is flown by a German crew, of course.

Shades of the Hindenberg

The diamond hunting zeppelin crashed after a gust of wind broke it loose from its mooring mast. One crew member was injured.

That leaves only two other zeppelins in the world, in Germany and Japan. It would take 18 months for the German company, Zeppelin, of course, to build another one.

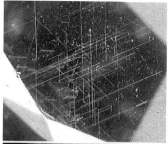

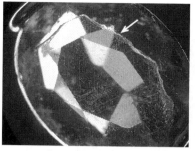

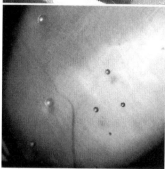

Bogus Bubbles

The top three photos above are of a garnet and glass doublet, a stone that was often used to imitate other gems before the advent of modern synthetics. This imitation was invented in the 19th century, and was used perhaps into the 1930's. I still see them in old jewelry.

Garnet is the only gemstone that will fuse directly to glass, without glue. The garnet top gives this imitation higher luster and more durability than glass. Even though the garnet is red, it's only a thin sliver and the stone takes on the color of the glass, which can be any color.

Usually the garnet covers just the table of the stone, not the whole crown (top). In the top center photo, the arrow points to the ragged border of the garnet slice.

What makes this photo so cool are the classic needle inclusions in the garnet, shown in the close-up at top left. This little bit of garnet exhibits a profusion of oriented needles that are diagnostic for red garnet. The needles are of a mineral called rutile that formed inside the garnet and lined up with its crystal structure. Needles in the same plane cross each other at 70° and 110°.

Also present are a lot of gas bubbles, as seen in the top right photo, formed by trapped air in the fusion plane between the garnet and the glass.

Gas bubbles always indicate some sort of fakery; they do not occur in natural gems, other than amber, the volcanic glass obsidian, and meteoric impact glass moldavite. So this garnet and glass doublet shows the real and the fake together.

The bottom photo shows gas bubbles very clearly. You can even see the shadows of the bubbles. It's a photo of a stone with a glass dome covering a thin iridescent layer on the bottom. The gas bubbles are in the glass. It's attractive, with a vague resemblance to opal, but It really doesn't look like any natural gem.

Clarification

Ever wonder why you always see nice clean aquamarines and usually see emeralds with eye-visible inclusions (even though emerald and aquamarine are the same material, beryl) I can't really tell you why – that's mother nature. But I can tell you what to expect.

Gems are classified into 3 clarity types.

Type I stones are often flawless or nearly so. Aquamarine, topaz, tanzanite, and green tourmaline are in this category.

Type II gems have moderate inclusions. Examples are garnet, sapphire and ruby, spinel, and amethyst.

Type III stones are almost always included, often heavily. Emerald and red or pink tourmaline are in this category.

These facts of nature are taken into account when evaluating gemstones: an aqua with inclusions that in an emerald would make emerald-lovers deliriously happy will make aquamarine aficionados frown.

Double Vision

One of the first things a gemologist tries to determine is to which family of crystal types a gemstone belongs.

Transparent gems fall into two broad categories: singly refracting and doubly refracting. (Refraction is the bending of light.) Doubly refracting gems split a beam of light into 2 rays which take different paths through the stone; singly refracting gems do not. (See *Light and Magic* on p. 191.)

The quickest way to check for single or double refraction is to look at the gem under a microscope, looking through the gem at the back facets. Doubly refracting gems have double images of the facet junctions, as seen in this photo of a peridot. Double images of anything else inside the stone, such as cracks or little inclusions of foreign material, or even dirt particles on the back of the stone can be seen. The two sets of doubled white lines in the upper right of the picture are small abrasions on the facet junctions of the peridot.

Peridot and zircon show strong doubling. Other stones show this effect less, that is, the separation between the two images is less. Of the commonly seen transparent gemstones, diamond, garnet, and spinel are singly refracting, and do not show doubling, and everything else is doubly refracting.

Bubbles That Aren't Bogus

I've told you before that gas bubbles in a gemstone are usually proof that the stone is man-made.

But there are exceptions. At left is a photograph of a moldavite, a natural stone with bubbles. Moldavite is a natural glass formed by the impact of a meteor. Like man-made glass, it can have gas bubbles in it.

Moldavite is a bottle-green stone first discovered in what is now the Czech Republic in 1787. It's named for the Moldau river, now called the Vlatava. Like most glass it is soft and has low brilliance so it has little to recommend it other than novelty.

Other natural gems with bubbles are obsidian, volcanic glass, and amber, naturally hardened tree sap at least 1 million years old.

3 gas bubbles are visible in the right photo. The wavy ribbons are flow structures, like you see momentarily when you stir a viscous liquid like honey.

Deep Thought

It don't mean a thing if it ain't got that bling.

The Doctor Is In

This one's not about how I selflessly come in for a few hours on my days off to take care of you. It's about doctoring diamonds.

Diamonds with eye-visible black inclusions can be "clarity-enhanced". A hair-fine hole is drilled with a laser to reach the black spot. Then the diamond is soaked in acid to remove it.

If the resulting cavity looks white and is too visible, it can be filled through the drill hole with a special glass that matches the diamond's optical characteristics and it will have a much lower relief. This is like the cracks in an ice cube that look white when they are air-filled, but disappear in a glass of water as the water penetrates them.

The two photos below are of customers' diamonds that have been laser-drilled. These customers were unaware that their diamonds had been doctored.

Laser-drilling is easily spotted under the microscope.

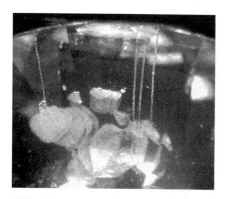

This diamond has been drilled in 4 places from the top, clearly visible. The original inclusions, the white areas now, must have been particularly black and nasty.

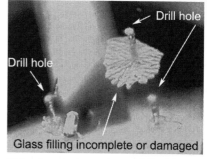

Glass filling incomplete or damaged

This diamond has been drilled in three places and one of the resulting cavities has been filled. The glass filling was either incomplete or has been damaged, possibly by ultrasonic cleaning.

The treated areas are not eye-visible in either diamond.

Battleship Silver

"The practice of donating silver services to the new battle-ships and cruisers of the United States by the States or cities after which the vessels are named, is now deeply rooted."

— The Jewelers' Circular and Horological Review, April 28, 1897, from an article titled *The Silver Service of the "Oregon."*

There were battleships named for all the states of the lower 48, the first the USS Texas in 1895 and the last the second USS Missouri in 1944. All were presented with silver services by their namesake states.

The first USS New Jersey was commissioned in 1906 and presented with a silver service in 1907. She was de-commissioned in 1920 and sunk as a bombing target in 1923.

The 119 piece silver service made by Tiffany was transferred to the second USS New Jersey commissioned in 1943, now a floating museum on the Delaware River in Camden. The silver service is in the Governor's mansion, Drumthwacket. (Can't you just hear Daffy Duck saying "Drumthwacket"?) 59 pieces of it were loaned to the ship for its 70th anniversary in 2013 (after some coaxing).

Treasure Map

A papyrus map dating from 1200 B.C. inspired an Australian gold miner of Egyptian heritage to search for the gold mines of the Pharaohs.

The map was found in Luxor in 1820, but the miner saw it in a museum in Turin, Italy. It is believed to be the oldest geological map in the world. The map shows where the ancient Egyptian gold mines were in the area from the Nile to the Red Sea south of Luxor.

The map led to a pot of gold in the hills near the Red Sea, worth about $4 billion so far, and they've just started.

Rose de France

You may hear of a gemstone called Rose de France. It's a pale pink amethyst. The name originates in Argentina where *Rosa de Francia* was in vogue in in the 1930's, set in 18 karat gold jewelry.

Light colored amethyst is abundant and inexpensive.

The Wearable Heaviness Of Being

Diamond is the densest known substance. It packs more atoms into a given space than anything else. This accounts for it's incredible hardness.

Rock Of Ages

Diamonds are old.

Diamonds themselves can't be dated, but inclusions of other minerals that formed at the same time and were incorporated in the diamond as it grew can be. Dating is done by comparing ratios of certain radioactive elements with their decay products. The rate of decay is known, so the age since formation can be calculated.

Most diamonds are about a billion years old. But one rough diamond of 270 carats has been dated at 3.3 billion years, the oldest known.

Government Shuts Down Gold Mines

The U.S. began mobilizing for war in 1940. In early 1941, the Office of Production Management (OPM) issued Preference Orders that gave mines deemed essential for war production priority in acquiring machinery and supplies. Gold mines were put at the bottom of the list so they couldn't buy new machinery.

In 1942, after Pearl Harbor, there was a severe shortage of skilled labor in nonferrous metals mining caused by expanding production and losing workers to the draft. On October 8, 1942, the War Production Board (WPB), successor to the OPM, issued Limitation Order L-208 closing down all gold mines to free up their workers for mines classified as essential.

The order was revoked June 30, 1945.

In 1950 a number of gold mines sued, arguing that the order constituted a taking of private property without compensation in violation of the Fifth Amendment.

The case eventually found its way to the Supreme Court, which ruled against the gold miners 7-2 in U.S. v. Central Eureka Mining Co. June 16, 1958.

Something Lost In Translation

Garnets are a complex family of related minerals that occur in all colors except blue, since no one has found a blue garnet yet. The different families mix with each other and so new types of garnet are regularly found.

Malaia garnet is an orange gem that was discovered in Africa around 1970. The discoverers were prospecting for rhodolite garnet, which was all the rage in Japan at the time, and kept coming up with these orange pebbles which the Japanese buyers deemed trash. Malaia is Swahili for prostitute or trash. It was later found that these stones were a new type of garnet, a mixture of two families not seen before and it has become a sought after gemstone. But the name Malaia stuck.

Nothing Lost In Translation

Coober Pedy is one of those odd Australian place names. It's a famous opal mining town. The name was given by the Aborigines. It means "white man in a hole".

I wonder what some of our local Indian names mean.

278 The First Engagement Ring

The Romans gave betrothal rings, but the first diamond engagement ring was given to Mary of Burgundy by Archduke Maximillian of Austria in August of 1477. The ring had thin flat diamond pieces in the shape of her initial, M. They were married the next day, August 18, 1477.

Mary died in 1482 at 25 after a fall from a horse.

Pressure Tactics

When scientists want to explore the world of ultra-high pressure, they use a device called a diamond anvil cell, invented in 1958.

Two diamonds with the points flattened are set tip-to-tip with a metal gasket around the tip area to form a tiny chamber. A simple screw pushes the diamonds together, creating enormous pressure on the test materials in the chamber.

Since the diamonds are transparent, lasers can be shined through them to heat the samples and measurements and observations can be made. With this benchtop device, pressures of over three million atmospheres, or 22,000 tons per square inch, have been obtained.

Literal Translation

Turquoise comes from the French *Pierre Turquoises* which means Turkish stone. Turquoise does not come from Turkey. From the 13th, century turquoise came from Persia (modern Iran) but entered western Europe through trade with Turkey. The finest turquoise still comes from Iran. When the Shah abdicated the Peacock Throne, desperate Iranian immigrants to the U.S. flooded the market with Persian turquoise.

Amethyst comes from the Greek *amethustos* which means not to be intoxicated. It was believed that amethyst would prevent drunkeness.

Diamond comes from the Greek *adamas*, which means unconquerable. the English adamant comes from the same root.

Lapis Lazuli, a dark blue opaque stone, means blue rock in Latin. From lapis, rock or stone, comes our word lapidary, a gemstone cutter. Lazuli, which derives from the Persian *lazhward* , meaning heaven, sky, or blue, gives us the English azure. The finest lapis lazuli has since ancient times come from Afghanistan. Lesser quality material is mined in Chile. Ultramarine pigment was made from powdered lapis lazuli until the mid 19th century.

The Greek word for amber is *electron*, from which comes electricity. Amber produces static electricity when rubbed with a cloth. Amber is the naturally hardened sap of pine trees that is at least 1 million years old. Commercial amber comes from the area around the Baltic Sea and from the Dominican Republic. A recent discovery of amber in central New Jersey has yielded specimens with entombed insects from which DNA has been extracted and analyzed. (Sorry, no pet dinosaurs yet.)

There are two wholly unrelated minerals each of which is properly called jade: jadeite and nephrite. The names of both mean kidney.

When the Spanish conquistadores blitzed the Aztecs they found a green stone the Indians believed helped in disorders of the kidneys. And so they brought back to Europe *piedra de hijada* or "stone of the loins". This became jade, via French, in English. The Latin translation was *lapis nephriticus*, or "kidney stone", from which we get "nephrite".

Meanwhile, the Chinese, unknown to the Europeans, had been carving jade for thousands of years. Soon after the Spanish introduced jade from the Americas to Europe, Chinese jade also showed up. But the name "jade" was established before Chinese jade was known in Europe.

Both the American and Chinese jade were of the type we now call nephrite. Jadeite was not discovered by the Chinese until later, in the 18th century, being imported from Burma.

The two types of jade are similar in appearance and were confused with each other and with similar materials, such as serpentine, a common jade substitute, until the advent of more modern science.

Both nephrite and jadeite occur in all colors. The inexpensive olive green jade you often see is nephrite. The mottled light green and white inexpensive bangle bracelets you see are jadeite. Intense green, highly translucent jadeite of uniform color is incredibly expensive. Such a jadeite bangle bracelet recently sold in Hong Kong for over $1 million.

2767   Waste Management

Scarab bracelets have links of oval domed stones of different colors. The stones are incised with lines in what looks like an abstract pattern. Actually It's supposed to be a scarab beetle, also known as a dung beetle.

Our scarab stones are descendants of ancient Egyptian carved amulets. The beetles were sacred to the ancient Egyptians. They believed that the dung beetle represented the god Khepri, who pushed the sun across the sky,

The Egyptians made their scarab amulets from such gem materials as lapis lazuli, carnelian, and turquoise. They also used faience, a fired colored glaze.

Dung beetles eat animal dung, rolling it into a ball and burying it. These insect pooper scoopers perform a valuable eco-logical service, cleaning the land and enriching the soil .

The Kimberly Big Hole

In 1866 a shepherd in South Africa found a pebble that turned out to be a 21 carat diamond, beginning the South African diamond rush.

In 1871, a cook for a diamond prospector was sent to a nearby hill to dig as punishment for being drunk and turned up an 83.50 carat diamond.

Soon thousands of miners arrived and the hill disappeared into a huge pit. A town sprang up around the pit, first called "New Rush" then renamed Kimberly, for the British Secretary of State for the Colonies, the Earl of Kimberly, in 1873.

The Kimberly Big Hole was dug by hand with picks and shovels to a depth of around 500 feet. It has an area of 42 acres. It has been billed as the largest hand-dug hole ever made, though recent research gives that title to the Jagersfontein mine.

Claims were 30 Cape feet square. A Cape foot is 1.033 English feet. With adjacent claims being dug to different depths, there were problems with cave-Ins. The wires in the top photo were used to haul buckets of dirt from the claims out of the pit to extract the diamonds. Below is the Big Hole today.

Underground mining succeeded open pit mining. By the time the mine closed on August 14, 1914, over 3 tons of diamonds had been recovered.

The Largest Check Ever Written

Barnett Isaacs was born in the East End, a poor area of London, in 1851. He was raised in an apartment above his father's second-hand clothing store. It was a tough neighborhood and his father taught him and his older brother Harry to box early, with twice-a-week sessions in the store or outside. They both quit school at 14. Harry worked as a bartender and bouncer at his brother-in-law's tavern, called the King of Prussia while honing his skills as a magician. Performers from the nearby Cambridge Music Hall frequented the tavern which led to gigs in music halls billed as The Wizard. Barney joined the act and one night when Harry took too many bows, a stagehand yelled "Barney too" which carried over to other shows and evolved to his stage name Barney Barnato.

In 1872, a cousin, David Harris, borrowed money from his mum and went to Kimberly to get rich in diamonds. Harry went to South Africa later that year, appearing in October in a hall in Dutoitspan with his magic act. It was well reviewed but after a while his act petered out and he went to work for a diamond dealer. He didn't do well but nonetheless Harry wrote letters to Barney telling of the opportunities in South Africa.

David Harris didn't do well either but he won £1400 by putting a coin on a number in a saloon that offered free drinks to gamblers. He immediately returned home, paid back his mum and entranced Barney with with tales of riches to be made there. A plus was that there was no prejudice against Jews and everyone spoke English. Barney had taken over his brother's job as bouncer and bartender and had managed to save £100. Friends gave him a gold watch and his brother-in-law donated 40 boxes of cigars and Barney sailed for Cape Town in July, 1873.

When he arrived 27 days later, he paid £5 to a Boer to carry his things in an ox cart and walked beside it the 600 miles to Kimberly, taking 2 months. He found his brother living in a tent, broke and dejected. A week later, when Payne's Traveling Circus came to Kimberley, Barney took on The Champion of Angola, a huge Portuguese boxer for a prize if he could last 3 rounds. The 5'3" Barnato climbed into the ring dressed in a loud jacket with bowler hat and wire-rim spectacles, to the laughter of the crowd and promptly floored him. According to one account, Barney then topped off his victory by juggling his hat and 3 bottles of beer then recited a soliloquy from Hamlet in his Cockney accent standing on his head as the crowd roared.

Barney bought and sold whatever he could find, and eventually met Louis Cohen, a cousin and a kopje walloper, someone who went from claim to claim in the diamond fields and haggled for stones with the miners. Louis and Barney went into partnership, renting a corrugated iron shanty next to a bar in Dutoitspan. Louis stayed in the "office" buying from thirsty miners who needed cash for a drink and Barney made the rounds of of the diamond diggers, haggling for stones.

The problem was in finding diggers who would sell at the right price. Barney bought a broken down horse from a successful and secretive walloper who was leaving for Europe for £27, 10 shillings, a large sum and the asking price. Barney had noticed that the horse stopped of its own accord at every digger's tent on the labyrinthine route.

The partnership eventually faltered and Barney moved in to a small room in the London Hotel, a seedy hotel in Kimberly his brother Harry had managed to acquire.

In 1876, the Barnato brothers used £3,000, all their capital, to buy four claims in the Kimberley mine. By this time, the soft "yellow ground" had been dug up and sifted leaving the hard "blue ground" underneath. The miners believed that a flood had left the diamonds on top of the hard ground. But Barney learned from geologist William Atherstone, who had identified the 21 carat Eureka Diamond, the first found in South Africa in 1867 (on the De Beers farm), that diamonds came up from the depths in volcanoes and the blue ground was the volcanoes' root and probably contained more diamonds. (The yellow ground the miners dug up was weathered blue ground.) The first weeks of mining the blue ground produced very little, then the diamonds started to come — £2,000 a week and £100,000 by the end of the year. The Barnato brothers were rich. They started buying other claims in the Kimberley mine and by 1888, owned most of them and sought to dominate all diamond mining. But there was a competitor.

Cecil Rhodes was a sickly child, one of 12 of the Reverend Francis Rhodes of Hertsfordshire, north of London. He went to South Africa in 1870 to join his brother, a cotton farmer, with £3,000 loaned by his aunt. He was 17.

Cecil ran the plantation while his brother went to Kimberly and bought three claims near the original De Beers farm. In 1871, Rhodes joined his brother in the diamond fields. The brother went off to look for gold and Rhodes ran the diamond diggings. Rhodes with partners started buying up claims in the De Beers mine until he controlled it. There were now two kings of diamonds, and there could only be one.

The French Company (Compagnie Française des Mines de Diamants du Cap de Bonne Espérance) owned a crucial part of the Kimberley mine. Barney already owned a fifth of the shares of the French Company and wanted the rest. Rhodes arranged financing with the Rothschilds and in 1887 a bidding war broke out between Barnato and Rhodes to buy up shares of the French company. They struck a deal. With Barney's acquiescence, Rhodes bought the French company for £1,400,000 then sold it to Barney for £300,000 plus 70,000 shares, a fifth, of Barnato's company, Kimberley Central.

To raise money for the coming battle for control, Barney threatened to sell shares of Central as a public company in London for £1. This would have ruined both of them and the rest of the diamond companies with cutthroat competition, precisely the situation Rhodes and Barnato were trying to avoid with their maneuvers to monopolize the mines. To buy time, Rhodes played an historic trick on Barnato.

Rhodes planted rumors that he was short of money and needed to sell some diamonds to raise cash. Barney agreed to buy them. To prevent him from dumping them on an already flooded market, Rhodes then tipped the table on which the carefully sorted rough diamonds were exhibited and they poured into a bucket. It took 6 weeks for Barnato's company to resort them into 126 categories. This gave Rhodes time for the next phase of his plan.

Rhodes began buying up Central shares bidding them up from £14 to as high as £49. Even some of Barney's steadfast pals sold out at those prices. By March of 1888, Rhodes owned 3/5 of Central and Barney saw the handwriting on the wall. Barney agreed to exchange his shares for shares in De Beers and a life-governorship on its board.

However, in August, 1888, a group of dissident shareholders in Central challenged the merger in court on a technicality of differences in the companies' charters. The judge ruled in favor of the dissidents. Rhodes and Barnato between them owned the majority of shares in Central and they put Central in to voluntary liquidation in January, 1889. De Beers offered the highest bid for Central's assets and on July 18, 1889 wrote a check for £5,338,650, the largest check ever written. (Over $637 million in 2015 dollars.)

De Beers then controlled 95% of the diamond market. Rhodes went on to become Prime Minister of the Cape Colony. One of his companies administered the area named for him, Rhodesia. Rhodes died in 1902. The Rhodes Scholarships were established the same year from a trust set up in his will.

Barney went on to be elected as a member of parliament for Kimberley in 1889.

Barney continued his acting. He joined an amateur theatre company in Kimberly and played Iago In Othello. After a heckler interrupted Othello the Moor when he declaimed "Haply, for I am black" saying "Then go and wash your face," and the actor quit the stage, Barney appeared in blackface to continue the performance, stormed to the footlights and said he would deal with anyone who dared interrupt *his* Othello. The disturbance continued and when the curtain came down, he rushed into the audience and gave the heckler a thrashing. Louis Cohen describes in *Reminiscences of Kimberly* Barney playing a role in a play, The Bells, how Barney delivered the line "'Ow the dogs do 'owl at Daniel's farm–'ow they 'owl" in his Cockney accent as "a monstrous inexactitude considering the animals were as absent as his h's."

Barney maintained his interest in boxing also, establishing an amateur boxing club in 1878. Boxrec, a boxing web site, lists Barney as a referee in two fights in 1884 and 1891.

Barney became increasingly paranoid and unhinged and he was convinced to return to England in 1897 for a rest accompanied by his wife and a nephew. As the ship neared the Island of Madeira, Barney suddenly cried out "they're after me" climbed up on the railing and jumped overboard, according to a child who witnessed it as quoted in *The Last Empire* by Stefan Kanfer. A ship's officer jumped overboard after him but it was too late; he was floating face down, drowned. "Coroner's Jury at Southhampton Finds he Died from Drowning While Temporarily Insane" headlined The New York Times June 19, 1897.

Barney's partner and cousin Louis Cohen had an acid pen. In *Reminiscences of Kimberly* he so maligned diamond magnate, J.B. Robinson that he sued him for libel in London in 1911. "It was alleged in the book that Sir J.B. Robinson's early career had been that of a fraudulent dealer, swindler and coward," reported the Sydney Morning Herald, Nov. 24, 1911. Cohen lost and was fined £1000 and forced to withdraw his book from bookstores and he went bankrupt. Then in 1914, Robinson brought charges of perjury for conspiring with a witness in the libel case, it being shown that at the time of the events in his testimony he was only 10 years old and was a student in Glasgow. Cohen was convicted and sentenced to three years.

Barney's nephew was murdered in 1898. See *The Cat Who Came to Dinner* on p. 21. Of course, there is a Barney Barnato cocktail. See *The Ghost Ingredient is Back* on p. 11.

Diamond Crooks Cop Plea

DeBeers, the South African diamond monopoly, pleaded guilty to a criminal antitrust indictment filed by the Justice Department in 1994 and agreed to pay a $10 million fine. They were accused of conspiring with General Electric to fix the price of industrial diamonds.

Debeers executives had not been able to enter the U.S. for fear of arrest. This cleared the way for DeBeers to do business directly in the world's largest diamond market. DeBeers had been doing business in the U.S. via intermediaries, since, as a monopoly, it would violate U.S. anti-trust laws. Government investigations of DeBeers monopolistic practices go back to World War II.

Industrial diamonds, diamond abrasive, are essential in manufacturing just about anything. For instance, carbide tools used in machining can only be shaped by diamond abrasives.

In 1940, after the Nazis overran France and began bombing Britain, the possibility of DeBeers' stockpile of industrial diamonds in London falling into enemy hands had to be considered.

The Roosevelt administration asked DeBeers to sell 6.5 million carats (1.43 tons) of diamond abrasive to the U.S. for war production. And DeBeers refused! It couldn't countenance such a large stockpile outside its control.

Finally, the U.S. threatened that it couldn't supply airplanes to England if DeBeers wouldn't sell the diamond abrasive with which to make them. The British government pushed DeBeers and 1 million carats were reluctantly provided. Moreover, DeBeers raised prices for the diamonds by reducing quality, so more diamonds were needed achieve the same production.

The U.S. Continued to press DeBeers for the remaining 5.5 million carats, but by this time, the crisis had passed. *(Continued next page).*

Meanwhile, in late 1943, agents in Germany informed the OSS (Office of Strategic Services, the wartime CIA forerunner) that Germany had only an 8 month supply of diamond abrasive. The OSS then discovered that tons of industrial diamonds were somehow being smuggled into Germany.

The OSS determined that the diamonds could only have come from one mine in the Belgian Congo. An agent sent to investigate found that the diamonds were being smuggled from that mine in Red Cross parcels and sold to Germany at 30 times the market price.

The Congo was run by the Belgian government in exile in London which was entirely under British control. The mine was policed by DeBeers with elaborate security. This damning, though circumstantial, evidence of trading with the enemy was, and is to this day, hotly denied by DeBeers.

In late 1944, the U.S. War Department dropped the investigation since the smuggling could only have been done with the co-operation of elements of the British Government; the division in charge of this vital war material was staffed entirely by former DeBeers executives. The matter was deemed too sensitive to pursue during the war.

The OSS was disbanded after the war and the matter was never resolved.

Blue White Special

Many of you have, or have a relative who has, a blue-white diamond. Unfortunately, there is no such thing as a blue-white diamond. This persistent myth will not go away.

Many diamonds light up blue under ultraviolet light. This is called fluorescence. Since there is an ultraviolet component in daylight (think sunburn), lower color diamonds, those with slightly yellowish tints, that also have strong blue fluorescence, are thought to have a slightly improved, whiter color.

Diamond firms in the 1930's sought out these diamonds and marketed them as "blue-white". This term was prohibited by the Federal Trade Commission in 1938.

The advertising must have worked. Over seventy years later, people still talk of "blue-white" diamonds, although the term has been transformed from an off-white diamond that looks better than it should to a diamond to die for.

In a GIA (Gemological Institute of America) study, members of the trade and civilians were asked to grade color in diamonds of the same colors with and without fluorescence. The civilians could not tell the difference and the trade members only from the bottom.

Yet wholesale price lists still indicate a premium for lower color diamonds with strong blue fluorescence and a discount for fluorescent high color diamonds.

The only time fluorescence affects the appearance of a diamond is if it makes it look hazy in daylight. Such diamonds are fairly uncommon. I've only seen a few in the course of repairs.

Helen of Ploy

You may see "helenite" advertised, purported to be made by melting the ash from the 1980 eruption of Mt. St. Helens in Washington state. One would think that the volcano had provided these inexpensive impossibly green stones to atone for killing that stubborn old codger, Harry Truman (no relation), who refused to leave his cabin.

The GIA found helenite to be man-made glass, containing little or no volcanic ash. They melted ash from the volcano and it came out black. Especially telling was a huge difference in melting temperature between their ash glass and helenite.

Nonetheless, a company (see *Luxe et Veritas* on p. 93 and p. 215) still touts helenite in ads in magazines like Scientific American and Discover saying "Helenite is produced from the heated volcanic rock of Mount St. Helens."

Obsidian is natural volcanic glass, usually black. You may have seen it in Southwestern silver jewelry as snowflake obsidian, black obsidian with white patches of a type of quartz or black Apache tears. (See p. 180.)

Other natural glasses include moldavite, a yellowish-green material of meteoric origin (see p. 201), and Libyan desert glass, whose provenance is unknown.

And for the sake of completeness there's trinitite, the glass formed on July 16, 1945 from the desert sand by the explosion of the first atomic bomb, at Trinity Site, New Mexico. This green unnatural glass is slightly radioactive and it's a federal crime to take it from Trinity National Historic site.

Hair Jewelry

"HAIR ORNAMENTS--Ladies wishing hair made into bracelets, pins (which are very beautiful), necklaces or ear-rings, can be accommodated by our Fashion Editor. A very large number of orders have recently been filled, and the articles have given great satisfaction."

This is an excerpt from Godey's Lady's Book of 1857, a popular women's magazine of the pre Civil War era. The magazine offered to make jewelry from readers' hair. Prices ranged from $3-15 for breastpins, earrings. rings, necklaces, and fob-chains. There were also patterns and instructions for do-it-yourselfers.

Hard times in early 19th century Sweden led to the revival of the Nordic traditional craft of making jewelry from hair in the village of Vamhus. Harkullor, hair ladies, traveled from there to northern European countries to earn money to send home. This started the 19th century fashion of hair jewelry.

Hair jewelry was made in a variety of techniques. Table work used a small table with a hole in the center. Weights were attached to the hair which hung down through the hole to keep the hair taut and the hair was then braided, around a mold for hollow tube shapes.

In palette work, hair was glued flat to paper, then cut out and arranged to form flowers or scenes and put under a glass cover in a setting.

Hair flowers were made by wrapping hair around a rod and securing it with a fine wire. Hair flowers could be arranged into wreaths.

Men wore watch chains made from hair. Napoleon wore one made from the hair of his wife, Empress Marie Louise. It is listed in his will.

In the 1853 Crystal Palace Exposition in New York, hair jewelry was displayed as well as a tea set made entirely from hair.

Queen Victoria wore hair jewelry and after the death of Prince Albert in 1861 she wore mourning jewelry made with his hair. The fashion died with her at the dawn of the 20th century.

But in Vamhus they still make hair jewelry.

Silver Lining

Samsung, the giant Korean company, now sells a washing machine that puts a little silver in the wash and sterilizes your clothes without hot water.

A small device in the washing machine, called the "Ag+ Nano System", uses electricity to spray hundred-millionth-of-an-inch silver particles on the clothes from two small sticks of pure silver in the machine, literally giving your clothes a silver lining. Clothes are said to be 99.9% germ-free and stay that way for up to a month.

The head of the division that developed the technology had his office workers take off their socks, then washed one in a regular machine and the other in the new one. After wearing their socks for a day, the employees were asked to give them the sniff test. One was smelly and the other odor-free.

The washing machine sells for $1150. Samsung also makes a refrigerator and an air-conditioner with a silver coating on the walls, said to keep food and air fresh by killing bacteria.

Cutting Edge Technology

Specially cut synthetic diamonds are used as ultrasharp scalpel blades for surgery. Budget about a thousand bucks for the knife and $350 for resharpening.

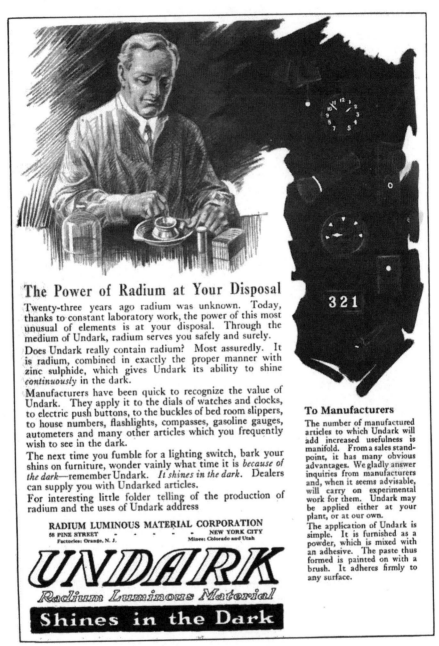

The Power of Radium at Your Disposal

Twenty-three years ago radium was unknown. Today, thanks to constant laboratory work, the power of this most unusual of elements is at your disposal. Through the medium of Undark, radium serves you safely and surely.

Does Undark really contain radium? Most assuredly. It is radium, combined in exactly the proper manner with zinc sulphide, which gives Undark its ability to shine *continuously* in the dark.

Manufacturers have been quick to recognize the value of Undark. They apply it to the dials of watches and clocks, to electric push buttons, to the buckles of bed room slippers, to house numbers, flashlights, compasses, gasoline gauges, autometers and many other articles which you frequently wish to see in the dark.

The next time you fumble for a lighting switch, bark your shins on furniture, wonder vainly what time it is *because of the dark*—remember Undark. *It shines in the dark.* Dealers can supply you with Undarked articles.

For interesting little folder telling of the production of radium and the uses of Undark address

RADIUM LUMINOUS MATERIAL CORPORATION
58 PINE STREET - - - - NEW YORK CITY
Factories: Orange, N. J.   Mines: Colorado and Utah

UNDARK
Radium Luminous Material

Shines in the Dark

To Manufacturers

The number of manufactured articles to which Undark will add increased usefulness is manifold. From a sales standpoint, it has many obvious advantages. We gladly answer inquiries from manufacturers and, when it seems advisable, will carry on experimental work for them. Undark may be applied either at your plant, or at our own.

The application of Undark is simple. It is furnished as a powder, which is mixed with an adhesive. The paste thus formed is painted on with a brush. It adheres firmly to any surface.

1921 ad for Undark. The Radium Luminous Materials Corporation was reorganized as U.S. Radium in 1921.

211

Luxe et Veritas

From the Jewelers' Circular, August 7, 1918:

A $4.50 Cake Plate for $4.95

With that element of "fourflush" still characteristic of a few department stores, a Wisconsin store advertised 'in this sale we are offering at department store prices the same high class merchandise prided by all silversmiths,' and then offered what the store said was a $6 cake plate for $4.95.

A jeweler called the matter to the attention of the local vigilance committee,* which found that the identical cake plate—same manufacturer, same pattern, same everything—was regularly on sale at three other stores for $4.50.

The owners of the store, already familiar with the fact that there is a strong truth-in-advertising law in that State, had the manager of the jewelry department up "on the green carpet," and other stores were thus protected against such competition.

*The Jewelers Vigilance Committee, founded in 1917 and still very active.

278   **Lux et Veritas**

In that same magazine is an ad for paint for glow-in-the-dark watch dials.

Luma
Radium luminous compound

We absolutely guarantee that only radium is used to activate Luma, no mesothorium, radiothorium, ionium[1], nor polonium being added.

Radium paint was used for glow-in-the dark watch dials. The radium was mixed with zinc sulfide which glows from the radioactive particles the radium emits.

The United States Radium Corporation set up shop in 1917 in Orange, New Jersey. It employed women to paint watch dial numbers with their radium paint brand, Undark (which did have mesothorium added). In addition to watches, U.S. Radium had a contract to paint instrument dials for the U.S. Army in World War I.

The women were told to point the brushes with their lips for the delicate task. In the process, they ingested small amounts of radium.

At the Radium Dial Company in Peru, Illinois the workers were told "if you swallow any radium, it'll make your cheeks rosy." The women would paint their nails and teeth for a glow-in-the-dark laugh. In Switzerland the dial painters could be recognized at night because their hair glowed.

The women dial-painters began to get sick with aplastic anemia, bone cancer, and a painful deterioration of the jaw dubbed "radium jaw", with many deaths.

In the early 1920's U.S. Radium contracted with a Harvard physician and researcher to examine its workers. He found symptoms of radium poisoning in almost all the workers, some severely afflicted.

Arthur Roeder, president of U.S. Radium, disputed the findings, suppressed the 1924 report by refusing permission to publish it, set up a bogus examination of one of the girls that found her in good health, and smeared the girls who had died by claiming they had died of syphilis.

The Orange health department contacted the Consumers League, a non-profit concerned with consumer and workplace issues, (founded in 1899 and still active), which led to an investigation of the deaths of four dial painters between 1922 and 1924 by the Essex County Medical Examiner, who issued a report in 1925 finding that radium poisoning was the cause of the deaths.

The word got out to potential employees and U.S. Radium closed its Orange factory in 1926 and moved to New York City, but with reduced production.

Five of the dial painters filed suit against U.S. Radium in 1927; it had taken two years to find an attorney who would take the case. After a January,1928 hearing, the national press picked up the story of the "Radium Girls"

In April, the judge adjourned the case until September because U.S. Radium said its witnesses would be going to Europe on vacation. The Radium Girls' attorney protested in vain that the women were dying and might not live until then.

At this point a Harvard M.D. On the board of the Consumers League contacted Walter Lippmann, influential columnist for the New York World. He excoriated the delay of the suit of the dying women — some of the women were too weak to raise their hands to take the oath in court. Lippmann's editorial and other negative publicity convinced the court to reschedule the trial for early June, 1928. Shortly before the trial, U.S. Radium settled with the Radium Girls for $10,000 each, $600 a year, and payment for legal and medical expenses, past and future, but denied any responsibility[2]

The Radium Girls all died by the early 1930's. Their case helped establish the right of workers to sue for labor abuse and promoted occupational safety regulations.

The U.S. Radium site was contaminated by waste from the extraction of radium from ore and became a superfund site. It was cleaned up from 1997-2005.

Radium was used in watch dials into the 1960's, but applied safely. Today, tritium or promethium is used in luminous dials

Bizarrely, there is a punk rock band named Undark and the Radium Girls.

1. Obsolete terms for radium 228, thorium 230, and thorium 228. Radium 226, with a half-life of 1600 years was used for watch dials. Radium 228, mesothorium, was added because it was cheaper, $32,000/gram vs. $120,000/gram for radium; it was a byproduct of gas mantle manufacturing. It quickly decays into thorium 228 which emits the alpha particles necessary for luminescence, but which itself decays away within a few years.

2. From a letter by Arthur Roeder, president of of U.S. Radium to the Commissioner of Public Health of the City of New York June 18, 1928:

The fact that we settled these suits in no way is indicative of the merits of the complainants contentions, or that we admit responsibility or liability. From a legal aspect there is very little question that we had a perfect defense, both from the standpoint of the Statute of Limitations [2 years] and from the fact that there was no negligence on our part.

Radium Craze

There was a "radium craze" beginning around 1903. Radium was touted as the cure for what ails you. Radium was put in candy, soda, toothpaste, face creams, suppositories(!), and sundry tonics and elixirs. Even Al Jolson plugged the Radio X pad that "worked wonders" for the crooner's throat.

There was Radium Spray "The new combination bug killer, disinfectant, and furniture polish." (You could drink it, too.)

The radium craze ended with the death of Eben Byers, a wealthy socialite and amateur golf champion. After injuring his arm in 1927, he drank some 1400 bottles of Radiothor radium water in three years. He died in 1932. The Wall Street Journal headlined "The Radium Water Worked Fine until His Jaw Came Off".

Eben Byers is buried in a lead-lined coffin in Pittsburgh.

State Gem

The old central American civilizations, the Olmec, Aztec, and Mayan, carved jade artifacts out of translucent blue and blue-green jadeite. But the source of this gem was not known until recently.

Floods in Guatemala in 1998 caused landslides that exposed the jade deposits and washed jade boulders as big as buses into rivers.

The jade deposits are in an area as big as Rhode Island. It seems there's always something out there the size of Rhode Island, like that iceberg a few years ago. But they never find anything the size of New Jersey. That may be a good thing.

Close Encounters
of the Canine Kind

We've had doggie jewelry, and "waste management". This one is about thinking inside the dog.

It seems that an Arizona pooch swallowed a black South Sea cultured pearl earring. Two days later it was returned, undamaged. The color was a little different but it was still round and had high shine like its partner. The major difference was the size: it was 15% smaller.

There are reports of an ancient practice of cleaning pearls by feeding them to chickens. Modern experiments have shown that this can work. A uniform thin layer is removed from a pearl without killing the shine. Don't try this at home.

Before   After
Dog   Dog

The Mother Lode

40% of all gold ever mined has come from one location in South Africa, the Witwatersrand Basin, extending for 200 miles south of Johannesburg.

Using 1/10th of a gram of the gold, scientists measured parts per billion quantities of a radioactive isotope of the element rhenium and its decay product, osmium, and dated the gold at 3 billion years old.

But the rocks the gold is in are 300 million years younger than the gold and this has scientists scratching their heads trying to figure out how it got there.

Johannesburg is now on the site of the original gold discovery in 1884.

Precious Metal

At the top of the Washington Monument is a 5 pound pyramid of aluminum, which in 1885 was an exotic metal costing $1 an ounce. Aluminum in the 19th century was made from corundum, aluminum oxide, which you know as ruby and sapphire in its gem quality.

The pyramid was exhibited at Tiffany, where people were allowed to carefully step over it so they could claim they had stepped over the top of the Washington Monument.

The aluminum pyramid was to have served as a lightning rod. After a lightning strike in June, 1885 damaged the stone at the top, platinum tipped copper rods were installed around the aluminum pyramid. In 1934, it was discovered that lightning had blunted the tip of the pyramid and there was some melted aluminum fused to its sides and taller copper rods were installed.

The Corundum Hill Mine in North Carolina was then the primary source of commercial aluminum oxide. Industrial grade rubies and sapphires were crushed and made into aluminum. The mine petered out around the turn of the century and today aluminum is made from bauxite ore, but you can still go to North Carolina and find rubies and sapphires.

Black Holes

If you notice that granny's diamond seems to have a black hole right in the center it's because it's an old mine or old European cut diamond. (See p.196.)

The apparent hole is caused by these diamonds having a large flat on the bottom instead of coming to a point. Light just passes through the flat and leaks out the bottom of the diamond instead of being reflected back to the eye, so it appears black.

White Holes

Ever wonder why all diamond jewelry has holes underneath the diamonds?

For one thing it saves weight, making pieces less cumbersome and less expensive. But mainly it's so you can keep the diamonds clean. Gunk on the bottom of a diamond kills the shine. (See *Sanitation Dept.* on p. 193.) Closed back settings can't be completely sealed and stuff can get down around the diamond. If food gets in there it will rot and smell.

Singularity

Older jewelry, dating from the Sixties back, often has small single-cut diamonds. Single cuts have 17 facets rather than the 58 facets of full cuts. Actually, they ought to be called "half-cuts", since they are diamonds that have been blocked, the first part of the cutting process, but not brillianteered, the final part.

You can see from the diagrams that if you grind facets on each rib where the facets of the single-cut meet, you will turn it into a full-cut.

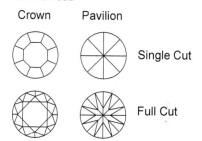

Crown   Pavilion   Single Cut / Full Cut

Black Dermatagraphism

Yes, it really has a scientific name, that black smudge that gold jewelry sometimes leaves on your skin. It's caused by fine particles, usually in cosmetics, rubbing off some of the metal. Very finely divided metal looks black. It can also be caused by chemicals, especially chlorine, attacking the copper and silver that is part of the alloy in 14 karat gold.

Fossil Fuel

Diamond is pure carbon. We know this thanks to the wonders of modern science. It had been known since 1694 that diamond burns completely, leaving no ash. In 1796 English chemist Smithson Tennant discovered that diamond burns to carbon dioxide, proving that diamond is pure carbon.

Luxe et Veritas

I told you about the company that sells cubic zirconia jewelry without saying what it is and making false claims about its properties (p. 93) and "helenite", that they claim is made from Mt. St. Helens volcanic ash, despite a GIA analysis showing it is not. (p. 209)

This time it's pearls. They're selling imitation pearls without saying they're imitation as required by Federal Trade Commission rules, although you could figure it out by a careful reading of the ad copy. The ad is also full of garbled science and misleading claims.

The ad is for "Australian Pacific Golden Pearls". This terminology is illegal. By FTC rules. You can only call a natural pearl by the word "pearl" alone. Cultured or imitation pearls must be labeled "cultured pearl" or "imitation pearl" or something similar. This is done throughout the text of the ad.

The ad starts out by saying they went to Broome, Australia, famous for South Sea cultured pearls, to do research. It gives a short, incorrect history of Broome. It says that fishermen discovered large oysters in the waters off Broome "just before 1900". Actually, they were discovered in 1882. The ad states "after this discovery, Broome soon became the dominant pearl trading post in the world and literally 80% of all worldwide pearl trading passed through Broome." Actually, Broome was famous at that time for mother-of-pearl, the inside of the oyster shell, which was made into buttons and other ornaments, not for pearls. Cultured pearls came on the market in 1921, so pearls of that period were natural pearls, and they mostly came from the Persian Gulf. And golden cultured pearls come from Indonesia and the Philippines.

Their people didn't bring a calculator along to Australia. Talking about Australian (cultured) pearls, they say that they "are often 11-14 mm — about 8 times the size of a standard cultured pearl." Standard cultured pearls are 5 - 8 mm. You do the math.

Cultured pearls are made by inserting in the oyster a mother-of-pearl bead along with a bit of tissue from another oyster. The oyster then plasters the bead with nacre, the lining of the shell. South Sea pearls are left in the water for 2 to 3 years.

The ad says the company's "bioscientists" create their pearls by "extracting the seed pearl from young fresh oysters and speeding up the natural process by which the nacre coats the pearl." If the bead is removed from the oyster, any subsequent nacre coating cannot be done by a natural process.

They go on to say that their "pearls" are "organically micro-coated in the laboratory with the same nacre that coats naturally grown pearls."

I doubt that they are coating it with nacre. Nacre is composed of thin plates of aragonite, a form of calcium carbonate, with a protein the oyster secretes, called conchiolin between the plates. The oyster also secretes other proteins, perlucin, which causes the calcium carbonate to form crystals of aragonite, and lustrin, a stretchy substance that adheres to the aragonite. This forms a brick and mortar structure that makes the nacre tough. This is too complex to be made in the lab, and I could find no references in the gemological literature to synthetic nacre. You'd think their bioscientists would know this.

The ad then states that their "pearls" have "a much more consistent shape than ordinary pearls that have to be extracted from 4-5 year old oysters that are dead." If you can get a dead oyster to grow a pearl, let me know; maybe we can get dead elephants to grow ivory, and we'll all get rich.

They also claim that their "pearls" are "less porous so you don't have to worry about perfumes or or cosmetics discoloring" them. Pearls don't discolor because they are porous. They discolor because they are made from calcium carbonate, which is easily attacked by chemicals. My guess is that those "pearls" don't discolor because they're covered with plastic like other imitation pearls.

And, of course, they're not available in stores.

Olden Goldies	Gold Nugget
The first gold coins were struck during the reign of King Croesus of Lydia, now western Turkey. Croesus reigned from 560 to 546 BC.	In 1854 the largest gold nugget ever found was in California at Carson Hill above the Stanislaus River. It weighed 195 pounds and was valued at $43,534 then.

Aureus Interruptis

How convenient! I can switch over to catch the gold price on Bloomberg from the comfort of my barcalounger during commercials. It's in the crawler at the bottom of the screen. But if there's breaking news, forget it. The breaking news banner goes up right over the crawler, and stays there until it's at soybeans or wheat, long past gold. And the news keeps breaking for as many rounds as it takes for me to give up. Usually, the news is about some boring stock market thing.

Break the news over the talking head, for the love of Mike!

Breaking news: Bloomberg moved the breaking news banner above the crawler, leaving only the talking head's head.

Update: Sometimes the crawler goes away, but it was changed so you can get the gold price in a window at lower right every 4½ minutes.

Breaking news: I got an Ipad — talk about barcalounger compatible! Now I can check the gold price at will on my own web site.

Heat Wave

Diamond conducts heat better than any other material, even copper or silver. Ordinary diamonds have carbon atoms with 6 neutrons, (carbon 12), but about 1% of the atoms have 7 neutrons (carbon 13). Scientists have succeeded in creating pure carbon 12 and making diamonds from it. These diamonds conduct heat much better than ordinary diamonds. Pure carbon 12 diamonds are used as heat sinks in advanced electronic equipment.

This is the pamphlet I hand out in the store

Selling Your Gold

Gold is $1100 an ounce, so if I have an ounce of old gold jewelry, I'll get $1100, right?

Well, you don't have an ounce of gold. The postal scale you used to weigh it uses the wrong kind of ounce. You have an avoirdupois ounce; precious metals are weighed in troy ounces.

A troy ounce, named for Troyes, France where it is said to have originated long ago, is about 10% larger than the ounce you know about.

Now that you've made your weight correction, you still don't have an ounce of gold. Your jewelry is 14 karat gold. The gold price you hear is for pure gold, 24 karat. 14 karat gold is 14/24ths , or 58.3% gold, so you only have .583 ounce of gold.

Well, not really. Your 14 karat gold will be bought at 13½ karat, or 56.25% gold. Prior to 1981, it was legal to sell 13 or or 13½ karat as 14 karat. This was permitted by the National Gold and Silver Marking Act of 1906.

At that time assay technology was crude, so the Act allowed items containing solder to be 13 karat and those without solder to be 13½ karat, yet be marked 14 karat. Today, gold solders are "plumb", actually 14 karat, but back then they were lower karat because they lacked the technology to lower the melting point of the solder without lowering the amount of gold.

In 1981, an amendment to the Act tightened tolerances to within 7 parts per thousand for jewelry containing solder and 3 parts per thousand for that without solder.

At any rate, you know no one will put in more gold than is absolutely necessary and you know that some people will always cheat. So 14 karat jewelry sold for scrap is always bought at 13½ karat. It's the same for 10 or 18 karat, too — it sells at ½ karat less.

Now that we have ounces sorted out, you can forget about them. You will sell your jewelry by the pennyweight.

There are 20 pennyweights to the troy ounce. Most jewelry weighs well under an ounce so it is more convenient to use pennyweights rather than fractions of an ounce.

You will be paid so much per pennyweight for your old gold. The price will be adjusted for the karat of gold. You will get more per pennyweight for 18 karat than 14 karat because 18 karat contains more gold; it is 18/24ths or 75% gold. Conversely, you will be paid less for 10 karat gold.

The price you get will be based on the market price of gold when you sell it. The market price of gold fluctuates every minute during trading hours which are around the clock weekdays, since Asian markets are open when the New York and London markets are closed.

The price you receive for your old gold is strictly for the salvage value of the raw material, the gold. You buy jewelry and you sell metal. It will be a fraction of what you paid for the jewelry new since, like any other manufactured product, the people who make it, ship it, insure it, and sell it make a living, just like you.

But the scrap value of the gold in jewelry is a much larger fraction of its retail price than for other products. This is simply because gold is so expensive that other costs are relatively small in proportion.

The price you will receive for your old gold is set by each jeweler. The jeweler makes a profit, of course. But the profit percentage should be modest since the numbers are large – thousands of dollars – and the sale is certain, unlike new jewelry that may sit for years.

Since those thousands of dollars are tied up to maintain the capacity to buy, even brand-new salable jewelry you sell gets scrapped. It would tie up too much money to put it in the case for sale and, in this economy, who would buy it? That's the flip side of high gold prices.

Generally, the only interest is for the gold in jewelry. Any gemstones or small diamonds should be removed and returned to you. The stones in most commercial jewelry have little resale value. Some of the small diamonds aren't even worth removing. Unless you have a truly fabulous piece of jewelry, it may be difficult to find a jeweler who is interested in buying it as a piece of jewelry rather than scrap gold and you will probably get considerably less than you paid. Again, it's about tying up money in a poor economy. And with everyone selling jewelry the market is flooded, a buyer's market.

The jeweler sells your gold to a refinery to be melted and chemically turned back into pure gold. This involves very corrosive acids or chlorine gas; it is not something that is done in the back of a store. The jeweler receives less than the market value of the gold, since the refinery has to make a profit, too.

Your gold will be tested to be sure it is gold and to determine its karat. Gold is tested for karat by rubbing the item across a black basalt stone to get a streak and then putting a little drop of acid on the streak to see if it dissolves. This is the origin of "acid test".

The acid is called aqua regia, Latin for noble liquid, so named because it will dissolve gold. Aqua regia is formulated in a variety of proportions to dissolve different karats of gold. If the streak stays with 14 karat acid and dissolves in 18 karat acid, the gold is 14 karat.

The acid test cannot distinguish between 14 karat and slightly subkarat pieces, usually certain types of old jewelry. Old charm bracelets with large disk charms are always 13 karat. Suspect subkarat jewelry will be bought for 13 karat, about 7% less, with the difference made up to you within a week if it checks out with an x-ray fluorescence analyzer, a $19,000 ray-gun that precisely reads metal content.

There are other karats of gold than those familiar in the U.S., 10, 14, and 18 karat. Often gold is marked with a number indicating its purity rather than its karat number. See table below.

Mark	Karat	Typical Origin
333	8	Germany
375	9	England, Ireland
417	10	U.S.
583/585	14	U.S. Russia
750	18	Most of world
800	19	Portugal
875	21	Middle East
917	22	India
999	24	China, S.E. Asia

You can also sell platinum and silver for scrap. Silver is only about 1.5% the price of gold, so you will need a lot of it to add up. A few pieces of silver jewelry will only bring a few dollars. Old silver coins and sterling flatware, knives, forks and spoons, will bring quite a bit due to their weight.

Flatware, dishes, candlesticks, etc. will be marked "sterling", not just so and so silver company. English sterling will be marked with a lion with a raised paw. Some European silver is marked 800, 830, or 835, meaning 80-83.5% silver. Sterling jewelry is often marked "925" because sterling silver is 92.5% silver, by definition. Although "sterling" has connotations of excellence or superiority, in this context it just means the 92.5% alloy of silver and copper.

You will get more for platinum jewelry than for gold. Platinum is 90-95% pure and almost 70% more dense than 14 karat gold. The combination of higher purity and more weight than for a comparable gold piece will translate into a higher price.

On the Road Again

Reckless Driving

In 1907 the speed limit in New York City was 10 mph. This was so slow that no cars actually obeyed the law. To demonstrate this the Warner Instrument Company installed a giant speedometer, 10 feet high and 4 feet wide with foot-high numbers on a car and drove it around Manhattan at the legal limit.

According to an article in The Automobile June 6, 1907 titled *To Prove the Absurdity of Speed Laws*, the the car set out down Broadway from 63rd to 60th street at 10 miles per hour. It was passed by every automobile, street car, and buggy.

In another test run up Broadway from 66th street for a mile showed only three horse-drawn vehicles obeying the law. But, "on the other hand, the Autometer was passed by three automobiles, four street cars, and three horse vehicles, all violators of the law."

Samuel M. Butler, secretary of the Automobile Club of America, said that the law is so absurd it gives license to reckless driving.

Defense Dept.

Air Force One, the president's plane, is equipped with gold-plated reflectors. Gold reflects 99% of infrared radiation (heat). This confuses a missile's heat-seeking system.

Knockoff

Forget those fake Rolexes and Gucci handbags. That's small potatoes. A Chinese (of course) automobile company knocked off a Ferrari. Only 6 of this 1967 Ferrari were made. The seventh was seized by the European Union in transit in 2006, so you missed your chance for a 90% discount on these prestige wheels.

Rolling Stones

Can't get no satisfaction because your Rolls doesn't stand out from the pack? Accessorize with cubic zirconia-studded wheels. If you can afford the $332,750 Rolls Royce Phantom they're designed for, what's another quarter million bucks?

There are 21 CZ's per spoke in the 5 spoke wheels. It all adds up to 63,000 carats or a little under 28 pounds. That's only 4 bucks a carat. Cheap!

One would think that flashy wheels would clash with the old-world elegance appeal of a Rolls, but they're designed for Rolls' most important customers, hip hop kings of bling. In fact, in that world, they're considered conservative.

As they say. there's no accounting for taste. In cars or music.

Gone in 60 Seconds

The New York Times reported extensively on the New York City subway opening on October 27, 1904.

A ceremonial sterling silver and ebony controller lever made by Tiffany in a mahogany case was brought aboard and fitted to the motor and Mayor George McClellan started the train at 2:33 P.M. The mayor liked it so much he drove the train all the way from City Hall to 103rd St. in Harlem, under the watchful eye of the motorman.

At 7:02 P.M., a man boarded the subway at 28th St. At 7:03 he noticed that his $500 horseshoe pin with 15 diamonds was gone. He reported the theft to police at 30th St., "and they sent out an alarm and notified Police Headquarters. The thieves will be looked for and the pawnshops watched."

Paint Job

A Honda Odyssey has become the first car to be completely covered in gemstones. Sort of.

The car has been slathered with 70,000 carats of Kyoto Opal. Kyoto Opal is a man-made opal impregnated with plastic, so it can be bent and cut into thin sections. The opal was crushed and combined with paint. The result is a white sparkly car.

The paint job is $88,000. The car is extra.

Bloomer War

7000 BICYCLES carried over from 1897 must be sacrificed now. New High Grade, all styles, best equipment, *guaranteed*, $9.75 to $17.00. Used wheels, late models, all makes, $3 to $12. *We ship on approval without a cent payment*. Write for bargain list and art catalogue of swell '98 models. Bicycle free for season to advertise them. Send for one. Rider agents wanted. Learn how to Earn a Bicycle and make money.

This is an ad from the J.M. Mead Cycle Co. of Chicago in the April 2, 1898 Literary Digest. Regular prices for bicycles were $35-50, 2-3 weeks pay. Sears advertised a $19.75 "Special Wheel" that is "equal to any bicycle you can buy anywhere at $40 to $50."

This was during the bicycle craze of the 1890's.

The high-wheel bicycle, the one with the huge front wheel and tiny back wheel, (also called the "ordinary" or the "penny-farthing" from the relative sizes of those coins) was dangerous: if you fell off, you had a long way to fall. The "safety" bicycle with two wheels of the same size, pneumatic tires, and a chain drive was invented in the 1880's and ushered in the golden age of the bicycle.

There was a bicycle show in Madison Square Garden in 1896. The New York Times reported extensively on it:

An Enormous Crowd Throngs the Madison Square Garden

A Wonderful Exhibit of Wheels

Never So Many Machines, Bicycle Accessories and Appointments Shown Before

The Garden Brilliant with Electric Illumination—Pretty Decorations and Designs

The Columbia Bicycle company exhibited "a wheel most elaborately finished in silver and with carved ivory handles finished by Tiffany...reputed to have cost $5000." The Syracuse Bicycle featured "an imposing and gorgeously decorated Indian of the Syracuse tribe distributing souvenirs."

The League of American Wheelmen (LAW) was formed in 1880 and was instrumental in lobbying for paved roads. Albert Pope, the manufacturer of Columbia Bicycles and owner of key bicycle patents, had formed the League. In 1892 the League collected 150,000 signatures on a petition to establish a national road department which was presented to the Senate.

The petition was signed by the Chief Justice and State Governors, and was endorsed by eminent corporations and civic organizations. In response to the petition, the Office of Road Inquiry was founded in 1893 which ultimately led to the creation of the Federal Highway Administration.

The individual sheets of the petition were assembled into one ribbon 1400 yards long, wound on two giant oak spools. It is 7 feet tall,weighs 600 pounds, and is stored in the National Archives.

Women enthusiastically took up bicycle riding but voluminous Victorian dresses were unsuited to cycling and women started wearing bloomers, baggy pants first popularized by suffragette Amelia Bloomer in 1851.

Mary Sargent Hopkins, the editor of The Wheelwoman, complained in the New York Times December 23, 1894:

Bloomers and Knickerbockers Mrs. Hopkins Condemns

Short Skirt and Leggins Proper

The Garb of Man Makes a Fool of a Woman, She Declares, and She is Waging a War Against It.

A speaker at an 1895 medical convention in Detroit recommended the bicycle for women for "moderate use in cases of acute diseases. An hour's wheeling three times a day is ample." But he commented that bloomers "lessened the respect of mankind for womanhood and blemished the landscape."

The Bachelor of Arts, a University of Michigan publication, wrote in May,1895 of a student who, finding it inconvenient to change clothes after cycling, wore her bloomers around the boarding house where she lived. Mrs. Eames, the owner of the boarding house objected and the student agreed to only wear her bloomers when cycling.

"But Miss Brown of the Medical School cried 'tyranny!' when she heard of it, and put her bloomers right on and sallied forth into the street, and declared war. Some of the professors' wives who ride bicycles sided with her, and declared it to be the constitutional right of every woman to wear bloomers with or without bicycles whenever she would." Mrs. Eames then declared she would have no bloomers worn in her house. Thus started the Ann Arbor "Bloomer War."

"The Bachelor's opinion is that only pretty women should wear bloomers at any time."

Autoing Has Come to Stay

"Has the automobile, or, to put it more broadly, mechanical road-traction, come to stay, or must it ultimately meet the fate that seems already to have overtaken the bicycle?" This is the question posed in an article titled *Future of the Automobile* in the Literary Digest, August 17, 1907.

The article quotes Motor Talk editor George Mertz Slocum that whereas ten years ago a horseless carriage "caused windows to fly open, crowds to press the curb..." But "To-day a splendid equipage, horse-drawn, will cause the crowd to stop and take notice, while the surging mass of automobiles rush past unnoticed."

Slocum asks if a gray-haired financier he saw with his daughter with a baby could substitute a bicycle. "The chauffeur tipped his leather cap, opened the plate-glass door; the three sank into the luxuriously upholstered seats, the driver hopped behind the wheel, and a moment later they were gliding quietly down the avenue."

"Autoing bids to youth with the cry of speed, wild excitement, and captivating romance; to the middle-aged with the beckonings of the tour, of the glories of nature, of the keen enjoyments; and to the aged with the soothing balm of comfort and luxury, of health and good-cheer, of strength and hope. Autoing has come to stay."

1902 ad

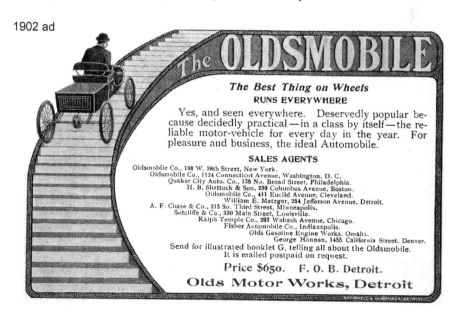

The **OLDSMOBILE**

The Best Thing on Wheels
RUNS EVERYWHERE

Yes, and seen everywhere. Deservedly popular because decidedly practical — in a class by itself — the reliable motor-vehicle for every day in the year. For pleasure and business, the ideal Automobile.

SALES AGENTS

Oldsmobile Co., 138 W. 38th Street, New York.
Oldsmobile Co., 1124 Connecticut Avenue, Washington, D. C.
Quaker City Auto. Co., 138 No. Broad Street, Philadelphia.
H. B. Shattuck & Son, 239 Columbus Avenue, Boston.
Oldsmobile Co., 411 Euclid Avenue, Cleveland.
William E. Metzger, 254 Jefferson Avenue, Detroit.
A. F. Chase & Co., 215 So. Third Street, Minneapolis.
Sutcliffe & Co., 330 Main Street, Louisville.
Ralph Temple Co., 293 Wabash Avenue, Chicago.
Fisher Automobile Co., Indianapolis.
Olds Gasoline Engine Works, Omaha.
George Hannan, 1455 California Street, Denver.
Send for illustrated booklet G, telling all about the Oldsmobile.
It is mailed postpaid on request.

Price $650. F. O. B. Detroit.

Olds Motor Works, Detroit

The Golden Spike

On May 10, 1869 the transcontinental railroad was completed. The Union Pacific and the Central Pacific railroads met at Promontory Summit, Utah Territory. Leland Stanford, president of the Central Pacific used a silver-plated maul to care-fully tap a ceremonial golden spike into a prebored hole in a special tie made of polished Californa laurel.

David Hewes had the golden spike made. He was a San Francisco entrepeneur and friend of Leland Stanford. The spike was 5 5/8 inches long and had over 14 ounces of 17.6 karat gold.

The spike was engraved on two sides with the names of officers of the railroad companies and with the wrong date, May 8, the planned date. Several hundred men had seized a train carrying a vice-president of the Union Pacific demanding to be paid and this delayed the arrival of the Union Pacific locomotive.

Another side was engraved *The Pacific Railroad ground broken Jany 8th 1863 and completed May 8th 1869.* The fourth side was engraved *May God continue the unity of our country as the railroad unites the two great Oceans of the world. Presented David Hewes San Francisco.* The top of the spike was engraved *The Last Spike.*

There were three other ceremonial spikes put into the laurel tie: a silver spike from Nevada, a gold and silver plated spike from Arizona, and a second gold spike ordered by a San Francisco newspaper.

After the ceremony, the laurel tie with the ceremonial spikes was removed and replaced with an ordinary pine tie and an iron spike was provided. Both the spike and the maul were wired to the telegraph line so the final blows could be "heard" by the nation.

Stanford swung at the last spike but missed and hit the tie. A rail worker finally drove it home and a Western Union telegrapher tapped out D-O-N-E at 12:47 p.m.

Just before the ceremony, a large sprue, the runner of metal from the castiing pour, that had been deliberately left on the point of the golden spike was removed. David Hewes had it made into four rings and seven inch long spike watch fobs.

The golden spike was returned to David Hewes and he donated it to the newly built Stanford University in 1892.

A second golden spike made at the same time was acquired from the Hewes family by the California State Railroad Museum in Sacramento in 2006.

The laurel tie disappeared in the San Francisco earhquake of 1906.

An immediate consequence of the completion of the transcontinental railroad was that the cost to transport the mail from coast to coast went from $1100 per mile per year to $200.

Horse Sense

This graceful and practical Automobile does the work of six horses at an average cost for gasoline of $35.00 a year (10,000 miles). Board alone for one horse costs $180.00 a year, so the economy is very evident. Price $650.00
— 1903 ad for Oldsmobile.

$650 adjusted for 26.32X inflation to 2012 is $17,108. $180 comes to $4738 or $395 a month. "Board costs seem to range around $400 per month for most areas of the country" according to horsechannel.com

Deep Thought
Pride is for others, honor for
yourself

Riding the Rails

The Harris 20th Century Railroad Attachment "transforms the ordinary bicycle into the most practical and durable device for obtaining high speed on railroad tracks," in an early 20th century Sears catalog.

You can still ride the rails on your bike. Just buy a conversion kit and you can ride on (hopefully) unused tracks. But watch out for a greaser, a pin sticking up beside one rail on a curve that activates a grease pump when the train wheel depresses it. A bike wheel won't and you'll be derailed.

$5.45

Happy Anniversary!

Here's an anniversary you'll want to celebrate: the installation of the first parking meter 80 years ago. Park-O-Meter No. 1 was installed on the southeast corner of what was then First Street and Robinson Avenue in Oklahoma City, Oklahoma on July 16, 1935.

Cars would park all day, or even for weeks, stifling downtown business and the city fathers asked Carl Magee, editor of the Oklahoma City News, to help find a solution. Magee invented the parking meter to solve the problem.

Despite opposition, stores saw an increase in business as the meters forced a turnover of cars (at a nickel an hour) and parking meters quickly spread through the city.

Carleton Magee left his law practice of 17 years in Oklahoma City in 1919, moving to Albuquerque, hoping the drier climate would help his wife's lung problems. He had always dreamed of owning a newspaper and he bought the Albuquerque Morning Journal, the state's largest newspaper, from U.S. Senator Albert Fall.

Magee began investigating political corruption in New Mexico. There was a lot to investigate. He began by exposing the diversion of funds from the state Land Office to Fall's campaign.

Fall angrily threatened to break him. Five previous editors had been threatened and silenced, but Magee kept investigating corruption in spite of physical threats.

In 1921, Fall resigned his Senate seat to become Secretary of the Interior under President Warren G. Harding. Magee found out that Fall was spending large amounts of money to improve his New Mexico ranch. His investigation ultimately led to uncovering the Teapot Dome scandal, the sensation of the era, in which Fall was convicted in 1929 of accepting bribes from oil executives in exchange for leases on the U.S. Naval Petroleum Reserves at Teapot Dome, Wyoming, and Elk Hills, California.

Due to Fall's pressure, the newspaper's banks called notes and refused to renew Magee's loans, forcing the sale of the paper. Magee promptly founded another paper, Magee's Independent, a weekly, in 1922. Within a year the name was changed to the New Mexico State Tribune and it became a daily paper.

Magee continued to investigate political corruption, angering powerful Republican leaders in San Miguel County. A district judge, David Leahy, ordered Magee to stand trial on a trumped up libel charge against a New Mexico Supreme Court justice. Even though the justice testified for Magee that he had not been libeled, Leahy ordered a directed guilty verdict and sentenced Magee to prison.

But New Mexico governor James. F. Hinkle, a Democrat, immediately pardoned Magee and set aside his conviction and sentence. Then Leahy found Magee in contempt of court for violating his order not to write about the trial and for calling the judge "corrupt" in print and sentenced him to a year in prison and a stiff fine. Again, the governor immediately pardoned Magee and set aside the sentence and fine.

In 1923, the Scripps-Howard newspaper chain bought the New Mexico State Tribune, keeping Magee as editor.

In 1925, while Magee was being interviewed by another paper in a hotel lobby, Judge Leahy stormed in, knocked Magee down and kicked him, breaking several ribs. Lying on the floor, Magee pulled a revolver he carried and fired two shots. One shot hit Leahy in the arm, but the other killed a bystander. Magee was tried and acquitted of manslaughter but was haunted by it the rest of his life.

In 1927, Scripps-Howard transferred Magee to Oklahoma City as editor of the

Oklahoma City News. Carl Magee died in Oklahoma City in 1946 at 73.

Today, Park-O-Meter No. 1 is on display in the Statehood Gallery of the Oklahoma Historical Society.

Road Rage

Motorists were not well received in the early days of the automobile. In 1904 the Automobile Club of America proposed that members arm themselves.

An article in the Literary Digest from August 27, 1904 titled *Shooting Automobilists* quotes the secretary of the club that in rural areas, even though speeders are few, "farmers and even officers of the law have without sufficient cause or justification frequently fired on or held up automobilists" and imposed fines that are "highway robbery."

Newspaper comment seemed to favor the country folk. The Washington Post would bet "dollars to doughnuts on the rustics" in a shooting match with automobilists. The Philadelphia Ledger commented that motorists who ignore a summons to stop by an officer be treated as fugitives. "the defiant chauffeurs are so numerous that there is danger that all automobilists will be regarded as outlaws."

Another paper reported that tramps from large cities are "posing as rural sheriffs, holding up speeding automobilists and assessing substantial 'fines' on the spot."

The New York Times said that law officers have found that reckless motorists pay no attention to an order to stop, and they should be treated as "fugitive chicken thieves or escaping misdemeanants."

"It is not a crime to shoot at automobiles in northern Illinois provided you do not hit the occupants of the car." This is from the December, 1905 edition of Motor Talk, a Detroit journal. An Evanston policeman stopped an auto by shooting the tire. He was held on $5000 bond but the grand jury refused to indict him.

There were "telephone traps" in which the law would phone ahead to the next town so reckless automobilists couldn't escape.

In Nova Scotia, a 1908 amendment to the 1907 Motor Vehicle Act allowed every local jurisdiction to make its own rules of the road. Most allowed cars on the road only one day a week, not necessarily on the same day. This made it impossible to travel far in some areas. This stayed in force until 1911.

The Evening Telegram, St. John's Newfoundland on March 26, 1908 reported the deliberations on the amendment in Halifax. A Cape Breton M.P. suggested that permission be given to "shoot down automobilists on sight just as sheep-killing dogs are shot."

A Tale of Two Grilles

Here's the latest toy for toffs, a $2.4 million special edition of the Bugatti Veyron Grand Sport, the L'or Blanc (that's French for white gold). It features porcelain accents, including a caviar tray, of course.

VW bought Bugatti in 1998, along with Lamborghini and Bentley. Bugatti makes 50 cars a year. The curvy white car with blue stripes looks like it drove out of the movie Tron, except for its ugly grille. It was a special order for an Arab businessman.

Remember the Edsel? It was called an Oldsmobile sucking a lemon. The Bugatti looks like it just spit the lemon out.

Next up a four door with a 1000 horsepower engine for around $1.4 million.

Golden Chariot

A Porsche 911 covered with 40 pounds of 22 karat gold worth $600,000 was stolen in Moscow in 2009. The owner had decided to sell it and a buyer found on the Internet took a few laps around a parking lot, then took off. After waiting 20 minutes for him to return, the owner called the police.

Moscow police said that reports of the theft were false. There were no Porsche thefts reported that day. The owner had called about a problem with the customer concerning the value of the car and the police did not get involved. They also said that the car was only painted with gold-colored paint and was worth $90,000, the price of a Porsche.

The car was found a short time later. Close-up photos clearly show plates of gold, some deeply engraved, secured with screws covering the car.

Keep on Truckin'

Saw this on the back of a dump truck.

⇐ Grateful   Dead ⇒

Stick Shift

You hop in your Bentley on a hot summer day, grab the shift knob and burn your fingers on the hot leather. What to do?

Accessorize with a diamond-studded gear shift. A company offers a Bentley shift with 30 carats of diamonds set into a metal center strip on the front of the leather-covered shift knob.

The diamonds are pavéd into 10 ounces of 18 karat white gold. The car costs $165,000; the gear shift is $150,000.

The company used 2.5 mm diamonds (about .055 carat) took 100 hours to make it. This is enough information for me to determine what it cost to make.

I'll sell it to you for $75,000 and make a fortune on it, and that's with fine diamonds.

Deep Thought
Do you know what you're talking about?

Highway Robbery

There are thousands of temples in Bali, elaborately carved with various demons, gods, and spirits of their Hindu religion.

The soft sandstone carvings erode quickly and new ones are constantly being done, some with more modern themes. Below is a scene of a bandit holding up a motorist, thought to be from an American movie according to an article in the Literary Digest July 7, 1928.

Another carving is of a Dutchman on a bicycle, with a lotus blossom wheel. (Indonesia used to be the Dutch East Indies.) X-rated scenes from the Kama Sutra and swastikas, an ancient Hindu symbol, are also seen.

Celestial Navigation

You can now get the voices of Star Wars on your Tom-Tom GPS. Darth Vader, Yoda, C-3PO, and Han Solo will guide you if you aren't Jedi enough to use the Force.

"I am altering the route. Pray I do not alter it further."

"Turned wrong you have. A u-ey hang you must."

"Sir, the possibility of successfully navigating the New Jersey Turnpike is approximately 3720 to 1!. We're doomed!"

"The light turned yellow — jump to light speed!"

Speeding Ticket

Eleanor Wilson McAdoo, wife of Treasury Secretary William McAdoo (see *Wall Street Closed* on p. 111) and daughter of the President got a speeding ticket November 19, 1915, reported the New York Times.

Actually it was a telephone summons by a magistrate after the "motor cycle guardian of the Washington Road" reported that he chased the car the 14 miles from Savage, Maryland to the Baltimore city line for 17 minutes, or 50 miles an hour.

The Maryland speed limit had just been raised from 25 to 35 miles an hour. Her chauffeur paid a $25 fine on November 22.

First Auto

William Howard Taft was the first President to have an official automobile. In January, 1909, President-elect Taft asked Congress for $12,000 for two automobiles. The appropriation was originally in a funding bill that wouldn't go into effect until July, but at Taft's request the funds were put into that year's Urgent Deficiency bill so the cars would be available by inauguration day, March 4*

The House passed the Deficiency bill but on January 21, the Senate struck out the automobile appropriation. The House put presidential autos back in the bill with the understanding that the funds would come out of a reduction in funds for the White House stable rather than new spending.

In debate on the bill it was suggested that the 354 pound Taft wanted the autos so as to prevent cruelty to animals. After some wrangling the House passed the bill on February 2.

In the Senate debate, Senator Joseph Bailey of Texas was ardently pro-horse and Senator Benjamin Tillman of South Carolina pro-auto, although not speeding autos.

"Down in my county when these things got to 'puff-puffing' around on the roads we had three of four runaways. Women and children were hurt. Finally, when a man hitched up and started out he put his trusty shotgun alongside him. When he saw one of the things coming he put his gun to his shoulder and the automobile stopped. Those automobile fellows got mighty polite after that."

— *Tillman's Motormania Cure,* The New York Times February 5, 1909.

The Urgent Deficiency bill passed February 9, after the Senate endorsed the conference committee report.

Taft bought a 40 horsepower White Steamer and a 48 horsepower Pierce-Arrow limousine and he test-drove both before his inauguration. Although he rode in a horse-drawn carriage to the inauguration, he took the Pierce-Arrow to the inaugural ball.

* The Twentieth Amendment moved the presidential inauguration from March 4 to January 20. It was ratified in January, 1933 but took effect in October. This resulted in Franklin Roosevelt's first inauguration being held March 4, 1933 and his second January 20 1937.

Hot Wheels

Hot Wheels, the toy car brand of Mattel, celebrated its 40th anniversary and its 4 billionth car by commissioning a diamond-encrusted muscle car.

The 1:64 scale car is cast in 18 karat white gold. 2700 white and blue diamonds weighing 22.94 carats cover the car. The hood opens to reveal black and white diamonds set in the engine. The tail lights are set with rubies.

The custom made presentation case sports 40 white diamonds. $140,000.

I wouldn't roll it past the dog.

Keep on Truckin'
Decals for your muscle truck

Thumbing a Ride

On July 27, 2014, a hitchhiker set out on a highway near the airport in Halifax, Nova Scotia and was picked up in two minutes on a trek to cross Canada to Victoria, B.C., a journey of 3,870 miles.

HitchBOT, a robot, arrived in Victoria August 17 where it was given a ride in a ceremonial war canoe by Songhees Indians and attended high tea at the Empress Hotel the next day.

Frauke Zeller, a professor of computational philology (!) at Ryerson University in Toronto and David Smith of McMaster University in Hamilton put together HitchBOT from odds and ends: a plastic beer cooler body, swimming pool noodle arms and legs and a cake saver head to protect its LED face. Yellow gloves, rubber wellies, and a garbage can lid hat complete its outfit. It's 3½ feet tall, weighs 18 pounds and speaks with a female sounding voice but is "gender neutral." A child booster seat built into its butt enables it to be buckled into a car.

It is equipped with GPS, 3G wireless connectivity, a camera that takes random shots every half hour which are posted online after being screened and it records conversations after asking permission.

A tablet computer in its stomach is its brain. It can carry on a conversation with its speech recognition software. "Do you love me? Do you know the origin of the universe? What's your favourite football team?" It asked a group of children. If it can't understand the conversation, it is programmed to just chatter, saying that sometimes it gets carried away.

When it's picked up it directs its ride to its web site for further instructions. It can recite from Wikipedia about the areas it is passing through. It has solar panels but instructions on its body say it can be plugged into a car's cigarette lighter to be recharged.

It took 18 rides to cross Canada. Along the way it went camping, fishing, went to a pow wow, and crashed a wedding, dancing with the bride on the groom's shoulders. Hitchbot interrupted the bride while she was thanking her friends for attending saying "I like to make friends."

It was on Facebook, Instagram and Twitter:

"Hitched my first ride! A lovely couple offered to help me out. Look out, New Brunswick -- Here I come!"

"Speaking human is difficult for me, and I only recently learned it. I find inner peace by staying quiet for a bit."

"I need to recharge, Hitchhiking is tough."

"I'm on a boat. Well, a ferry to be exact. Victoria, I'm on my way."

HitchBOT's creators said the idea was to explore the role reversal of humans helping a robot instead of the other way around.

Yellow Fellow

The Yellow Fellow was the most famous bicycle during the 1890's bicycle craze. It was a bright yellow bicycle made by the E. C. Stearns Bicycle Agency in Syracuse, N.Y. The Yellow Fellow was heavily advertised. On August 14, 1896, Eugene Neidert, a vaudeville trick riding cyclist, rode up the steps of the Capitol in Washington on a Yellow Fellow which generated national attention.

Stearns teamed up with newspaper publisher William Randolph Hearst to set up the Journal-Examiner Yellow Fellow Transcontinental Relay, named for two of Hearst's papers, the San Francisco Examiner and the New York Journal, then engaged in a circulation war with Joseph Pulitzer's New York World.

The 3000 mile cross-country trek began in San Francisco at noon on August 25th, 1896. Each rider on the relay was accompanied by a back-up rider and carried the packet, a leather pouch with a dispatch from Major General Nelson Miles at the Presidio in San Francisco to Major General Thomas Ruger at Governor's Island, New York. The dispatch was engraved on a gold plate and enclosed in a silver case. Also enclosed was a certificate to be signed by the governors of each state on the relay route.

Big Bill Rishel, a legendary bicycle racer living in Salt Lake City was tapped by Hearst to manage the 900 mile leg of the relay across Utah from Truckee, California to Rock Springs, Wyoming.

Rishel and a companion had scouted a route across the Great Salt Lake Desert, riding with ease 62 miles on the hard salt until they ran into mud flats that rain had turned into a quagmire. They had to carry their bikes most of the rest of the hundred mile trip, taking 23 hours.

Nonetheless, Rishel scheduled the route across the desert, the most direct route to Salt Lake City. When the riders were in Nevada, a rainstorm made the mud flats they were approaching impassable. Rishel made a last minute change of route, informing all by telegraph, detouring north around the Great Salt Lake to Ogden. The riders were then supposed to go south into Salt Lake City.

There was intense rivalry between Salt Lake City and Ogden, to the point of plots to hijack the packet. Salt Lake city riders had prepared a ruse to bypass Ogden and divert the packet to Salt Lake City, but an honest rider scuttled the plot.

Meanwhile, the Ogdenites were determined to deny honors to Salt Lake City. North of Ogden, an Ogden rider with the packet bypassed Ogden, picking up the route to the west of both cities. Ogden cut off its nose to spite its face, but had the schadenfreude satisfaction of leaving the governor and Salt Lake City waiting in vain.

Responding to a snarky article in the Ogden Standard, Rishel said in a letter to the Salt Lake Herald, September 1, 1896 "To the editor of the Ogden Standard: 'It is a waste of lather to shave an ass'".

The packet arrived at the headquarters of the New York Journal on Park Row in Manhattan on September 7, 1896. The journey had taken 13 days, 29 minutes, 4 1/5 seconds. The packet was opened by New York Postmaster Charles Dayton who found inside a letter announcing the race whose envelope was covered with the postmarks of all the places through which the relay passed and also the signatures of their postmasters.

Big Bill Rishel moved on to automobiles, championing the salt flats for racing and establishing the route of the Lincoln Highway across them. He was an early automotive pioneer, organizing the Salt Lake Auto Club. He became the automotive editor of the Salt Lake Tribune and championed auto tourism in the west. He died in 1947 at 77.

Bicycles in those days had no brakes. An article in the New York Times July 19,1896 headlined "The Necessity For Brakes Becoming More Apparent", and cited deaths of riders on a tandem bicycle: "powerless to check their momentum when danger was discovered, they were hurled into eternity." A November 29 article was titled "Brakes on Bicycles to be the Rule Next Year."

Speed Limit

Montana had no speed limits until 1974 when the national 55 mph limit was enacted to save gas. When the government threatened to withhold highway funds for states that kept speeding, Montana fined speeders $5 for "wasting a natural resource." The ticket didn't go on a driver's record and you could just hand the trooper a $5 bill.

Jn Passing

Help Yourself

Remember those tacky ads on match-book covers? Learn to be a cartoonist! A TV repairman! 90 lb. weakling getting sand kicked in your face? Build muscles and get the girls.

This has now morphed into the $8.5 billion a year self-help industry selling you books and audiotapes. Even The Donald wants to teach you how to get rich in real estate (and make him richer in the process).

Self-help can all be boiled down into 4 categories:

How to get your head screwed on right
How to lose weight
How to get rich
How to get women.

I suspect that if you have to buy the book, you won't be a thin, rich, well-adjusted lady-killer.

If you really want to get rich, write a self-help book.

The best ad I've seen follows, below.

Want to get rich? Order your Acme home counterfeiting kit today! Cut out the middle-man and make your money directly. Exclusive manual press will also give you a workout – lose weight while you make money! You can never be too rich or too thin! (Includes get out of jail free card courtesy of Parker Brothers.)

Zen and the Art of Canine Maintenance

Concentration! Urination! Defecation! It's the concentration part that's hard. Do it already, dog! Grrrr.

While we're in Zen mode, Here's a Haiku.

Winter, white coats grass
Doggie footprints in the snow
Poopsicles behind

Atomic Secret

I vaguely remember watching a 15 minute TV show called Atom Squad as a kid. All I remember is men walking around in radiation suits in a mist. I've asked many people of the right age, but no one remembered it.

Google did. It popped into my head just now and I googled it up, no sweat. It was a 1953 TV show that aired daily, live, for 15 minutes. It was about the Atom Squad, a secret government agency that tracked down villains hatching nefarious cold war plots involving atomic stuff.

In a July, 1953 episode, *The Trouble at Fort Knox*, the bad guys contaminate the gold at Fort Knox with radiation. The Atom Squad decontaminates the gold and goes after the evil-doers.

This is the plot for Ian Fleming's Goldfinger, published in 1959. Coincidence? (See *New Gold Rush* on p. 115.)

Ninaology

Cartoonist Al Hirschfeld, who died in 2003 at 99, was famous for his pen-and-ink caricatures of Broadway stars and for hiding "Nina", his daughter's name, in the lines of the drawings. He would put the number of Ninas next to his signature. You had to really look to find them.

During World War II, the army used his cartoons to train bomber pilots to spot their targets by looking for the Ninas.

A 1966 anthology included a drawing of Nina called *Nina's Revenge* with no Nina's but with 2 Als and 2 Dollys (his wife).

Artificial Stupidity

What's with those fake people who answer the phone when you call the bank or credit card company? I wouldn't have called if I had a question so simple that someone who flunked the Turing test could answer it, so I just keep pressing 0 until I get a real person. I would do it even if I thought a fake person could answer it, on principle, so I don't know why they bother to hire fake people.

This will Make Your Skin Crawl

Nokia has patented a tattoo that vibrates when your cell phone calls. The tattoo would use ferromagnetic ink that would be magnetized once the tattoo has healed.

Your cell phone would signal the tattoo when a call comes in and your skin would vibrate. You could program the phone to give you different vibes for phone calls, text messages, emails, or your mother calling.

Don't answer the call from the Borg.

Machismo

National Twit Paris Hilton wasn't in jail 10 minutes before she freaked out (and conveniently got religion). Why couldn't she take it like a man, like Martha Stewart?

228

Loaner Cat

Sberbank, the largest bank in Russia, will lend a cat to 30 lucky home mortgage customers.

There is a Russian superstition that If a cat is the first one to enter a house it is considered good luck and a bad omen if it refuses. If the cat curls up in a corner, it will become the Red Corner, the place for religious icons.

"Order a cat for your housewarming, and bring happiness and luck to your home," says the bank's web site. You can choose from 5 different cats. The bank's promotional video shows van labeled *Cat Delivery Service* dropping off the cat.

The cats are loaned by their owners, including bank employees, and have to be returned after two hours.

There is an 8 page densely worded terms and conditions document you have to sign first.

Irritations

• Credit card statements folded so that the perforated part you have to tear off to send in with the payment is so close to the fold in the paper that it always tears with a jagged edge.

• Decline of the fudgesicle. Fudgesicles circa 1957 lived in a dry ice freezer, the kind with the foot-thick doors on top. For a nickel, you would get a rock-hard, deep chocolate treat. It came with a wrapper with a red ball on it that stuck to it so that it was impossible to remove completely. It was so dense, it lasted for an hour. In a pinch it could be used as a hammer.

Now a fudgesicle is like frozen mousse. Why, you can actually bite off a piece! One shudders to think what they've done to the orange creamsicle.

• Labels on the outside of clothing. I tediously cut the threads holding that leather patch with the brand name on the side of jeans. If I could figure out how to get the label that says "Rockport" off the back of my shoes, I would. I won't buy shirts with a logo embroidered on the pocket. (You lose this chukker, Ralph!)

• While we're in the closet, there are plenty of "relaxed fit" pants on all those shelves in department stores. But Some men do not have a big belly and are gluteus minimus, not gluteus maximus. There. I said it. I'm thin and I'm proud.

Mercury Made From Gold!

Hey, wait a minute…it's supposed to be the other way around. Can't get rich that way. You flunk alchemy 101.

A January 28, 1952 article in Life Magazine reported a new lamp for more precise measurements with an interferometer. An interferometer works by passing a beam of light through two partially silvered mirrors. Part of the beam bounces around between the mirrors before passing through them and part of the beam goes straight through.

When the beams are focused on a screen the slightly delayed bouncing beams are out of sync with the ones that pass straight through and they interfere with each other giving light and dark rings.

As the mirrors are moved apart, new rings appear at the center as old ones disappear off the outside of the screen. The rings are separated by ½ wavelength of the light used, so by counting the new rings, the change in distance between the mirrors can be measured. Light wavelengths are measured in billionths of a meter so we're talking really teeny here.

The key is to use a light with few wavelengths, or colors. Regular white light has a zillion colors. The cadmium lamps used until then produced rings that were a little fuzzy because there were a number of wavelengths of light.

The Bureau of Standards made a new light using a single isotope of mercury, mercury 198. The mercury was made from gold. A roll of gold foil was put it a nuclear reactor and bombarded with neutrons for a year. The result was 1/500th of an ounce of gold was transformed in mercury 198 which gives off light 400% sharper than cadmium, enabling measurements to a billionth of an inch.

It's less of a pain to get the mercury than it sounds. A 1958 article in Nature says that only a fraction of a milligram of the mercury is needed for the lamp "and this isotope can now be produced quite cheaply from gold." Today, lasers are used as monochromatic light sources.

But — listen up alchemists — you can reverse the process and make gold from mercury in a nuclear reactor. After 23 hours you can get 3/10 of a cent worth of gold. But the reactor costs $200 an hour.

The Handwriting on the Wall

"The words of the prophets are written on the subway walls
And tenement halls" — Simon and Garfunkel, The Sounds of Silence

Excavation of Pompeii, buried in 20 feet if pumice and ash by Vesuvius in 79 A.D. uncovered walls full of graffiti. Here are some of the printable ones.

The gladiatorial troop hired by Aulus Seuthus Certus will fight in Pompeii on May 31. There will also be a wild animal hunt. The awnings will be used [for shade].

Faithful Caesius loves M...

Serena hates Isidorus

Farewell, Victoria, and everywhere you wish may you sneeze well.

I should like my jewel to be ready at 3 o'clock.

The united fruitmen with Helvius Vestalis urge you to make Marcus Holconius Priseus duumvir [magistrate] with judiciary power.

If anyone does not believe in Venus, they should gaze at my girl friend.

Atimetus got me pregnant.

What a lot of tricks you use to deceive, innkeeper. You sell water but drink unmixed wine

Chie, I hope your hemorrhoids rub together so much that they hurt worse than when they ever have before!

We have wet the bed, host. I confess we have done wrong. If you want to know why, there was no chamber pot.

O walls, you have held up so much tedious graffiti that I am amazed that you have not already collapsed in ruin.

Var Inte Ond*

Ogooglebar is a Swedish colloquialism for ungoogleable, can't be found on the web by searching. The Language Council of Sweden had planned to make *ogooglebar* officially Swedish, since everyone was using it until Google's lawyers objected.

Google insisted that it be defined as "something that cannot be found on the web using Google" as opposed to any old search engine. They wanted the trademark symbol added, too.

The Council decided to drop the word from the official lexicography rather than redefine it after lengthy email exchanges with Google's lawyers became too much of a hassle.

They should try *inte bada bing* instead. Maybe Microsoft's lawyers are more enlightened.

One would think Google would be thrilled to be the eponym for web search. Their obstinacy is enough to make you weep into your facial tissue.

* Don't be evil, courtesy of Google Translate.

SEO No Help For CEO

Can't remember the exact name of the web site? No worries. Just google — excuse me, search the web — for "jewelry newsletter" — it's in the first 5, top of the first page. Same for Bing, Yahoo, and AOL. Google says that's out of 41,300,000 results. That sounds far-fetched, but 25 pages in it was still jewelry newsletter listings.

Getting to the top of the list is called Search Engine Optimization, and companies charge big bucks to do it, from $300 to $5000 a month and $100-300 an hour consulting fees.

SEO involves keywords, meta tags, and descriptions. For instance, next to the title of the site, *The Jewelry Box*, it says "a jewelry store newsletter with wit and attitude, very differinternet." It says that because I put it in as a description. I do the web site myself, or, rather, the software does it.

But I paid no bucks to be top of the list. It just happened. You'd think riches would flow from being top of the list on Google, but it ain't so. Ah, well. No inbucks, no outbucks. And no help for the running out of green before you fade to black problem.

Squeeze and Tease

After discovering that 25% of television viewers changed channels when the credits rolled at the end of a program, NBC compressed the scroll into 1/3 of the screen. The rest of the screen was used for "promo-tainment", promotional spots for upcoming shows. The network debuted this format in 1999, dubbed "squeeze and tease."

Grin and Bear It

"On Whit-Tuesday, 1786, there was celebrated at Hendon, Middlesex, a burlesque imitation of the Olympic games. One prize was a gold-laced hat, to be grinned for by six candidates, who were placed on a platform, with horse collars to exhibit through. Over their heads was printed:

Detur Tetriori;
or
The ugliest grinner
Shall be the winner

Each party grinned separately for three minutes, and then all united in one grand exhibition of facial contortion. An objection was lodged against the winner on the ground that he had rinsed his mouth with vinegar."
— *All the Year Round,* Charles Dickens' weekly, 1888.

Grinning matches, making grotesque faces for a prize standing on a table with your head through a horse collar, had been going on for more than a hundred years before this account.

A mocking essay by Joseph Addison in his paper The Spectator September 18, 1711 notes an advertisement in The Post-Boy for an event on October 9 featuring a horse race for a prize of a plate worth 6 guineas, a lesser value plate for a race of asses, and "'a gold ring to be grinn'd for by men'"

Addison says the contests "in which the

asses and the men are concerned, seem to me altogether extraordinary and un-accountable." He "would advise a Dutch painter to be present at this great controversy of faces, in order to make a collection of the most remarkable grins that shall be there exhibited."

Addison then gives the account of a gentleman who, seeing the same ad, entertained a coffee house with the story of a grinning match he had witnessed. He references celebrations on the taking of Namur (in modern Belgium during the Nine Years' War), which would place the event in 1695. The prize was a gold ring.

A swarthy Frenchman happened by and "looking upon the company like Milton's Death, grinned horribly a ghastly smile." But, lest a foreigner take the prize, it was decided upon a second trial that "he was master only of the merry grin."

The next contestant "excelled in the angry grin," but the prize ring had been offered by a Whig (constitutional monarch-ist) Justice of the Peace and the contestant was said to be a Jacobite (favoring restoration of the absolute monarchy of Catholic James II) and when he refused to take an oath of loyalty to King William III was disqualified.

A ploughman nearly won the prize with "such a hideous grimace that every feature of it appeared under a different distortion" until it was revealed that he had practiced with verjuice (juice of sour fruit) and was discovered to have a crabapple on him during the contest and he was disqualified as a cheat.

The prize went to a cobbler, Giles Gorgon, whose first grin "cast every human feature out of his countenance, at the second he became the face of a spout; at the third a baboon; at the fourth the head of a bass-viol; and at the fifth a pair of nut-crackers."

The "country wench" he had wooed for five years without success was "so charmed with his grins and the applauses which he received on all sides, that she married him the week following, and to this day wears the prize upon her finger, the cobbler having made use of it as his wedding ring."

They still grin today, although it's called gurning. At the Egremont Crab Fair in Cumbria on the northwest coast of

England is held the World Gurning Championship, complete with horse collars. "Top Gurn" Tommy Mattinson won again for the 15th time in 2013.

The Fair has been held since 1267 and is named for the crab apples that the Lord of Egremont gave away. Today, sweet apples are thrown to the crowds lining the street in the Parade of the Apple Cart.

Tommy Mattinson gurned for the Queen, and she gurned back.

Deep Thought

Few men have virtue to withstand the highest bidder.
— George Washington

Men Go Topless!

Before 1936, it was illegal for men to go topless. Men's bathing suits then were wool with a tank top and trunks, one or two pieces, often with a belt.

In 1935, 42 men were arrested in Atlantic City for wearing topless bathing suits. "We will not have gorillas on our beach," the judge said according to one account.

In the 1934 movie *It Happened One Night* Clark Gable takes off his shirt revealing a scandalous bare chest — no undershirt! Urban legend has it that sales of undershirts plummeted after that.

By 1936 topless men were allowed on the beach. A June 3, 1936 article in the New York Times said that an amendment was proposed to the Coney Island code of ordinances "permitting the wearing of topless bathing suits by men on city beaches this summer. The amendment went to committee for study."

Evidently boys were not required to wear tops. A July 8, 1922 article in the Literary Digest titled *A Swimmin'-Hole for City Boys* has a photo of boys at a swimming pool without tops.

In Toronto in 1936, 24 men arrested for going topless on the beach were acquitted on a technicality when a law student pointed out that they were on the beach and not bathing as stated in the wording of the law.

Close Encounters
Of The Canine Kind

I figured out why dogs sniff each other's butts: if you're going to smell someone, you might as well smell where it smells the most.

Dogs are hardly fastidious. Rotting garbage? Lemme at it. Road kill, chipmunk pee, poop of any kind: up close deep sniffing. Unidentifiable blech on the road, roll it around in the mouth for a while to get the full effect, then roll in it. I once took the dog for a walk and she picked up a piece of chewing gum on the road, chewed it for while, spat it out, then picked it up again the next day for another chew.

But if you break wind, the dog will look at you with disgust and move to the other side of the room. But there is hope. See *Waste Management* on p. 42.

Fat Men's Ball

The first annual ball of the Fat Men's Association of the City of New York was held at Irving Hall December 20, 1869.

Tickets were sold to the public, who watched from galleries above the dance floor, to raise money for the Fat Men's annual picnic in Norwalk, Connecticut.

The guest of honor was seven year old Thomas Conway (80½ pounds) introduced by the president of the Association John Fiske (358 pounds).

Music was provided by Claudio Grafulla, the March King before Sousa, conducting the Seventh Regiment Band, which was much in demand at the time for social events. The band played *The Fat Men's March*, specially composed for the occasion by Grafulla.

Dancing began at 9:30, with the Fat Men and their wives, some of whom were as hefty as their mates, dancing "waltzes, mazourkas, schottiches, reels, and even jigs," without incident due to "extra propping-up of the floor" according to the Louisville Daily Express, December 21, 1869.

About 11:30 was the grand march which "terminated in the supper room, where the fat men found themselves at home, and joined heartily in their devotions to the voracious deity from whom they derived their inspirations and their fat," according to the New York Times, December 21, 1869.

After the feast, the dancing resumed, ending at 2 or 3 in the morning. "Altogether it was an elegant affair," said the Times.

New York City - Fat Men's Ball - Introduction by Messrs. Fisk and Stout, of Master Thomas F. Conway, aged seven, and weighing 81 pounds, to the guests.

In 1867, Smith Barnum (350 pounds), a cousin of P.T. Barnum, and Sidney Smith (317 pounds), held a picnic of fat men to help a friend whose hotel at Gregory's Point in Norwalk, Connecticut was not doing well. The picnic was a success and the Fat Men's Association was founded, with Sidney Smith the first president.

A picnic was held the next year and the year after that invitations were sent to fat men in other towns in Connecticut and also New York City, which founded its own chapter of the Association.

In 1874, Philetus Dorlon (250 pounds), a legendary oysterman in the Fulton Market in New York bought the hotel and renamed the location Dorlon Point.

The New York Fat Men took a steamboat up the Sound to join their Connecticut brethren for the annual picnics. The New York Times covered the 1877 picnic:

Fat Men on a Frolic
A Feast of Fun and Roast Clams
Heavy weights at Norwalk Point — A Scale That Weighed Nothing Less Than Two Hundred Pounds — The Attack on the Roast — Scenes at the Table — A Solemn Election.

90 men stepped on the scale which wouldn't register under 200 pounds, the minimum for membership. Two women also qualified.

At the picnic they consumed 110 bushels of clams and oysters, 300 chickens, 400 lobsters, 60 pounds of bluefish, 3 barrels of sweet potatoes, 2 barrels of white potatoes, and 1000 ears of corn. After the picnic, the Fat Men elected officers of the Association.

In 1883, the Times reported a scandal:
War Among the Fat Men
The Connecticut Society Divided by Unholy Strife.

In 1879, Willard Perkins (425 pounds) succeeded Charles Bradley (300 pounds) as president of the Association. In 1881, Perkins moved the picnic along with the president's chair, to Roton Point, where a hotel offered 10% off. Bradley and his friends refused to go and, lacking a quorum, new officers were not elected and in 1882 no picnic was held.

One of the perks of the president of the Association was a 4 foot 6 inch cane and each president put on it an engraved gold plate. Perkins said that Bradley demanded the cane so he could remove the gold plate he had paid $35 for and replace it with a brass one. Bradley said that when he put on his gold plate, the jeweler told him that all the other plates from other presidents were brass and his was the only gold one.

Five days later, on August 31, 1883, the Times reported the situation resolved. In an article titled Adipose Men at Dinner the subhead was "Bloodshed Narrowly Avoided Owing to Good Counsel and the Day is Passed in Peace."

Bradley had scheduled the picnic at Dorlon Point. Perkins had intended to come to the picnic to make a speech "and if need be sacrifice for principle's sake his 425 pounds," but he was persuaded to instead resign from the Association, and he shipped the cane and the chair to Dorlon Point. The picnic was held and Philetus Dorlon was elected president.

The Connecticut Fat Men's Association was much diminished by the turn of the century. An October 10, 1899 article in the Los Angeles Herald says that only 12 members were left, down from 200.

The obituary in the New York Times, August 20, 1901 of Erastus H. Lewis, 330 pounds when president of the New Jersey Fat Men's Association, notes that the Association was then defunct.

Lewis was 440 pounds when he died on August 17 at 57, down from a peak of 520, as noted an article titled Extreme Obesity in the 1901 Journal of the American Medical Association

Lewis, from Jersey City, was buried in a bespoke casket 6'9" long and 3'1" wide. A special hearse large enough to hold it had to be sent from New York City. Former members of the Fat Men's Association served as pallbearers.

Mycology Dept.

A newly discovered mushroom found in Borneo that looks like a sponge has been given the scientific name of Spongiforma squarepantsii. It's round and naked, though.

Deep Thought

Do you only listen to people who tell you what you want to hear?

Generation Gap

A January 14, 1946 ad for Fleer's Candy Coated Gum by "Der Bingle"* [Bing Crosby] was titled How to Handle Parents.

Parents are positively people! Try to remember, they have a lot of problems, and of course I don't mean you. When dad hides your lipstick, or Mom insists that you take sad sack Elsie to the Prom, don't pout...speak out. give 'em the benefit of the doubt...they want to understand.

All parents are strong characters. but you'd be surprised how they respond to kind treatment. Give 'em a little gush when they do something solid. (Crosby kids please note!) Remember, you'll be a parent yourself some day!

In a November 25, 1946 Fleer's ad, Crosby reversed course with an ad titled How to Handle Teenagers.

Teensters are positively people! Try to remember, they have a lotta problems...mainly parents. When their jive talk gives you the heebie-jeebies, and their rootin'-tootin' clothes (Look who's talking!) make you despair for 'civilization'...better bear up and shut up. They'll grow up and get over it, even as you and I.

"Scratch most teen-agers and you'll find a solid citizen. And when they sound off with ideas for improving the world we made...well, maybe us parents could learn sumpin' if we'd stop snooting the kids and listen.

The ad was "...one of a series presented by Fleer's to promote better understanding among families, friends, and nations."

The ad series featured the stars of the day: Kay Kyser, Harry James Perry Como Alan Ladd, Ray Milland, and Joan Crawford. The ads promoted tolerance of different people, but without Der Bingle's jive talk.

* Bing Crosby learned to pronounce German and made propaganda radio broadcasts aimed at German troops in World War II. His German listeners dubbed him "Der Bingle", which caught on in America.

Beneath the Gate of Heaven

Under a granite headstone in the Gate of Heaven Cemetery in Hawthorne, New York, about an hour away across the Tappan Zee Bridge, lies a secret of buried treasure that was taken to the grave. It is the grave of Arthur S. Flegenheimer, the prohibition and depression era mobster known as Dutch Schultz.

Flegenheimer took the nom de guerre Dutch Schultz from an especially brutal member of the Frog Hollow gang in the Bronx of the 1890's. And he lived up to his namesake, being responsible for 135 mob killings.

Manhattan special prosecutor Thomas E. Dewey (who defeated Harry Truman in the famous Chicago Tribune newspaper headline in 1948) was investigating Schultz, and Schultz went before the Mafia Commission to propose killing Dewey. The Commission rejected his proposal. Schultz theatened to do it himself.

The Commission tasked its hit squad, Murder Inc., headed by Albert Anastasia, to dispose of Schultz. On October 23, 1935, Schultz and three associates were ambushed at the Palace Chop House in Newark.

Schultz survived until the next day, and with a 106° fever chattered for over two hours in a disjointed stream-of-consciousness ramble that was taken down by a police stenographer. The most quoted line is the enigmatic *A boy has never wept nor dashed a thousand kim.* He was 33.

A legend of $7 million in thousand dollar bills* and gold coins in a 2x3 steel box buried in the Catskills village of Phoenicia, New York, a favorite Schultz getaway, sprang up after his death. The source was probably his lawyer, J. Richard "Dixie" Davis, but the legend became considerably embellished over time: there is a map, it's buried beneath a tree with an X on it by a creek, and so on.Treasure hunters to this day come to Phoenicia looking for Schultz's hoard.

The novel Billy Bathgate by E. L. Doctorow was based on the last days of Dutch Schultz.

* High denomination bills, 1, 5, and 10 thousand dollars were last printed in 1945 and President Nixon suspended distribution of bills larger than $100 in 1969 to help fight organized crime. They are still legal tender.

Deep Thought

Worry is the interest paid by those who borrow trouble.

— George Washington

Downstairs Upstairs

The Equitable Life Assurance Building (see *Less More Money Than You Could Ever Spend* on p. 103) at 120 Broadway was completed in 1875. At 130 feet It was considered by some to be the first skyscraper. It was the first building with elevators — "5 steam elevators constantly in motion" touted an 1875 ad, along with "Fire-Proof Building". Of course, the building was completely destroyed in a fire, in 1912.

A new 391 foot building was built on the site, opening in 1915. On May 5, 1920, Howard Le Chevalier Roome, a Yale football star in 1905, won a bet by climbing the 40 stories of of the Equitable Building from the sub-cellar to the cupola in 8 minutes, 52 seconds, taking the 940 steps two at a time.

During an elevator strike, Roome accepted a bet at the Racquet and Tennis Club* that he could not climb the stairs in under 40 minutes. The bet was for $1000 with $100 for every minute under 40. He won $4100 ($48,134 in 2015 dollars).

The next day, Roome was challenged by a 55 year old man, Charles H. Ingersoll, co-founder with his brother of the Ingersoll Watch Company, who claimed to have climbed 440 steps to his office in under 6 minutes. Roome accepted the challenge but Google turned up no record of of the contest.

* The Racquet and Tennis Club, 370 Park Avenue, now as then, refuses to admit women members.

Gender Bender

In a quirk of the English language, a singular personal possessive pronoun referring to a singular indefinite pronoun is gender-sensitive. In case you didn't catch my drift, here's an example.

Anyone who is bored by the grammar lesson may read (a) his (b) her (c) his or her comic book instead.

Since this is a mixed class, neither (a) nor (b) will work, and (c) is so awkward I hate to use it. It used to be grammatically correct to use just "his" with the understanding it could be hers, too. It may still be grammatically correct, but it isn't politically correct. (Sssh, I sneaked* one in on p. 99.)

The marriage problem was solved by adopting "Ms." We need a similar solution for the gender problem.

"Hiser" or 'heris" would work, but they sound terrible. "Hrh" ("hraitch") would shorten it, but sounds even worse, and the Brits might see it as lèse majestié. Maybe we should just legalize using the plural "their", since everyone does it anyway, but pronounce it "dere", from the Brooklyn dialect, so we won't sound like one of dose ignorant people.

* The past tense of "sneak" is "sneaked". Use it or you'll sound like a dumb snucker.

tlhIngan maH!*

What is Person 1's race? Mark X one or more boxes. This is question 9 on the 2010 census. There were 11 boxes, and you could write in *Other Asian* such as Hmong, Laotian, Thai, etc. or *Other Pacific Islander* such as Fijian or Tongan.

You'd think this would surely cover every race. But just in case you could check a box for *Some other race* and print it in 19 characters max.

Thousands of census forms were filled in with other races that included Borg, Klingon, and Vulcan.

The penalty for wrongful disclosure is 500 credits.

* we are Klingons!

Trash Talk

London installed 25 talking trash cans in 2011. The cans thank you, sing, applaud, or burp when you do your civic duty to keep Britain tidy. The response can be tailored to the location. Liverpool will get trash cans that sing Beatles songs, Covent Garden, opera.

In Sweden, a talking can was used three times more than a nearby dumb can. Finland has been trash talking since 2009. A dozen Helsinki cans will talk back to you in Finnish, Swedish, Japanese, English, German, Polish, and Russian

Monopoly Money

There have been a couple of makeovers for Monopoly since you played it as a kid.

The new Monopoly comes with Visa debit cards instead of real fake money. You put the card in slots in an electronic reader for credits or debits. (Batteries not included.)

The old tokens are gone. McDonalds french fries, Starbucks coffee, laptop computer, jet plane and a labradoodle (replacing the scotty) are a few of the new ones. One of the zillion new editions goes

back to the original circular board.

And, talk about inflation, when you pass go you get $2 million, not $200. Rich Uncle Pennybags, the Monopoly mascot with the top hat and cane, is nominally under-capitalized. (See *Santa Loses Title!* on p 33.)

Antisubmarine Warfare

The Swedish Peace and Arbitration Society (SPAS) is a non-governmental organization dedicated to peace and disarmament.

There have been a number of incidents of Russian submarines invading Swedish waters over the years, the latest in 2014. SPAS lowered a neon sign (with a copyright notice!) in waters outside Stockholm. The homophobic Russians will be greeted with a pink outline sailor in white jockey shorts gyrating his hips with flashing pink hearts in the background. The sign says "Welcome to Sweden. Gay since 1944" (when Sweden legalized homosexuality) in English and Russian. It also broadcasts "This way if you are gay" in Morse code.

The Ninny Factor

Breaking news on the ninny front. I opined in *The Ninny Factor* on p. 130 that 20% of people are dingbats or doofuses, nincompoops or ninnies. I underestimated.

"Does the Earth go around the Sun, or does the Sun go around the Earth?" That was the question asked by the National Science Foundation in a 2012 survey. 26% got it wrong.

Hats Off

I live in New Jersey, so I don't see a lot of cowboy hats. But through the magic of television, I am occasionally transported out west, to the land of cowboy hats.

Looks like a great hat to keep you in the shade in a sunny clime. They don't look too waterproof, though, but I guess it doesn't rain a lot there. But it can get windy. You never see anyone wearing a cowboy hat with a chin strap and you never see hats tumbling along with the tumbleweeds.

But what's most striking about cowboy hats is that the wearers never seem to take them off when they come indoors. You see real people scenes of line dancing, beer drinking, and country singing with hats on.

It seems to me that a real 19th century cowboy would doff his hat when he came inside. Audie Murphy did. After all, the sun only shines outside.

Hats On

I'm not a hat person, although I wear a knit cap and earmuffs when I walk the dog in the very cold.

The list of hats is astounding. Bearskin, baseball (front, back, sideways), beret, bowler/derby, bonnet, boater, balaclava, breton, feed cap, homburg, mortarboard, yarmulke, trilby, pillbox, chitrali, hijab, wimple, tricorne, turban, railroad, pith helmet, night cap, dunce cap, miter, tarboush, top hat, cai non, deerstalker, ivy cap, porkpie, cloche, pickelhaube (the Prussian helmet with the spike), snood, tyrolean, toque, fez, fedora, coonskin, shako, sombrero, gaucho, tam o'shanter, digger, panama, and zucchetto (the Pope's yarmulke) are just a few.

Most hats aren't very functional. The bicorne (admiral's hat — Napoleon wore his sideways), top hat, mortarboard, and fez come to mind.

The fedora (see Stetson ad next page) was de rigueur from the 30's through the 50's. Old photos of baseball games show men in the stands wearing fedoras (and jackets and ties). My dad had one, though he didn't wear it much. Hats seem to have tapered off in the 60's, maybe because JFK didn't wear them. Both he and Eisenhower wore top hats en route to his inauguration, but Kennedy rarely wore hats afterwards.

And there's the ultimate hat, your crown, Your Majesty.

Of course, hats are important for keeping secrets. See the ad for Stetson hats from Life Magazine April 5, 1943 next page.

I'm not sure what the significance of all these hats is, but people take hats seriously. Maybe it's because the ego is located in the head.

The most notorious mad hatter was 15th century Prince Vlad Dracula of Wallachia (yes, that Dracula). He had the turbans of visiting Turkish ambassadors nailed to their heads because they wouldn't remove them as a sign of respect.

A more recent mad hatter was Richard Nixon. In 1970, he got a bee in his bonnet about spiffing up the White House guards by dressing them in comic opera hats. It was laughed out in about 6 months.

Hats are very important in religion. If you want to start a new religion, you'll need a prophet, a book, and a splendid hat. My vote for best sacerdotal headgear goes to Katherine Jefferts Schori, head of the Episcopal Church. She wears a new age red miter with purple swooshes and a white circle.

As I said, I'm not a hat person, but if I become one, I'll wear an ivy cap. That's the tweed flat cap with the front of the hat nailed down to the brim. My dad had one of those, too, and he wore it.

It's over 200 years too late, but I found another hat story, on p. 266.

Loose Talk
can cost Lives!

"...sails tonight, world's biggest, packed with troops... Berlin waiting"

Keep it under
your
STETSON

Stetson "Playboy" America's most popular hat raw edge, narrow band, springy light-weight felt.
Now made by the exclusive
Stetson Vita-felt* Process…$5.00
Reg. U.S. Pat. Off.

By Fiat
Fiat is Latin for "let it be done"
- Fiat money — What's in your wallet?
- Fiat lux — Let there be light.
- Fiat luxe — Let the the consumption be conspicuous
- Fiat numerus unus — Make it so number one.
- Fiat Punto — Let there be a really small car.
- And, of course, Fix It Again Tony.

(Thanks to Paul Solman of NPR's The Business Desk for the Punto one.)

How to Rate an "A" on
a Date Between Classes

That's the caption on this ad for Stetson hats in Life Magazine October 6, 1947. "The two college men above are very well-dressed indeed—one in his Stetson *Campus* for stepping out with his best girl, the other in his Stetson *Casual* for shuttling between classes."

"*But switch the hats*—and you kill the effect of both. Just as one suit won't do for all occasions. so one 'Jack-of-all-trades' hat won't always fill the bill."

She wears a Stetson, too, the *Mistral*, $6.95.

Did your classmates look like this?

Max Headroom

A few days before the deposed last emperor of China, Pu Yi, was due to be installed as the emperor of the Japanese puppet state of Manchukuo in 1934, it was discovered that he couldn't sit up straight inside his $20,000 American armored limousine wearing his top hat. The solution was to tie down the springs under the seat with wire, gaining four inches.

President Hoover's Postmaster General Walter Brown had the same problem for the 1928 inauguration:

"For the inaugural parade he [incoming Postmaster General James Farley] may use, if he so desires, the official high-hat limousine of the Postmaster General's office, purchased for the retiring Postmaster General, Mr. Walter Brown. If the limousine proves too low for his high hat, the precedent established by Mr. Brown will permit him to put in for another one at Government expense as soon as he takes office. Mr. Brown's need of a limousine with adequate high-hat room expires at this time, and the car reverts to the Government."
— The New York Evening Post, February 1, 1933

238

You Haven't Seen Anything Yet

That's the title of an article in the February 8, 1960 Life Magazine heralding scientific breakthroughs possible in the 1960's.

The article starts with a project called Ozma using radio telescopes at Green Bank, West Virginia: maybe ET will call in.

Cheap, Almost Limitless Power. Nuclear fusion, magnetohydrodynamics, thermocouples, supercooled computers and power lines and fuel cells are all possible.

Abolition of Want. "Completely automated factories before long may be capable of producing an abundance of goods, clothes and housing hitherto unthinkable." Photosynthesis may enable production of almost limitless food "without the 'middle man' of green plants." Maybe we can even make food from coal and petroleum.

Medical Breakthroughs. Prolongation of life, curing cancer, artificial life possible.

Space. Circle the moon, a manned space platform, solar sails.

Electronics. "A telephone exchange for a whole city may soon fit into a single room."

Pure Science. Maybe we'll finally figure out the theory of everything.

Big Game Hunter

When 19 year old Texas cheerleader Kendall Jones posted photos of herself on Facebook next to animals she killed hunting in Africa, a lion, a hippo, a leopard, a zebra, a white rhino, and an elephant, there was immediate outrage, including death threats. Facebook took down her page along with a "Kill Kendall Jones" page.

Facebook wit Jay Branscomb then posted a photo of Steven Spielberg with a Triceratops from the movie Jurassic Park with the caption "Disgraceful photo of recreational hunter happily posing next to a Triceratops he just slaughtered. Please share so the world can name and shame this despicable man."

The post garnered 10,000 likes and 6,000 comments, some clearly in on the joke:

"Poor animal! Triceratops are endangered! Soon they will be gone like the dodo bird and ET, the Extra-Terrestrial."

"For all of the anti-hunters out there, This was a meager minor sized tri-top. I shoot Brontosaurus 15 times as tall.."

But as I said in *The Ninny Factor* (p. 130) (See also the article about someone picking up the fake ice cream on the rug next to the fake kids and thinking it was real on p. 63) that anyone who deals with the public knows that, say, 20% of people are dingbats or doofuses, nincompoops or ninnies:

"Steven Spielberg has absolutely no respect for animals. Posing in front of this poor dead animal like that. Barbaric."

"Like, OMG how could you kill an innocent (c)reature like that???!!! What did it ever to do you???!! Like, what is wrong with you???!!"

"Disgusting! I bet he only kept the horns!"

Back to the Future

In an article titled *A Warning to Air-Ship Investors*, the January 2, 1909 issue of the Literary Digest quotes the December 10, 1908 Engineering News that charlatans engaged "in floating gold-mine stocks or in perfecting various impossible 'electric' processes, may turn in the near future to the promising field of aerial navigation." Better to avoid the whole business.

The article says that carrying freight by aeroplane will be far too expensive, and that the risks will "limit passenger traffic to the field of sport and amusement."

"It is altogether probable that a few years hence aeroplane flights will be a drawing card at county fairs and other public occasions, just as ordinary balloon ascensions have been for a century past...but it will have just as little relation to the serious, practical, every-day business of carrying freight and passengers for the great workaday world as have the hundred horsepower automobiles that break speed records in

France or America."

As for war, the flying machine "offers an ideal mark to the bullets of the enemy. Its limitations of weight forbid its protection by any sort of armor... with modern infantry rifles discharging projectiles with an initial velocity of 2,700 feet per second, and with light artillery fitted to discharge a perfect hail-storm of bullets having equal velocity and range, the rise of an air-ship at .any point within several miles of a hostile army would be merely the signal for its immediate destruction."

But it might be useful behind the lines: "If, however, an aeroplane can be developed which can ascend and alight at any desired point, it might be made use of to carry messages back and forth between the posts of an army operating in the field."

Last Words

This obituary appeared in The Record in August, 2014. The names have been changed to protect the guilty.

John Doe of Bloomingburg, NY, a long time area resident of Middletown, NY, passed away on Wednesday, August 6, 2014 at the home of Jane Doe, his ex-wife *whose house he whole-heartedly built and is thankful he will never have to perform another renovation on again. At the end, he never wanted nothing from nobody.* He was 61.

An *uneducated* graduate of Westwood High School, Westwood, NJ, class of 1972, John went on to become a skilled and proud carpenter *with Carpenter's Local # 279, although he was unsure of how proud the union was of him since he was chronically out of work. By some miracle he did acquire enough pension credits to retire early.* He was also an avid automotive technician, cook, and fisherman. *Always believing that you should get yours, he never got his and spent the majority of his time and resources supporting his unappreciative family and friends. Never one to yell, he would only raise his voice to unskilled college graduates so you could get his point.*

Survivors include his daughter Mary Doe of Middletown, NY; two sons, Tom *"no sense of humor"* Doe of New York, NY, and Jack *"free is for me"* Doe of

Middletown; his half-brother, Sam Smith and his wife Joan of Westwood, NJ; his *"good for nothing"* but beloved sister, Colleen Jones and her husband Joe of River Edge, NJ; three grandchildren, and several cousins, nieces, and nephews.

At the request of John, *he would prefer that no one gawks at him while he is deceased, so* a private family ceremony will be held at the convenience of the Doe family.

For more information on private ceremony, please reach out to a member of the family.

In lieu of flowers and arrangements, please perform one act of kindness to someone in need.

This was the obituary in the Record/Herald News in New Jersey. It was submitted to his hometown New York paper, the Times Herald Record which refused to publish it as written. John wrote his own obituary, dictating it to the son with no sense of humor. The family was ok with it, even the good for nothing sister — he was a kidder to the last — since, after all, they were his last words, and the family was paying for the obituary.

The family then submitted a morbidly correct version with the italicized portions removed to the Times Herald Record.

Global Warning

"A surface layer of water 100 meters thick, covering most of the oceanic basin between Labrador and Greenland, was found to be about five degrees Centigrade warmer than normal. This represents an additional heat reservoir of tremendous proportions and one that is bound to have far-reaching climatic effects."

This is from an article in Science, November 16, 1928 by Lt. Commander Edward H. Smith who commanded the Coast Guard Cutter Marion's Expedition to the Arctic.

The Marion Expedition measured depth, ocean currents, temperature and salinity from July 7 to September 18, 1928, with over 2000 measurements taken at 191 stations over an 8100 mile course. A detailed technical report was published in three parts in 1931.

Edward H. "Iceberg" Smith became interested in arctic oceanography in 1919 while assigned to the International Ice

Patrol, an organization formed in response to the sinking of the Titanic in 1912.

After the Marion Expedition, Smith was assigned to the Rum Patrol, intercepting whiskey smugglers during prohibition. In his spare time he studied at Harvard and was awarded a PhD in geologic and oceanographic physics in 1930.

In 1931 he went on the arctic expedition of the Graf Zeppelin, a rigid hydrogen-filled German airship on a 136 hour mission for mapping, upper air meteorological observations, and measurement of the earth's magnetic field. He was the only American invited.

Smith was promoted to rear admiral in 1942. He retired from the Coast Guard in 1950 and became director of the Woods Hole Oceanographic Institution the same year. He died in 1961 at 72.

Keeping Up With the Smiths

City directories listed people and their addresses. New York City published city directories from 1786 to 1934.

Immigrants were not listed until the mid 19th century. Before 1933, The directories listed only heads of households and other employed adults. The 1933 directory was unusually thorough, listing all adults in a household.

The Literary Digest January 28, 1933 reports "Once and for all the ancient rivalry of the New York Smiths and the Cohens is settled. The Smiths win."

It took 94 feet of type, at 14 lines per inch, to list all the Smiths. The Cohens were 10 feet shorter. The Browns took third place with 67 feet. The Joneses couldn't keep up, finishing behind the Millers, the Johnsons, and the Williamses.

John Bull, Al Capone, Enrico Caruso, Charles Chaplin, Christopher Columbus, Oliver Cromwell, Jack Dempsey, Henry Ford, Robin Hood, Jesse James, Helen Keller, Harold Lloyd, Mary Pickford, Paul Revere, Bernard Shaw, Woodrow Wilson, and John Doe were all New York residents.

The directory was funded by the Emergency Unemployment Relief Committee, a philanthropic organization. The directory provided 200,000 work days for 800 canvassers beginning at the end of 1931. The main problem was the estimated 1 million people who moved while the directory was being compiled.

Killer Cat

Towser, a cat at the Glenturret distillery in Perthshire, Scotland, is in the Guiness Book of Records as the world mousing champion. The grain used in distilling attracts mice.

Towser the mouser was a long-hair tortoiseshell and in her 24 years at Glenturret she caught an estimated 28,899 mice, averaging 3 a day, according to Guiness, whose auditors watched her for a few days. Towser always brought the mice back to the still house every morning.

Glenturret erected a bronze statue of Towser on the distillery grounds.

A plaque below the statue reads:

TOWSER
21 April 1963 — 20 March 1987
Towser the famous cat who lived in the still house Glenturret distillery for almost 24 years. She caught 28,899 mice in her lifetime World mousing champion Guiness Book of Records

Back to the Future

What We Shall Be Like in 1950 is an article in the Literary Digest January 10, 1931.

"...Tomorrow's Business (New York), published by the Shaw-Walker Company, presents twenty definite prophecies made by the National Educational Association."

Here are some of the predictions for life in 1950:

— A system of health and safety that will practically wipe out preventable accidents and contagious diseases.

— Universal air transportation at low cost.

— The perfection of the insurance system to give universal protection from disaster, unemployment, and old age.

— The organization of industry, business and agriculture to minimize uncertainty and depression.

— Hospitalization and medical care will be available for all who need them.

— Educational service, free or at small cost, will be available from the earliest years of childhood throughout life.

— The free public library v/ill grow in importance, leading the way toward higher standards of maintained intelligence.

— Crime will be virtually abolished by transferring to the preventive processes of the school- and education the problems of conduct which police, courts, and prisons now seek to remedy when it is too late.

— A system of housing that will provide for the masses homes surrounded by beauty, privacy, quiet, sun, fresh air, and play space.

— There will be a quickened appreciation of the home as a center of personal growth and happiness.

— The shorter working week and day, so extended that there will be work for all.

— Ethical standards will rise to keep pace with new needs in business, industry, and international relations.

— The religious awakening will grow in strength until most of our citizens will appreciate the importance of religion in the well-ordered daily life.

— A flat telephone rate for the entire country at moderate cost.

And in sports news
279 Welsh Outsmurf Irish 2 to 1

In June, 2009, the Welsh Smurf team blitzed a nightclub in Swansea, Wales with 2510 Smurfs, smashing the Guiness world record for smurfing.

British online costume seller Jokers' Masquerade organized the record attempt, mostly by nearby university students. Each Smurf had to be checked to make sure no skin showed through the blue to comply with strict Guiness rules.

By 11:00 there were under 2000, but a last minute surge of Smurfs after the bars closed settled the record at 1 A.M.

This doubled the previous record of 1253 Smurfs set by Castleblayney, Ireland last year.

Monkey Business

English photographer David Slater went to take pictures of crested black macaques, endangered monkeys, in a national park on the Indonesian island of Sulawesi. The animals were friendly and inquisitive. Slater walked with them for three days.

The macaques were investigating an unattended camera, looking at their reflections in the camera lens when one of them managed to push the button. The sound intrigued him and he kept pushing the button taking hundreds of pictures, most of them out of focus, but some of them perfect simian selfies, which went viral.

Wikipedia put Slater's photos on its Wikimedia Commons site as in the public domain for a free download because an animal took the picture and animals can't copyright.

Slater was not amused. He complained repeatedly to Wikimedia, which refused to take the photos down. Slater sued but the U.S. Copyright Office ruled in favor of the monkey.

Hello Darling!

If you hear that while you're out for a stroll in the park in Sydney, Australia it's probably a parrot.

Escaped parrot pets have been teaching their wild kin to talk. Whole flocks of wild galahs, cockatoos, and corellas are learning phrases like "What's happening?", "Hello cockie", and "Who's a pretty boy then?" And the birds are teaching their offspring to talk, too.

Parrots don't forget, either. One girl stubbed her ingrown toenail and her pet bird still reproduces that mighty shriek 30 years later.

Give 'em Hell Harry

Miss Truman is a unique American phenomenon with a pleasant voice of little size and fair quality. She is extremely attractive on stage. Yet Miss Truman cannot sing very well. She is flat a good deal of the time—more so last night than at any time we have heard her in past years.
— Review by Paul Hume of Margaret Truman, the President's daughter, in the Washington Post December 6, 1950.

Mr. Hume:

I've just read your lousy review of Margaret's concert. I've come to the conclusion that you are an "eight ulcer man on four ulcer pay."

It seems to me that you are a frustrated old man who wishes he could have been successful. When you write such poppycock as was in the back section of the paper you work for it shows conclusively that you're off the beam and at least four of your ulcers are at work.

Some day I hope to meet you. When that happens you'll need a new nose, a lot of beefsteak for black eyes, and perhaps a supporter below!

[Columnist Westbrook] Pegler, a gutter snipe, is a gentleman alongside you. I hope you'll accept that statement as a worse insult than a reflection on your ancestry.

H.S.T.
— Letter from President Truman to Hume December 6, 1950.

The Post did not publish the letter, but it became public after Hume told a colleague about it. Hume took it gracefully as the outburst of an over-protective father. Margaret said "Mr Hume is a very fine critic, He has a right to write as he pleases."

Some years later Hume visited Truman and had a "wonderful visit", with Truman showing him about the library. "I've had a lot of fun out of you and General MacArthur over the years. I hope you don't mind",Truman told him.

Illegal Immigrant

In 1924, Osbert, a stag fleeing hunting hounds in West Kent, jumped into the English Channel. Halfway to France, he was rescued by a French ship and taken to Dunkirk.

The captain of the ship was threatened with a fine for carrying an animal without a license. He appealed to The Ministry of Agriculture which determined that Osbert wasn't of the French deer type, so he didn't exist and recommended that he be shot.

But the police said it was out of season for deer and he could get into trouble. Dunkirk officials then contacted the English Ministry of Agriculture asking to send Osbert back home but were informed that this would have required a six month quarantine.

A restaurateur from Le Toquet bought Osbert, but not for venison. He set Osbert free in a park.

Osbert died in 1933.

Lip Floss

Lt. Gen. Gaishi Nagaoka (1858-1933), the father of Japanese aviation, had a mustache 20 inches long. When he died, "To his death bed came his son and reverently clipped the mustaches away. They were bound with white silk, laid on a satin cushion in a separate casket and buried with all honor in a separate burial mound," according to Time Magazine, May 8, 1933.

He was honored in Kudamatsu, Japan with a statue.

The world record mustache goes to Ram Singh Chauhan of India at 14 feet according to the Guiness Book of World Records. It was measured on the set of Lo Show dei Record, an Italian TV show, in Rome on March 4, 2010.

Up to Snuff

Tradition dies hard in the U.S. Senate. There are still two small lacquered leather snuff boxes decorated with Japanese scenes. They were made circa 1860. The snuff boxes are are on each side of the rostrum to facilitate bipartisan snuffing.

Isaac Bassett, Senate page and assistant doorkeeper for 64 years from 1831 to his death in 1895, tells of vice-president Millard Fillmore being so annoyed by the interruptions of Senators dipping into a large snuff box then kept on his desk that he demanded that it be put somewhere else and Bassett suggested two boxes on either side of the chamber.

Bassett said that by 1887 only a few Senators used snuff. But a December 26, 1937 article in the Reading Eagle says that four or five Senators used snuff then, with more on rainy days, going through four ounces every two weeks. Today the snuff boxes are still kept filled, although no Senators come up to snuff.

On the fiftieth anniversary of his appointment as a page, the Senate presented Bassett with a gold and silver snuff box.

Snuff is finely ground tobacco that is gives the mucous membranes inside the nostrils a quick hit of nicotine. Sneezing while snuffing is considered the mark of an amateur.

But if you'd rather just have an old-fashioned chaw instead of hifalutin snuff, there are still spittoons on the Senate floor.

Dictator

Pliny the Elder reports that Julius Caesar could dictate to his secretaries four letters at once for serious matters and up to seven for lighter fare.

Author and naturalist Pliny, Gaius Plinius Secundus, died on August 25, 79 A.D. in Stabiae, near Pompeii, while trying to rescue a friend by ship from the eruption of Vesuvius, probably of natural causes. Caesar died on the Ides of March, 44 B.C. definitely of unnatural causes. They were both 56.

Pajama Game

In the first blitz, the Germans bombed London from Zeppelins, hydrogen filled rigid airships in World War I. From May 1915 to August 1918, 51 raids dropped over 5,000 bombs across England, killing 557 people and causing £1.5 million damage. Although that was minor in the scale of the war, it did have an impact on British fashion.

The thought of rushing outside in the middle of the night in embarrassing nightclothes caused a "Zeppelin boom in British pajamas" according to an article in the Literary Digest January 1, 1916.

No more Hair curlers in bed: no woman "will take the risk of being 'zepped' in these," says the Digest quoting the Chicago Post. "No stage-hero in his most admired pajamas-scene is better attired today than the average 'bedroom' Londoner."

Men's pajamas are plain but "the October, 1915 model of the 'female pajama' comes in a pink *crêpe de chine,* cut on a more or less mannish angle and frilled at the waist and ankles with delicate-tinted silk ribbon."

"Pink and blue are the prevailing colors, tho there is some talk, say the shopkeepers, of introducing a 'Joffre gray.' It's a more invisible color."*

* Marshall Joseph Joffre was a French general in World War I. The French were slaughtered in their highly visible red uniform trousers until the adoption of blue-grey uniforms in early 1915.

Deep Thought

Don't see yourself, be yourself.

O Weinachtsbaum

'Twas the night before Christmas, when all thro' the house
Not a creature was stirring, not even a mouse;
The stockings were hung by the chimney with care,
In hopes that St. Nicholas soon would be there;
— From *The Night Before Christmas* published anonymously in in the Troy, New York Sentinel on Christmas Eve 1823, attributed to Clement Clarke Moore.

An article in the New York Times from the day after Christmas, 1883 noted a decrease in Christmas tree sales which it attributed to the revival of the Christmas stocking. The article says that this was due to the recent invention of the Smith Christmas Stocking. This was an elastic stocking that could hold both the meager gifts of the poor and the abundant ones of the rich without looking under or over filled.

Before the Smith stocking was only the New England stocking, so small it wouldn't suffice for even the poor, and the Chicago stocking, so large it stretched the budget of most to fill it.

The Smith stocking also conveniently had a metal compartment in the toe for molasses candy*, gooey stuff that had been a problem.

Saint Nicholas, a 4th century Greek, is credited with the origin of the Christmas stocking. A poor man with three beautiful daughters could not afford dowries for them and so they could not marry and would likely become prostitutes.

St. Nicholas, hearing of this situation, entered the man's house through the chimney and left a bag of gold coins in each of the girl's stockings that were hung from the mantelpiece to dry. There are other variations of this 1700 year old tale, but this one sounds the best.

In 1850, Godey's Lady's Book (see *Hair Jewelry* on p. 210) reproduced a woodcut of the British Royal family, first published in 1848, standing around their decorated Christmas tree. Godey's removed Queen Victoria's tiara and Prince Albert's moustache to make the image more generic. This illustration was widely circulated, reprinted in 1860, and is credited with the adoption of the Christmas tree in America by the 1870's.

The Times lamented the decline of the Christmas stocking and the adoption of the Christmas tree:

"The German Christmas tree — a rootless and lifeless corpse — was never worthy of the day, and no one can say how far this spirit of rationalism which begins with the denial of Santa Claus, the supernatural filler of stockings, and ends with the denial of all things supernatural, has been fostered by the German Christmas trees, which have been so widely adopted in this country."

The tradition of an orange in your Christmas stocking symbolizes the gold St. Nicholas put in the girls' stockings. It dates to the 1880's when railroads first made oranges from California and Florida available in other parts of the country year round.

By the way, *tannenbaum* means fir tree in German. The Germans decorate a Weinachtsbaum (with weinachtsbaumschmuck).

* Molasses candy — one cup of molasses, two cups of sugar, one tablespoon vinegar, a little butter and vanilla, boil ten minutes, then cool it enough to pull. *(Continued next page.)*

"Candy-pull (American), a candypull is a party of both sexes at which molasses or sugar is boiled and pulled by two persons (whose hands are buttered) to give it proper consistency, and then mixed and pulled again, till it becomes true candy."
— A Dictionary of Slang, Jargon & Cant Embracing English, American, and Anglo-Indian slang, Pidgin English, Tinkers' Jargon and other irregular phraseology (1897).

Gangsta Rap

My buddies wanted to be firemen, farmers or policemen, something like that. Not me, I just wanted to steal people's money!

These few dollars you lose here today are going to buy you stories to tell your children and great-grandchildren. This could be one of the big moments in your life; don't make it your last!
— John Dillinger

Back to the Future

"The computer will touch men everywhere and in every way, almost on a minute-to-minute basis. Every man will communicate through a computer, whatever he does. It will change and reshape his life, modify his career and force him to accept a life of continuous change."
— Willis Ware, in a paper presented at the Rand Corporation in March, 1966.

Ware (1920-2013) was a computer pioneer, working with mathematician John von Neumann, legendary early computer theoretician, at the Institute for Advanced Study at Princeton after the war.

279 Waste Management

Oh, crap! Another pillar of eternal truth has crumbled. Thomas Crapper did not invent the toilet. Bummer!

Sir John Harington (1561-1612) invented the flush toilet. Harington was a writer, courtier, and godson to Queen Elizabeth I.

In 1596 he published *A New Discourse of a Stale Subject, Called The Metamorphosis of Ajax*. This was a takeoff on "a jakes", Elizabethan slang for privy. In the work he had drawings of a toilet titled *A Plaine Plot of a Privie in Perfection*.

Harington had the toilet, which he named the Ajax, installed in his house. Queen Elizabeth had him put one in Richmond Palace. Some accounts say Elizabeth sat on that throne, others that she was too embarassed by the flushing noise to use it.

Thomas Crapper (1836-1910) was a British plumber who patented improvements for the toilet and popularized toilets with sanitation showrooms. He put his name on his wares in raised letters, i.e. *Crapper's Valveless Waste Preventer*.

Thomas Crapper & Co. is still around: "Producers of the world's most authentic period style sanitary ware."

The word "crap" is middle English for chaff, grain husks, and long predates Thomas Crapper. The first usage of "crap" to mean bodily waste is an 1846 reference to a "crapping ken" for a privy. "Ken" was slang for a house or building.

Scott Paper Company marketed the first rolls of toilet paper in 1896. I don't know what people used for the previous 300 years and I don't want to know.

Cleavage Between Unions

In October, 1946 a jurisdictional dispute in Hollywood between two unions, the Conference of Studio Unions (CSU), carpenters whose job was making the parts of sets, and the International Alliance of Theatrical and Stage Employees (IATSE), prop makers whose job was to assemble the sets the carpenters had made, led to a violent strike.

With 45 unions in Hollywood, there were squabbles over who was allowed to do what. One dispute was between the make-up artists' union and the costumers' union over which had jurisdiction over falsies, bra padding for actresses in need of a lift. An arbitrator assigned rubber falsies to the make-up union and cloth ones to the costumers.

Deep Thought

Grass is long. Life is short.
— Sign advertising lawn mowers.

Attention!

The average attention span declined to 8 seconds in 2012, down from 12 seconds in 2000.

The attention span of a goldfish is 9 seconds. Were you able to make it through this article?

In Flanders Fields

In Flanders fields the poppies blow
Between the crosses, row on row,
That mark our place; and in the sky
The larks, still bravely singing, fly
Scarce heard amid the guns below.
— In Flanders Fields

This haunting poem was written by Canadian physician Lt. Col. John McRae in 1915 after the funeral of a friend who died in battle and became the elegy for that terrible war.

Moina Michael, a professor at the University of Georgia, on leave during the war to work for the YWCA was inspired by McRae's poem. After the war, when teaching a class of disabled servicemen, she came up with the idea of selling silk poppies to raise funds for veterans. Due to her efforts, the red poppy is now the iconic symbol for Veterans Day.

But the Flanders poppy at the time was considered a weed.

"'In Flanders fields the poppies blow'— but they are not to be allowed to do so on or near the dump heaps of Kearny, N.J." according to an article titled *Fighting Flanders Poppies* in the Literary Digest, Jan. 14, 1922.

"The federal horticultural board has adjudged them a nuisance and a pest to agriculture and ordered them plowed under, until they haven't the heart to rise again. The poppies were brought over in earth ballast, shipped in France by troop transports. They threaten to overrun surrounding gardens and truck farms," from an article in the California Garden, February, 1922.

"'The reason the poppy blooms in France and Belgium is because the farmers can't get rid of it,' said Harry H. Shaw, pathologist of the federal horticultural board", quoted in an article in The Spokane, Washington Spokesman-Review, Dec 10, 1921.

Don't confuse the Flanders poppy, *Papaver rhoeas* with the opium poppy, *Papaver somniferum,* source of opium, morphine, heroin, and the poppy seeds on your bagel.

Poppy seeds are about 3 bucks a pound and come from various countries with Turkey the number one producer.

They used to be grown in California. World War II cut off imports of poppy seeds and the price soared from 7 to 50 cents a pound and California farmers set out to meet this very profitable demand. This attracted the attention of the Federal Bureau of Narcotics resulting in the Opium Poppy Control Act of 1942 banning the growing of opium poppies.

The California growers were allowed to harvest the crop planted before the law when it matured in 1943. But California continued to issue permits to grow the poppies. The Division of Narcotics Enforcement of California cited a letter from the state Attorney General to the State Director of Agriculture saying that the variety of poppy grown for edible seed "is actually not suitable for producing opium." This is not true, however, virtually all poppy production was for seeds, save for a hapless farm laborer in Holtsville ("The Carrot Capital of the World") who fortified his coffee by boiling it with the seed pods of the opium poppies he grew as was the custom in his native village in India.

Thus began the California "Poppy Rebellion". After lawsuits contesting the constitutionality of the law (taking of property without due process and intrastate only commerce) a special three judge court upheld it in August, 1944 and the remaining poppy crops were destroyed.

Today you can plant seeds and grow opium poppy flowers in your garden and the narcs won't bother you. Probably.

By the way, don't eat that poppy seed bagel before you get drug-tested for your new job. The tests are so sensitive that the minuscule amounts of opiates in the seeds will trigger a false positive and you'll be arrested as a dope fiend. A Pennsylvania woman had her newborn daughter taken away in 2010 for 5 days because she tested positive after eating a poppy seed bagel before entering the hospital. She sued and was awarded $143,500 damages in 2013.

John McRae died January 28, 1918 of pneumonia. He was 46. He is buried in Wimereux Cemetery in France.

Deep Thought

To see things clearly, first open the mind's eye.

Eric Sloane

As an anodyne to these distressing times, read Eric Sloane. If we designated people as living national treasures like the Japanese, Eric Sloane (1905-1985) would have been one.

Born in New york City, Sloane as a boy learned to hand-paint signs from neighbor Frederic Goudy, the noted type designer. In 1925 he stole his family's Model T and headed west, ending up in Taos, New Mexico, and was introduced to the Taos Art Colony, home of many famous painters, where he took up oil painting.

He returned to new York in 1933 and worked as a painter at the amusement park on Coney Island and also painted aviation murals at the restaurant of the Half Moon Hotel, where pilots from nearby Roosevelt Field came to eat. The pilots admired his work and soon he was painting markings and fuselage art on the airplanes of aviation pioneers. He also painted scenes with airplanes and sold them to the pilots who flew them. Sometimes he traded his paintings for rides and he began painting sky and clouds. Amelia Earhart bought one of his "cloudscapes".

Sloane became recognized for his paintings of the sky and drew illustrations for flying books, was contracted to write and illustrate a book about clouds and weather by a publisher in 1941, and was hired by the Army Air Corps to write and illustrate several works. His largest cloud painting occupies a wall at the Smithsonian Air and Space Museum in Washington DC.

His interest in weather led him to research old almanacs and diaries and he became immersed in early American life, leading to his publishing and illustrating many books on the subject, as well as paintings.

Sloane died of a heart attack in New York on March 5, 1985 on the steps of the Plaza Hotel on the way to meet his wife for lunch. He is buried in Kent, Connecticut at the Sloane-Stanley Museum

Diary of an Early American Boy, American Yesterday, A Reverence for Wood, A Museum of Early American Tools, An Age of Barns, and *Our Vanishing Landscape* are a few of his delightful 19 books about the way we were. The books are illustrated with his pen and ink sketches.

It was only yesterday. See you tomorrow.

Written in the Stars

The source for many of the articles in this book is The Literary Digest. The Literary Digest, *A Weekly Compendium of the Contemporaneous Thought of the World,* was founded in 1890 by Isaac Funk and published by Funk & Wagnells.

It offered opinion and news analysis from around the world, with sections on science, business, literature, the arts, poetry, and religion, a perfect time capsule of the way we were. It even had a chess section and *The Lexicographer's Easy Chair* for grammatical questions.

It was famous for correctly predicting every presidential election from 1920 to1932 from its polls. However, in 1936 it predicted a landslide for Republican Alf Landon, with the final poll October 31, showing Landon in the lead 1,293,667 to 972,879.

Roosevelt trounced Landon, taking every state except Maine and Vermont. The magazine was discredited because of the poll and went out of business in 1938. The episode led to new scientific methods of public opinion research. Gallup correctly predicted the election and also predicted the failure of the Literary Digest poll.

In the September 19, 1936 issue, the weekly poll tabulation of 254,718 put Landon ahead almost 2 to 1. But there was also an article about the All American Astrological Convention in Chicago predicting a Roosevelt victory:

"Landon's sun is under the sign of the Virgin, overshadowed by Neptune. He is between Neptune and Saturn. Neptune may trick him into believing he will win; Saturn will hold him back. The signs are against him."

Fiat Lux

The Centennial Light, the world's oldest light bulb has been burning continuously since 1901. The 4 watt hand-blown carbon filament bulb lives at fire station #6 in Livermore, California.

The bulb has moved four times along with the fire department. For a 1976 move the cord was cut for fear of the disturbance of unscrewing it. It was rewired 22 minutes later. That interruption and a few others over the years have been deemed by Ripley's Believe It Or Not to have not dimmed its continuously burning record.

Hair Oil

Crudol is "nature's hair tonic." It's "crude oil made pleasant to use." "Crudol removes dandruff, feeds the scalp and nourishes the hair roots, promoting the luxuriant growth of fluffy hair."

— Ad in The Literary Digest, July 22, 1911.

Psychic Edgar Cayce (1877-1945) was a believer in hair oil with his Crudoleum hair treatment, made from Pennsylvania crude oil.

In a 1972 study of 45 users of Crudoleum 29% reported complete to moderate hair restoration and 71% little to none.

You can buy Crudoleum hair treatment today for $12.49. Or maybe you'll prefer Pennsylvania Crude Oil Scalp Treatment, 16 oz. for $14.95 on Amazon.

Pennsylvania oil is sweet crude — low sulfur. But the Internet touts sulfur in your snake oil as the cure for hair loss. The contradiction is enough to make you tear your hair out.

But why put up with messy petroleum? Try the Evans Vacuum Cap. "Used for 10 minutes twice a day, will produce a normal growth of hair where a vestige of follicle life exists." From a June 4, 1903 Literary Digest ad.

A lever activated the vacuum, cropped out.

Coincidence

When it was announced that the names of the missing were available on the Internet, I looked to see if one of my customers who worked in the World Trade Center was on the list. He wasn't.

I went to the store that afternoon (it was my day off; I only work a half day) and waiting for me was his father-in-law, who had come in for a watch battery. A strange coincidence.

He worked on the 99th floor of the South Tower. When the first plane hit the North Tower, he took the elevator down. He ignored the instructions to go back up, and, shortly after, when the second plane hit his building, he was able to get out.

But the father-in-law tells of an even stranger coincidence.

He was in the army in World War II, in the Pacific. In 1944, he had come from New Caledonia to New Zealand, passing through on his way to New Guinea as a replacement in the 43rd division.

On his first weekend pass, he was let off in downtown Auckland. He saw an older gentleman standing on a corner and went up to him to ask directions. The man spoke in a familiar accent, that of the soldier's Yugoslavian grandparents.

Yes, the gentleman was from Yugoslavia; in fact, it turned out, from the same village as the grandparents. Not only did he know the grandparents, he was their foster son. He had been orphaned and raised in their home

Gangsta Rap

"They call Al Capone a bootlegger. Yes, it's bootlegging while it's on the trucks, but when your host at the club, in the locker room, or on the Gold Coast hands it to you on a silver tray, it's hospitality."

"Capitalism is the legitimate racket of the ruling class."

— Al Capone

279 Never Cheat an Elephant

That's the title of an article in the Literary Digest August 12, 1933. Navy Captain Harold A. White told this story to New York Sun columnist Bob Davis:

A 100 year old elephant (?) in the Saigon zoo, a present of the King of Cambodia, spends coins tossed to him to buy peanuts and bananas from a vendor. One of four French sailors tossed the elephant a lead slug. The elephant was suspicious, investigated the coin for a while, then gave it to the vendor, who promptly threw it back.

The elephant fixed him with a stare and the four left. They came back an hour later and the elephant investigated each of them with his trunk, accepted a handful of peanuts from the counterfeiter, ate them, then pointed his trunk at him and blasted him with a couple gallons of water, knocking him flat.

Snake Oil

1903: "Wash your fat away with Howard Obesity Ointment. It removes fat from that part of the body to which it is applied — restoring the natural bloom of youth, leaving no wrinkles or flabbiness." $1.00

2012: "Slimming Seaweed Weight Loss Cream (buy 1 get 1 free). A Super concentrate weight loss cream to go after stubborn high fat areas like the stomach, thighs, back of the arms, neck and much more." $33.95 (5 bucks off).

1903: "100 persons cured every day of rheumatism by Magic Foot Drafts [pads]. Magic Foot Drafts open the pores of the feet, the largest in the body, and by means of the intricate capillary development of the blood vessels here, draw out and neutralize by alkaline reaction the acid poison accumulations in the blood reaching and permanently curing rheumatism in every part of the body." $1.00. Free trial.

2012: "The Verseo Detox Foot Patch is the original all-natural patch that you can wear overnight to revitalize your system, which may need relief from heavy metals and other toxins. The patch provides an unparalleled and effective external cleansing experience that can relieve arthritis pain, increase energy, reduce stress, improve circulation, enhance mental focus and concentration, soothe headaches and more." 30 for $24.95

1903: Buffalo Lithia Water, Buffalo Lithia Springs, Virginia. "The experience of the medical profession with this water in the treatment of Bright's disease, albumenaria, gout, rheumatism, renal calculi, inflammation of the bladder and all uric acid troubles has been highly satisfactory. voluminous medical testimony on request."

2012: Lithia Water from Lithia Springs, Georgia "America's Legendary Health Elixir". "Scientific research has discovered Lithia Water enhances health and increases human life span. Lithia water protects brain from toxins, oxidants & dementia, lithium in Lithia water stimulates brain cell growth & health, Lithia water stimulates elevated moods & reduces depression, Lithia Water removes toxins, uric acid & heavy metals from body." Case of 12 half liter bottles, $29+ $12.50 shipping.

The Well-Clothed Soul

"The soul is no longer a mystery. Its organ has been discovered and can be developed with mathematical exactness…It is the first scientific Text-book on the Soul ever published."

This is from a 1913 ad for a book *The Soul: Its Organ and Development From Man to Superman* by Jasper William Corey, M.D.

Corey says in the book that the two hemispheres of the brain are actually two brains. He says that since right and left handed people have speech and motor functions on the opposite hemisphere of the brain, "The great fact has thus been conclusively proven that all of the seven mental faculties of the human mind are located in one hemisphere of the brain."

So what's in the unused half of your brain? Your soul! "In speaking of the two hemispheres of the brain they shall hereinafter be termed the Human Brain and the Super-human brain, the Human Brain being the organ of the mind and the Super-human Brain being that of the Soul."

According to the ad, the book has good paper, clear type, silk cloth binding, and gold letters. "Booksellers and Librarians say it is first class. The Soul should be well clothed."

Jasper William Corey
He looks well-clothed but not a happy soul.

Deep Thought

If I can do it, it's not art.

— New York City Mayor Rudolf Guiliani.

(See *Skullduggery* on p.31)

American Idol

A Korean businessman has come to the U.S. to buy idols "to be used in the heathen temples of his country as well as in China." It seems that the Koreans liked some sample idols that had been sent there. This news is from an article in the March 7, 1903 issue of The Literary Digest.

The article quotes the Chicago Tribune that England and Germany have long had a monopoly on "the trade in Buddhas, Krishnas, Sivas, Ganeshes, and Jumjums."

The Digest then quotes a tongue-in-cheek article from The Philadelphia North American that "At last the skill of the American artisan is recognized in the realms of poetic legend. Philadelphia idols will glower in the dim, scented gloom of far-off temples," and "The shaven bonze will swing his censer before images made in Jersey City and Tacony."

But The New York Christian Herald felt otherwise: "Merchants who send rum and other intoxicating liquors to heathen lands are little likely to have any compunction of conscience about sending idols."

And it will be a problem for the Christian missionaries sent to Korea to "have the idolatrous worship they are laboring so hard to destroy galvanized into new life by such importations."

Marching Boots

A January 3, 1914 article in The Literary Digest quotes the St. Louis Republic about a large goose farm in Illinois. The farm fattens geese hatched elsewhere and the farmer's son travels to Tennessee and Kentucky to buy them.

The geese are often in small flocks scattered here and there in the hills and they must be marched on foot many miles to the nearest railroad.

To prevent sore geese feet, the birds are fitted with shoes by driving them through soft tar and then into sand. When the tar hardens it forms a hiking boot for the geese.

This is an ancient practice. Geese were herded into Market Square in Nottingham, England to be sold for the Feast of St. Matthew perhaps a thousand years ago.

Some of the geese were marched a hundred miles in their "shoes". The annual Goose Fair in Nottingham, was officially recognized in 1284 when King Edward I granted Goose Fair a charter to mark the Feast of St. Matthew.

Today the Goose Fair runs four days at the beginning of October, with entertainment, exhibits, and rides, like our state fairs. Over a million people attend.

Truth in Labeling

In 1916, the Canadian Parliament moved temporarily to the Victoria Museum nearby in Ottawa.

" Work has not yet been completed upon the new senate chamber, and, whether by accident or design, the placard which stood above the door still remains in the chamber. It reads: 'Hall of vertebrate fossils (temporary exhibit).' "

— From the Manitoba Free Press Feb. 7, 1916 as quoted in the Literary Digest March 4, 1916.

Fore!

Early golf balls were made of wood. But in 1618 the featherie ball was invented. A featherie is a leather pouch stuffed with chicken or goose feathers.

Enough feathers to fill a top hat were boiled and stuffed into the wet leather pouch. The pouch was held in a frame which was held against the chest while pushing the feathers into it with a stick. Then the pouch was stitched closed. As the ball cooled, the feathers expanded and the leather shrank giving a hard, compact ball. A coat of paint finished the ball. The balls were seldom round, being ovate or egg-shaped.

The method was slow and the balls were costly, $10-20 equivalent today.

William Berwick & Company made the first featherie golf balls in Great Britain under a 1618 license from King James I. the license was for 21 years and they made about 200 balls a year.

Featherie balls had good flight characteristics. The stitching acted something like dimples on a modern ball, although this was not known at the time. They were used until the mid 19th century when they were superseded by the gutta percha ball.

The workers who made the balls were said to suffer from feather plucker's lung, a disease caused by dust from the feathers.

The Roaring Twenties

Osculation is the sincerest form of flappery.
— Life Magazine, 1928

Papers, Please

In July, 2010 Nathan Wayne Pugh walked into a Wells Fargo bank in Dallas carrying a Whataburger bag, told a teller he wanted to "make a withdrawal", and passed her a note:

"Look if you don't want to die then you should do as this note says This is not a bag of food This is a bom, so just put money in an envelope and do not make any move till after I have left for ten mintis"

The teller told him he would have to show identification to get the money. He handed the teller his Wells Fargo debit card. The teller asked him how much money he wanted and he told her $2000. He would need to show a second ID for that much the teller said and he pulled out a state of Texas ID card with his name on it.

The teller said she only had $900 in the drawer and would have to go to the back of the bank to get the rest. He decided to settle for the $900, which he put in his shirt pocket, then retrieved his ID and went to walk out.

Of course, the teller had pressed the silent alarm and two police officers were at the entrance to the bank. Pugh then grabbed a woman with a child from behind with a choke hold and told her to put the baby down and cooperate or he would kill her.

The woman wrestled the 49 year old five foot six robber to the ground and the police officers rushed in and arrested him.

Pugh was paroled in 2009 on a 25 year sentence for aggravated robbery in 1996 and had been convicted of cocaine possession in 1990 and served 6 years of a 10 year sentence.

Pugh was sentenced in March, 2011 to 102 months in prison beginning after he finished the 25 year term for which he was on parole.

Deep Thought

It is amazing what you can accomplish if you do not care who gets the credit.
— Harry S. Truman

Rent-a-Cat

Mark Twain would hide from publicity during the summer. In 1907 he rented a house in Tuxedo Park, New York as his getaway.

Nonetheless, someone discovered his hideaway and while walking the grounds around the house found him seated under a tree in his trademark white flannel suit petting a kitten.

An account in the Literary Digest from November 2, 1907 quotes *The Sunday Magazine* [a syndicated newspaper magazine].

"Where did you get it?" asked the intruder.

"I rent it from a neighbor. You see, I can not afford a cat — not even a young one."

It turned out Mark Twain actually did rent the kitten for the summer.

"What does he pay for it? Nobody knows what Mark Twain pays for anything. All the world is interested only in what Mark Twain is paid."

A Hitch at the Cemetery

That's one of the headlines in an article in the Toronto Daily Mail and Empire from April 24, 1899.

Leo Whitton, "The Canadian Colossus" died in Macclesfield, England on April 10, 1899, aged 41. Whitton was indeed colossal, weighing 715 pounds, with a 26 inch neck and 7 feet around at the waist.

He died while on exhibition at a pub and a window and a portion of the front had to be removed to get him out in his coffin. The coffin was too large for a hearse and a "tradesman's lorry was requisitioned."

After four attempts at the cemetery the coffin was found to be too large to fit in the grave. It was too heavy to be lifted back onto the lorry to be taken back to town. "Hence the mourners had to wait around while additional grave-digging operations were carried out."

Whitton was married to a normal size woman and had five children, all also normal.

The Doctor is In

An October 26, 1923 article in the Literary Digest titled *Do We Pay Doctors Too Much* quotes an editorial in *American Medicine (New York)*. In brackets are figures adjusted for 13.84X inflation to 2015.

"It has been determined repeatedly in

the courts and rather generally accepted, too, that $20 [277] per hour is satisfactory remuneration for the average medical man;...$10 [138] a fair examination fee, which ordinarily does not require over thirty minutes; and $5 [69] for ordinary treatments which do not require over fifteen minutes. However, many specialists charge $25 [346] for an examination and $10 to $15 [138-208] for treatments."

The editorial was about a paper by Dr. Louis I. Harris, director of the Bureau of Preventable Diseases of the New York City Health Department.

"It seems that Dr. Harris was trying to make the 'high class' physician realize his responsibilities to the middle and poorer class of patient who can and is perfectly willing to pay a moderate fee, but who is being driven to such substitutes as the Cornell Clinic and the Life Extension Institute because of private office fees which he can not meet."

The Life Extension Institute offered examinations only at low cost, the Cornell Clinic (now Weill Cornell Community Clinic) offered low or no cost medical treatment.

279 Help!

SOS does not mean *Save Our Ship* or *Save Our Souls*. It was an arbitrary Morse code signal adopted in Germany in 1905 and then by the second International Radiotelegraphic Convention in Berlin as an international standard in 1906.

The Morse sequence *dit dit dit dah dah dah dit dit dit* is sent run together without letter breaks. Three shorts, three longs three shorts is easy to remember. It happens to correspond to the letters SOS in Morse code (also VTB, but SOS sounds better.) Actually SOS should be written SOS, with a bar above it to indicate a continuous sequence.

The first use of SOS was by the Cunard liner Slavonia which foundered on rocks near Flores Island in the Azores on June 10, 1909. The passengers and crew were rescued the next day by two ships responding to the SOS.

Mayday as a distress signal was coined in 1923 by a radio officer at Croyden Airport in London. He got "Mayday" from the French "m'aidez", "help me," since much of the Croyden air traffic at that time was with Le Bourget airport in Paris.

At Last! The Cure for the Common Cold

"To cure your cold, tie a woolen wrap around the head, well down on the forehead and over the cranium in back. Leave it there all night. Drink a hot rum or hot wine—or, in America, hot lemonade—and perspire all night. In the morning the cold in the head will be gone."

This is the prescription from Dr. Louis St. Maurice, from an article in the Literary Digest February 7, 1920 titled *Back to the Nightcap?* quoting the Chicago Tribune. The article also was in the Milwaukee Journal on the same date.

The problem is that people have abandoned the nightcap. When nightcaps were worn by everyone, before the end of the 18th century, no one ever had head or chest colds, grippe, or influenza: no mention of these ailments appears in literature prior to the 18th century according to Dr. St. Maurice*.

Wet feet are not responsible for colds, colds are caught at night when "the head is exposed to the cold current of air that comes in from the window and is sucked up the chimney or around corners."

Moreover, now we need head protection even more than before. "The average brain to-day is larger and heavier than it was a hundred years ago." But the size of the cranium has not changed in 2000 years; the skull is getting thinner to make room for the larger brain. "Eventually, perhaps in another couple of hundred years, we shall have a race with skulls as thin and frail as eggshells, so that everyone will have to wear constantly head-guards like your American football players or as aviators wore at the beginning of the war."

So put on your nightcap. "Even the silk and lace boudoir-caps that milady wears nowadays are better than nothing."

* Dr. St. Maurice evidently didn't read Noah Webster (1758-1843). Not the dictionary but *A Brief History of Epidemic and Pestilential Disease,* published in 1799. Webster identified 44 influenza epidemics beginning in 1174.

Webster believed that the flu was "evidently the effect of some insensible qualities of the atmosphere," calling it an "electrical quality." All the epidemics occurred just before or just after volcanoes or earthquakes to which he attributed the atmospheric changes

It is not known if Webster wore a nightcap to bed.

How to Wash Ostrich Feathers

To wash ostrich feathers: make a suds of Ivory Soap and lukewarm water, dip the feather in and draw it through the hand a few times. If very dirty wash through two suds, then rinse through several bowls of clear water.

When clean draw through the hand until almost dry, then place it on the thigh and slap it with the hand to bring it out fluffy.

It takes some practice to do this, but by experimenting with a poor feather the proper way to handle a good one can soon be learned.

— Ad for Ivory Soap, 1907.

Deep Thought

Courage is fear holding on a minute longer

— General George S. Patton

280   The Limits of Radio

That's the title of an article in the Literary Digest from April 7, 1923. While it may be possible to call someone in Australia from London from a "radiophone office", other notions are physically impossible

"Perhaps the one which appeals to the imaginative mind most often is that soon the ordinary land-line telephone will be obsolete, and every one will carry a pocket radiophone, by which they can call up whom they like."

Not going to happen. Not enough wave-lengths for the million phones in use in England and you would need to a carry large dynamo for enough power to carry any distance. You wouldn't have any privacy, either. Radio waves travel in all directions so anyone could listen in.

End Times

The Watchman, a Boston religious weekly (published 1876-1913) notes that some men are teaching that the moral deterioration of the times is a sign that the second coming is near.

"They accumulate the proofs of an increase of wickedness with a zest that constrains one to believe that they are rather glad of it. If that is the Christian temper we have misread the New Testament."

— Quoted in the Literary Digest January 9, 1897.

Language Isn't Fixt

You rarely see discust that the evolution of English hasn't stopt. Altho it may look here as if some letters have been dropt and another affixt, everything has been spelt correctly. Surprized? This was the way we wrote from the 1910's into the 1930's.

Women Why Be Thin?

Dr. Rivard's Flesh Producing Treatment for women guaranteed to increase your weight 15 to 30 pounds. Neck, arms, shoulders beautifully rounded. Very moderate cost. Quick, sure, safe. Nothing like it ever offered before.

— 1902 ad

A Proper Burial

The Literary Digest quotes Harper's Weekly on May 25,1907 telling of a West Point cadet who was instructed to draw up plans for a railroad viaduct running from one hill to another over a stream.

The cadet presented his drawings, one of which was a sketch of the bridge and surrounding landscape. Two men were sitting on the bridge with legs dangling, fishing in the stream.

The drawing was returned with an order to take the men off the bridge.

The drawing was returned and the men had indeed been removed from the bridge: they were shown fishing from the bank of the stream.

The drawing was returned again with specific orders to remove the men.

In the third version of the drawing the men were gone. Two graves with tombstones complete with epitaphs had been placed on the bank of the stream.

The cadet was James McNeil Whistler, most famous for painting his mother. Whistler wasn't military material and was dismissed from West Point in 1854 by the superintendent, Col. Robert E. Lee.

Deep Thought

The greatest act of faith is when a man understands that he is not God.

— Oliver Wendell Holmes Jr.

The game of life is hard to play. I'm gonna lose it anyway — from *Suicide is Painless*, the theme from MASH.

Lured to Ruin at Monte Carlo
Suicides Hushed Up While Rare
Winnings, Much Advertised,
Attract New Dupes
— The New York Times March 31, 1912

The Times article tells of a wealthy French couple who, having lost everything at the tables, committed suicide by turning on the gas in their apartment. The authorities "treated their chauffeur liberally" and "dispatched the bodies under cover of night to the victims' home. All expenses were paid and the public was none the wiser."

In another suicide an elderly man shot himself on a park bench and police carried him off in less than five minutes.

The Literary Digest from February 19, 1927 says that suicides were once common in Monte Carlo and quotes "A Retired Croupier" writing in *The Elks Magazine* that in 1872, "a little black rowboat, loaded with corpses, would set out once or twice a week, deposit its burden a few miles off shore and return empty." "Things were so bad that the only way to stop the suicides was to make them kill themselves somewhere else."

By 1927, the suicide rate had plunged. You couldn't buy the means to do yourself in: poison and revolvers could not be had in Monaco. And if you bring your own, "it is likely they will disappear from your baggage while you are away playing at the Casino," writes the Croupier.

Those who lost everything and had no money even to return home were given a viaticum: some money, a train ticket and an escort out of Monte Carlo.

Suicide was bad publicity for the new casino. The Croupier relates an incident of a man stopped on the verge of shooting himself. François Blanc, founder of the Monte Carlo Casino, happened by and rushed up to him, shook his fist in his face, and said "Sir, you are no gentleman; if you wish to shoot yourself, go home and do it, not here."

Mrs. USA
In 1957, Miss Maryland won the Miss USA contest to go on to represent the country in the Miss Universe pageant.

Rumors immediately started that Leona Gage was married, which she initially denied, but admitted the next day.

The 21 year old was married to an Air Force Sergeant at 14 and had two children. She said she only had $2 to her name and needed the $4,000 worth of prizes.

She was stripped of her title but was deluged with offers and she appeared on the Ed Sullivan show just days after. She accepted an offer as a showgirl in the Tropicana in Las Vegas at $200 a week. She appeared in minor roles in a few films. She was troubled, with drug and child abuse problems. She was married six times and died in 2010 at 71.

Abuse of Power
Adèle D'osmond, Comtesse De Boigne (1781-1866) knew the French royals and just about everybody else of her era.

In *Memoirs of the Comtesse de Boigne* (Vol. I 1781-1815), she tells a story of Wilbraham Bootle, a wealthy Englishman engaged to a Miss Taylor "who could bring her husband nothing but a pretty face."

At a dinner at Lord Camelford's, the British minister in Rome, conversation turned to someone who had climbed St. Peter's Basilica to the cross on top of the dome, over 400 feet high. The cross sits on top of a gilded ball.

Bootle said nothing could induce him to attempt such a feat. Miss Taylor insisted that he do it for her.

Two days later the company assembled to watch Bootle climb to the cross, which he did "with great coolness" and when he came down he kissed Miss Taylor's hand and said:

"Miss Taylor, I have obeyed the whim of a charming girl. Permit me now in return to give you a piece of advice: if you wish to keep your power, never misuse it. I wish you all prosperity, and now goodbye." And he left Rome.

The Comtesse reported that she saw Miss Taylor 10 years later and she was still unmarried.

Deep Thought
He who can take advice is sometimes superior to those who give it.
— From a Chinese fortune cookie

The Hunchback of Smuggler's Game

There is an old superstition that rubbing a hunchback's hump brings luck. This proved to be the undoing of an ingenious smuggler who made 27 trips across the Atlantic and the Canadian border with large quantities of jewelry hidden in bicycle tires, chocolate candy, artificial fruit, and plumbing fixtures. He even crossed the ocean escorting a casket he claimed contained his brother. The body had 43 rings on its fingers.

In September,1900 customs inspectors asked politely to rub the hump of a hunchback debarking from the SS Trave in New York who initially assented, then drew back as they approached. This aroused their suspicions and he was taken back on the ship and searched. The hump turned out to be plaster holding in place a package of several hundred pieces of jewelry wrapped in cotton.
— From the memoirs of customs agent William Henry Theobald, 1908.

Bandwidth

According to the Treasury Department Bureau of Statistics, from an article in the Literary Digest December 23, 1899, there were 1500 submarine cables linking all the continents. Their total length was 170,000 miles and they carried 6 million messages a year. With land telegraph added in, there were 835,000 miles carrying 1 million messages a day.

There were a series of chess matches by telegraph between the United States and Great Britain held from 1896 to 1911, (with 3 year hiatus from 1904-1906). A message during the match sent from the House of Representatives in Washington to Parliament in London during the 1898 match received a reply 12½ seconds later. The Brits won.

The Victorian Age

The Literary Digest of January 9, 1897 quotes the *Handelsblad*, an Amsterdam paper, as to what "the age of steel and steam will be called by future generations."

"Not only in England, but throughout the world, our century will be called the 'Victorian Age,'"

Queen Victoria celebrated 60 years on the throne in 1897. She died January 22, 1901 at age 81.

Big Blue Marble in Space

The earth's a big blue marble when you see it from out there — from the theme song of Big Blue Marble, a children's TV series 1974-1983.

Long before the iconic "Earthrise"* picture of a blue earth floating in the void above the moon taken on the Apollo 8 lunar orbit mission, Dec. 24, 1968, it was known that the earth would look blue.

Astronomer Vesto Slipher (1875-1969) of the Lowell observatory in Flagstaff, Arizona determined that the earth would appear blue by analyzing spectrograms of the light from earth reflected off the moon.

Slipher presented this finding at the George Darwin lecture to the Royal Astronomical Society in London in 1933 where he was presented the Society's gold medal.

* The picture was actually taken sideways due to the orientation of the orbiter and rotated 90°

Sabbath Sticks

An act of the Parliament of Scotland March 6, 1457 said that football and golf should be "utterly condemned and stopped."

It seems that sports was getting in the way of archery practice for the war against England: "a pair of targets should be made up at all parish churches and shooting should be practised each Sunday."

The ban on "ye golf" was renewed by parliament under James III in 1470 and again under James IV in 1491. The wily Scots got around the ban with Sabbath sticks, walking sticks with a handle that was a golf club head. The Sabbath stick would simply be reversed to play a few holes when no one was looking.

With the signing of the Treaty of Perpetual Peace in 1502, the war with England ended and the ban on golf was lifted.

In 1592, the City of Edinburgh banned golf on the Leith links on Sunday "in tyme of sermonis." In 1618 King James VI decreed that golf may be played on Sundays after attendance at services. (1618 also saw the first introduction of the featherie ball, see *Fore!* on page 251)

In 1599, a foursome in Perth were caught golfing at the wrong time on Sunday. From the records of the Kirk Session (Presbyterian ecclesiastical court):

"Nov.19, 1599.—John Gardiner, James Bowman, Laurence Chalmers and Laurence Cuthbert confessed that they were playing golf on the North Inch in the time of the preaching afternoon on the Sabbath. The Session rebuked them, and admonished them to resort to the hearing of the Word diligently on the Sabbath in time coming, which they promised to do."

The Sabbatarians still prevail on the islands of Lewis and Harris (famous for Harris tweed) in the Outer Hebrides off the northwest coast of Scotland where Sunday golf is still banned

Lord Leverhulme, William Lever of Lever brothers soap, bought the Isle of Lewis in 1918. In 1923 he donated a 68,000 acre estate which included the main town of Stornoway to the community to be administered by the Stornoway Trust, whose ten elected trustees determine, among other things, when golf can be played on the grounds of the Trust's tenant, the Stornoway Golf Club. They have so far kept the ban.

But the Sunday golf ban only applies to members of the Stornoway club, who would have their membership revoked if they played on Sunday. Non-members play on Sundays. The golf police are off on the Sabbath.

The Harris Golf Club maintained its Sunday golf ban but was awarded £64,000 by SportScotland, a government agency, in 2009 despite possible violation of equality laws. "SportScotland said it recognised a rest day for staff but hoped golfers could use the course and leave a fee in an honesty box," reported UK Wired News in 2010.

It was only recently that Sunday ferry and air service to the Outer Hebrides from the mainland was allowed. In 2011, a Sunday ban on liquor at the Stornoway Golf Club was overturned by the Sheriff court.

Two golfers are caught red-handed by clergy in *The Sabbath Breakers* by English painter John Charles Dollman, 1896

The Eagles' Eagle

Philadelphia's football team and 1926 NFL champions the Frankford Yellow Jackets went bankrupt and stopped playing halfway through the 1931 season.

James R. Ludlow "Lud" Wray and De Benneville "Bert" Bell, University of Pennsylvania football teammates, paid $2500 for the assets of the Yellow Jackets and took over the Philadelphia NFL franchise. They named the new team the Eagles from the blue eagle symbol of the NRA, the National Recovery Act.

The NRA was a 1933 New Deal law that established fair practice codes for wages, hours, and prices. Businesses that subscribed to the codes displayed the poster with the blue eagle with the slogan "We Do Our Part." The NRA was ruled unconstitutional by the Supreme Court in 1935 saying it attempted to regulate commerce that was not interstate and also that the executive branch usurped legislative powers.

The Eagles lost their first game to the New York Giants 56-0 in 1933. Bert Bell went on to become NFL Commissioner in 1946, an office he held until his death in 1959.

Prussian Blue

A baker in Berlin violated Prussia's blue laws by "playing worldly airs on the piano during church-time." According to an article in the Literary Digest January 2, 1897.

It was his wife's birthday he told the policeman who had heard the sacrilege, "But the officer insisted that the family must make merry to the tune of the 'Old Hundred,' 'In the Hour of Trial,' or of similar inspiring music. The baker, taking no notice of the warning, played 'Pop Goes the Weasel' and 'The Dude's March,' and a summons was served."

The Moral Gown

In 1921, a reaction began against the scanty dress of the flappers. The YWCA distributed literature saying "Working Girls Responsive to Modesty Appeal" and "High Heels Losing Ground Even in France."

Worthies In Philadelphia sent a questionnaire to over a thousand clergymen asking their opinion of proper and modest dress for women. From the responses they designed a "Moral Gown", loose-fitting with sleeves just below the elbow and a hem 7½ inches above the floor.

Various states proposed bills regulating women's dress, including a bill in Utah forbidding skirts higher than 3 inches above the ground with penalties of fine and imprisonment.

The French were perplexed. The New York Times February 17, 1921 quoted French comment in a article titled *Paris Gibe at Moral Gown*. "These crazy fellows in America are always trying to suppress something. First it is alcohol, then it is tobacco and now it is liberty to dress as one pleases."

The "moral costume for women... appears somewhat to resemble a sack... All the precepts of earth and even of heaven will change nothing of the morality or immorality of women's dress. For women will always do what they want to do, and, above all, what other people don't want them to do."

Hemlines fell with the stock market in the Great Depression. See *Off the Chart* on p. 126.

Is Sex Necessary?

Mr. Herbert Televox was a robot first built in 1927 by the Westinghouse Electric Company. It could pick up the phone and listen to instructions given by different notes blown on a pitch pipe and acknowlidge with a series of buzzes.

Televox could wirelessly turn appliances on or off or check if the furnace was too hot in a home. Industrial uses included controlling electric loads for the power company. Three Televoxes, Adam, Cain, and Abel ("Eve being omitted because the automatic kingdom has not been divided into two factions"), were employed by the War Department in Washington to report and control reservoir levels.

The New York Times reported June 4, 1928 "Mechanical man now can also talk. Televox gets vocal cords to call up employer and tell him latest news." A few sentences were recorded on film, like a movie sound track. Now it would answer the phone with "Televox speaking" and could initiate a phone call: "this is the Televox calling for Main 5000." The rest of the conversation would then be with buzzes.

Mr. Televox made a special appearance at the American Booksellers' Association convention in 1930. When asked what his favorite book was, he replied *Is Sex Necessary?* a book by humorist and cartoonist James Thurber.

The Man Who Saved Christmas

In 1918 during World War I, the Council of National Defense, an agency that oversaw industry to support the war effort, was considering a ban on the production of Christmas toys to encourage people to buy war bonds instead.

Toy manufacturer A.C. Gilbert, inventor of the erector set and founder and president of the Toy Manufacturers of America, went to Washington for a meeting of the Council including the secretaries of Commerce, War, and Interior. He brought toys with him, including erector sets, a miniature submarine, and a steam engine.

The Secretary of the Navy got on the floor to play with the toy submarine and other council members played with the toy engines and built an erector set bridge.

"The greatest influences in the life of a boy are his toys," Gilbert told the Council. Toys were not banned and Gilbert became known as "The Man Who Saved Christmas." He was memorialized in a 2002 movie of the same name starring Jason Alexander.

Alfred Carlton Gilbert (1884-1961) was from Salem, Oregon. He attended what is now Pacific University, excelling in sports. He then obtained a medical degree from Yale. While at Yale he won a gold medal in the pole vault in the 1908 Olympics.

Gilbert retired in 1954 and published his autobiography, *The Man Who Lives in Paradise,* which is still in print.

Don't Yank the Crank

Early telephones had a little crank on the side you would turn to generate a current to ring the operator. These were obsolete by the turn of the 20th century, except for the obstinate French, as an article in the June 13, 1908 Chicago *Western Electrician* made clear, quoting the Paris correspondent of the New York Times:

"Hitherto excitable Frenchmen whiled away the time while awaiting Central to answer by grinding furiously at the crank bell call. The new system denied them this form of relief. The result was that their pent-up feelings found outlet in imprecations and wild gesticulations. In many cases the telephones were damaged by poundings and shakings and had to be removed." The French Minister of Telephones said that "the highly trained Americans" could master the new automatic signaling system but the French "need the safety valve of the old-fashioned bell."

The last crank telephones in the U.S. were removed in 1983 from Bryant Pond, Maine. The family-owned Bryant Pond Telephone Company, with a switchboard in the owner's living room, was bought out and upgraded. A last ditch "Don't Yank the Crank" campaign was unsuccessful.

Pride

Here's a war story from a customer and a friend.

He's a taxi driver in the local area. One day he picked up a woman who demanded that she be taken to her doctor. When he asked the doctor's address, the lady said she didn't know, but said that the doctor was the leading doctor in his specialty, and why didn't he know where the famous doctor's office was? Then she asked "how long have you been driving?" That was the wrong question. My friend declined the ride.

Then the woman demanded that he call her a taxi. "Ok," he said, "you're a taxi."

That's the only time I know of that old Vaudeville line being used in combat.

Prejudice

A long time ago I was overseas in the Air Force. One of the guys in our outfit was extremely prejudiced. He would go out of his way to use *those* words. You know the ones, the ugly, hurtful words, emphatically delivered and with a twist-the-knife sly smile of satisfaction.

He was from Texas, and he was especially denigrating of Hispanics in general, and Mexicans in particular.

He went home a few months before the rest of our group and sent us a letter. He told us how great it was to be a civilian again and that he was getting married to "a cute little girl of Latin extraction."

¡Felicitaciones!

280   Heavy Reading

At 16.21 words per square inch (25.13 x 10^9/km^2 for you scientific types), this book has more than twice the literary nutrition as the the average book, with no fat. A bargain!

You've Got Mail

At 12:01 A.M. January 1, 1913, the Woodrow Wilson Club of Princeton mailed 11 pounds of apples to Governor and President-Elect Woodrow Wilson. The mail carrier raced to Wilson's home nearby and delivered the apples at 12:04. At 12:05 A.M. Six eggs were mailed from St. Louis about 18 miles northeast across the Mississippi to Edwardsville, Illinois, and were returned by mail baked into a cake at 7 P.M. A pitchfork was mailed in Louisiana for 38¢. 1000 bricks, 6,000 pounds, were wrapped in 11 pound packages, the parcel post weight limit, and mailed from Gary, Indiana. In Atlanta, a doctor mailed a roast in the morning from his downtown office to his wife at their home. It arrived still cold at 11:00 A.M. These were some of the first packages delivered on the first day of parcel post. Over 4 million packages were shipped that day and 300 million the first 6 months. The weight limit was raised to 20 and then 50 pounds by the end of the year.

The New York Times headlined January 26 "Baby Boy by Parcel Post. Rural Carrier Safely Delivered 10¾ Pound Infant to Grandmother." The baby, just under the 11 pound limit, was mailed from Batavia, Ohio a mile for 15¢ and was insured for $50. Several other children under the higher 50 pound limit were mailed in the next several years until the Post Office put an end to the practice. The First Assistant Postmaster General ruled that "children did not come within the classification of harmless live animals which do not require food and water while in transit," after a 9 year old girl entered the main post office in Washington, D.C. requesting to be mailed to Kentucky reported the Times June 14, 1920.

In 1918, the Post Office made an experimental shipment of "more than 2900 pounds of eggs, butter, and honey, in addition to 400 newly hatched chicks, to New York from Lancaster, Penn." reported the Times in an article titled "Farm-To-Table Post", April 14, 1918. The 100 mile trip took 12 hours. Postage was $31.61 on which the Post Office made $12 after expenses. This profit and more was standard at the time: "Mail Trucks Earn Four Times Their Cost", headlined Automotive Industries magazine December 26, 1918.

Parcel post was started in Europe in the 1880's and the U.S. initiated international parcel post service with an 11 pound weight limit in 1887. So why the delay for domestic parcel post? "In point of fact there are but four strong objections to the parcels post, and they are the four great express companies," Postmaster General John Wanamaker (see *Prix Fixe* on p. 44) wrote in Report of the Postmaster General in 1891.

Adams Express, American Express, United States Express, and Wells Fargo dominated the parcel business. They were a politically potent cartel, with interlocking ownership with each other and the railroad companies, and opaque pricing. The Cambridge Sentinel (Mass.) reported March 12, 1910 on the express companies outsize profits and dividends. And high prices. The New Zealand parcel post would ship a 10 pound package to London, 12,000 miles, for 75¢ whereas the express companies charge a dollar to ship the same package the 3,000 miles from Boston to London. "Monopoly and greed have fastened their tentacles on this country as on no other in the world and are blighting the fairest Democracy upon which the sun has ever shone." *(Continued next page.)*

Prior to parcel post, there was a 4 pound weight limit for mail and mail was only delivered to the door in cities. In rural areas, home to two thirds of Americans, mail had to be picked up at the nearest post office, usually at a general store in a town, often a long trip over poor roads. The National Grange and other farmers organizations lobbied for Rural Free Delivery over opposition by general store merchants, who would suffer from the loss of traffic, and RFD was inaugurated in 1902.

This transformed rural life with catalogs from mail order companies. But with the 4 pound weight limit, little could be mailed. Orders had to be shipped by rail which required pick up at a train station. Some mail carriers filled the void by picking up and delivering these packages as a side business. The mail wagons were often half-empty. Although this was stopped in 1904, the Post Office took notice of the possibility of lucrative extra business.

After the Hepburn Act of 1906 brought the express companies under the jurisdiction of the Interstate Commerce Commission, the ICC investigated and issued a damning report in 1912 of inflated prices and incomprehensible rate structures. This and political changes in Congress led to lengthy Senate hearings (with long discussions about mailing eggs) in 1912 and finally passage of the Parcel Post Act that August.

Flint Stones

All persons in the united American States who are able to inform the Congress of any quantities of flint stone, or of any persons who are skilled in the manufacture of FLINTS, are requested to apply in person, or by letter, to the Board of War and Ordnance, at the War Office, in Market street, near the corner of Fourth street.

— Virginia Gazette, July 5, 1776

The flintlock musket was the primary weapon in the Revolutionary War. The 5 foot long muzzle-loaded smoothbore gun fired a ball with black powder. A shaped piece of flint was held in the vise-like hammer. When the trigger was pulled, the flint in the spring-loaded hammer struck the frizzen, an L-shaped piece of steel, causing sparks. The frizzen snapped back, uncovering the flash pan which had been loaded with a small amount of powder. The sparks ignited the primer powder and the flash passed through a small hole, the touch hole, in the barrel and ignited the main gunpowder charge.

The weapon had two positions for the hammer, a safety position, half-cock, so the flash pan could be loaded without fear of accidental discharge, and the cocked position, ready to fire. The term "flash in the pan" comes from a failure of the primer to ignite the main charge. "Going off half-cocked" was a failure of the half-cock ratchet mechanism causing premature firing.

Flints had to be replaced after 8 to 10 shots and soldiers carried 6 to 12 spares, so you can see the urgency of this notice at the beginning of the Revolutionary War, just a day after the Declaration of Independence.

Prying the Lid Off

A January 6, 1934 article in the Literary Digest summarizes a food industry study.

"Of the 500 bottles and jars tested, ninety six proved unscrewable in the hands of housewives, tho fifty-six were later removed by the housewives with the aid of such rough-and-ready devices as hitting, prying, heating the bottle and in some instances calling in the husband."

"Incidentally, some of these jars baffled even husbands. Forty defied all efforts to open them."

Thank You For Smoking

In Edmonds, Washington a jewelry store robber found he couldn't outrun the law.

In May, 2010 a man entered the store and after browsing for engagement rings, demanded all the rings after showing what looked like a gun in his waistband.

The man fled the store with $75,000 in rings and a group of people gave chase.

Losing ground, the man threw the gun, which turned out to be fake, at his pursuers. Then he threw away the rings, but, panting heavily, he was soon caught and surrounded. The crowd held him until police arrived.

It turned out the getaway was so easily foiled because the man only had one lung.

Futurama

I was born in the forties, so this is the future. Where are the spaceships and ray-guns? Why doesn't my car fly?

Well, at least they found out what causes cancer (everything). And they can cure it in mice!

Sock it to Me

"On his word of honour, Mr. Leopold von Sacher-Masoch undertakes to be the slave of Mrs. von Pistor, and to carry out her wishes for a period of six months."

This is the first clause of a contract signed December 8, 1869. Sound masochistic? Leopold von Sacher-Masoch is the original masochist, the guy masochism is named for, and for good reason. "On the occurrence of any misdemeanor or negligence or act of Lèse-majesté, the mistress (Fanny von Pistor) may punish her slave (Leopold von Sacher-Masoch) in whatever manner she pleases...On her behalf, Fanny von Pistor undertakes to wear furs as often as possible, especially when she is behaving cruelly."

Leopold von Sacher-Masoch was born in 1836 in Lviv, Ukraine, then called Lemberg and part of the Austrian Empire. In 1848 the family moved to Prague. where he learned German, the language of his writings. He studied at the University of Prague and at the University of Graz in Austria, then moved back to Lemberg where he was appointed a professor of history at the University of Lemberg. He became a writer of historical non-fiction, then novels. In 1870, he quit his job as a professor and published his most famous work, *Venus in Furs,* a novella based on his affair with Fanny Pistor. The word whip or whipping occurs 74 times.

In 1873, he married Angelika Aurora Rümelin. She was a 27 year old glovemaker. She had written letters to him under the name of Wanda von Dunajew, the dominatrix in Venus in Furs. She took the name Wanda von Sacher-Masoch. Leopold wrote another contract with Wanda similar to the first one with Fanny. Leopold even tried to arrange liaisons for his wife with other men to further humiliate himself. Wanda indulged his fantasies, including lots of whipping, without enthusiasm. After a first child died, they had two sons in 1874 and 1875. They moved about as Leopold tried to earn a living by writing. He edited various magazines in Graz, Budapest, and Leipzig as well as publishing novels. Wanda also published novels under the name of Wanda von Dunajew. Wanda was too normal and in 1883 she left him and moved to Paris with another man, a journalist who had been hired by Leopold at the review he edited, Auf der Höhe (At the Pinnacle) in Leipzig. Leopold obtained a divorce in 1885.

Auf der Höhe went out of business in 1885 and Leopold was

Image on Sacher-Masoch's Leipzig stationery

rescued by a translator who worked at the magazine, Hulda Meister, who bought a home in Lindheim, Germany with inherited money. Two sons were born to the couple and they married in 1890. They moved to Mannheim in 1890 where Leopold worked as a critic and editor at two newspapers. The same year, Richard von Krafft-Ebing added "masochism" to his *Psychopathia Sexualis* damaging Leopold's reputation. The family moved back to Lindheim in 1891.

In Lindheim he organized educational clubs to counter entrenched anti-Semitism (the Lutheran Pastor of Lindheim had written an anti-Semitic book), as well as libraries, theaters, and orchestras.

Leopold von Sacher-Masoch died March 9, 1895 at 59. Altogether he wrote 80 novels,100 novellas and essays and 8 plays and was awarded the French Legion of Honor. He was admired by such authors as Victor Hugo, Emile Zola, and Henrik Ibsen.

If you go to Lviv be sure to stop in at the Masoch Cafe. Under cathouse red lights, a leather-clad waitress will handcuff you and give you a few strokes with a whip if you want. You can have hot wax dripped on you, too. Décor is decidedly kinky with whips, chains, and handcuffs on the walls, which are also for sale as souvenirs at the gift shop.

Outside the cafe is an unusual statue of Sacher-Masoch by a Ukrainian sculptor unveiled in 2008. You'll get a giggle if you put your hand in his left pocket.

No Shit!

Korean dictator Kim Jong-il, who died in 2011,was quite the talented guy. The first time he played golf he scored 38 under par with 11 holes-in-one, after which he retired from the game.

But his god-like qualities didn't stop at golf. A North Korean web site once claimed he neither urinated nor defecated according to a December 19, 2011 article in the Guardian.

Rabbit Food

There really are rabbits the size of dogs. A German man, Karl Szmolinsky, raises German Gray Giants in Eberswalde, near Berlin. One of his rabbits, Robert I, won the prize for Germany's biggest rabbit at 22 pounds in an agricultural fair in 2006.

Robert was featured on a South Korean children's TV show which was seen in North Korea. Shortly after, a convoy of Mercedes from the North Korean embassy in Berlin showed up at Szmolinsky's home.

The North Koreans saw the giant rabbits as an answer to their chronic food shortage. Szmolinsky agreed to sell some of his best rabbits to North Korea for breeding stock, for a bargain price, 80 Euros, 60% off. Twelve rabbits, 4 males, including Robert I, and 8 females were flown to Pyongyang in December, 2006.

A giant rabbit would yield about 15 pounds of meat, enough to feed 8 people and, of course, they breed like rabbits.

But they eat a lot and Szmolinsky says the right diet is important: "I feed them everything - grain, carrots, a lot of vegetables. At the moment they're getting kale." They have to drink a lot of water, too, or they get constipated.

Szmolinsky was supposed to travel to Pyongyang to advise the North Koreans, but they canceled the trip at the last minute. Szmolinsky found it suspicious that the cancellation occurred right after a banquet for Dear Leader Kim Jong-il and he thinks rabbit was on the menu.

But Robert II, 24 pound son of Robert I, is still safe in his hutch.

The Guinness World Record for the biggest rabbit went to Darius, a Continental Giant rabbit from Worcester England in 2014. Darius is 4 feet 4 inches long, weighs 49 pounds, and eats 360 carrots, 30 apples and 15 cabbages a month, costing about $4000 a year.

Deep Thought
Don't be so strong it makes you weak.

All Creatures Great and Small

All things bright and beautiful,
All creatures great and small,
All things wise and wonderful:
The Lord God made them all
— Cecil F. Alexander, Hymns for Little Children, 1848.

Of all the terrible things that have happened in my lifetime, I don't know why this strikes me as one of the saddest.

The October 27, 1947 Life Magazine had an article titled *Hunting the Polar Bear.* The subhead was "In the icy waters of the Arctic, Norwegian sealers kill a she-bear and capture her broken-hearted cub."

The Norwegian sealer *Harmoni* came back from a 30 day hunt with 11 polar bear skins and the cub. The skins were worth $100 each ($1061 in 2015) and the cub $500 to a zoo.

Today, only Canada allows trophy hunting of polar bears; the Inuits are allowed to sell their subsistence hunting quotas to outsiders. Cost for a 10 day guided hunt is $35,000. Mothers with cubs are forbidden to be killed. The skins may not be imported into the United States. Norway completely bans polar bear hunting.

The United States put polar bears on the threatened species list in 2008 and then governor of Alaska Sarah Palin sued the government claiming that there were plenty of polar bears, that the science predicting melting of sea ice was unreliable, and that the listing would affect oil and gas drilling in the polar bears' habitat. In 2011, a U.S. district judge ruled against Palin. 280

Broken-hearted cub, realizing that his mother is dead, embraces her. Little bear remained in this position all day and night, whimpering and refusing proffered food.

Back to the Future

The illustration above is T*he Telephonoscope* from Albert Robida's 1892 science fiction novel *The Twentieth Century. The Electric Life.* It's a multi-channel flat-screen TV, with news and commercials.

Robida (1848-1926) was a prolific French illustrator and author of science fiction. *The Twentieth Century* and *The Twentieth Century. The Electric Life* envisioned life in 1952 and 1953. In addition to the telephonoscope, modern marvels included trains in elevated pneumatic tubes, a videophone, flying zeppelin transport, *aerocars* that look like amusement ride cars, and meals and mail delivered by pneumatic tube. And he foresaw the social and political emancipation of women.

In an 1887 book, *War in the Twentieth Century*, Robida imagined a French-German war in 1945, with airships bombarding armored vehicles, and chemical and biological weapons.

The background image on the back cover is Robida's *Leaving the Opera in the Year 2000.*

Deep Thought

Reputation is built in years and destroyed in minutes.

264

It's Greek to Me

A lot of stuff is, especially whatever's going on in Greece.

The expression "It's Greek to me" traces back to Shakespeare's 1599 play *Julius Caesar*, in which one of Caesar's assassins remarks to another that he was left out of the loop when Cicero, a Roman Senator who was also assassinated, spoke Greek describing Caesar having a seizure.

So what's Greek in other languages? The Swedes stick with Greek, for the Finns it's Hebrew, in Yiddish, Aramaic, Cambodian to the Vietnamese, French or Arabic to the Turks, fish-egg language in Iceland, and Chinese in just about every other language, including Greek.

So what's inscrutable to the inscrutable Chinese? In Mandarin it's God's writing and in Cantonese chicken intestines.

Maybe Caesar should have paid attention to the chicken intestines. He was told to "beware the Ides of March" by Spurinna, a haruspex — one who foretold the future by reading animal guts.

Kill Junk Mail, Save Trees

That's the motto of PaperKarma, a new free phone app that will let you "Just snap your junk mail away." You just take a picture of the offending missive with your phone: "We automatically contact the Mailer and remove you from their distribution list."

PaperKarma has a huge database of junk mailers with the contacts for their "suppression lists," required by FTC rules to keep track of unsubscribe requests. PaperKarma will follow up with users to make sure the junk pile has shrunk.

Boondoggle

Scoutmaster Robert Link coined this word for the braided leather items made by the Boy Scouts. A boondoggle was presented to the Prince of Wales at the 1929 Boy Scout World Jamboree in London.

The word came to symbolize makework as in the Depression-era headline in The New York Times on April 4, 1935: "$3,187,000 Relief is Spent to Teach Jobless to Play ... Boon Doggles Made".

Maverick

Samuel Maverick (1803-1870) was a colorful Texan (Maverick County is named for him). In 1847 he took 400 head of cattle as payment for a debt. He left them on the open range in the care of a slave named Jack who neglected to brand the new calves. When he sold them in 1856, the cowboys who rounded up his cattle called all the unbranded ones they found "mavericks" and the word passed into the dictionary as a non-conformist.

The Lord Tweeteth

God opened a Twitter account, @TheTweetOfGod.

• To those of you taking the SATs tomorrow:BCCDECDABBCDEABCDEEBB CEBADEBCDEACBDEACBEDACBCAD.

I damn well better see you in church on Sunday.

• Your prayer has a current wait time of 400 million years. We apologize for the inconvenience.

• Watching "Jurassic World" really made Me nostalgic for the era between day six of creation and Noah's Ark, when they lived.

• Everything happens for a reason you make up afterwards.

• Life is a never-ending battle between the dumbasses and the smartasses.

• America is the greatest country on earth when it come to telling everyone it's the greatest country on earth.

David Javerbaum, former executive producer and head writer of *The Daily Show* started the holy (or unholy) tweets in 2010, which led to a book,*The Last Testament: a Memoir by God*, which in turn led to the Broadway play *An Act of God* which opened in 2015.

No Buss Bonnet

"Lady W. a writer in the Worcester Gazette complains bitterly to lady X. of the modern fashion of making bonnets.—She concludes thus:—'For my part, I cannot say, that I feel perfectly easy about the matter; for as true as I now live, I have not had a single kiss, since I first wore the Bonnet; nor do I so much wonder, for it is not possible for any creature, except it be a horse, or some other long-snouted animal, to come *near enough* to perform the act.'"

— An article titled *Fashionable Bonnets* in the Weekly Companion and the Commercial Centinal, Newport, Rhode Island January 12, 1799.

Close Encounters
of the Canine Kind

National Dog Bite Prevention Week® is the third full week in May, sponsored by the U.S. Postal Service. There are 70 million dogs in the U.S., so there are a lot of dog bites, 4.5 million according to the American Veterinary Medical Association.

Children and postmen are the most vulnerable. The Post Office reports that 5700 mail carriers were attacked in 2014, with Los Angeles leading with 416, Houston second with 67, and San Diego third with 47.

According to a 2013 Post Office media advisory, "The appearance of a well-trained dog owned by one of your letter carriers will help dispel the myth that Postal employees don't like dogs."

Prevent the Bite, a Palatine, Illinois organization founded by a woman who needed 100 stitches after an attack by a neighbor's dog in 1999 when she was 7, offers an educational materials kit on how to avoid dog bites.

Hockey Pucky

The first hockey pucks in the 19th century were made from frozen cow dung.

Ms. Piggy

The Elizabeth A. Sackler Center for Feminist Art at the Brooklyn Museum presented the Sackler Center First Award, honoring women who are first in their fields, to Miss Piggy June 4, 2015.

Piggy joins Supreme Court Justice Sandra Day O'Connor and author Toni Morrison in feminist fame.

The award was presented by Elizabeth Sackler. In her acceptance speech, Piggy said "Starting today, moi IS a feminist!" and that she was a "proud porcine-American feminist."

She then had a conversation with the original Ms., Gloria Steinem, in which she declared she would stay a Miss, saying she loves Ms. "But changing your name is just impossible, really...Actually, I would prefer it if people just called me 'Your Highness' or 'Your Majesty'". She then said that she never got an Oscar because the Academy has never recognized pigs or farm animals as eligible.

She wrote an essay for Time Magazine titled *Why I am a Feminist Pig*. As for questions of "whether moi deserves such an honor...some might say that moi is just a mere Hollywood celebrity who cares more about her appearance, her star billing, and most especially her percentage of the gross, than about women and women's rights. To which I can only respond 'Oh yeah!?!' by which I mean that moi is now and has always been and ardent feminist and champion of women's rights."

Told in her youth on the farm that life would be "nothing but mud, sweat and tears", she achieved her dreams and now lives in Hollywood, "where there is still a lot of mud, sweat and tears, but the hours and compensation are much more attractive."

So how can a pig be a feminist when pig is associated with male chauvinists? Species-ism — all pigs are not chauvinists. There are male chauvinist pigs as well as humans "and, on very rare occasions and at their own peril, male chauvinist amphibians."

Fortunately, The Sackler Center didn't see the January, 2005 cover of Playboar magazine with Miss Piggy posed provocatively on a motorcycle with the caption *Miss Piggy This Little Piggy Likes to Get Dirty.*

Free at Last

In the Old Hill Burying Ground in Concord, Massachusetts is a gravestone with this epitaph:

God wills us free; man wills us slaves.
I will as God wills; God's will be done.
Here lies the body of
JOHN JACK
a native of Africa who died
March 1773 aged about 60 years
Tho' born in a land of slavery,
He was born free.
Tho' he lived in a land of liberty,
He lived a slave.
Till by his honest, tho' stolen labors,
He acquired the source of slavery,
Which gave him his freedom;
Tho' not long before
Death, the grand tyrant
Gave him his final emancipation,
And set him on a footing with kings.
Tho' a slave to vice,
He practised those virtues
Without which kings are but slaves

This is one of the most famous epitaphs in history, written by Daniel Bliss, a loyalist lawyer from Concord just before the Revolutionary War who thought it was hypocritcal for those who espoused freedom from England to deny it to their negro slaves.

John Jack first turns up in church records as "Jack, Negro." He belonged to a shoemaker, Benjamin Barron, who died in 1754. His estate passed to his widow. Listed in the inventory of the estate was:

"One Negro servant named Jack £120"
"One Negro maid named Violet, being of no value."

John Jack raised £120 from earnings as a shoemaker to buy his freedom from his master's widow. In 1761 he bought from her daughter Susanna four acres of land and two more acres from someone else. Both deeds state he is a free man.

He worked at odd jobs for farmers and made shoes in the winter. Ailing, he sensed the end coming and made his will in December, 1772. In it he bequeathed everything to Violet, then living with Susanna Barron. But Violet was still a slave and could not legally own land and his properties passed back whence they came, to the Barron family. Daniel Bliss was appointed in the will as executor.

Daniel Bliss was born in Concord in 1740 and graduated from Harvard in 1760 and was admitted to the bar in 1765.

On March 20, 1775, Bliss allowed two British officers into his home in the center of Concord to recconoiter rebel activities and report back to General Gage. The presence of British spies was noted by the townspeople who threatened to kill him and his guests. Bliss was able to escape with the British officers late at night by a circuitous route.

He left his wife and children behind and arranged for his brother Samuel, also a loyalist, to go to Concord and salvage what he could and get his family to safety. Samuel was arrested on May 12, accused of guiding the British search for military contraband in Concord on April 19th that culminated in the Battle of North Bridge at Concord and the beginning of the Revolutionary War. He produced four witnesses who testified that he was in Boston on April 19 and he was released and fled to Boston.

Both he and his Brother Daniel received commissions in the British army and setttled in New Brunswick, Canada after the war, both doing very well.

The primary source of this article is *John Jack, the Slave and Daniel Bliss, the Tory*, a paper presented to the Concord Antiquarian Society in 1902 by George Tolman. Tolman says that one of the British officers who spied from Bliss's house in 1775 sent the epitaph home in a letter and it was published in a London newspaper and that the epitaph was copied many times and translated into many languages.

The original gravestone was broken and lay on the ground by the grave until 1830 when Rufus Hosmer, a lawyer and son of a fiery patriot who had stood up to refute a loyalist speech by Bliss at a Concord town meeting in 1774, sponsored a faithful copy that still stands today.

Tolman sums up eloquently:

"But for this poor slave, without ancestry, without posterity, without kindred, of a despised and alien race, a social pariah, his title to immortality is found only in his epitaph, which has made him, to his own race, the prophet of that great deliverance that was to come to them in blood and fire, a century after he had worked out his own emancipation."

Rest in peace John Jack.

The Sayings of Chairman Joe

Well, I'm finally thunk out of *Deep Thoughts*. While I refresh myself at the well of wisdom, here's a review of pithy profundities past. All are original except the last 18.

Don't count new money for old things or old money for new things

Reputation is built in years and destroyed in minutes.

A good deal on a bad diamond is no bargain.

Buy for yourself, not for the approval of others.

To see things clearly, first open the mind's eye.

If you seek the unusual, don't look in the usual places.

If everything is a bargain, nothing is a bargain.

Discount means cheap stuff cheap, not good stuff cheap.

Image is bought, reputation earned.

If you want jewelry, don't shop where they just sell merchandise.

Things are worth what you can sell them for.

The cheaper the merchandise the louder the advertising.

If the results are wrong, the rules are wrong.

Don't see yourself, be yourself

Tomorrow's antiques are here today.

The point of having money is to not have to worry about having money.

If others tell you what is in your self-interest, it is in their self-interest.

It's not about the rules, but who gets to make the rules.

Pride is for others, honor for yourself.

Bumper sticker slogans won't fix car wreck problems.

Don't criticize others for what you hate in yourself.

Wisdom is knowing when smart people say dumb things.

Good principles make bad dogma

It is what it is, whether you believe it or not.

Don't be so strong it makes you weak.

Do you know what you're talking about?

The Constitution, like the Bible, means whatever you want it to.

The Bible like the Constitution, means whatever you want it to.

Don't deny the problem because you don't like the solution.

We pay actors so much because we need them to tell us who we are,

It's not how high the taxes but if you get what you pay for.

It don't mean a thing if it ain't got that bling

A fool knows the price of everything and the value of nothing.
— Adapted from Oscar Wilde, who said it of a cynic.

We are a rich Nation; we can afford to pay for security and prosperity without having to sacrifice our liberties in the bargain.
— President Franklin D. Roosevelt, Fireside Chat, April 14, 1938

Those who control the present control the future. Those who control the future control the past. — George Orwell, 1984.

It is difficult to get a man to understand something when his salary depends upon his not understanding it — Upton Sinclair

Few men have virtue to withstand the highest bidder. — George Washington

The greatest act of faith is when a man understands that he is not God.
— Justice Oliver Wendell Holmes Jr.

Worry is the interest paid by those who borrow trouble. — George Washington

If I can do it, it's not art — Rudolf Guiliani

It is amazing what you can accomplish if you do not care who gets the credit.
— President Harry S. Truman

Courage is fear holding on a minute longer. — General George S. Patton

A fool and his money are soon elected. — Will Rogers

He who can take advice is sometimes superior to those who give it.
— From a Chinese fortune cookie

Grass is long. Life is short. — Sign advertising lawn mowers

I believe that people would be alive today if there were a death penalty
— Nancy Reagan

It is always the big thief who shouts the loudest about the little thief.
— Hazen Pingree (1840-1901. Detroit Mayor and Michigan Governor.)

It is impossible to defeat an ignorant man in argument.
— William Gibbs McAdoo, Treasury Secretary 1913-18

The great enemy of the truth is very often not the lie, deliberate, contrived and dishonest, but the myth, persistent, persuasive and unrealistic.
— President John F. Kennedy

The amount of energy necessary to refute bullshit is an order of magnitude bigger than to produce it.
— Computer programmer Alberto Brandolini. I didn't dress it up as a deep thought, but I'm promoting it to wisdom after the fact. Counts as the half a deep thought in the introduction.

Notes

Izzy and Moe (6)

There are many variants of the Einstein/Epstein story, one from the ATF (Bureau of Alcohol, Tobacco, Firearms and Explosives) cited on the SUNY Potsdam site, has the bartender insisting the name was Epstein, and two in books have the same story but with the verification of the name from the back of a picture of Izzy hanging on the wall. This one from the St. Petersburg Times Jan 13, 1929 seems the most plausible. The picture versions may have been conflated with another episode in Brooklyn in 1922. See *Face on Barroom Wall Was Izzy's*.

Both Time Magazine and the Pittsburgh Press in articles on Izzy's book in 1932 report that Izzy said he quit the Bureau in 1927, resigning because he didn't want to transfer to Chicago. But the Times, in addition to reporting the pair being dropped, also says that in 1925 that the Anti-Saloon League tried unsuccessfully to have Izzy and Moe reinstated.

Izzy and Moe along with another agent were arrested by deputy sheriffs in Providence, Rhode Island on September 8, 1922 on charges of assault and held on $10,000 bail.

The New York Times reported September 9, 1922 that civil suits were filed by near beer dealers "charging that prohibition agents are 'rushing' bartenders, intimidating them with revolvers, using 'extreme, vile, vulgar, obscene and filthy language' and even assaulting near-beer dispensers." This was the coda to the hostile reception they received in Rhode Island.

"Saloon keepers simply laughed when served a summons to appear in front of the United States commissioner of Prohibition. In one instance, an irate bartender threw a pitcher of whiskey in Izzy's face. All made it clear they planned to ignore any legal proceedings brought against them." — Forgotten Tales of Rhode Island by Jim Ignasher

"Dry authorities assert it will be a fight to the finish with the liquor interests," said the Times article.

The Advance News of Ogdensburg, N.Y. Reported in Moe Smith's obituary that due to animosity between prohibition agents and the police he was turned down when he applied to join the police after his prohibition agent career.

Izzy and Moe, A television movie starring Jackie Gleason as Izzy and Art Carney as Moe was made in 1985.

Medicinal Beer (3)

Volstead had one vice, chewing tobacco, consuming a pound a day according to the book *Weird Minnesota*.

The Fools of Bruges (10)

There are numerous accounts of Maximilian calling the people of Bruges fools. This one is from the De Halve Maan web site. All accounts mention a parade, some with "merrymakers and fools". Many say it was a parade in Maximillian's honor. If so, it would probably have been before 1488 when Bruges imprisoned Maximilian for 11 weeks over issues of high taxes and local autonomy. Perhaps it was in 1479 after defeat of the French with Flemish help. The Procession of the Holy Blood was a longstanding tradition and a major event so it seems likely that this was the parade referred to.

Fowl Play (11)

The article concluded with a note from the editor of the Hawke's Bay Herald:

"Except that all journalistic knowledge runneth to the contrary, we should have concluded from the above account that the Scotch reporters have been emulating their American compeers."

An article in another New Zealand paper titled "Depraved Poultry" supplied the name John Turner and the amount. The article was in Papers Past, a collection of digitized newspapers from the National Library of New Zealand. Unfortunately, while the article was in English, everything else was in Maori and I couldn't figure out which paper the article was from.

The Oban Times in Scotland did not respond to an email inquiry about the case.

Smelling the Roses (15)

The Japanese have a rose scented chewing gum, *Otoko Kaoru*, "man scent." A poll by a Japanese deodorant maker of younger women showed that 89% have caught a whiff of BO from men on commuter trains, with older men especially stinky. The Japanese even have a word for old man smell, kareishuu.

Potlikker Politics (22)

In a letter to the editor of the New York Times February 23, 1982, Georgia Lt. Governor Zell Miller, referred to a recent article about a 1935 Huey Long filibuster in which the Times called potlikker "pot liquor."

"Only a culinarily-illiterate damnyankee (one word) who can't tell the difference between beans and greens would call the liquid left in the pot after cooking greens "pot liquor" (two words) instead of "potlikker" (one word) as yours did. And don't cite Webster as a defense because he didn't know any better either."

Shoe Leather (23)

The American Licorice Company in Chicago says on its web site that it provided the shoe for the film but IMDb, "the world's most popular and authoritative source for movie, TV and celebrity content," says Hillaby's in Pontefract, West Yorkshire, England made the licorice (or liquorice) shoe.

Ring Around the Collar (40)

In 1864 the first all female labor union, the Collar Laundry Union, was founded in Troy.

The Krementz one-piece collar button was inspired by a demonstration of the manufacture of Remington rifle cartridges from one piece of metal at the 1876 Centennial Exhibition in Philadelphia.

Other collar buttons were made from two or more pieces riveted or soldered together.

The Krementz button was made from superior 14 karat gold overlay and advertised to the trade as if a button was sawn in two pieces and put in acid a thin shell of 14 karat gold would be left, whereas with competitor buttons there would be "a few formless morsels of a brownish metal."

Krementz successfully defended its collar button patent in a Supreme Court case in 1893.

Krementz was a storied jewelry manufacturer of quality gold-filled jewelry founded in 1866. Krementz was bought by Colibiri in 1997. Colibri went bankrupt in 2009 and the Krementz name vanished with it.

Zip Your Lip (43)

In case tempis has fugited by the time you are reading this, Beverly Hills 90210 was a TV show that aired from 1990 to 2000, and it would always get a laugh when I used it as my zip code when asked while checking out at a store.

Skullduggery (31)

London diamantaires estimated the true value of the skull at $14-20 million at 2007 exchange rates.

Shoddy Goods (41)

An inferior type of shoddy with shorter fibers was called mungo.

The 1902 article says that an all wool suit cost 4 times as much as one made with wool, cotton, and shoddy.

An Indian web site says that shoddy is 30% of India's woolen industry but that the product is of such low quality that it is used mainly domestically and exported to poorer countries.

Pardon My French (48)

A perfume ad in the October 27, 1952 Life Magazine touts Chantilly, Le Parfum Idéal, and Quelques Fleurs (a few flowers). But at least the ad is from a real French perfume company, Houbigant.

Cosmetology (49)

This newspaper had extensive coverage of the death of George Washington a month before on December 14, 1799. There was reprinted the funeral oration by Major General Henry Lee given on December 26 and a letter from Martha Washington.

Send Frenchie to Mars (51)

Burma Shave couldn't sell Albert Einstein, either. Einstein used regular soap for shaving. When asked why, he replied "Two soaps? That is too complicated!"

It must have worked. "Why is it I get my best ideas while shaving?", he said.

Shirt-Waists are for Pantywaists (55)

Ladies shirtwaists were often called simply "waists"

Bad Relations (60)

The Law of Inverse Proportion: The bigger the lady the daintier the jewelry.

A Poser (64)

From the web site of Jewelers of America, a trade organization:

"Intentionally over-valuing items on appraisals is considered illegal under Federal Trade Commission (FTC) guidelines and unethical by all nationally recognized appraisal organizations. The value assigned to the piece of jewelry should not be inflated beyond what is considered a fair retail selling price."

The Debtor Strikes Back (68)

I paid off all my credit cards in 2011, a 10 year project tracked on a spreadsheet. Banks do not loan to very tiny businesses. A friend with a lot bigger business than mine got a Small Business Administration loan only after a lengthy bureaucratic ordeal.

Cash advances on credit cards was the only financing option for me.

Bulletin from the Department of Good and Evil (72)

Chase did this to my wife. They raised the minimum payment from $150 to $375. After a phone call with lots of shouting, Chase relented and gave her a 5 year payoff with a flat monthly payment of $150 at the old 6% rate. Then they mysteriously lowered the interest to 2%.

I had been corresponding via email with Elizabeth Warren, then at Harvard. I saw her on a TV show talking about credit cards and on a whim I sent her my article *The Debtor Strikes Back* (p. 68). She replied "Great story."

I told her about the Chase minimum payment with no opt-out and she was surprised. I even sent her a scan of the notice. I assume the reduction to 2% was her doing, although she did not respond to a subsequent inquiry about it in a letter.

I was pissed. I emailed ABC, NBC, CBS, Fox, and assorted newspapers. The Philadelphia Inquirer responded and did an article about us and the Chase minimum payment. From the article, a recently unemployed woman in Michigan contacted me with the same problem, but she could not get Chase to budge.

In February, 2013, a check arrived for $25, my wife's share of the settlement.

My Little Chickadee (75)

Fields made a short film in 1932, *The Dentist* that had the bushy beard gag. Several birds fly out and Fields goes after them with a shotgun. You can watch the 22 minute film on Youtube.

By the way, Fields' real name was William Claude Dukenfield

Special Effects (76)

While governor of New Mexico Territory, Wallace granted amnesty to Billy the Kid in exchange for grand jury testimony about the murder he had witnessed. After what was supposed to be a token arrest, the district attorney refused to honor the deal. Billy the Kid escaped from jail and continued his outlaw ways until he was killed by Lincoln County sheriff Pat Garrett in 1881.

The banner underneath the poster says *Ben-Hur Drives Sheik Ilderim's "Stars Of The Desert" To Victory in the Antioch Circus, Defeating His Arch-Enemy Messala*

Gaiety Girls (77)

"...the light and sparkling music, the beautiful scenery, the clever acting, and the attractive pageantry being universally admired. The dialogue is described as sparkling, epigrammatic, with well-rounded wise saws, mixed up with no end of drollery." — 1896 review of *A Gaiety Girl* in the Evening Post (New Zealand).

The Magic Flute (83)

An article in Time Magazine from Dec. 2, 1935 says that Barrère paid $1000 for his 14 karat flute and $3000 for the platinum flute. However, an exhaustively detailed and impressively researched biography of Barrère, *Monarch of the Flute* by Nancy Toff, (Oxford University Press, USA 2005) gives the $450 and $2600 figures.

Three platinum flutes, the first ever made, were made in London in 1933.

Pumping Iron (88)

As a publicity stunt, after Sandow's show at the Trocadero, wealthy women could pay $300, which would be donated to charity, to go backstage to feel his muscles. One woman fainted and had to be revived with smelling salts.

While Sandow was in Venice in 1893, just before he was called to England for the Sampson challenge, he attracted the eye of E. Aubrey Hunt (1855-1922), an American painter, who painted him in the Coliseum as a Roman gladiator wearing a leopard skin and sandals.

The 8'6" high x 5'6" wide painting was acquired by Joe Weider, founder of the International Federation of Bodybuilders and founder of the Mr. Olympia contest. The painting now hangs in The Joe and Betty Weider Museum of Physical Culture at the University of Texas.

A full-size plaster body cast of Sandow (sans fig leaf) was commissioned by the the British Museum of Natural History in 1901. Sandow presented one copy to his friend Dr. Dudley Sargent at Harvard, which is lost. Another copy is on display at the USA Weightlifting Hall of Fame in York, Pennsylvania.

The original cast is in the basement of the British Museum. Arnold Schwarzenegger had a copy of it made at great expense.

A tiny ad for a Sandow photograph in the April 19, 1902 Literary Digest mentions a bronze statue of him at Harvard University in the same pose as the British Museum cast. The ad implies that the bronze is not life size.

Luxe et Veritas (93)

This article about the ad that inspired a gemologist colleague of mine to call the company and get them to admit that "DiamondAura" was actually cubic zirconia had some interesting consequences.

As usual, I posted the newsletter, Holiday '05, for download on the web site, and thought nothing more about it.

In November, 2005 I got an email out of the blue from a criminal defense attorney in Texas. He had a client accused of some sort of gemological fraud. He had read the article in the newsletter and wanted some more information on diamonds and diamond imitations.

When I got my web site statistics I noticed that traffic had tripled, due to downloads of the newsletter and 450 people had used "DiamondAura" as the search term that brought them to the site. When I googled DiamondAura, the link to the newsletter was on the first page. So people who searched for DiamondAura were treated to a second opinion.

Then I got three more emails, from a woman in California and two men in Texas, saying they had read the newsletter article and had decided not to purchase DiamondAura.

In January, 2006 I got a phone call from a couple in California. They had bought DiamondAura under the impression that it was actually man-made diamond and had taken it to a number of jewelers who had told them it was cubic zirconia. They were mad. They called the FBI and complained and sent them the newsletter article.

Cool!

Trial of the Pyx (105)

In case you can't read the writing on the 1707 trial plate, it is as follows:

The Standard comixed of XXII Carrets of fine gold and II Carrets of Allay in the Pound w.[t] Troy of Great — Brittain made the 25.th of June, 1707.

Not Guilty (95)

Joseph Mirsky Esq. passed away in October, 2011. I did not know him. I did correspond with Joseph Mirsky, Assistant United States Attorney in Houston.

Depression Gold (100)

Roosevelt's national bank holiday was precipitated by a bank holiday in Michigan on Feb. 15, forced by the imminent failure of a large bank when Henry Ford would not subordinate his deposits at the bank to a loan from the Reconstruction Finance Corporation.

This sparked a run on banks everywhere, with an increase of 30% of currency in circulation as depositors pulled their money out, and bank holidays were declared in many other states.

A rush to gold depleted the gold stocks of the Federal Reserve Bank of New York from the mandated 40% of the money supply to 24%.

Roosevelt's first fireside chat on the radio on March 12, just a week after his inauguration, so reassured the populace that when the banks reopened the next day, people lined up to put their money back.

Less More Money Than You Could Ever Spend (103)

Jamie Dimon had his pay cut in half in 2012 as punishment for a $6 billion loss, but he still made over 9 times more than his newly humbled 1911 compatriots.

Pennyweights (104)

The grain is the only unit that is the same in the troy, avoirdupois, and apothecaries' systems.

Wall Street Closed (111)

National banks chartered by the government issued their own currency, national bank notes, until 1935, backed by bonds deposited with the Treasury. The Federal Reserve Act allowed commercial paper as additional backing for new money.

Sterilization of gold along with the Fed doubling banks' reserve requirement causing a contraction of the money supply was one cause of the recession in the Depression of 1937-38. In 1934, large gold inflows to the U.S. were caused by the devaluation of the dollar by changing the gold price from $20.67 to $35 an ounce by the Gold Reserve Act of 1934. The Chicago Daily Tribune Dec 30, 1936 headlined "U.S. Sterilizes $14,835,000 Imported Gold."

"The tremendous increase in the monetary gold supply of the United States in the last three years had created a vast amount of idle funds in the banks which are regarded as the potential base of an unsound credit expansion. The surplus reserves now total approximately 2 billion dollars."

"Under the treasury's 'sterilization' policy all gold acquisitions will be so handled that they cannot affect bank reserves. The program provides for the sale of treasury bills in an amount corresponding to the gold acquired. By this scheme funds equal to the amount of the new gold will be siphoned from the money market."

"If the United States begins to lose some of its gold the plan will go into reverse, with the treasury purchasing bills and restoring funds to the money market in an amount equivalent to the gold moving out of the country."

Where have You Gone Ferdinand Pecora? (131) One account has Lya Graf sent to Orianenberg in 1937, but Orianenberg was closed in 1935, succeeded by Sachsenhausen. Another source says her name was Schwartz and that she was half Jewish.

Practical Money Skills (120)
"Do not let any calamity-howling executive with an income of $1,000.00 a day … tell you that a wage of $11.00 a week is going to have a disastrous effect on all American industry."
— President Franklin Roosevelt, Fireside Chat June 24, 1938

In 1992, New Jersey raised the minimum wage from $4.25 to $5.05, while in neighboring Pennsylvania it remained at $4.25, the Federal minimum.

UC Berkeley economist David Card and Princeton economist Alan Krueger* surveyed fast-food restaurants along the border between the two states twice over 11 months and published a study in 1994, *Minimum Wages and Employment: A Case Study of the Fast-Food Industry in New Jersey and Pennsylvania.* The study found that there was no change in employment in higher wage New Jersey, contradicting conservative dogma.

But nothing puts a dent in the hard-headed. Forbes published an article on December 31, 2012 titled *Why Raising The Minimum Wage Kills Jobs.*

* Assistant Secretary of the Treasury for Economic Policy 2009-2010, Chairman of the Council of Economic Advisers 2011-2013

Message From The 1% (132)
I like the "everybody who's got the right to vote" blt.

Pocket Change (136)
"The Secretary may mint and issue platinum bullion coins and proof platinum coins in accordance with such specifications, designs, varieties, quantities, denominations, and inscriptions as the Secretary, in the Secretary's discretion, may prescribe from time to time."
— From 31 USC § 5112 - Denominations, specifications, and design of coins.

All other coins described in the law had specified denominations. The platinum coin was added in 1996.

"Contrary to some media reports, minting a trillion dollar platinum coin would not raise the debt limit. Rather, it would add a trillion dollars to the general fund of the treasury without requiring additional borrowing, effectively delaying the date when the debt limit is reached."
— Philip Diehl, former director of the mint, who wrote the law along with Mike Castle (R-Del). The quote is from an email published on an American Enterprise Institute blog, Jan. 8, 2013.

The N Word (147)
An investigative panel of the Southern Baptist Convention terminated Richard Land's call-in radio show in April, 2012 for racially charged remarks about the Trayvon Martin case, in which an unarmed black teenager was killed in Florida by a man on patrol for a neighborhood watch group. He was also accused of plagiarism, reading from a Washington Times article about the case without attribution.

Truth to Tell (147)
The Sarah Palin "Death Panel" posting on facebook was called "The lie of the year" for 2009 by Politifact.

Palin I can understand — she's a nincompoop. But Grassley knows better and he is dishonorable. He gave a lame explanation after the fact that people would be freaked out by mentioning death and money together.

Ultracrepidarianism (133)

I got this amazing word from a commentary by Jon Nadler, a senior analyst at Kitco, a large Canadian refinery and bullion dealer, in 2010. In an article called *The Creeping Art of Ultracrepidarianism* he gave as an example conspiratorial commentaries about how the LME, London Metals Exchange, has no gold in its vaults. This is true. However, this should be expected since the LME only trades in base metals.

In March, 2009, Lisa Miller wrote an article in Newsweek titled *Why Investors are Hoarding Gold* in which she interviewed Jon Nadler among others. Lisa Miller was the religion editor at Newsweek. She is an accomplished journalist on religious and social matters, but with no credentials in precious metals. John Nadler's bio on Kitco says his "33-year career has focused exclusively on the precious metals market and its physical investment products." While I'm sure he understands the gold coin and bullion market, I doubt that he has any experience buying granny's gold in a store. Kitco will not buy scrap gold from private individuals and even if they did, he wouldn't be the one doing the buying.

On July 29, 2009 I was on the Brian Lehrer show along with Lisa Miller to discuss "the rush to invest in gold and what you should know before taking that old bracelet or watch to a 'sell-your-gold' party." The previous segment ran over and I got one comment in to the effect that generally the only interest was in the gold, not the jewelry. Lisa Miller said that people who sold their gold for scrap should get 8% less than the market price.

This is an ultracrepidarian opinion. It is possible for selling gold coins or bars, which are not scrap to be refined (they are what scrap gold is refined into), and are traded at a small buy/sell spread. The gold price you hear is for pure gold, 24 karat.

14 karat gold is nominally 14/24ths, or 58.3% gold, but scrap gold is bought from the jeweler at ½ karat less, 3.5% less for 14 karat, since until 1981 it was legal to make 14 karat as low as 13 karat and a lot of scrap is old stuff. The jeweler gets less than market value even after the ½ karat deduction (the refiner makes a profit). Also, some items marked 14 karat are as low as 10 or 12 karat (it's called cheating), the jewelry has to be reported to the police and held for a period of time (people steal it), 15 days in my town, and there's all kinds of weird stuff that comes in. I lose 2-3% on subkarat gold, weird stuff, and inevitable mistakes. No one can or does work on 8%.

I once had a New York dealer who buys from stores but who also has a retail operation solicit my business. He told me he pays 4% more than I do at retail on 47th street, the most competitive location in the world. (There is a 15 day holding period in New York City also.)

I emailed Lisa Miller with this information along with a link to the pamphlet I hand out at the store, *Selling Your Gold* (p. 216), after the show, but she did not reply, I have to presume because she is somebody and I am nobody.

I also fault the Brian Lehrer show for featuring Lisa Miller as an expert. There are plenty of people the show could have put on who know what they are talking about. 47th street is a subway token away from the show's studios.

Lisa Miller got her ultracrepidarian 8% notion from not knowing enough about gold to know she misunderstood Jon Nadler from whom I got the word itself, coming full circle.

Jon Nadler left Kitco in February, 2013 to a chorus of good riddances since he was too bearish: "Gold bugs gloat after Nadler and Kitco part ways" said Mining.com.

Original Intent (144)

My analysis was my own, but I subsequently found the quotes below.

"A historically-grounded analysis of what was actually debated in 1787-1789 can only conclude that the status of the militia was always what was in dispute, and not the private rights of individuals." — Historians Brief to the Supreme Court in Heller.

"Under longstanding linguistic principles that were well understood and recognized at the time the Second Amendment was adopted, the 'well regulated Militia' clause necessarily adds meaning to the 'keep and bear Arms' clause by furnishing the reason for the latter's existence." "The purpose of the Second Amendment, therefore, is to perpetuate 'a well regulated Militia.'" "The amendment's unmistakably military language protects the right of the people to serve in a well-regulated militia and keep and bear arms for such service." — Linguists brief to the Supreme Court in Heller.

All able-bodied men were required to be in state militias and to supply their own weapons: a musket, bayonet and belt, two spare flints, a cartridge box with 24 bullets, and a knapsack. Men owning rifles were required to provide a powder horn, 1/4 pound of gun powder, 20 rifle balls, a shooting pouch, and a knapsack, according to the Second Militia Act of 1792.

The draft of the amendment that explicitly mentions military service as the rationale for the right to bear arms seems to me the smoking second amendment gun, as it were.

I'm constantly amazed how otherwise sensible people spout nonsense about guns (and gold). I once knew a man who believed (in the cold war '70's) that when the Russians invaded, 1 million hunters would defeat them with their Second Amendment guns. That's about 66 divisions, or 3 army groups. The logistics alone are staggering — think D-Day with 156,000 men. And this is from someone who owned a manufacturing business with 20 or so employees, a practical guy.

I'm amused by the notion that if you have to register your guns, the government will take them away. The government won't have to take your guns away. It can just make it illegal to have them so you won't be able to use them. Do you think the cops will be on your side? But when civilization collapses, your neighborhood warlord will take away your guns (and your gold).

In Miller, the Court decided unanimously that a sawed-off shotgun transported across state lines was in violation of the National Firearms Act of 1934 because it was not registered as required by the act, and, because a sawed-off shotgun was not a weapon suitable for a militia, it was not protected by the Amendment. But It also said that the National Firearms Act did not violate the Second Amendment. This seems to imply that if a weapon were suitable for a militia, and properly registered, it would be ok, an individual right to bear arms — if you're in a militia?

Romney Flunks Make-up Exam (150)

The Corporation for Public Broadcasting received $445 million in federal funds in 2014, which it distributed to public broadcasters, 15% of public broadcasting revenue, the rest coming from private grants and audience donations. Romney said he would eliminate funding for PBS in the October 3, 2012 presidential debate, then quickly added "I like PBS. I like Big Bird. I like you, too," to moderator and PBS news anchor Jim Lehrer. But Sesame Street gets two thirds of its revenue just from licensing and royalties — toys, games, books, T-shirts etc., and would hardly be affected by a cut in federal funding of PBS.

The Corporation for Public Broadcasting was founded in 1967. We continue to fund it because it's a national treasure: Sesame Street, Nova, Masterpiece Theater, Frontline, Antiques Roadshow, Nature, This Old House, American Experience, Wait, Wait, Don't Tell Me, Morning Edition, All Things, Considered, and On the Media are just a few of its gems. The Muppets, including Kermit and Miss Piggy, got off the dole in 2004, hired by Disney.

The Fourth Estate (160)

Time quotes McWilliams in an article titled *NEW YORK: Mr. McNazi* Sept. 23, 1940:

"Adolf Hitler is the greatest leader in the history of the world."

"Herbert Hoover is mentally deficient and Roosevelt is an amateur Englishman, a Jew, and the leader of the fifth column in this country."

"America suffers from effeminacy; it is time to get strong."

"I intend to get a huge following and run the Government like a factory, appointing all the key men. I may not be President but I will have absolute control."

"The Jews are in control and demand complete intellectual subserviency. To combat this, I would ship all the Jews to some place such as Madagascar."

"As far as violence is concerned in my methods, I will only say that I must have control."

"I look on every newspaperman as a prostitute. I have a blacklist of the worst ones and they will be taken care of. The newspapers and magazines will be run with a firm hand. We'll make a real free press."

"Once in power, I will down all dissident opinion."

The Militant Moderate Manifesto (137) and **Shootout at the Circle K Ranch** (170)

Below is an excerpt from a letter by President Eisenhower to his brother Edgar Newton Eisenhower, November 8, 1954.

"Now it is true that I believe this country is following a dangerous trend when it permits too great a degree of centralization of governmental functions. I oppose this--in some instances the fight is a rather desperate one. But to attain any success it is quite clear that the Federal government cannot avoid or escape responsibilities which the mass of the people firmly *believe* should be undertaken by it. The political processes of our country are such that if a *rule of reason* is not applied in this effort, we will lose everything--even to a possible and drastic change in the Constitution. This is what I mean by my constant insistence upon "moderation" in government. Should any political party attempt to abolish social security, unemployment insurance, and eliminate labor laws and farm programs, you would not hear of that party again in our political history. There is a tiny splinter group, of course, that believes you can do these things. Among them are H. L. Hunt (you possibly know his background), a few other Texas oil millionaires, and an occasional politician or business man from other areas. Their number is negligible and they are stupid."

Dobson, Falwell, Robertson, et al. (154)

The BP oil spill started April 20, 2010. On June 16, after almost 2 months and millions of gallons of oil fouling the Gulf, BP executives met with the President and agreed to set aside $20 billion for damages.

On June 17, BP CEO Tony Hayward appeared before a A House Energy and Commerce subcommittee.

The senior Republican on the committee, Joe Barton of Texas said:

"I'm ashamed of what happened in the White House yesterday. I think it is a tragedy of the first proportion that a private corporation can be subjected to what I would characterize as a shakedown, in this case a $20 billion shakedown. I apologize. I do not want to live in a country where any time a citizen or a corporation does something that is legitimately wrong, is subject to some sort of political pressure that is, again, in my words, amounts to a shakedown. So I apologize"

Exactly the Reverse (156)

Conservative — a liberal who was mugged. Liberal — a conservative who lost health insurance. This was actual friendly political banter with a conservative customer with my punch line about health insurance delivered a week later. "Touché," was his reply.

"Capitalism is the exploitation of man by man. Yes? Well socialism is exactly the reverse."

— Colonel Stok, Russian head of intelligence in Berlin in Len Deighton's *Funeral in Berlin*, (1964) quoting a Czech joke.

Yellow Peril (157)

Rocky Mountain Jim was killed on June 19, 1874 by Griffin Evans. There are five different accounts that disagree over the nature of the dispute, but all agree that liquor was involved.

Isabella Bird rode her horse astride, not sidesaddle, as was the custom for women, and wore a split skirt. She threatened to sue The New York Times for saying that she dressed like a man.

Bird was inducted into the Colorado Women's Hall of Fame in 1895.

Shaving Shovels (158)

Of course there is a man who actually shaves with a shovel. A Russian English teacher from Nizhny Novgorod shaves with a sharpened shovel and also scissors and a hatchet — anything sharp. He claims to have never used a razor. He says he was inspired by his grandfather's tales of soldiers using whatever they could find to shave with in World War II.

Goldwater (181)

German scientist Fritz Haber, winner of the 1918 Nobel prize for the synthesis of ammonia (and reviled developer of poison gas), tried without success in the 1920's to extract gold from seawater to help Germany pay back its war reparations.

Waste Management (204)

For a quick tour of the Egyptian pantheon google up *Ramses the Second is Dead, My Love* by the Fugs in the 1968 album *It Crawled into my Hand, Honest.*

The First Engagement Ring (203)

The source for the ring being in the shape of an M is the Reader's Digest web site.

The legend is that the Romans specified the third finger of the left hand for betrothal rings because they believed the *vena amoris* ran from the finger to the heart. All fingers have this vein, and there are no concrete sources for this, but it sounds good.

Lux et Veritas (212)

Radium paint was patented by Tiffany gemologist George Kunz in 1903.

The Hamilton Watch company, Lancaster, Pa. (I grew up 2 miles from Hamilton Watch) used fine-pointed pens to apply radium to their watch dials and the dial painters were instructed not to put the pens in their mouths according to an interview with a 102 year old dial painter by Jack Brubaker posted on Lancaster Online May 9, 2014. She said that no one got sick from the radium although it did get on their hands and in their hair, glowing in the dark.

Radium poisoning can be diagnosed by detecting radon in the breath.

Undark was sold as a do-it-yourself kit for $3.

One of the founders of U.S. Radium, Dr. Sabin Arnold von Sochocky died of radium poisoning in 1928 at 45.

Marie Curie, the discoverer of radium in 1906, died of aplastic anemia caused by radium poisoning in 1934 at 66

Bloomer War (219)

In the *L.A.W. Bulletin and Good Roads* May 28, 1897 were printed two letters on the problem of "ballooning skirts":

"The Skirt lined with a firm, substantial lining: goods and lining turned to form a two inch hem. Stitch firmly. Skirt must not be too full. Three yards and three-quarters is the maximum width I can safely and comfortably use on my wheel. My Winter bicycle skirt was lined with the heaviest of rustic cambric. This Spring many are using moreen."

"Pin your skirt together on the lower edge, in centre of front and back between the feet, with a safety pin; or, better, cut the clasps from and old pair of men's gloves, having about 1½ inches of the leather attached in a strip, and sew them on the inside of the lower edge of skirt in centre of back an front."

In 1899 a few automobiles were exhibited at the Madison Square Garden bicycle show. The next year was the first automobile show at the Garden and the last bicycle show.

The League of American Wheelmen barred Negro members at it's convention in 1894. However some clubs ignored the ban.

The print at the upper right reads: "If they have no roads they are savages for the road is the creation of man and a type of civilized society".

First Auto (225)

Senator Benjamin Tillman was a notorious racist. As Governor of South Carolina he was responsible for Jim Crow laws, saying "We have done our level best [to prevent blacks from voting] ... we have scratched our heads to find out how we could eliminate the last one of them. We stuffed ballot boxes. We shot them. We are not ashamed of it."

The Negro "must remain subordinate or be exterminated".

These are two of the milder Tillman quotes, from Wikipedia.

Grin and Bear It (231)

"A Grinning match took place in June near Bridlington, England, for a quantity of tobacco. There were three competitors for the prize, all of whom were speedily seized with the most painful symptoms, in consequence of their violent contortions and two of them died in a few days. The other survived only a few days longer, whose father on going to visit him, was so shocked with his appearance, that he took to his bed and never rose again."
— The Sprig of Liberty (Gettysburg) August 24, 1804.

This bizarre incident was originally reported in the Times of London June 11, 1804 according to *A Brief History of the Smile* by Angus Trumble, which also quotes it. (*Cont.*)

Oddly there is an American band called The Grinning Match that plays "funky fresh" music.

Hats Off (237)
Audie Murphy actually played the bad guy in the 1959 movie *No Name on the Bullet*. He wore a black hat, too. I don't remember if he took it off indoors, though.

Hats On (237)
In the Stetson ad, the large type is the original image but has been made smaller to save space. The small type under the man and under the hat has been made larger for readability, redone in the same font and style.

Napoleon's bicorne hat was bought at auction in 2014 for $2.4 million by a South Korean. Napoleon wore it at the battle of Marengo in Italy in 1800. The hat was sold by the royal family of Monaco to raise money to fix up their palace.

Welsh Outsmurf Irish 2 to 1 (242)
Yes, there is a global Smurfs Day. In 2011 SONY started it on June 25, the birthday of Smurfs creator Peyo

According to a SONY press release on July 2, 2011, "adjudicators from Guinness World Records confirmed that a total of 4,891 people dressed as Smurfs in 11 locations simultaneously around the world, claiming a new title for Largest Gathering of People Dressed as Smurfs within a 24-hour Period in Multiple Venues."

Peyo (1928-1992) was a Belgian comic artist named Pierre Culliford. He created the Smurfs in a comic series in 1958.

Waste Management (246)
John Harington said "Treason doth never prosper: what's the reason? Why, if it prosper, none dare call it treason."

In Flanders Fields (247)
The state flower of California is a poppy, Eschscholzia Californica, the California Poppy. You can't get high from it, though.

Eric Sloane (248)
Eric Sloane oil paintings sell for $40-60,000

Written in the Stars (248)
The poll mailed 10 million questionnaires. 2.3 million were returned. The mailing list was chosen from the magazine's subscription list, car registration lists, telephone books, and club membership lists.

From this poll, the Digest predicted that Landon would win 57.1% of the popular vote and win the electoral college 370 to 161 Roosevelt clobbered Landon with 60.8% of the vote and 523 to 8 electoral votes .

The poll's list was skewed toward the more wealthy, who could afford cars, magazines, phones, and club memberships in the Depression. In past polls in more prosperous times there was not such a great divergence of interests between wealthier and poorer voters.

Never Cheat an Elephant (249)
Elephants live 50-70 years. The record is 86 for a Taiwanese elephant who died in 2003. So I think we can take the 100 year figure as a bit of hyperbole.

Snake Oil (250)
In 1910, the U.S. Attorney for the District of Columbia, acting on a report by the Secretary of Agriculture, seized 36 half gallon bottles of Buffalo Lithia Water imported from Virginia, charging that it was misbranded and violated the Food and Drugs Act.

The case went from the Supreme Court of the District of Columbia (changed to the District Court for the District of Columbia in 1936) to the Court of Appeals of the District of Columbia, and finally to the Supreme Court in 1915. In 1917, the Supreme Court ruled against Buffalo Lithia Water, citing a 1914 article from the Journal of the A.M.A. that a person would have to drink 200,000 gallons of lithia water a day to get a therapeutic dose [for gout].

The brand then became Buffalo Mineral Water.

American Idol (251)
The Jumjum are a people from south Sudan. They worship the god Dyong who lives in the sky and sits on a horse. I presume the Jumjum reference is to an idol of Dyong.

Help! (253)
SOS superseded CQD. CQ was and is used in radio as "calling all stations." The "D" was added by the Marconi company in 1904 to be used only for distress calls. CQD was sent as separate letters.

The Limits of Radio (254)

"Murray, Ky. (Special.)—Nathan Stubblefield, the local electrician, who has invented a wireless telephone gave a practical test of his system here."

"Several Stations were established in different parts of the town and messages were successfully received at a distance of a mile. Stubblefield believes he can soon send and receive messages at any distance. The apparatus used is of his own make, except for the receivers, which are similar to those used on ordinary telephones."

This article titled *Talks By Wireless 'Phone* is from The Afro-American Ledger (Baltimore), January 11, 1902.

Stubblefield (1860-1928) also demonstrated his wireless telephony in Washington and Philadelphia in 1902. He continued to experiment in the field, obtaining a patent in 1908. He became a recluse and died of starvation in 1928.

You Bet Your Life (255)

Evidently suicides at Monte Carlo were common knowledge at the time. In a speech about the Panic of 1907 titled *Thou Shalt not Steal* at the Civic Forum at Carnegie Hall February 4, 1908, William Jennings Bryan said "measured by the number of suicides caused by the New York Stock Exchange, Monte Carlo is an innocent pleasure-resort by comparison."

Is Sex Necessary? (258)

Maybe it is. A 2014 poll in the U.K. by Middlesex University found that 1 in 5 people would "have sex with an android."

However, androids were not polled.

Panic Ad (258)

Below is the text of the ad in case it's too small for you to read.

"Panic is a take-off. A mimic Wall Street Stock Exchange. Full and delirious excitement — Flurries, Corners, Failures and Fortunes. Fun and noise from start to finish. Panic is played with a deck of 65 handsome cards representing 8 different kinds of Wall Street stocks with 8 cards each and an extra card known as the "Panic." Price 40 cents at your dealers or from us postpaid. Sample card with instructions FREE. Everyone likes Panic. Ask for it of your dealer today. Copyrighted 1903."

"Panic Card Co,, Detroit, Mich. and Topeka, Kan."

The Moral Gown (258)

If it isn't immoral music dooming us to perdition, it's immoral dress. University of Florida president Albert A. Murphree said in 1921 "The low-cut gowns, the rolled hose and short skirts are born of the Devil and his angels, and are carrying the present and future generations to social chaos and destruction."

Things loosened up by 1958 when University co-eds were permitted "to wear Bermuda shorts on campus uncovered by raincoats." But only on Saturdays.

Heavy Reading (259)

The pages measure 8 x 4.8" inside the margins, or 38.4 sq. In. There are 280 pages in the body of the book with the notes. 38.4 X 280 = 10,752 sq. In. There are 174,242 words, so the software tells me. That works out to 16.21 words/sq. in.

There are 1.55×10^9 sq. in. per km². $16.21 \times 1.55 \times 10^9 = 25.13 \times 10^9$ words/km².

A publishing site says a good 6" x 9" non-fiction book has 300 words per page or 7.81 words per sq. in.

Sock it to Me (262)

Wanda von Sacher-Masoch published her memoirs, *The Confessions of Wanda von Sacher-Masoch* in 1907.

Leopold von Sacher-Masoch did not want a religious burial, an unusual practice for the time, and he was cremated. His widow wanted his ashes buried in Graz, but the city refused. The urn with his ashes was stored in a neighboring palace in Lindheim which burned to the ground in 1929. This gave rise to the joke "only a masochist can enjoy being cremated twice".

All Creatures Great and Small (264)

Cecil Frances Alexander (1818-1895) was an Irish woman. She wrote about 400 hymns in her lifetime.

Palin's lawsuit was joined by the National Association of Manufacturers, the U.S. chamber of Commerce, the National Mining Association and the American Iron and Steel Institute.

Web sites for the companies that offer polar bear hunting expeditions show grinning men posing with their weapons next to bears they killed, some bloody. One especially macho guy is shown posing with his bear holding the high tech compound hunting bow he used to kill it.

Name Index

Subject Index

293

Made in the USA
Middletown, DE
31 October 2015

Made in United States
North Haven, CT
25 October 2024

59422617R00141